Penguin Books
The Astrologer's Handbook

Frances Sakoian has been a practicing astrologer for over
years. Her well-published predictions on the U.S. space flights and
other current events have earned her considerable publicity in recent
years. She is now head of the New England School of Astrology.

Louis S. Acker began studying astrology at the age of nineteen at the
headquarters of the American Federation of Astrology. His association
with Mrs Sakoian began in 1962 and they started writing *The
Astrologer's Handbook* in 1969.

They have also written *The Astrology of Human Relationships*.

THE ASTROLOGER'S HANDBOOK

Frances Sakoian and Louis S. Acker

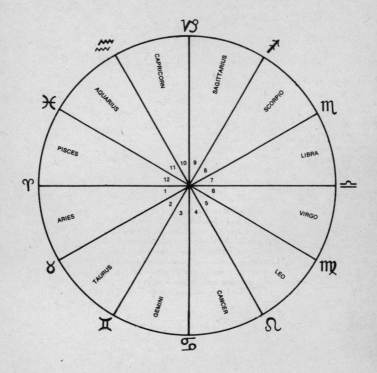

PENGUIN BOOKS

Penguin Books Ltd, Harmondsworth, Middlesex, England
Penguin Books, 625 Madison Avenue, New York, New York 10022, U.S.A.
Penguin Books Australia Ltd, Ringwood, Victoria, Australia
Penguin Books Canada Ltd, 2801 John Street, Markham, Ontario, Canada L3R 1B4
Penguin Books (N.Z.) Ltd, 182–190 Wairau Road, Auckland 10, New Zealand

First published in Great Britain by Peter Davies Ltd 1974
Published in Penguin Books 1981

Made and printed in Great Britain by
Richard Clay (The Chaucer Press) Ltd, Bungay, Suffolk
Set in Monophoto Times

Contents

Introduction

The eagerness with which increasing numbers of people are delving into astrology is a healthy sign of a powerful hunger for a more meaningful way of life. Still, one might reasonably ask, is astrology as it has been practiced a worthy instrument to satisfy that hunger? There are serious and sympathetic people who believe that it is not. In many ways Western astrology has become debased in its resources, subject to commercial distortion, and reduced to simple gossip by sign, planet, and house.

Happily, insightful astrologers, who were first surprised, then delighted at the skyrocketing interest in their art, have started to respond to this renewal of interest by attempting to renew astrology itself. This book, *The Astrologer's Handbook*, represents a significant effort on the part of two experienced astrologers to clarify and rebuild the potentially magnificent but threatened structure concerned with man's correspondence to "cosmic consciousness."

How did astrology come to the state in which we now find it? The reasons date at least to the mid-seventeenth century, when man began to think of himself as more important than God, and the rise of scientific supremacy began. One of the major effects of the new thinking was that nature, previously at one with every order of phenomenon in the universe, became desacralized, and as the dimension of Divine Intention was cast aside, the world became metaphysically two-dimensional rather than three-dimensional. Astrology, which had had no misgivings about which was higher, God or man, of course became the target of the rising opposition. Soon astronomy and astrology split from each other, and the new "scientists" started issuing edicts against astrology through a corrupt—and politically oriented—church.

The attempts to tear down such a profound understanding of what each man is placed on earth to do could not eliminate astrology, but they did drive it underground. For centuries it peeped out only in the old almanacs, persisting more as an oddity than as a vital art. So astrology survived, but the disaster was that for several hundred years it lost contact with other intellectual disciplines. That was a costly isolation, and, in fact, even today the skeptical astrologer is still a rarity. Denied the rigorous pruning that a strong metaphysics would have given, astrologers and clairvoyant geniuses have had no assistance in discriminating between fantasy and revelation. The inspired insights that have occurred in the intervening centuries have gone unjudged; mistakes have been perpetuated as blindly as truths.

Times have changed since astrology was rejected by science and the church alike. Jacob Needleman says in his *New Religions* (Doubleday, 1970), "Things are different now, and the present interest in astrology can be as much a sign of the incipient spiritual search as was, for example, St. Augustine's turning away from astrology in his day." But even now astronomy remains at odds with astrology, or more accurately it ignores astrology. The father of a successful young astrologer I know is a well-known astronomer. I understand that the subject is simply never brought up between them. It is interesting, however, that when science bothers with astrology at all it demands, before anything else, statistical proof of the correspondences between individuals and the configuration of certain planets at their birth. This is surely appropriate, because what science does have to offer contemporary astrologers is precisely its methods of statistics. Applied to astrology, these techniques could be of real help in distinguishing fantasy from divine revelation. Scientists in general may never be able to enter the intuitional domain of astrologers, but through participation in a common search for truth they might come to acknowledge instead of ignore its existence.

With so many overblown testaments abroad today, all extolling astrology for the wrong reasons, the art's honest values are overshadowed. I surely make no claim to know absolutely the true from the mistaken or the exaggerated; what endears astrology to me is that during my study of it I found a forbearance and even a compassion toward people who could not help doing what they do. Astrology is valuable to me because it balances the hint of fatalism with the reality of being able to read the forewarnings in a chart and then to attempt to transcend them by "rightminded" actions taken in the light of the chart. This important dimension of astrological thinking is akin to the wisdom of the *I Ching*.

The Astrologer's Handbook has rich material for beginner and expert alike. Chapter 1, "For the Astrological Beginner" shows the novice how much information he can gain about himself if he knows no more than the day on which he was born, and it indicates to him how much more he can learn about himself if he has the precise hour and minute of his birth. The expert reader will be especially interested in the material on the major aspects. In this book, for the first time, the characteristics of squares and oppositions are not lumped together as "unfavorable" but are delineated specifically as two kinds of opportunities to work and to learn. Further, the characteristics of squares are distinguished from the features of oppositions and both of these from conjunctions, and so on for all the major aspects. The bulk of the *Handbook* is devoted to delineations of each aspect combination, Sun square Moon, Sun square Mars, and the squares of the Sun to all the rest of the planets, Sun trine Moon, trine Mars, and so on.

In working out this new material on the major aspects, the authors adhered strictly to the classic rules of astrology, bending every effort to stay close to the concepts that are at the foundation of the art. Thus, we may surely recognize this ambitious book as a genuine contribution to classic astrology prepared by two modern astrologers with faith in the ancient laws.

Needless to say, the new delineations of Sakoian and Acker are still to be tested, both by themselves and by other competent practicing astrologers. The discrimination between imaginary and real messages from "on high" requires that the best intellects in the field be brought to bear over long periods of time. Such discrimination is more than one or two people can safely attempt alone. Thus, we should remember that the stimulating new material in *The Astrologer's Handbook* is more in the nature of announcement than pronouncement.

In the past few years teaching has become a major activity in the busy life of Frances Sakoian, first in small private groups, then in a private school of astrology with the able assistance of Louis Acker. In the summer of 1970, Mrs. Sakoian accepted the invitation of Dr. Harry L. Morrison, President of the John F. Kennedy University at Martinez, California, to offer an accredited course in astrology. It is to be hoped that this is but the first of many such opportunities for astrology to reenter the academic world. Changes are occurring today, and among the hopeful signs in an age of change is the exciting possibility of a real renewal of astrology at its very core.

MINOR WHITE

Preface

The sudden wealth of books on astrology reflects the current upsurge of interest in this subject. However, most of these books, both the new ones and the reissues of the old, concentrate for the most part on the history of astrology per se and/or on interpretations of the Sun signs, the rising signs (Ascendants), perhaps the planetary signs (Moon in Virgo, Mercury in Gemini, etc.), and an explanation of the significance of the houses. None deals comprehensively not only with all this but also with the aspects. None sets forth, in detail, the meaning of each aspect and how it can be used in understanding the entire horoscope.

A prime requisite for interpreting a horoscope is the knowledge of how to read aspects correctly. This book for the first time makes that information readily available and understandable to the student and/or practitioner of astrology.

In addition to dealing with the Sun signs, rising signs, planetary signs, and houses, *The Astrologer's Handbook* outlines logical, step-by-step methods for interpreting the meaning of the various aspects through the fundamental rules of astrology, and thus provides the student with a valuable exercise in the interpretation of horoscopes. The usual practice of lumping the aspects into general categories of favorable or unfavorable has been avoided; instead, conjunctions, sextiles, trines, squares, and oppositions are treated separately.* Thus it is shown how each type of aspect imparts its own characteristic coloration to any combination of aspects, planets, nodes, or angles. For instance, the square and opposition are considered stress aspects, yet they are not stressful in the same way. The square deals with obstacles in the path of the native's ambition, while the opposition is concerned with relationship problems.

---

* While the inconjunct and parallel aspects also qualify as major aspects, these will be dealt with in a separate work.

Another topic covered is how the motions of the planets involved in the aspect affect the meaning of the aspect. Whether an aspect is applying or separating, approaching or departing, and whether its orb is exact or wide, is a major factor in determining an aspect's strength and significance.

This book does not include a bibliography since it was written from personal knowledge and experience. It lays no claim to being infallible but is the product of pooled resources which it is hoped will prove of lasting value.

There is no area of human experience which is not touched upon in some way by astrology. This book is intended to provide insights into the laws of consciousness whereby the reader can comprehend that he is an integrated unit within the larger framework of consciousness in which all of us live.

Years of experience have proved that astrology is a valid discipline with vast potential for enriching an understanding of all phases of life. For this reason we believe the present work can serve as a basic text for the eventual teaching of astrology in colleges and universities.

How to Use This Book

This book is designed to provide the layman, the astrological student, and the practitioner of astrology with the information necessary for interpreting horoscopes.

Horoscopes cast by computer are available for those who do not have the time or the inclination to learn the mathematics involved in casting an accurate horoscope. The computerized horoscope will be mathematically exact and the readout will include a list of all the aspects in the natives' horoscope and all the planets in their signs, printed on a horoscope wheel. A computer-cast horoscope of the kind mentioned is obtainable from:

ACA,
Box 395,
Weston,
Massachusetts 02193,
U.S.A.

For this purpose the following particulars are required: your name, address, place of birth (town, county, and country), date of birth (day, month, and year), and time of birth (local time, A.M. or P.M.; if unknown a solar chart will be cast). A charge of U.S. $3.85 (this price includes air mail postage) is made by ACA for this service.

You can cast your own horoscope manually by following the instructions in Chapter 2 and checking your results by comparing them against the example given.

Having acquired your horoscope, either by computer or by your own calculations, you are ready to proceed with its interpretation. Read the part of Chapter 3, "Sun Sign Potentials," that applies to your horoscope. Next, study the chapter on the houses, which represent the departments of one's life. Then read Chapter 4, "Rising Sign Overlay Patterns," which explains how the native projects himself in each department of life. And then read your planets in the signs and houses (Chapter 6).

As a first step in interpreting your aspects, read Chapters 9–11. Bear in mind the orb allotted to each of the major aspects and the possibility of an aspect's being "hidden" (this occurs when one planet is in the last degrees of one sign and the other planet is in the first degrees of another sign).

Finally, you are ready to interpret the individual aspects of your horoscope. First, find out which of the five major aspects you are dealing with—conjunction, sextile, square, trine, or opposition. Determine the planets or points in the horoscope involved and make a note of which comes first in the following lineup: Sun, Moon, Mercury, Venus, Mars, Jupiter, Saturn, Uranus, Pluto, North Node, South Node, Ascendant, Midheaven, Descendant, Nadir. Then turn to the chapter on the aspect involved and look up the appropriate planet or point. For example, if you have a sextile formed by Venus and Neptune, look at "Venus Sextile Neptune" under "Sextiles of Venus" in Chapter 13.

To aid in horoscope interpretation, the chapters on the exaltations of the planets and on dispositors can be utilized as additional factors.

Part I
BASIC ASTROLOGY

CHAPTER 1

For the Astrological Beginner

Sun Signs

A horoscope is a map of the position of the planets in the heavens at the exact time and place of your birth. This map represents a circle of 360°, the path that the Sun appears to follow through the sky (actually the plane of the Earth's orbit around the Sun), which astronomers call the ecliptic. Astrologers divide this path into twelve 30° sectors. These are the twelve "signs of the Zodiac," or "Sun signs." They indicate in which sector the Sun was found at the time of your birth. For instance, if you were born in the early part of October, then the Sun would have been in the seventh sign, Libra. Your "Sun sign," therefore, would be Libra.

The Zodiac most commonly used in Western astrology is determined by the vernal equinox. This is the position of the Sun (about March 20 of each year) when the days and nights are of equal length. The vernal equinox is defined in astronomy as that point in space where the plane of the Earth's orbit around the Sun, the ecliptic, intersects the plane of the Earth's equator extended into space. It occurs when the Sun moves from a position south of the equator to a position north of the equator in its apparent motion along the ecliptic as seen from the Earth (which we know is actually revolving around the Sun). In astrology, this moment is known as 0° of Aries. It marks the beginning of what is known as the "tropical Zodiac," the most commonly used Zodiac in Western astrology and the one on which this book is based.

In astrological terminology, a horoscope is called by many names: nativity, natal chart, natus, chart, map, wheel, etc. However, the signs of the Zodiac always follow an unchanging pattern: Aries, Taurus, Gemini, Cancer, Leo, Virgo, Libra, Scorpio, Sagittarius, Capricorn, Aquarius, and Pisces.

CHART 1

The Cardinal Ingresses

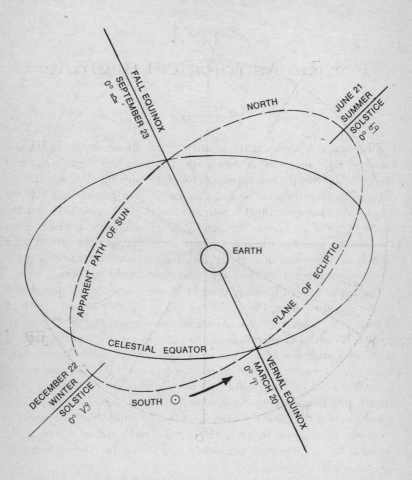

A cardinal ingress is the entry of the Sun into one of the signs of the cardinal grouping or quadruplicities. The signs are Aries, Cancer, Libra, Capricorn, indicating the beginning of the four seasons which are demarcated by the vernal equinox, the summer solstice, the fall equinox, and the winter solstice.

CHART 2

The Natural Zodiac

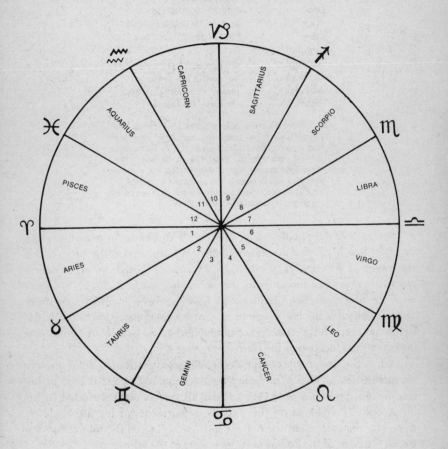

Approximate Dates of the Sun Signs*

Aries	March 21–April 19
Taurus	April 20–May 20
Gemini	May 21–June 21
Cancer	June 22–July 22
Leo	July 23–August 22
Virgo	August 23–September 22
Libra	September 23–October 22
Scorpio	October 23–November 21
Sagittarius	November 22–December 21
Capricorn	December 22–January 19
Aquarius	January 20–February 18
Pisces	Februray 19–March 20

* Note: Because of leap years, time zones, and other factors, the exact day and time when the Sun enters a particular sign of the Zodiac varies slightly from year to year. The exact time when the Sun enters a sign of the Zodiac for a given year and locale must be ascertained by means of an *Ephemeris*. (See section on the manual casting of the horoscope, on page 25.)

The sun is in either one sign or another; it cannot be in two signs. The dividing line between two signs is called a cusp—hence the often-heard statement, "I was born on a cusp." In the case of those born on or near a cusp it is necessary to compute the horoscope mathematically to determine the Sun sign. (See Chapter 2 on how to erect a horoscope, or make arrangements for the horoscope to be cast by computer.) For the calculation to be accurate, one must know the month, day, year, hour (minute, if possible), and location of the birth.

Each of the twelve signs of the Zodiac represents certain unique positive characteristics as well as unique negative characteristics of human behavior and development. Everyone has all twelve signs included in his horoscope. Their effect on the various departments of his life is determined by the position of the planets in these signs and the interaction between the signs of the Zodiac and the houses of the horoscope.

Houses

Like the signs of the Zodiac, the houses divide the horoscope into twelve segments. Each house is fundamentally related to one sign of the

Zodiac. The houses, however, are defined by the Earth's 24-hour rotation on its axis, whereas the signs of the Zodiac are defined by the Earth's yearly revolution around the Sun. Like the Sun signs, the houses are also divided by lines called cusps. The First House cusp or Ascendant is found by determining that point in space where the eastern horizon at the time and place of birth intercepts the ecliptic. Thus any one of the twelve signs which lie along the ecliptic could be found on the eastern horizon. Time and location of one's birth, therefore, determine which of the twelve signs will be rising.

The rising sign is also known as the Ascendant. It indicates one's manner of self-expression, character, abilities, and appearance. It describes one's early environment.

Following the First House cusp are the Second through Twelfth houses, which represent different departments of practical affairs: money, marriage, profession, the domestic scene, friendship, etc. (See pages 82–95 for a complete description of the jurisdiction of each house.)

The most important of these houses are called the cardinal, or angular, houses. They consist of the Ascendant (First House or rising sign), the Fourth House cusp (or Nadir, where the plane of the meridian passes underneath the Earth and intersects the ecliptic), the Seventh House cusp (or the Descendant, defined as the point where the western horizon intersects the ecliptic), and the Tenth House cusp (or Midheaven). The Midheaven, also written M.C., is defined as that point where the meridian —the line passing from north to south through a point directly overhead called the zenith—intersects the plane of the ecliptic. The other eight house cusps are spaced at approximately equal intervals between these four angular house cusps.

Each house cusp bears a sign of the Zodiac (see Chart 4). The sign will determine the way the department of life ruled by that house will be expressed in the life of the individual.

If your birthday is October 8 and you were born at 4:00 P.M., your Sun sign would be in the Eighth House. This puts Libra on the Eighth House, Scorpio on the Ninth, Sagittarius on the Tenth, Capricorn on the Eleventh, Aquarius on the Twelfth, Pisces on the First (commonly called the Ascendant), Aries on the Second, Taurus on the Third, Gemini on the Fourth, Cancer on the Fifth, Leo on the Sixth, and Virgo on the Seventh. This combination would give approximately Pisces rising. These calculations are not an accurate way of setting up the horoscope but a means of checking for errors in the original casting.

CHART 3

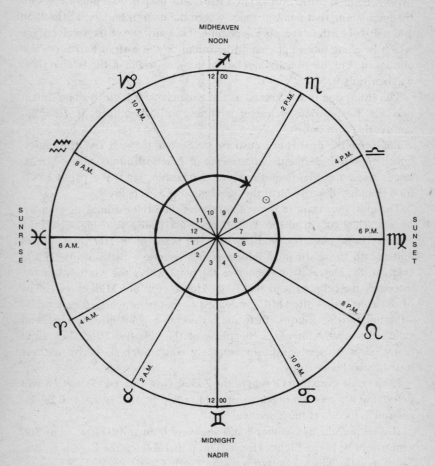

CHART 4

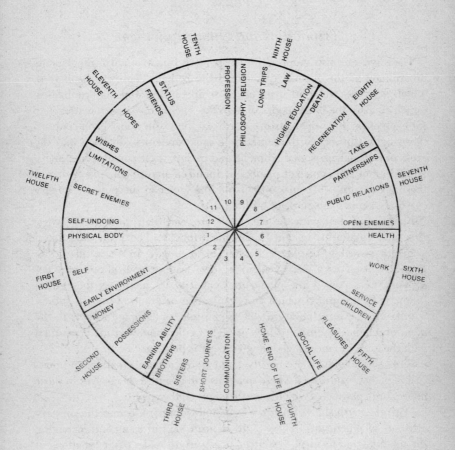

After determining and reading about your Sun sign and the houses, read Chapter 4 on the overlay patterns, which describes the characteristics of the Sun as they are related to and modified by the rest of the Zodiac. For instance, if you are a Libra, apply your horoscope to the Libra overlay.

Triplicities and Quadruplicities

The signs are also grouped into two more fundamental arrangements determined by the geometric layout of the Zodiac. These are triplicities, which deal with the tendencies of the temperament, and quadruplicities, which concern the basic modes of activity. There are four triplicities, one for each of the four elements fire, earth, air, and water, and each contains three signs. Conversely there are three quadruplicities, dividing into the areas of cardinal, fixed, and mutable, and each of these contains four signs. Should a preponderance of planets be found in signs belonging to one of these groupings, it becomes an outstanding factor in the person's quality of expression in some phase of his life.

First, let us deal with the elements: fire, earth, air, and water. Aries, Leo, and Sagittarius belong to the fire triplicity. The individuals born under them seek to display leadership in some way. In Aries, this desire manifests itself as a decisiveness in spearheading new efforts and endeavors. Leos possess the managerial capacity for acting as the central dramatic figure around which an organization or group of people gather. Sagittarians have the ability to act as spiritual, philosophic leaders in the areas of religion, philosophy, law, or higher education; they are concerned with the ideas around which human society is built.

Fire sign individuals are positive, aggressive, ardent, creative, and masculine in their expression. These qualities will manifest themselves in those houses or departments which have fire signs on the cusp.

With the earth signs, Taurus, Virgo, and Capricorn, comes the primary attribute of practicality. These signs indicate skill in using and managing the material and financial resources necessary to make other functions of human life possible. In whatever houses the earth signs are found, one will manifest the quality of practicality.

Taurus's practical quality appears as the ability to accumulate and manage money and other material resources. In Virgo, practicality is evidenced as intelligence and skill in labor and constructing those material objects essential to man. It is also concerned with properly maintaining our most

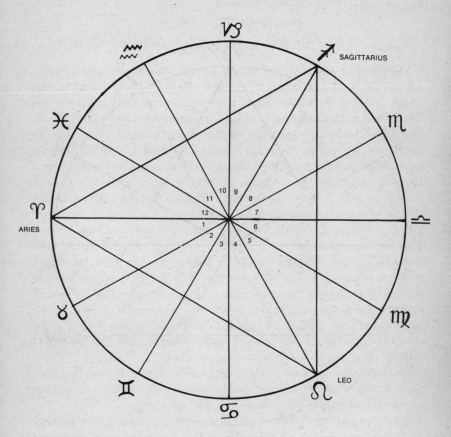

CHART 5

Fire Triplicity (120° △ Trine Aspect)

Always count 30° from one sign to the next sign.

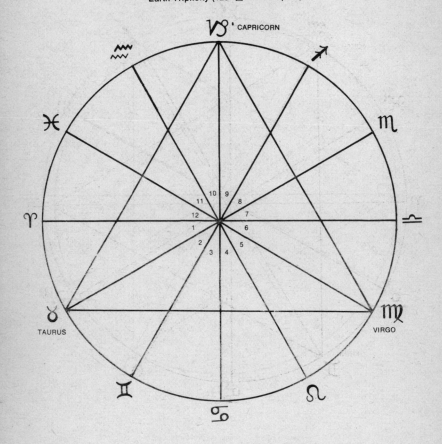

CHART 6

Earth Triplicity (120° △ Trine Aspect)

Always count 30° from one sign to the next sign.

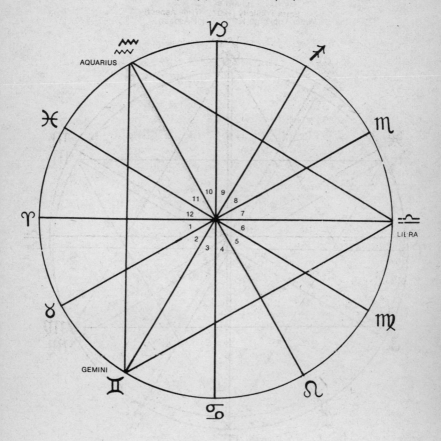

CHART 7

Air Triplicity (120° △ Trine Aspect)

Always count 30° from one sign to the next sign.

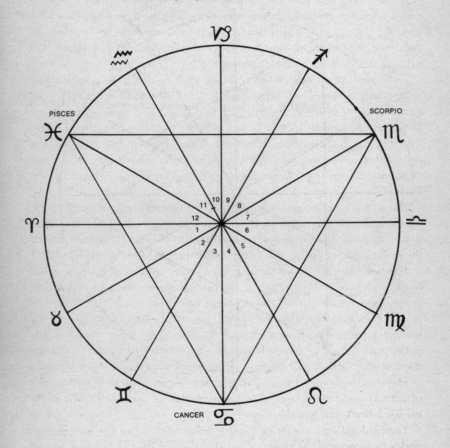

CHART 8

Water Triplicity (120° △ Trine Aspect)

Always count 30° from one sign to the next sign.

valuable material possession, our physical bodies. With Capricorn, there is the practical ability to organize and manage vast business and governmental enterprises. Or, on a more mundane level, the ability to structure and organize ordinary business affairs.

The air element, or air triplicity, consists of the signs Gemini, Libra, and Aquarius. They deal with the intellectual capacity of man, which includes communication and social interrelationships. The air signs manifest strong mental abilities and intellectual attributes in one form or another. In whatever department of your horoscope the air signs are found you will evince social and intellectual qualities.

In Gemini, this intellectualism shows itself as the ability to acquire, utilize, and communicate factual information. A certain originality from repatterning of ideas is often present. In Libra, these qualities are manifested as the ability to weigh and balance, making just comparisons. There is also a strong social awareness which leads to natural ability in psychology and related disciplines. In Aquarius intellectuality is expressed as an intuitive grasp of universal principles, along with a concern for the universal well-being of humanity.

The water signs, or water triplicities, are Cancer, Scorpio, and Pisces. Concerned with the realm of emotion and feeling, they deal with sensitivity, intuition, and the deeper psychic aspects of life. In whatever houses the water signs are found, one's deep emotions will be manifested.

This quality of emotion appears in Cancer as strong feelings about home and family. In Scorpio, it appears as strong feelings concerning death, joint resources, and the deeper occult mysteries of life. In Pisces, it is shown as a strong mystical feeling toward the Infinite and as unconscious telepathic communication with other people. (This includes a sympathetic awareness of the environment.) Such sensitivity leads to extreme impressionability, so that Pisces is strongly influenced by the unconscious.

The quadruplicities are groupings of four signs. They deal with modes of activity and with adaptability to circumstances and are known as the cardinal, fixed, and mutable signs.

The cardinal signs are Aries, Cancer, Libra, and Capricorn. People born under them possess the ability to act directly and decisively upon present circumstances. They have a realistic grasp of the immediate situation and its potentials for action. In whatever houses or departments of life the cardinal signs are found, one likes activity and is capable of initiating and organizing new enterprises. Positively expressed, these signs manifest constructive initiative, but on the negative side, there can be busybody tendencies and thoughtless actions.

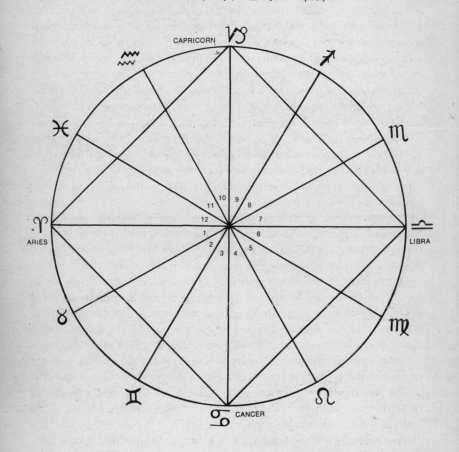

CHART 9

Cardinal Quadruplicity (90° □ Square Aspect)

Always count 30° from one sign to the next sign.

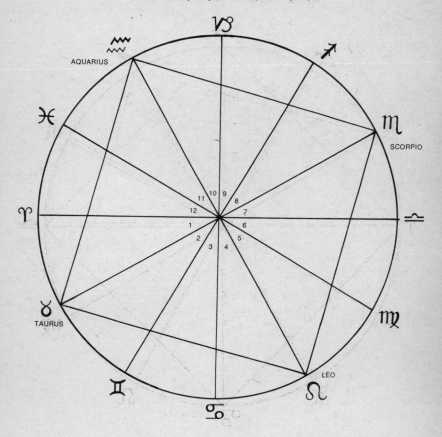

CHART 10

Fixed Quadruplicity (90° □ Square Aspect)

Always count 30° from one sign to the next sign.

CHART 11

Mutable Quadruplicity (90° ☐ Square Aspect)

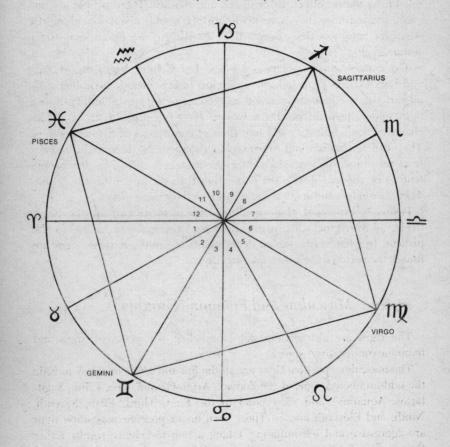

Always count 30° from one sign to the next sign.

The fixed quadruplicity consists of Taurus, Leo, Scorpio, and Aquarius. Those born under these signs achieve results through persistence and determination; their success comes through unwavering perseverance over an extended period of time. They are goal oriented and in this sense concerned with the future. The positive attributes of fixity are constancy and reliability; the negative, stubbornness and rigidity. These people are not easily swayed once they have made up their minds about something. In whatever houses or departments these fixed signs are found, one exerts sustained effort.

The mutable quadruplicity is composed of Gemini, Virgo, Sagittarius, and Pisces. These signs indicate a richness of experiences in dealing with all varieties of circumstances, and an accompanying mental ability. Those born under them adapt themselves to the exigencies of life and like chameleons are able to meld into their circumstances and surroundings. They can be flexible and ingenious in emergencies. This ability comes from previous experience in similar circumstances. Mutable sign people tend to be concerned with the past rather than the present or the future. They should be careful not to get trapped in their memories.

Positively expressed, these qualities appear as resourcefulness; negatively, as worry, neurosis, nervousness, and the inability to live in the present. In whatever houses or departments of life the mutable signs are found, the person will express adaptability.

Masculine and Feminine Groupings

The signs are also divided into masculine (or positive) signs and feminine (or negative) signs.

The masculine/positive signs are all the fire and air signs. They include the odd-numbered signs of the Zodiac (Aries, Gemini, Leo, Libra, Sagittarius, Aquarius) and correspond to the First, Third, Fifth, Seventh, Ninth, and Eleventh houses. Those born under positive/masculine signs are aggressive and self-initiating, taking action to achieve results rather than waiting for things to come to them. Wherever these signs are placed in your horoscope, in these areas you are likely to take initiative or go after what you want.

A strong preponderance of planets in masculine signs indicates a self-propelling person with positive aggressive tendencies. In a man's chart such a preponderance is favorable. However, in a woman's chart it can

CHART 12

Masculine Signs ♈ ♊ ♌ ♎ ♐ ♒

Negative Signs ♉ ♋ ♍ ♏ ♑ ♓

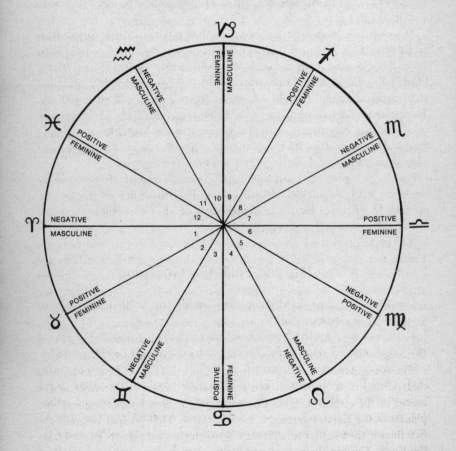

indicate an inclination to be more aggressive than is traditionally considered appropriate for her sex.

The negative or feminine signs include all the earth and water signs. They are the even-numbered signs of the Zodiac (Taurus, Cancer, Virgo, Scorpio, Capricorn, and Pisces) and correspond to the Second, Fourth, Sixth, Eighth, Tenth, and Twelfth houses.

These negative/feminine signs indicate passivity. At times, however, persons born under them are capable of acting forcibly, although they usually wait for things to come to them before taking action. In this respect, they are passive and interact with what happens to come their way. They work by a principle of attracting what they desire rather than attempting to go out and conquer it.

If a strong preponderance of planets occurs in negative passive signs, the person probably will not manifest himself aggressively but can possess great strength in terms of passive endurance. A grouping of negative signs in a woman's horoscope makes her more feminine and is considered appropriate for her sex. In a man's chart it can encourage effeminacy and lack of aggressiveness.

Aspects

The eight planets we are concerned with in astrology, as seen from the Earth, all rotate at different speeds around the Sun in approximately the same plane in space. As a result of these planetary motions, various angles, measured in degrees, minutes, and seconds, are formed between the planets as seen from the Earth. An angle is defined as that fraction of a circle formed between two intersecting lines. The number of degrees between two imaginary lines connecting two planets with the Earth forms the angular relationship between those planets with respect to the Earth.

These angular relationships are called aspects. In geometry, an angle is that portion of a circle between two straight lines that intersect at the center of the circle. Imagine that two straight lines connecting any two planets to the Earth intersect at the birthplace. That portion between the two lines is the angular relationship between the two planets as seen from the Earth. Certain degrees of angularity are very important to astrology; $0°$, $60°$, $90°$, $120°$, $180°$, for example, are the major aspects, known as conjunction, sextile, square, trine, and opposition respectively. (There are also several minor aspects, which are not dealt with in this book.)

Major Aspects

An aspect is the angle formed between two points in the horoscope and may be formed by two planets to each other or by a planet to some other point in the horoscope.

Aspect	Degrees Apart	Symbol	Influence
Conjunction	0 (in the same degree)	☌	variable (expression, action)
Sextile	60	✳	good (opportunities, ideas)
Square	90	□	Adverse, inharmonious (goals and ambitions)
Trine	120	△	favorable, harmonious (creativity, expansion)
Opposition	180	☍	inharmonious (relationships)

The conjunction is the direct lineup of two planets as seen from the Earth. In an ideal conjunction 0° separates the two planets. However, an aspect has an orb, or orb of influence—the amount by which the two planets involved can deviate from the exact number of degrees of the aspect and still be considered to have an aspect influence.

In the case of the five major aspects, a deviation of plus or minus 6° from the exact number of degrees in the aspect is allowed. (This is known as an orb of 6°.) Should the Sun or Moon be involved in the aspect, an orb of 10° is allowed.

The conjunction (☌) is a very dynamic aspect, since it marks a strong focalized potential for expression along with a tendency for direct action and self-dramatization. The two planets in a conjunction indicate a specific psychological characteristic in the person (which can be ascertained by reading first the chapter on conjunctions and then the section on the specific planets conjuncting; see, for example, "Mars Conjunct Uranus" on page 302). If you want to interpret the aspect further, study Chapter 9 on interpreting and integrating aspects.

The sextile (✳) aspect is 60° or one-sixth of a circle. The position of a planet in a sign is determined by degrees and minutes of degrees measured from the beginning of a sign. This distance can never be more than 30°0′ since there are never more than 30° in a sign. Planets in sextile aspect are placed two signs apart and occupy approximately the same number of degrees in these signs within an allowable difference of plus or minus 6°. However, if one of the planets is in the very beginning of a sign and another planet is in the last degrees of another sign, the two planets may still be within a 6° orb of being 60° apart, forming what is known as a hidden aspect. In this case, the signs occupied by the planets are adjoining, whereas in the case of most sextiles at least one sign intervenes between the two signs occupied by the two planets which form the sextile aspect. The sextile represents an easy flow of opportunities or ideas that, if acted upon, will help realize the individual's goals.

The square (□) aspect is a 90° angle relationship. Planets in square aspect generally occupy the same number of degrees in signs which are three signs apart (or have two signs between the signs occupied by the planets). If there is only one intervening sign, the aspect is called a hidden aspect. A square indicates the areas in the individual's life where adjustments must be made and where he must expend tremendous effort to realize gains.

The trine (△) aspect is an angular relationship of 120° or one-third of a circle between two planets. Planets in trine aspect generally occupy the same number of degrees in signs which are four signs apart (or have three signs between them). In a hidden aspect there will be only two intervening signs. The trine is an aspect of creativity and expansion; it is the most fortunate of all aspects.

The opposition (☌) aspect is an angular relationship of 180° between two planets. Planets in opposition generally occupy approximately the same number of degrees in two signs directly across the Zodiac from each other; they are automatically six signs apart with five signs separating them. If there is a hidden aspect, only four signs separate the signs occupied by the two planets. An opposition aspect indicates a situation in which one must cooperate with others or break with them.

It is important to remember that signs, not houses, are counted in this process of determining what aspects are present in a chart, since a house may contain considerably more or less degrees than a whole sign. In the commonly used Placidian system of houses, it is possible in extreme northern latitudes for one house to contain two whole signs or for a single sign to be present simultaneously on the cusps of two houses.

CHAPTER 2

Basic Chart Calculation

If the ancient wisdom disclosed in the rest of this book is the soul of astrology, then accurate chart calculations could be called the heart of astrology, for without accurate charts as a guide one cannot utilize the ancient science at all.

Do not take chart calculations lightly. Normally about £25 of reference books, knowledge of mathematical interpolation, and a good half-hour to an hour of accurate calculations are necessary for each really accurate chart. If you are seriously interested in becoming a professional astrologer, you must master this science. This chapter gives a complete guide to calculating exact natal charts. However, if you are a beginner in astrology, or are unsure of your degree of interest, you might consider the computerized service developed by the American company, Astronomical Computations for Astrologers, Inc. ACA will send you a complete personal horoscope chart, together with a full list of astrological chart details. Each item is cross-referenced with the text of this book by page and number, so that it will be easy to interpret and study your own individual horoscope. The ACA charts are professionally prepared and accurate to within one minute. They are used by many experienced astrologers and teachers and will add personal excitement to your study of this book.

The bane of every good astrologer is the "approximate" chart. Do not use shortcut techniques unless you fully understand what accuracy is being lost, and what the implications are. Aquia, the technique described here, gives exact charts if followed exactly.

Information Needed

The astrology chart is a picture of the heavens at the moment you were born. The planets must be located first with respect to the stars (the

Zodiac), then with respect to the horizon (the houses). Thus it is necessary to have the exact birthtime (month, day, year, time) and birthplace (city, country). You should obtain this information as far in advance as possible to allow you adequate time to do an accurate calculation.

Necessary References

Ephemeris. This is a set of tables that give the planets' location by sign at noon or midnight (Greenwich Mean Time—GMT) for each day of each year. We strongly suggest *Raphael's Ephemeris* (Foulsham, 55p each year) or *Die Deutsche Ephermeride* (Otto-Wilhelm-Barth-Verlag, about £3.50 for each decade). Although published in Germany, this latter set is quite understandable to the English-speaking astrologer.

Longitude and Latitude

You must determine the longitude and latitude of the birthplace. There are several excellent books available for this purpose. *Philip's Record Atlas* and *The Times Atlas* (*Index*) are a cheap and an expensive version, respectively.

Time Changes

A knowledge of time zones and daylight, wartime, and summertime changes is needed to correct the birthtime to GMT. Doris Doane's *Time Changes in the USA, Time Changes in Canada and Mexico,* and *Time Changes in the World* (Professional Astrologers, Inc.) are the most accurate compilations of these changes.

Table of Houses

This table gives the house cusps from a time calculation. *Raphael's Table of Houses in Northern Latitudes* and *Table of Houses in Great Britain* are easily obtainable and quite adequate.

Additional Calculation References

Several books on chart casting techniques are available. Alan Leo's *Casting the Horoscope* (Fowler) and Margaret Hone's *Modern Textbook of Astrology* (Fowler) are very good.

Procedure

1. Assemble information and references. For this example I will use *Time Changes in the World, Philip's Record Atlas, Raphael's Ephemeris and Table of Houses.* As an example I will use July 7, 1942, Liverpool, 7:15 A.M.

2. Look up location in *Time Changes in the World* to check for summertime. On page 48 note that July 7, 1942, falls during World War II, when double summertime was in force in Great Britain, so two hours must be subtracted from the birthtime. Therefore, birthtime was 5:15 A.M. Greenwich Mean Time.

3. Look up longitude and latitude in *Philip's Record Atlas* to get location and time corrections. On page 66 note that the coordinates of Liverpool, England, are 53 25 N and 2 55 W.

4. Look up sidereal time for the day in question. This is the time shown on an imaginary star clock at Greenwich at noon. It reads 6 hours 59 minutes 17 seconds.

5. Perform calculation. Four items must be added or subtracted. Make sure all four are present. They are:

a. Sidereal time at noon GMT (step 4).

b. Difference in time between noon and birthtime GMT. In this case it is 6 hours 45 minutes (the difference between 5:15 A.M. and noon). The birth was *before* noon, so subtract the difference. If it was *after* noon, add the difference.

c. Sidereal correction. The formula is "ten seconds for each hour" of difference between birthtime and noon (b. above). In this example the formula reads 10 sec x 6¾ (six hours and 45 minutes) = 67 seconds. The same rule applies, as in b. Before noon = subtracting, afternoon = adding.

d. The longitude sidereal correction term, which is calculated according to this formula: multiply by four the degrees and minutes of longitude of the birthplace and call the result and seconds of time. In this example, we multiply 2° 55′ by four, and the answer is 11 minutes 40 seconds. Subtract if *west* of Greenwich, add if *east* of Greenwich.

Here is the calculation in tabular form:

	Hours	Minutes	Seconds
a. Sidereal time noon GMT (step 4)	06	59	17
b. Time difference	−06	45	
Result so far	00	14	17
c. Sidereal correction	−00	01	07
Result so far	00	13	10
d. Longitude correction	−00	11	40
Local sidereal time at birth	00	01	30

This is the final sidereal time accurate to one second.

6. You must now examine the appropriate table of houses to convert this sidereal time into the Ascendant and House cusps on the horoscope. For Liverpool, there is a table for that exact latitude. In the top left-hand corner of the columns you can see these columns:

Sidereal time	10	11	12	Ascen	2	3
hr. m. s.	♈	♉	♊	♋	♌	♍
0 0 0	0°	9°	24°	28° 12′	14°	3°
0 3 40	1	10	25	28 51	14	4

This means that when the sidereal clock at Liverpool reads 0 hours 0 minutes 0 seconds, the 0° of Aries lies due south, on the Midheaven, on the 10th House cusp. The 9° of Taurus is the cusp (or beginning) of the 11th Houses, while 24° Gemini is the start of the 12th House. The all-important Ascendant, where the Zodiac crosses the Liverpool horizon, is 28° 12′ Cancer, and the 2nd House begins at 14° Leo and the 3rd House at 3° Virgo.

Three minutes 40 seconds later, shown in the second line, all these positions had changed. The sidereal time we are interested in, 0 hours 01 minutes 30 seconds, lies in between these two, so it's a simple matter of interpolation to arrive at the correct result. Roughly, in your head, you can calculate that our time lies approximately midway between those shown in the table, so all the House cusps will be roughly halfway between the two values given. To be accurate, the time difference between 0 hours 0 minutes 0 seconds and the birth sidereal time is obviously 0 hours 1 minute 30 seconds, so the interpolation factor is

Cusps	10th	11th	12th	Ascen	2nd	3rd
Initial value	0° ♈	9° ♉	24° ♊	28° 12′ ♋	14° ♌	3° ♍
Next value shown	1° ♈	10° ♉	25° ♊	28° 51′ ♋	14° ♌	4° ♍
Approximate difference	60′	60′	60′	0° 39′	0°	60′
Difference x inter-polation factor of $\frac{90}{220}$	24′	24′	24′	16′	0°	24′
Correct cusps for this sidereal birthtime	0° 24′ ♈	9° 24′ ♉	24° 24′ ♊	28° 28′ ♋	14° ♌	3° 24′ ♍

$\dfrac{1 \text{ min } 30 \text{ sec}}{3 \text{ min } 40 \text{ sec}} = \dfrac{90}{220}$ which is then applied to the difference between the

House cusps and Ascendant.

The complete calculations can be seen on page 28. The opposite cusp values are exactly 180° from these values. Thus the 5th House cusp will be 9° 24′ ♏, the sign opposite ♉, which is the 11th House cusp.

7. A similar interpolation must be done to ascertain the exact planetary locations. In this case the sidereal time is not used, but the ordinary GMT determined in step 2. In our example it is 5:15 A.M.

Since the birth was before noon, the interpolation must be between the noon positions on July 6, the day before, and those on July 7 itself. In this 24-hour period, the moment 5:15 A.M. is $\dfrac{6 \text{ hours } 45 \text{ minutes}}{24 \text{ hours}}$ back along the

time track, or 405 ÷ 1440 minutes.

	Value on day before	Value on birthday	Difference (in min.)	Difference × $\dfrac{405}{1440}$	Final value
Sun	13/46 ♋	14/43 ♋	57	16	14/27 ♋
Moon	26/44 ♈	8/56 ♉	732	206	5/30 ♉
Mercury	22/36 ♊	23/34 ♊	58	16	23/18 ♊
Venus	10/06 ♊	11/16 ♊	70	19	10/57 ♊
Mars	13/51 ♌	14/28 ♌	37	10	14/18 ♌
Jupiter	5/57 ♋	6/10 ♋	13	4	6/06 ♋
Saturn	7/21 ♊	7/28 ♊	7	2	7/26 ♊
Uranus	2/54 ♊	2/57 ♊	3	1	2/56 ♊
Neptune	27/18 ♍	27/19 ♍	1	0	27/19 ♍
Pluto	4/33 ♌	4/49 ♌	16	5	4/44 ♌
(on page 39)	(June 30)	(July 10)	(in 10 days)		
N. Node	7/01 ♍	6/55 ♍	6	1	6/56 ♍
	(July 5)	(July 7)	(in 2 days)		

If the birth is before noon, you subtract the interpolation from the noon positions; if after noon, you add them to the noon positions. The one exception is when a planet is retrograde (shown by the planetary movement going backward from one day to the next); in this example, the Node (as ever) is retrograde, so the interpolation is added, even though the birth is A.M.

8. Births outside Britain. Step 2 must include examining the relevant time zone as well as summertime. If this example had been calculated for Boston, Mass., one hour would have been subtracted for wartime in the U.S.A., but another five hours added to correct Eastern Standard Time to

CHART 13

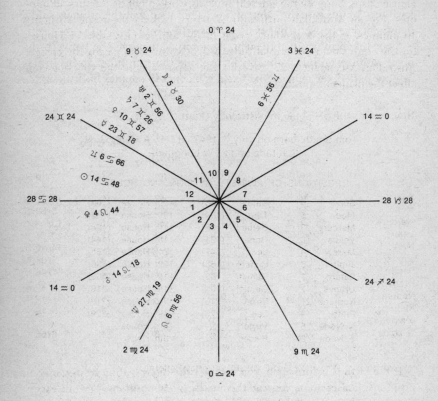

0 ♈ 24

9 ♉ 24

3 ♓ 24

☽ 5 ♉ 30

♅ 2 ♓ 56

♃ 6 ♓ 56

♄ 7 ♓ 26

24 ♊ 24

♀ 10 ♊ 57

14 ♒ 0

☿ 23 ♊ 18

♃ 6 ♋ 66

10 9

☉ 14 ♋ 48

11   8

12   7

28 ♋ 28

1   6

28 ♑ 28

2   5

♀ 4 ♌ 44

3 4

⚷ 14 ♌ 18

14 ♒ 0

24 ♐ 24

♇ 27 ♍ 19

☊ 6 ♍ 56

2 ♍ 24

9 ♏ 24

0 ♎ 24

GMT. Details for every country in the world are given in the Doris Doane books.

9. The 24-hour clock system. When calculating sidereal time for any birthtime, do remember that you can add or subtract 24 hours to the result in order to keep a positive result between 0 hours and 24 hours.

10. Birth in Southern Latitudes. The rule is quite simple. Add 12 hours to the sidereal time of birth and reverse the Zodiac signs given for the House cusps. Suppose the sidereal time, as worked out, is 8 hours 40 minutes. For an Australian birth, add 12 hours, making the result 20 hours 40 minutes. If the Ascendant, given in the appropriate table of Houses for the equivalent northern latitude, is 27° Taurus, this means the correct Australian Ascendant is 27° Scorpio, the opposite sign. But this does not affect the planetary positions.

Astrology Chart

Tom Smith, born on July 7, 1942, at 7:15 A.M. at 53° N Latitude and 2° W Longitude

POSITIONS OF PLANETS BY SIGN AND HOUSE

Sun	14°	Cancer	(38)*	12th House	(103)
Moon	5°	Taurus	(104)	10th House	(112)
Mercury	23°	Gemini	(115)	11th House	(128)
Venus	10°	Gemini	(131)	11th House	(144)
Mars	14°	Leo	(147)	2nd House	(155)
Jupiter	6°	Cancer	(165)	12th House	(180)
Saturn	7°	Gemini	(183)	11th House	(198)
Uranus	2°	Gemini	(201)	11th House	(212)
Neptune	27°	Virgo	(215)	3rd House	(219)
Pluto	4°	Leo	(226)	1st House	(229)
N. Node	6°	Virgo		3rd House	
S. Node	6°	Pisces		9th House	

HOUSE CUSPS (Overlay Pattern)

Cancer	is on your	1st House	(60)	Ascendant
Leo	is on your	2nd House	(60)	
Virgo	is on your	3rd House	(60)	
Libra	is on your	4th House	(60)	Nadir
Scorpio	is on your	5th House	(61)	
Sagittarius	is on your	6th House	(61)	

* Numbers in parentheses refer to the page in *The Astrologer's Handbook* where the explanatory information can be found for your horoscope.

Astrology Chart (continued)

Capricorn	is on your	7th	House	(61)	Descendant
Aquarius	is on your	8th	House	(61)	
Pisces	is on your	9th	House	(61)	
Aries	is on your	10th	House	(62)	Midheaven
Taurus	is on your	11th	House	(62)	
Gemini	is on your	12th	House	(62)	

ASPECTS

Sun Aspects

Sun conjunct Jupiter   (280) 8° orb, separating

Moon Aspects

Moon sextile Jupiter   (332) 1° orb, separating
Moon square Pluto   (360) 1° orb, separating

Mercury Aspects

Mercury square Neptune (364) 4° orb, applying

Venus Aspects

Venus sextile Mars   (337) 4° orb, applying
Venus conjunct Saturn   (297) 3° orb, separating
Venus sextile Pluto   (339) 6° orb, separating

Saturn Aspects

Saturn conjunct Uranus   (310) 3° orb, separating
Saturn sextile Pluto   (347) 3° orb, separating

Uranus Aspects

Uranus trine Neptune   (410) 5° orb, separating
Uranus sextile Pluto   (348) 2° orb, applying

QUADRUPLICITIES AND TRIPLICITIES

Chart has 2 Fire, 2 Earth, 4 Air and 2 Water signs and 2 Cardinal, 3 Fixed, 5 Mutable signs.

CHAPTER 3

Sun Sign Potentials

The Sun sign is the most important single factor in interpreting the horoscope. It indicates the way a person expresses his basic energy potential and his creative drive to grow and develop as an individual. The Sun sign also indicates the stage of growth represented by the native's present incarnation, as well as the lessons he must master.

The Sun sign determines the dynamic expression of the will, which is manifested through the activity of the other planets in the horoscope. The will, as it is modified by the Sun's influence, is the fundamental component of consciousness, coloring all other modes of activity.

ARIES

March 21–April 19

Cardinal, Fire
Rulers: Mars, Pluto

Key Words: initiative, activity, enterprise

Aries, the first sign of the Zodiac, is the sign of new beginnings. The Arian's present life indicates a new cycle in his personal evolutionary development. Arians are aggressive and direct in expressing themselves. The key phrase for Aries is "I am."

Arians are full of creative energy and enthusiasm (because Aries is a fire sign ruled by Mars and Pluto); and, because Aries is a cardinal sign, Arians initiate new activities, which keep them occupied until the novelty wears off.

These people have a tremendous psychological drive to prove themselves to themselves through action. Arians are not satisfied merely to intellectualize about their concerns; they are impatient to do something about them.

If Arians can learn to think before taking action, their energetic natures will enable them to accomplish much. However, their impulsiveness and inability to listen to the advice of others tend to involve them in difficulties. Arians are likely also to be impatient and do not always finish what they start, leaving follow-up activities to those with fixed and mutable signs.

Since they are highly competitive, Arians seek to be first and best in whatever they do. They make good leaders, seeking fame and recognition more than wealth and comfort. However, because of their desire for authority and superiority, they are sometimes overly aggressive and prone to use force rather than reason and diplomacy in dealing with others. If they do not possess the necessary wisdom and experience to back up their craving for leadership, they can appear foolish. Arians must be first! But much of their strength arises out of their refusal to admit defeat. They are never daunted by failure and will always seek new avenues of expression.

Arians need to learn the lesson of love, so that they can relate to others and reach out to them with consideration. By reflecting on the overall consequences of their actions, they can learn this lesson.

The more highly evolved Arian types possess great willpower, spiritual self-confidence, and regenerative ability, due to the Sun's exaltation in this sign.

TAURUS

April 20–May 20

Fixed, Earth   Key Words: possessions,
Ruler: Venus   determination, practicality

Taurus is the sign of purposeful determination and power. And, as it is also an earth sign, Taureans were born to achieve mastery over physical matter. The element earth teaches and guides them to become efficient in practical matters. They strive for spiritual truth by working with the practical aspects of life.

Taureans are fond of the good things of life and often focus their attention on material acquisitions. The key phrase for Taurus is "I have." Love of comfort, satisfaction, and pleasure is also a characteristic of people born under this sign. Whatever fulfills these needs has great value to Taureans, and they make an effort to possess it. Once they do, no earthly force can persuade them to attach their interests elsewhere. Taureans see to it that nothing interferes with what they want. They want money, not for its own sake, but so they can enjoy the things it enables them to purchase.

Since Venus rules Taureans, they have a high appreciation of form and beautiful things, especially those which appeal to the sense of touch. They are fond of good clothing and are genuinely impressed by others' appearances. They tend to use beauty too as a means to their ends.

The hub of the Taureans' universe is security, both emotional and material. Taureans withhold themselves from involvement until they have determined whether a person, situation, or relationship will be of use to them. However, out of their strong sense of loyalty they often burden themselves with the griefs and problems of their friends. They are intensely jealous, to the point of being absurd. They regard another person's affections as their property. This possessiveness is a result of their deep inner need, both emotional and mental, for security.

Since they have powerful and sensitive emotional natures, coupled with intellectual capacity, they are often miserable if they marry beneath their station.

They are not aware of inner motives, as a rule. Self-analysis is not important to them. They are endowed with a strong willpower, which enables them to make plans from a distance, perhaps even years in advance. Thus, they strive assiduously toward their goals, firm in their acquisitive instincts. Success usually follows their efforts.

Taureans have their own methods of doing things, and if one wants a smooth relationship with them, it is wise not to interfere with them or attempt to make them over.

GEMINI

May 21–June 21

Mutable, Air
Ruler: Mercury

Key Words: mentality, versatility, nonconformism

Individuals born under the intellectual air sign Gemini are ruled by Mercury and think and act swiftly. The key phrase for Gemini is "I think."

Since Mercury has to do with communication, Geminis must identify and classify. They must produce words and models in order for their contacts to be meaningful to them. Speech is especially important to them, serving as a framework for their activities. Words are anchoring or safety devices, as the mind jumps from one thing to another. Geminis' ease of speech is a positive attribute, but they must keep in mind the harm they can do by being chatterboxes.

They are thirsty for knowledge and eager to study. Generally, they have a highly developed learning capacity. Their inventive imagination qualifies them for professions in writing, experimentation, and criticism. Education is therefore necessary to them from the time they are born. If their training is poor, they often make life unbearable for others. If they are well educated, however, they tend to be charming and refined individuals.

Geminis' reactions are prescribed by the mood of the moment; hence the dual quality to their personality. Variety is the spice of life as they see it, and this philosophy makes them high-strung. Unless things go their way, they are likely to become depressed. Geminis are happiest when they have more than one dominant interest.

Their state of nervous awareness allows no intellectual or physical tranquillity. In emergencies, therefore, they rarely lose control, and their ingenuity provides unsuspected solutions.

Since Gemini rules the hands and arms, as well as the nerves, these people experience much pleasure when their hands are busy giving form to their ideas, and their ideas are plentiful!

Geminis must work to acquire calmness of mind as well as body. They might well begin by trying to keep their hands and feet still and to eat slowly. This discipline will enable them to maintain control even during angry moments or extreme nervous tension.

Geminis enjoy great popularity, largely because of their witty conversation, mental agility, sociability, courteousness, and intuition. However, they dislike being bound to any particular person or place. Their home life, therefore, leaves much to be desired. They are continually curious and always searching for personal intellectual security in the middle of their constantly changing experiences. They are fond of constant travel and changes of atmosphere.

Although they have no special attachment to material belongings, Geminis see money as power and freedom and feel an attraction to it. They may be thrifty with their own money but squander that of others.

As children, Geminis are so charming and ingenious that parents and educators are often blind to their defects. They should be trained early, since their objectionable traits are extremely hard to correct in later years. Once they are adults, education or discipline must come through their own volition. When this process occurs, this passion turns into creative energy and originality, which can be manifested in both business and the arts.

Geminis are the nonconformists of the Zodiac. Thus, they must maintain their separateness and remain different from those around them. They feel that if their potential is to be fully realized they must emerge from every possible kind of bondage. They rebel against the status quo, often breaking rules and resisting authority, never yielding their individuality to one place or to one person. They will never act because someone or convention tells them to do so. However, as they grow older, they come to realize that cooperation is necessary to self-fulfillment. As Dane Rudhyar says, the very air we breathe has been exhaled by someone else's lungs. The air signs bring the individual to realize his relationship to humanity's common lot.

If Geminis master their deficiencies and negative tendencies, the excellent potentialities they possess at birth will enable them to reach high objectives.

CANCER

June 22–July 22

Cardinal, Water   Key Words: domesticity, sensitivity,
Ruler: Moon   tenacity

Cancers were born under the sign of emotional sensitivity. The key phrase for Cancer is "I feel." This is the strongest of the water signs, favoring women more than men, since Cancer, of all the signs of the Zodiac, is most strongly linked to domesticity and homemaking.

Cancers possess highly developed protective and defensive instincts, which are aimed at material and domestic security. They are extraordinarily sensitive and fearful of ridicule. The crab shell, Cancer's symbol, represents the crust or armor which hides extreme sensitivity and shyness, as well as physical and psychological vulnerability. Cancers protect themselves from the possibility of emotional hurt by withdrawing and finding their security in solitude. This tendency is unfortunate because of their powerful need for home and children. Completion is not a reality for them until they are able to lavish their protectiveness on the family.

Because of their strong need for security, they will do whatever is needed to establish and serve that security. They seldom gamble unless they have safely put away their "rainy day money." Even then, gambling is rarely a means of livelihood, since they are reluctant to jeopardize their security. However, if their future stability depends upon taking a risk, they will take the risk—if possible, with someone else's money. But in that case Cancers would take great care to watch over the investment; they have a deep sense of responsibility toward others. They therefore pay their debts and expect others to do the same.

These people are very complex; at certain times they appear to have the strength of a giant and at other times they display the weakness of a child. This variability is due to the reversal of the Sun's direction in this sign: it stops in the northern skies and starts its trek southward. (Like the crab, heavenly bodies stand still in order to reverse their direction.) At that time we have the longest days of the year.

As a rule, Cancers are well-intentioned, but because of their inconstant Moon they are at one moment sweet and charmingly outgoing (especially when they have some objective in mind) and at the next melancholic, introverted, and distant.

They are noted for their diplomacy and seldom fail to achieve their goals. However, when they are hurt, they may behave in a nonsensical manner, being unable to collaborate with others. At times they can behave extremely childishly and stubbornly—and this is one of the major flaws they must work to overcome.

Although they appear gentle and tranquil, their inner thoughts are difficult to fathom. Since few people ever really comprehend how Cancers feel, they rarely get the necessary understanding from others.

Cancer children are by nature very tender, sweet and loving, willing to be helpful. Cancer mothers and fathers warm those who are lucky enough to be in their proximity. A word of caution: All Cancers should guard against bearing a smothering love.

Cancers desire the absolute possession of their beloved. It can be said of people under this sign that once a love is begun, it is never stopped. Resentment may make them cruel enemies, but they never stop loving. Theirs is the maternal love which brings out some of the complexities of this zodiacal sign. It is that of a mother who continues to love her sons even though she receives ill-treatment at their hands, so great is the maternal and paternal instinct of the sign. Cancers tend to be very much aware of their family trees. They are patriotic and have good memories for historical events.

They seek to avoid at all costs any mental or physical discomfort. Since neatness and cleanliness are conspicuous with this sign, it follows that they also dislike activities which prevent absolute cleanliness. They prefer a refined atmosphere.

Because of their powerful imaginations it is imperative for Cancers to avoid all thoughts of illness. They must also cultivate the courage to say yes or no at the appropriate moment. They need to control their tendencies to moodiness, intolerance, timidity, and excessive emotionality.

Cancers will not joke about themselves. They are inclined toward self-satisfaction and can be quite egotistical. On the other hand, they can be equally helpless in their determined, silent way. They have a great deal of personal vanity and like clothing and frivolities, which they use as tools to keep up appearances.

Cancers are masters of the art of passive resistance. This is a powerful weapon which, when wielded, makes the individual unapproachable.

With kindness, Cancers can be directed easily, since they are basically understanding. If they are forced, they become immovable.

They are averse to being told how to do things; they must complete tasks on their own, since the ideas of others confuse them. At times, they shun responsibility. However, if they work on an enterprise that promotes or requires it, they are punctual, exact, and efficient, willing to guide things through to a successful conclusion.

LEO

July 23–August 22

Fixed, Fire   Key Words: vitality, authority, power
Ruler: Sun

Leos were born under the sign of generosity and nobility of feeling. The sign Leo represents man's attempt at self-expression, the unfolding of the internal-power principle. Leo is a fire sign ruled by the Sun. Since it is the Sun's function to bestow upon the world heat, light, and life, it is the benefactor of every living creature. In our planetary system it is the center around which the planets rotate. Leos, then, are generous. They must have the spotlight and, once in it, they must shine. They enjoy being the center of attention.

Providence helps Leos when they need it most. New fields of action open at a time when there seems to be no visible solution to their problems. As the Sun infiltrates the darkest shadow, so it puts Leos in the light.

Leos' roots lie in the home and in their own personal independence. They feel the need to produce children both of their minds and of their bodies.

Leo rules the heart; therefore these people give of themselves generously through time, money, and knowledge, with no thought of the self.

They are strongly attracted to the opposite sex. Their love nature should be held in check, or serious heartache can be the result. (The French as a nation are ruled by Leo and afford ample illustration of this point.)

Leos are unconsciously drawn toward the idea that "the means justify the ends." Money is important only as a means of achieving their goals.

They assume that others possess a sense of integrity equal to their own, and consequently they are overly confident, frank, and outspoken. These traits cause them many interpersonal difficulties and they often lose friends.

They dislike repetition. Once they see the point, they become quite impatient, and often obstinate, in discussions. Those who disagree with a Leo's opinions should be tactful, for he will surrender so long as his dignity is recognized. He wants people to think well of him, and as he directs a great deal of energy to this goal, it is frequently achieved. Leos are very aware of the effect they have on others and study what to do in order to create a better effect. (This does not mean, however, that they are introspective or that they analyze themselves in order to improve their character.)

The role that they assume is a noble role, and their sense of the dramatic is so strong that they achieve nobility in playing this role, and thus create their own reality. But self-approval is also important to them—self-approbation replaces conscience. They will do anything they think is right—if necessary, sacrificing public disapproval for self-approval. If they are forced into a compromising situation, they will despise their work and neglect it.

The symbol of this sign is the lion, denoting majesty, power, and dignity. Leo is a kingly sign, and Leos express pride in every movement and a stateliness that will not escape the keen eye. Power will increase Leos' self-confidence amazingly, to the point where they seem actually to glow! As long as Leos feel that they are in a position of authority and responsibility, they will leave no stone unturned in order to justify the confidence that has been placed in them. Leos function well in positions of responsibility and management, expressing their creativity by setting policies. Leos whose desire for authority is unfulfilled may develop traits of indolence, laziness, impetuousness, and inconstancy.

Women born under this sign tend to dominate their marriages. They are like ferocious lionesses in defending their children. One may step on the toes of Leo mothers, but never on the toes of their children!

Leos are practical, philosophical, and spiritual. These qualities, along with their enthusiasm and inspiration, help them to mold public opinion. When Leos are controlled and informed, there are no others so powerful, useful, and capable of giving to their fellow men.

They have a reckless courage, but they never fight unfairly, no matter how great the advantages offered. In victory they remain magnanimous and in defeat stand unconquered. The key phrase for Leo is "I will."

VIRGO

August 23–September 22

Mutable, Earth   Key Words: discrimination,
Ruler: Mercury   methodicalness, service

For those born under the earth sign of Virgo, the hub of the universe is work. Since Mercury rules Virgos, they are forever seeking knowledge, which will bring matter under the control of the mind. Through this seeking, they learn that the mind of man is a good servant but a bad master, especially when the mind usurps the sovereignty of the spirit. Virgos have to learn that although the body must serve the mind, ultimately the mind must serve the spirit.

The symbol of this sign is a virgin with sheaves of grain in her hands. The sheaves represent the wisdom that is harvested in the fields of experience.

Virgos are meticulous in their work, paying a great deal of attention to detail and doing things carefully and efficiently. They like to bring order out of confusion. Because they value work and have a great deal of respect for it, they will go to great lengths to help a friend find employment but will seldom raise a finger to help someone who gets into difficulties because he refuses to work. To Virgos, the only true aristocracy is the aristocracy of the worker.

Virgos, however, are much too practical and intelligent to allow anyone to make martyrs of them. When the demands made on them become excessive and unreasonable, they say no, with conviction.

In its best form, this sign makes for efficiency and a brilliant performance of duty. At times, however, it bestows a narrowness of outlook: The individuals may be unable to talk about anything except their work, and they lack interest in anything that is not related to work.

Virgos subject their world to a microscopic analysis. Occasionally, they are engrossed with trivialities to the extent of becoming blind to the significance of the issue as a whole. Eventually, developed Virgos learn discrimination between the essential and the trivial. Once this power of making distinctions evolves, Virgos are able to become great scholars, constructive critics, excellent editors—all exacting perfection. The key phrase for Virgo is "I analyze."

However, Virgos should not mistake brilliant intellect, with its accompanying faculty of criticism, for heavenly wisdom. They must learn to be absolutely dispassionate in evaluating both their own performance and the performance of others.

They function at the height of their powers in careers that are related somehow to service. They are capable of great self-denial if they think their work is worthy of it.

Virgo also rules health. In this phase of their evolution, therefore, Virgos must learn that wise men do not exhaust their body energies by worrying, fretting, or overworking. Foolish fears and apprehensions can lead to semi-invalidism. Nevertheless, this sign has a marvelous physical resistance to disease, once the mind develops discipline. If Virgos can keep out of the clutches of disease, they become effective healing agents, exercising a splendid influence on the sick.

Virgo bodies reject all artificial food or medicine. Food is quite harmful to them when they are angry or in extreme anguish.

Because Virgo is an earth sign, Virgos admire material progress. They like good food and are fond of comfort and good clothes. Many people born under this sign are leaders in fashion. Virgos will inspect the labels on clothing to determine whether the article was manufactured by a reputable firm. No shoddy workmanship is passable for Virgos! However, they must learn to refrain from gossip and chattering about people who do not seem to approach their own particular standard of good appearance.

It is difficult for Virgos to accumulate large sums of money because of their excessive expenditures. They need to develop a system whereby they can avoid unnecessary expense, for while they are able to go on saving "sprees," the saving never lasts.

They are impressed by eloquent words strung together like pearls. These sounds are music to their ears and they prefer them to less subtle expressions of affection.

Many Virgo people are indifferent to love adventures and often remain voluntarily unmarried; no one measures up to their standards of perfection.

Married women of this sign possess a greater executive capacity than their partners. They place themselves as the real family heads, governing husband and everyone around, taking the responsibility for their homes and families.

LIBRA

September 23–October 22

Cardinal, Air
Ruler: Venus

Key Words: harmony,
companionship, balance

Libras are ruled by the planet Venus, which gives them charm and grace in expression, combined with a desire for popularity and the approval of others. The highly evolved natives of this sign will never compromise principle in order to gain approbation, because experience has taught them that ultimate humiliation is the result of such expediency.

Because Libra is a cardinal sign, Libras are concerned with the present and will initiate activities. But they usually seek the cooperation of others rather than continuing alone.

Libras have a special need for companionship in order to be fulfilled. However, they need to maintain their own individuality within the framework of their relationships. Marriage and partnerships are a primary concern of Libras.

Typical activities involve social relations and contact with the public. They can include the legal profession, public relations, art, the performing arts, music, and partnerships that require close cooperation.

Libras have a strong sense of justice and fair play arising from Saturn's exaltation in this sign. Thus they demand that their partners work as hard as they do. Contrary to what has often been said by astrologers, Libras are anything but lazy, because of this Saturn influence. The more highly evolved the individual, the more likely he is to be hard-working, especially after his 29th year (on account of the 29-year-cycle of Saturn and Saturn's exaltation in Libra).

Since Libra is an air sign, those born under it are intellectual and actively seek knowledge, new ideas, and mental stimulation. They are especially adept at analyzing what is occurring in the society around them. All matters pertaining to psychology and human relationships are of deep interest to them. For this reason they make good counselors and often seek to help people with their personal problems. They frequently play the role of peacemaker. The key phrase for Libra is "I balance."

These Venus-ruled natives rarely express anger, but when they do it is as though a tornado has gone through a room—they leave nothing unsaid.

They will tell you exactly what you said fifty years before and under what circumstances you said it. Yet, like the tornado their anger soon spends itself, leaving them shaken and ill.

SCORPIO

October 23–November 21

Fixed, Water   Key Words: regeneration,
Rulers: Mars and Pluto   resourcefulness, secrecy

In many ways Scorpio is the most powerful sign of the Zodiac because it is ruled by Mars and Pluto, while Uranus, the planet of sudden release of energy, is exalted in it.

More than any other sign, Scorpio deals with processes of fundamental transformation on all levels. This transformation can be on a high or low plane, depending on the motivation behind the change. However, as a rule, Scorpios work to improve the status quo.

Scorpios possess power, will, and intense emotional desires. Their life is likely to be a constant struggle to conquer desire through the creative use of the will.

Since this sign is strongly related to the desire principle and the sex drive, there is tremendous emotional force behind the Scorpio's romantic involvements. When out of proper control this can lead to possessiveness, jealousy, and violence. No sign can be so potent for good or evil as Scorpio.

Because Scorpios act with all their power, it is of utmost importance that they set out on the proper course from the start. They never deal with life superficially, and whatever they become involved with is generally of serious consequence. Sometimes their desire to do everything perfectly makes them unable to delegate responsibility, so they overwork themselves, seeking perfection in all details.

Highly developed Scorpios are the most ardent defenders of justice, even in the face of death. Unlike Arians, who are also ruled by Mars and Pluto, they have tremendous staying power because they are in a fixed sign. They will see any matter through to the bitter end, regardless of the required effort and sacrifice.

Although these people despise weakness in themselves and do not like to see it in others, they are often generous and compassionate and will extend themselves in order to help someone else. Scorpios expect, however, that the individual, once helped, will stand independently and continue to help himself.

They are not always diplomatic, since they believe in expressing their ideas and feelings with unfiltered truthfulness. They would rather remain silent than give a watered-down version of their true opinions and emotions.

They have an intense drive to investigate the nature of things and discover the causes behind any outward manifestation. Consequently, they excel in work involving detection, science, research, and occult investigations.

They tend to be highly secretive, and woe be unto those who give away their secrets or incur their wrath. In a battle they will give no quarter and expect none. If one takes up cudgels with Scorpios, he should be well fortified.

In appearance, they are generally of robust and strong build. They often possess keenly penetrating eyes and a strong aura of personal mystique and magnetism.

Their intuition is well developed, as a rule, giving them the ability to penetrate the inner thoughts of others and exact secret information from them.

When spiritually developed, Scorpios derive immense power from their ability to tap the fundamental, creative, regenerative forces of nature. Thus, their accomplishments can sometimes seem almost miraculous.

They are not inclined to fear death because they have a mystical understanding of the cyclic nature of manifestation. The key phrase for Scorpio is "I desire."

SAGITTARIUS

November 22–December 21

Mutable, Fire
Ruler: Jupiter

Key Words: aspiration, love of
freedom, exploration

Sagittarians, born under the sign of honesty and straightforwardness, are represented by the arrow that flies swiftly to its goal. Sagittarians deeply love liberty and freedom.

They are energetic and naturally outgoing, achieving their goals through the power of positive thinking. Since the beneficent Jupiter rules and preserves Sagittarians, help always appears when they need it, even if only at the eleventh hour.

Sagittarians are naturally serious thinkers, concerned with the well-being of society as a whole, as well as with their own lives. Even if they are uneducated in the formal sense, they are at home with abstract ideas, principles, and beliefs.

They place the spiritual law and the ethics to which they subscribe above personality. In their religious zeal they may, at times, overlook the personal side of life.

They are honest, just, and generous, because of their concern for the approval and harmony of the society in which they live. However, they may also have a tendency to be narrow-minded and bigoted if the social standards to which they subscribe are limited ones.

Although idealism is strongly marked in this sign, less evolved Sagittarians may be religious fanatics and blind adherents to established philosophies and dogmas. They must learn to advance beyond the lowest common denominator of the thinking of the current social, religious, and philosophical groups in the society to which they belong.

Sagittarians do not have a subtle approach to life. They often jump to conclusions without taking all factors into consideration. Since they are straightforward, their actions are unimpeachable. If one associates with Sagittarians, he had best grow a thick skin because he will hear the undiluted truth. They can be unmerciful to enemies. However, under anxiety they may become much depressed.

They have the ability to see the future by their understanding of current trends of thought, and their insights border on prophecy. They are especially aware that what appears in civilization is the result of man's thinking and motivation. The key phrase for Sagittarius is "I see."

Sagittarians expand into previously undreamed-of realms because there is a desire to viscerally know, to experience, to try their wings, and to have excitement through adventure. They travel far and fast, either geographically or in thought, or both. They like people to acknowledge their qualities and work, and since the creative urge is strong, they expand their egos through their creativity.

Women of this sign, as a rule, are not fond of domestic tasks and tend to be highly independent. Yet they do make charming and agreeable companions.

CAPRICORN

December 22–January 19

Cardinal, Earth   Key words: ambition, conservatism,
Ruler: Saturn   conscientiousness, organization

Since they were born under an earth sign, Capricorns will never be content merely to keep body and soul together. They have a persistent feeling that they must develop into something. They must have some accomplishment to point to, some property to look after, or some obligation to fulfill, which may be in business, politics, or the social or intellectual fields.

They have excellent intuitions and use them in their struggle to achieve personal independence and economic security. Like their symbol, the mountain goat, they are steady and surefooted. They love law and order and are dogmatic in their view that a rule is a rule and an order is an order. Since they are of the element earth, everything has to be sensible.

Capricorns have a knowledge of practical affairs, not through formal study so much as from reading articles and talking to people. Their prudent habits predispose them to utilize everything they see, hear, or learn, but they are not students per se. The key phrase for Capricorn is "I use."

Capricorns are never deterred by things that stand in the way of their climb to the top. Their extreme capacity for hard work is linked with their notion that success means material security, and they will work and plan for it. They feel, however, that the world has to give them something in return for what they have contributed.

They have great faith in their own power, and they are worldly and careful. Asking for no mercy from anyone, they drive a hard, but not unjust, bargain. They are extremely apt in finding solutions to the most difficult problems and are very successful as troubleshooters.

They are neat and methodical in their work and tend to be slave drivers at home. Their household, they feel, should be managed with precision, with everything in perfect working order.

Capricorns are excellent executives and remain in subordinate roles for a short time only. They may appear to be meek as lambs, but they can take the boss's place without snapping a finger if the opportunity arises.

They never voluntarily step backward. They move up by alternating security and ambition as their goals.

They desire money, because theirs is a long-lived sign. They fear being dependent on others when they are old. This need for security may cause them to have frugal instincts, which make them stingy and at times greedy.

They are old when they are young and young when they are old. As a child the Capricorn may have had difficulties with health, but once he passes the early years he can live to a ripe old age.

Because Saturn rules Capricorn, the natives have a tendency to be melancholic and, at times, lonely. Occasionally, they behave on the principle that the world is a place in which every man is for himself. Yet they have sensitive personalities and want very much to be appreciated.

AQUARIUS

January 20–February 18

Fixed, Air
Ruler: Uranus

Key Words: humanitarianism, independence, originality

Individuals born under the sign of brotherhood and fraternity have as their symbol the water-bearer, who spills out to mankind the life-force and spiritual energy. Since the planet Uranus rules Aquarius, friendship and companionship are extremely important to Aquarians. Those whom Aquarians befriend have their unswerving loyalty.

Born under a fixed sign, Aquarians have eccentric temperaments and are determined and stubborn. They sometimes feel that those who are listening to them are unreceptive and incapable of comprehending their ideas, and they tend to become annoyed when people fail to understand them. Then Aquarians argue, and when they do, they stir up opposition from others. They are capable of discarding these people from their intellectual circle. The key phrase for Aquarians is "I know."

There is no affectation or snobbery in the Aquarian personality but a dislike of spurious imitation and hypocrisy in any form. Aquarians operate as equals among equals. However, they are not dependent on their environments for their security, because they derive this from being in the company of others.

Persons born under Aquarius can be anything or nothing, but they are never lonely. The influence of Uranus promotes an honest enjoyment in meeting new people and exchanging ideas. Aquarians' group instinct will always direct them to where there are people, or else people will come to them.

Since Aquarians have friends of both sexes, they see no reason for giving them up, even after marriage. Because Aquarius is an intellectual air sign, those born under it relate to others on a mental level.

Aquarians love the beauties of nature, but they like to admire them in comfort. They long for material possessions but are not greedy. They are disinclined to engage in sports as a rule, except as observers. Their pursuits are more intellectual than physical.

Women with this sign should watch their tendency to exaggerate their problems. However, one can forgive them for their charm and brightness of expression make them very attractive.

The Aquarians' appearance of calmness is deceptive; their anxiety can even make them feel ill. Since they take their work very seriously, nervousness and apprehension seldom leave them. They do their best work with others or with organizations that attempt to bring about some ideal. In such pursuits, their excellent memory, creativity, knowledge, love of freedom, and humanitarianism find their outlet.

Their interest in and sympathy for human problems win the respect and confidence of those about them. Their sympathy is impersonal and their response intellectual, but once aroused, Aquarians are tireless workers.

PISCES

February 19–March 20

Mutable, Water
Rulers: Neptune and Jupiter

Key Words: compassion, universality, renunciation

Pisces is a sensitive sign and those born under it are extremely responsive to the thoughts and feelings of others. They unconsciously absorb the ideas and mental outlook of those around them.

They desperately want to do the right thing, but as a rule they do not have strong willpower. Therefore, they are easily influenced by external factors. They must learn to stand alone and face the unknown with a simple faith.

The symbol for Pisces is two attached fishes, one swimming upstream and the other downstream, implying the drastic duality of emotions in persons born under this sign. Pisceans apparently are unable to make up their minds.

Pisceans always seem to have a tired feeling, which prompts them to withdraw from intense effort and avoid sports. They are not combative. Their aversion to struggle often makes them indecisive in thinking and acting. They will generally suffer injury rather than fight for their rights. When their supply of patience is exhausted, however, they can become so provoked that it is impossible to calm them down. Pisceans can be stubborn and allow no one to reason with them.

Jupiter is one of the rulers of Pisces, and since this planet functions as a preserver, it gives Pisceans the faith necessary to maintain vitality and a sense of personal significance.

Their charm, humor, and sympathy open the gates of opportunity for Pisceans. Nevertheless, their kindly, moderate natures make it quite easy for them to get into the habit of allowing things to drift, which can be extremely annoying to others who are more practical. On the other hand, given the duality of this sign, they can be efficient and exact.

The Piscean temperament varies from being strongly optimistic to being acutely pessimistic. This can be irritating to those who are absorbed in the material world and cannot understand how people born under a sensitive sign can get lost in the business of living.

Generally, Pisceans are not ambitious for material or monetary acquisitions. However, in early life their aims appear to be materialistic, since Pisceans know instinctively that if the search for the self is to be successful, physical wants should not be a source of worry. They must learn to be more careful with other people's possessions, as well as their own.

Their awareness of the subtle undercurrents of human interactions gives them an air of aloofness. Pisceans are impelled to maintain their individuality—they must follow that still, small voice within. If they attempt to force their spirits into a harness that constricts their uniqueness, they are extremely unhappy.

Pisceans like to be enveloped in a dream world where they can forget the self. If this tendency can be developed, controlled, and directed, the result is an admirable dramatic ability. It sometimes produces the artist, poet, musician, or sculptor. Many excellent and creative dancers are born under this sign. Music appears to be a natural law to Pisceans, for the sign has also produced prominent and superb singers.

Since Neptune, the image-making planet, rules Pisces, Pisceans have overactive imaginations. They are able to perceive the difficulties in people's lives and they can foresee the painful effects of words and actions upon others. Pisces rules the feet, which is the area of the body traditionally dealing with the understanding of man.

Neptune sensitizes Pisceans to the whole of human suffering. Thus, they sincerely want to initiate healing and relief. Many of them choose to work in the most sordid conditions or accept anything that will lighten the load for others. Pisceans from all walks of life devote their strength and time, with no thought of personal reward, to the sick and desolate.

When Pisceans are themselves, they are unselfish, lovable, devoted, and eager to sacrifice themselves for those who surround them. The Piscean consciousness craves to reach out and become a part of all life, and the emotions are extended with compassion and tenderness to others. Pisceans are blind to all defects in those they love and trust.

Pisceans' character deficiencies are found in the area of fatalism; they must realize that they are not chained to any destiny not of their own making. They have to face themselves realistically in order to bring forth that which they can become.

They feel disoriented if they do not recognize and confront all complexities. Once they have done so, the self becomes absorbed in service, and the whole world is transformed into a radiant sphere, where even commonplace things seem to glow. The key phrase is "I believe."

CHAPTER 4

Rising Sign Overlay Patterns

The overlay patterns explain the meaning of the natural sequence of houses when a particular sign is rising. Space limitations permit only the most significant elements that emerge from a particular combination of sign and house to be treated.

Because the commonly used (Placidian) system of houses does not use houses of equal span, in an individual horoscope a sign is sometimes intercepted; that is, it is found within a house containing more than 30° but is not on the cusp or the beginning of that house. Also, a single sign can appear on the cusp of two houses when a house contains less than 30°. However, at least part of a sign will fall in the house that corresponds to its natural overlay pattern lineup. All horoscopes with Aries rising then have Taurus somewhere in their Second House, although another sign may be on the house cusp. This is the case except at the most extreme northern or southern latitudes, where the Placidian system of house divisions breaks down completely.

Aries Overlay

Aries on the First House Cusp

Arians project themselves with intense energy and with primal power. Their decisiveness enables them to act on their ideas the minute they are formed. Arians do not waste time. They are competitive and have the urge to excel in everything they do. They must continually prove themselves to themselves through action.

Taurus on the Second House Cusp

Arians' practicality and willingness to adapt to the methods of business or trade pay off in the ability to earn money. However, they tend to dissipate their earnings in luxuries. They attach special importance to the tools of their trade.

Gemini on the Third House Cusp

Arians like to be known for their originality and individuality. They are intelligent and versatile in expressing ideas and thrive on being considered so by others. They like to discuss their ideas with relatives and neighbors. They need, however, to focus and concentrate their thoughts in order to bring them to fruition.

Cancer on the Fourth House Cusp

Arians gain deep emotional satisfaction from home life. They are dedicated to their families, which are the bases of their operations.

Leo on the Fifth House Cusp

Arians are ardent in love. They identify strongly with their children and want to be proud of them. Their constant flow of creative energy is often expressed in art. They like to excel in sports and competitive games. They can be lucky in speculation, although as a rule they do not engage in it.

Virgo on the Sixth House Cusp

Care and precision characterize Arians' work, and in many respects it is of superior quality. Yet they often leave something unfinished because their perfectionist tendencies make it difficult for them to complete a task on time, or because their enthusiasm has waned.

Libra on the Seventh House Cusp

Often Arians marry without considering the major factors involved, and strife is a likely result. They tend to choose gentle and vulnerable marriage partners. Their mates are usually skilled in public relations and intent on presenting a good image to the world.

Scorpio on the Eighth House Cusp

Arians often have secrets and conflicts with respect to their partners' finances. There are likely to be problems concerning affairs of the dead such as wills and legacies.

Sagittarius on the Ninth House Cusp

Arians have strong, dedicated religious beliefs, which generally follow conventional patterns. There is a natural interest in philosophy and higher education. They are always longing for "greener pastures" and have periodic fits of wanderlust.

Capricorn on the Tenth House Cusp

Arians are ambitious and want to achieve professional prominence through competition. They do not always cultivate the patience needed to submit to those in the position to give them the promotions they desire.

Aquarius on the Eleventh House Cusp

Arians are capable of establishing many friendships and working well in groups, especially with young people. However, their individualism sometimes prevents their having many friends. They are also erratic in their associations.

Pisces on the Twelfth House Cusp

Arians have an unconscious spiritual wisdom that is not apparent on the surface. They possess an intense empathy for humankind, yet at times they feel alone. Confusion on the unconscious level may sometimes be their undoing.

Taurus Overlay

Taurus on the First House Cusp

Taureans can express their potential for power through their financial dealings, and through structuring material and resources. They love the good things of life and create beauty in some form.

Gemini on the Second House Cusp

Taureans make money from original ideas and practical thinking with respect to material resources. They are not confined to one financial outlet.

Cancer on the Third House Cusp

A maternal/paternal attitude prevails toward brothers and sisters and the neighborhood environment. There is much coming and going and fluctuation in communication. Taureans tend to travel in connection with business and financial affairs.

Leo on the Fourth House Cusp

Taureans express their power through the home and family. Generally, their homes are showplaces through which they express their creativity and status. They entertain lavishly, and those who come into their homes are treated with warmth and love.

Virgo on the Fifth House Cusp

These people express power through careful, analytical thinking and close attention to detail. They are also perfectionists in social matters, making certain that everything is in its proper place, scrupulously organized to the last detail. There is a tendency to be overly critical in affairs of the heart. Taureans want everything to be so perfect that their loved ones become ill at ease under the Taureans' constant scrutiny.

Libra on the Sixth House Cusp

Taureans are able to work effectively with others in matters of service. They seek harmony and cooperation with their co-workers, and this is probably one reason for their financial success. As employers they are just and treat their employees as equals.

Scorpio on the Seventh House Cusp

Taureans are attracted to power and status. They seek energetic partners, those who excel in creative expression and the power to accomplish. However, they must guard against jealousy, combativeness, and possessiveness with partners. Coinciding with the Scorpio need for regeneration where partners and the public are concerned is the need for spiritual detachment.

Sagittarius on the Eighth House Cusp

There is much legal activity in regard to wills, insurance, and joint finances. Taureans often profit through inheritance. Their partners usually are financially stable, and useful in the Taureans' progress toward the next "green field."

Capricorn on the Ninth House Cusp

Taureans are very traditional and conservative in religion and philosophy. Their philosophical outlook is restricted by materialism. Their humanitarian instincts are expressed through their professional work.

Aquarius on the Tenth House Cusp

There is a tendency to work in groups where matters of profession are concerned; hence, involvement with large corporations and group endeavors. Taureans like to have the reputation of being associated with prominent and stable, yet unusual and ingenious, people.

Pisces on the Eleventh House Cusp

These people express their compassion and sympathy by generosity to their friends. They enjoy sharing their aesthetic appreciation with friends. But friends can be a source of disillusionment to Taureans if they are unwise in their choice of whom to befriend.

Aries on the Twelfth House Cusp

Impulsiveness and headstrongness can be the cause of Taureans' undoing, although courage and decisiveness are their hidden support. They secretly initiate new activities in order to elude competitors.

Gemini Overlay

Gemini on the First House Cusp

Geminis are original and creative thinkers and tend to dominate their circles intellectually. They also have the power to visualize their ideas and express them scientifically. Since they tend to identify themselves with their ideas, their most dynamic form of expression is intellectual.

Cancer on the Second House Cusp

Geminis acquire money through their adaptability and their receptiveness to the people around them. They instinctively know what others need for growth and nourishment, and by responding to these needs they are often able to make money. Thus, their emotional and financial affairs are interrelated. Generally, they have something tucked away as a nest egg. They are emotionally tied to this and protect it at all costs.

Leo on the Third House Cusp

They express power through creative thinking and invest their ideas with great energy. Thus, they think in large and dramatic terms. Their mental ingenuity is often expressed in art. Their journeys are likely to have a pleasurable or creative purpose; they tend to travel to see those whom they love or with whom they are romantically involved.

Virgo on the Fourth House Cusp

Geminis prefer to and often do situate their professions and workshops in the home. They render service to their families and are fastidious and discerning in the home. Like the Moon, Geminis move around constantly and, if possible, combine visits with financial gain.

Libra on the Fifth House Cusp

Partnership is the channel for their creative power. Geminis are attracted to people of refinement, grace, and balance. They derive great aesthetic pleasure from listening to music and enjoy intellectual discussion in social interchange. They have artistic ability of which other people are usually unaware; their artistic creativity is as much mental as emotional.

Scorpio on the Sixth House Cusp

These Geminis have to regenerate themselves through the areas of work and service. Only by making their ideas effective in a practical way can they transform themselves and get a new start in life. Gemini rules the nervous system; and this Sixth House placement of the highly emotional Scorpio indicates that the expression or repression of desires strongly influences the natives' health. So there is a necessity to use the mind in such a way as to improve the health.

Sagittarius on the Seventh House Cusp

Geminis tend to emphasize ethical, religious, and philosophical values when choosing personal affiliations. They are usually lucky in marriage and have good relations with the public.

Capricorn on the Eighth House Cusp

Geminis have to earn their fair share in any sort of partnership or they deprive themselves of fulfillment. If they are lucky enough to get an inheritance, there is generally delay and the inheritance is often tied up in litigation. However, Geminis protect themselves by buying insurance.

Aquarius on the Ninth House Cusp

There is a tendency to be progressive, unusual, and freethinking in matters of religion, philosophy, and higher education. Geminis like to associate with people involved in these fields. They are curious about foreign cultures and seek out the unusual through travel and study. Since inspiration comes in sudden flashes, they go on long journeys suddenly, without much preparation.

Pisces on the Tenth House Cusp

Geminis tend to be "otherworldly" and visionary, and not always practical with regard to work and public reputation. They are elusive and hard to pin down in professional matters. Peculiar conditions are sometimes associated with their jobs and reputations, and there is always an element of mystery in their professional activity.

Aries on the Eleventh House Cusp

There is a constant effort to make new friends. Geminis are continually moving in a new group, leaving old friends behind and rejoining them at a later time. They tend to organize group endeavors. They are energetic in expressing their hopes and wishes and often try new and unusual methods of obtaining them.

Taurus on the Twelfth House Cusp

Geminis are likely to be affected by conditions from the past that do not change easily. There is a tendency to be more persistent on the unconscious level than on the conscious level. Geminis' self-undoing comes from their unconscious materialistic desires.

Cancer Overlay

Cancer on the First House Cusp

Cancers tend to be emotionally volatile. They expend a great deal of energy through their feelings and are romantic and dramatic in their emotional expressions. Their emotions are supported by their will, however. They identify strongly with their families and familial concerns.

Leo on the Second House Cusp

Cancers express power through financial matters, but they want their money to be used for their children, family, and home. They generally earn money by being placed in positions of authority.

Virgo on the Third House Cusp

Cancers are precise in speech, letter writing, and the formation of ideas, these ideas always being practical and workable. Journeys and short trips are meticulously planned and organized. Cancers are, however, critical of brothers, sisters, and neighbors.

Libra on the Fourth House Cusp

Cancers cultivate art, beauty, and refinement in the home and are emotionally attached to their household objects. They consider the family a partnership and insist on strict justice and fairness for all members;

otherwise emotional problems arise that will put everything out of balance and affect the peace of the household.

Scorpio on the Fifth House Cusp

The children of Cancers are subjected to intense emotionality. Although Cancers are very generous and provide the wherewithal for their children, their excessive concern may lead to domination if it is not controlled. They tend to be jealous of their loved ones. They are extremely sensual in their romantic lives. Actors with this overlay pattern express great emotional intensity on stage.

Sagittarius on the Sixth House Cusp

Since the native is generous in helping others, his spiritual self is able to mature through service. However, Cancers must be free to follow their own inspiration in work. They have a great belief in faith healing and the power of positive thinking. They will work hard and selflessly for others, believing that if they help one they help all.

Capricorn on the Seventh House Cusp

There is a tendency to be cautious and reserved in forming partnerships and to be shy in public relations. Since large crowds frighten them, Cancers do not like to remain in a crowd for very long. They are cautious in marriage. They tend to marry late in life and often for status.

Aquarius on the Eighth House Cusp

Cancers are interested in the spiritual side of life. Many of them have ability as mediums. They are uniquely connected with the goods of the dead. When friends pass away, the loss stirs them deeply, more than they demonstrate outwardly.

Pisces on the Ninth House Cusp

Religion plays a dominant role in the lives of these people, and their beliefs have a mystical connotation. Insights that seem to come from heaven help them solve their problems. Many Cancers have written books on mystical subjects that have emotional appeal. They like to take long journeys by sea.

Aries on the Tenth House Cusp

Cancers must work hard in their professions, and they channel an immense amount of energy to their jobs. They are impulsive in matters concerning work and public reputation. If they are employed, they can easily be hurt by harsh or unfair treatment of those in authority.

Taurus on the Eleventh House Cusp

Cancers have an attraction for artistic, stable, and wealthy people. This is one of the secrets of their own ability to amass wealth and financial resources. Very often they invoke the aid of their wealthy friends to finance their meticulously worked-out plans.

Gemini on the Twelfth House Cusp

Cancers' hidden support comes from their ability to keep their ideas secret. Thus, they provide their own impetus for growth; yet they have a self-destructive habit of discussing their emotional problems, verbalizing what should remain concealed.

Leo Overlay

Leo on the First House Cusp

While Leos project themselves with dignity, energy, and will, at times they are abrupt and overbearing. They are determined to express themselves wherever they see fit, and they will sometimes enter into and dominate a situation without being invited.

Virgo on the Second House Cusp

There is a tendency to be particular and exacting in money matters. Since they like teamwork in business, Leos will include their friends in their financial plans or perhaps make their money through large corporations or group endeavors.

Libra on the Third House Cusp

Leos express their ideas gracefully. They are friendly and just toward their brothers, sisters, and neighbors. They like to travel in luxury. If Leos are writers, they like to have partners in their literary endeavors.

Scorpio on the Fourth House Cusp

Leos do a lot of growling around their family; it's the nature of the beast. But the privilege to growl is confined to the king. Outsiders should not step on the toes of any member of a Leo's family or they will know what it is to have a lion at bay. Often there is a great deal of activity in the basements of Leos' homes or in their dens, and all Leos need their own private "dens" somewhere.

Sagittarius on the Fifth House Cusp

It is important to Leos to provide the best for their children, even to the extent of spoiling them. Leos are artistic and creative, and usually flamboyant. They enjoy giving lavish parties and will spend their last cent to present a spectacular evening. Involvement in sports or religion is characteristic, since one or both is a source of great pleasure for Leos. They especially like religious and philosophical dramas that give them insights into life's significance.

Capricorn on the Sixth House Cusp

Leos are intensely serious about their professions. Anyone who scoffs at their endeavors at work will again have a lion to deal with. When Leos work they work hard. Leos are organized in their work.

Aquarius on the Seventh House Cusp

In partnerships, Leos like to be free. They are humanitarian in public relations and enjoy creating the image of altruism. They have an instinct to centralize things in partnerships, and when they are married they want to know, for no rational reason, the whereabouts and activities of all. The king must know what his queen is up to!

Pisces on the Eighth House Cusp

Even though they know that death ultimately comes to all people, Leos do not dwell on the idea of dying. Conversely, they do everything possible to postpone the final day. Male Leos especially are frequent pill poppers, even if the pills are vitamins and minerals. Generally there are peculiar conditions concerning inheritances, and many times their inheritances are dissipated even before they receive them.

Aries on the Ninth House Cusp

Leos instinctively know that all things originate in the Eternal. As a result of their visionary thought, their creativity is often expressed dramatically. They do not want to be suppressed by traditional religious forms. Many of the medieval crusader-kings were Leos, and to this day Leos tend to be crusaders for their ideals.

Taurus on the Tenth House Cusp

Leos earn money primarily to support the high standards of living which fit their dignified self-images. They desire prominence and wealth.

Gemini on the Eleventh House Cusp

Leos choose as friends people who are intelligent and ingenious, whose ideas can help them attain the power they seek. They cultivate diversity and intellectual stimulation in their friendships.

Cancer on the Twelfth House Cusp

Leos seek seclusion and privacy in their domestic environments. They use their homes for contemplation and spiritual searching. Leos appear strong and unaffected by criticism, but actually they are surprisingly moody and emotionally vulnerable. They rarely show how deeply hurt they are by rejection and rebuff.

Virgo Overlay

Virgo on the First House Cusp

Virgos' mental acuteness is expressed in practical affairs. They are systematic and well organized in developing ideas and executing them. No detail is too small for them to notice or explain, and their success is due to this careful attention to fine points and details overlooked by others. Perfection is Virgos' goal, and there are no flaws in what they do. Quality supersedes quantity.

Libra on the Second House Cusp

Virgos tend to become involved in ventures with a partner, often the wife or husband. They have the ability to attract the money necessary to provide the beautiful and good things of life. The pattern of acquiring these things is irregular, however, since they alternate between frugality and extravagance.

Scorpio on the Third House Cusp

Virgos are energetic, extremely resourceful, and creative in their thought processes. Succinctness and frankness characterize their speech and communication. Words well said function as a balm for them and are beautiful music to their ears.

Sagittarius on the Fourth House Cusp

Spacious and comfortable homes are important to Virgos. They like to provide a place for everything and see to it that everything is in its place. While visitors are generously treated, Virgos are especially generous with their own families. Their families, indeed, usually get along better than most.

Capricorn on the Fifth House Cusp

Virgos are rather prudish concerning sex and romance. Although they appear to be cold, they are highly sexed. They frequently realize their ambitions through the one they love, or the children of their body and mind. They are extremely cautious in the realm of speculation and do not enter into "wildcat" schemes. They seek pleasures that are serious and contemplative and have the ability to enjoy hard work.

Aquarius on the Sixth House Cusp

These people are creative and original in their work. They treat co-workers as friends and enjoy group projects. However, they lose interest in a project if all the group members are not willing to see it through to its completion. They are generally methodical in their professions, employing original techniques, and humanitarian in their service.

Pisces on the Seventh House Cusp

Partners are often the avenue by which the natives expand into new fields; these partners enhance Virgos' human understanding and emotional involvement. Virgos attract people who are not nearly so well organized as they.

Aries on the Eighth House Cusp

Virgos are subject to accidents and fevers which can change their whole lives if they are not careful. Legacies often are involved in extended litigation. Disagreements arise in matters relating to joint finances. Since their opportunity for regeneration is through decisive action, their pattern is to initiate projects, as well as to complete those other people have begun.

Taurus on the Ninth House Cusp

The philosophy of Virgos is based on the beautiful and the practical. They take a down-to-earth view of social concepts and religion and are not likely to change their views easily on these subjects. They insist on the just handling of finances and relationships.

Gemini on the Tenth House Cusp

Virgos engage in professions that allow them to utilize both mind and hands to implement their original ideas, and these ideas bring them fame and recognition. They often become involved in more than one professional activity. Many of them work in the field of communications. This fulfills the Virgos' desire to be remembered for their genius.

Cancer on the Eleventh House Cusp

Virgos treat their friends as family members. They develop unusually strong emotional attachments to friends, as well as to the groups and organizations to which they belong. Their friends are invited into their homes, which become places of group activity.

Leo on the Twelfth House Cusp

Virgos possess astonishing strength that is not apparent until they are tested. This depth of willpower is their unconscious support. Their self-undoing may come from pride and hidden egotism.

Libra Overlay

Libra on the First House Cusp

Libras project their individuality through cooperation with other people; their personalities must be focused on and mirrored in those with whom they cooperate. Their actions express beauty and grace, along with discipline, sternness, and a strong sense of justice. Their strongest virtue is their ability to see any matter from the viewpoint of the people with whom they are dealing. Libras do not like to be alone; they feel lost when they are forced to rely entirely on themselves.

Scorpio on the Second House Cusp

These people are resourceful and energetic in their means of making money. They have the ability to transform worthless materials into something of real value. They spend the money earned from their inventiveness and ingenuity at a rapid rate. Nevertheless, they are more concerned that their possessions have aesthetic than monetary value. Their partners often provide the money for elegant objects to satisfy Libras' taste. However, they are ready to share these possessions with their partners, as well as their friends.

Sagittarius on the Third House Cusp

Libras are philosophic and visionary in the expression of their thoughts and ideas. They are concerned with religion and social values and esteem ideas in terms of their usefulness in the larger social order. They are generous toward brothers, sisters, and neighbors, even though they may be separated from them. Many times their short trips, whether mental or physical, take them to places they have not previously visited. They frequently receive messages from and communicate with people in faraway places.

Capricorn on the Fourth House Cusp

Since they want everything in its proper place, Libras are great disciplinarians and household organizers. Yet nothing is ever systematized to their satisfaction. Much work and responsibility are concentrated in the home. Although their families tend to be conservative and austere, it is important to them that their homes be recognized as contributing to the life of the community.

Aquarius on the Fifth House Cusp

Libras like exciting and singular loves. A great source of pleasure comes from the study of unique things, friends, and group activities. Their children are a peculiar mixture of originality and mental discipline, but their children's bodies are not always as strong as the will that is expressed through them. In art and the theater, structure is especially important to Libras, and they enjoy pieces that are both unusual and dramatic.

Pisces on the Sixth House Cusp

In matters of work and service, circumstances require unselfish devotion from Libras. They are sympathetic to co-workers and employees. Sometimes, however, they assume more work than they can effectively handle, thereby creating confusion and problems. They may become hypochondriacs if they are looking for an escape from their professional responsibilities. Their health is contingent upon their emotional state of being.

Aries on the Seventh House Cusp

Libras can be aggressive in order to gain the cooperation and attention of others. They also have the power to motivate other people into action without their being aware of it. The partners of any Libras must understand that if they want peace they must maintain a high activity level and work hard.

Taurus on the Eighth House Cusp

Libras will cooperate to help their partners earn money, but their love of beauty makes them prone to spend it on adornment. They also have the power to generate wealth from sources that are unknown to others. These persons usually die tranquilly, and begin and end things peacefully in general.

Gemini on the Ninth House Cusp

Libras demand that religion and philosophy be practical in application and logically comprehensible. Many Libras like to write about and discuss these matters. There are numerous comings and goings in relation to religious activities.

Cancer on the Tenth House Cusp

These people are acutely sensitive to their reputations and standing in the world. It is important to them to be considered responsible and respectable. In many ways there is a close tie between professional activity and the home life. Libras often have partners in their profession or business.

Leo on the Eleventh House Cusp

An external source of strength and security must be established. Therefore, Libras cultivate friendships with influential people of genius and creativity, since their own creative self-expression is often linked with these friends.

Virgo on the Twelfth House Cusp

Libras tend to bring about their own downfall by excessive worry and nagging about trivial points. Their hidden support, however, is their ability to devote meticulous attention to secondary details that others may well overlook. The substratum of their endeavors is well planned and organized.

Scorpio Overlay

Scorpio on the First House Cusp

Scorpios project themselves with energy and willpower and are willing to stake their lives to accomplish their aims. It is futile to attempt to convince them that something cannot be done, since Scorpios will do it or die trying. They fortify their objectives with a tremendous, fixed, emotional intensity. They have the ability to draw on hidden sources of power to attain their ends.

Sagittarius on the Second House Cusp

Generally, Scorpios have good luck in financial matters and know how to make money multiply. They expand their activities through money, and there are usually adequate financial resources to further their ends. They often provide financial support for religious and educational institutions. Sometimes they are economic theorists.

Capricorn on the Third House Cusp

Scorpios are careful in the expression of their thoughts. They never say or write anything unless there is a definite reason for doing so, which is why they have a reputation for secrecy. Since their words are carefully calculated for maximum impact, they can be harsh and exacting in their speech. This is where the Scorpio sting appears.

Aquarius on the Fourth House Cusp

The home environment is unusual and distinctive. As a rule, there is something out of the ordinary about Scorpios' homes, families, or both.

Rather than going to visit their friends, they like to have their friends come to them.

Pisces on the Fifth House Cusp

Scorpios are surprisingly sentimental in affairs of the heart; they serve their loved ones without thought of self. Their children and those they love are often a source of disillusionment to them. Scorpios gain pleasure from seclusion and from the study of mysticism.

Aries on the Sixth House Cusp

Scorpios are efficient, powerful, and original in tackling tasks that would seem impossible to others. Since they get more accomplished efficiently than do those born under any other sign, Scorpios appear to be self-propelled in all that they do. Being natural leaders, they have a tendency to be somewhat bossy to subordinates and co-workers. They extend a helping hand when others are in trouble, but they expect the aided individual to absorb the strength and self-sufficiency needed to continue on alone.

Taurus on the Seventh House Cusp

Scorpios attract marriage partners who have wealth to offer. They are cooperative in partnerships but expect some practical gain as a result. They spend money on lovely things that have quality. They also spend money on their partners and take great pride in the fact that they look well.

Gemini on the Eighth House Cusp

Scorpios are pregnant with ideas concerning joint finances. They are often occupied with thoughts and communications concerning death and the affairs of the dead. They are intellectually interested in mystery.

Cancer on the Ninth House Cusp

These persons are emotional and tenacious in the areas of religion and philosophy. They have foresight by means of psychic perception, yet they cling to family religion. As a rule, they prefer to travel by water.

Leo on the Tenth House Cusp

Scorpios are ambitious in their professions and proud of their standing in the community. They often achieve positions of leadership and authority and are admired for their accomplishments.

Virgo on the Eleventh House Cusp

Scorpios exert themselves for their friends, especially those who need help. They cultivate friends through their work and utilize the practical ideas and skills of their associates.

Libra on the Twelfth House Cusp

Scorpios who enjoy the seclusion of places of beauty are more refined and gentle than they would have one believe. Their hidden strength is their innate sense of justice and fair play, but their self-undoing may come from their unconscious desire for luxury.

Sagittarius Overlay

Sagittarius on the First House Cusp

Sagittarians project themselves with optimism. Their ambitions are geared to large-scale goals. They appear to be friendly, interested, and jovial. However, they have a tendency to take things for granted and to think solely in terms of their own affairs and frames of reference. Their power comes from their ability to influence other people to subscribe to a system of thinking that is arranged to provide them with all the advantages. Nevertheless, the Sagittarians' optimism is a source of inspiration to those with whom they have contact.

Capricorn on the Second House Cusp

Sagittarians are practical, responsible, and ambitious concerning money. They do not spend it foolishly or capriciously. They feel it should be used for things that have lasting value, and they are often quite frugal.

Aquarius on the Third House Cusp

In this position, Sagittarians are able to communicate ideas in exciting and ingenious ways. Their ideas come in flashes of intuition, but Sagittarians are capable of putting them to practical application. They are progressive in thought, insisting that ideas have a practical function based on values that have stood the test of time. They think in humanitarian terms. Unusual and peculiar relationships exist with brothers, sisters, and neighbors, who come unexpectedly in and out of Sagittarians' lives.

Pisces on the Fourth House Cusp

The homes of Sagittarians are often places of retreat, set aside for retrospection. Sometimes their houses are provided by institutions; they may live in rectories, ashrams, university-provided housing, etc. At any rate, they enjoy privacy in their homes.

Aries on the Fifth House Cusp

Sagittarians expend much energy in creative activity. They originate numerous concepts. In the realm of love and romance, they are passionate and aggressive. They like sports, especially those involving competition and combat such as boxing, wrestling, and football. They are dominating in their relationships with children, yet at the same time they may be generous.

Taurus on the Sixth House Cusp

Sagittarians' work is practical, but they enjoy projects they consider beautiful and artistic. They will work hard only if they can see a monetary gain from their efforts. Their health is generally robust, providing they do not overeat or become self-indulgent in any way.

Gemini on the Seventh House Cusp

Frequently, there is more than one marriage or partnership, since Sagittarians often have their eyes on greener fields. Even though Sagittarians are primarily loners, they attract people who are intelligent and versatile, and who can aid them in practical ways. They are astute and intelligent in public relations. However, they often prefer that their partners represent them and their ideas.

Cancer on the Eighth House Cusp

Sagittarians are intensely emotional regarding their own deaths. It is imperative to them to be remembered fondly after they die. They must make certain that their affairs are in order and that those they leave behind have ample provisions. In joint finances the partners generally earn money which Sagittarians use to bring about their own betterment.

Leo on the Ninth House Cusp

These persons may not appear to want fame, but their subconscious minds as well as their philosophy are somehow geared to attaining it and to achieving positions of importance in their respective fields of endeavor. Sagittarians give their philosophy the power of their being. Many take long journeys, either physically or mentally. Their eyes are always on distant goals.

Virgo on the Tenth House Cusp

Sagittarians are usually particular about their public images. They appear circumspect, efficient, and organized and in their professional roles may seem cold, aloof, and critical.

Libra on the Eleventh House Cusp

These people often obtain their goals by surrounding themselves with unusual, attractive, artistic, and gracious friends who are stable and prosperous. They are likely to marry a friend, a partner's friend, or a friend of long standing.

Scorpio on the Twelfth House Cusp

The Sagittarians' hidden support is their resourcefulness. They are able to perceive as valuable things that others have overlooked. They also know how to cultivate hidden talents in others. Their downfall can be caused by secret resentments and concealed love affairs.

Capricorn Overlay

Capricorn on the First House Cusp

Discipline, systematic endeavor, hard work, and patience are Capricorns' characteristics. Everything they do has a purpose and is designed to achieve some definite practical end. Capricorns are serious, austere, somewhat melancholy, and reserved.

Aquarius on the Second House Cusp

These persons make their money in original and unusual ways through groups and organizations. They are often associated with corporate enterprises, achieving financial success by producing the most costly innovations and the most ingenious techniques in their fields.

Pisces on the Third House Cusp

This position creates persons who are surprisingly cryptic and highly emotional in their thoughts and communication. Very often their ideas are based upon intuitive insights. Capricorns organize their plans and ideas secretly. They also like to be alone when doing mental work.

Aries on the Fourth House Cusp

Capricorns are aggressive in matters relating to home and family. The home is sometimes a battlefield for emotional spats. It is generally filled with mechanical devices and implements.

Taurus on the Fifth House Cusp

Capricorns are sensual and romantic in the affairs of the heart. They are consistent in their love and affection toward their children. They invest a great deal of pride in them, especially if the children's accomplishments result in higher status for the Capricorns themselves. They want their children to have the good things of life. They gain pleasure from luxurious surroundings and good food. They appreciate art, sculpture, and music.

Gemini on the Sixth House Cusp

Capricorns are versatile and ingenious in organizing their work and can handle several jobs at once. Their fraternal attitude toward co-workers and employees is one of the secrets of their management ability. They have numerous ideas on how to increase efficiency.

Cancer on the Seventh House Cusp

Capricorns are strongly attached emotionally to their spouses and partners. However, the fact that their partners also are often emotionally dependent on them presents problems at times. Capricorns are, moreover, emotional about their relations with the public and with dear friends, whom they regard as members of their family.

Leo on the Eighth House Cusp

Since Capricorns have Leo, the sign ruled by the Sun, on the Eighth House, they live a long time. (The Sun is the giver of life and it staves off death.) Even if they are generous, Capricorns like to control joint resources. They like to control the dispensing of the goods of the dead too; Capricorns are often executives in insurance companies.

Virgo on the Ninth House Cusp

The philosophy of Capricorns is based upon efficiency and hard work. They have practical ideas that can be utilized within the existing social structure. Any philosophy they respect must be consistent in every detail. Their awareness of detail and their capacity to do research contribute to the fine legal minds of some Capricorns.

Libra on the Tenth House Cusp

Capricorns often have partners in their professions. They are charming and skillful in winning over people who are in positions of power and thus gain promotions. However, possessing a strong sense of ethics in professional matters, they usually have good reputations and standing in the community.

Scorpio on the Eleventh House Cusp

These persons tend to surround themselves with dynamic, aggressive, and powerful friends, who can handle many of the difficult jobs they are too reserved to tackle. They have their private source of agents to carry out their purposes or wishes. Capricorns seldom choose weak individuals as friends.

Sagittarius on the Twelfth House Cusp

When they are alone, and removed from the business world, Capricorns are philosophically oriented. Their philosophy of life is the hidden support guiding and inspiring their thinking. Their undoing may come as a result of lofty aspirations which they are unable to fulfill in their present circumstances.

Aquarius Overlay

Aquarius on the First House Cusp

Aquarians are original, creative, independent, wishing to make their own unique contribution to the common good. They are at the same time fun-loving, people oriented, and friendly in an impersonal way. They are modest and do not like to call undue attention to themselves. They would rather be loved than admired. They find their source of power in group activity within a close circle of friends.

Pisces on the Second House Cusp

There is likely to be a laxity and an impracticality due to excessive generosity in professional and money matters. However, it is this generous spirit that often brings Aquarians good luck financially. Aquarians love the beautiful and good things of life, although this appreciation never makes them greedy.

Aries on the Third House Cusp

Aquarians may be aggressive and argumentative concerning their pet theories and ideas. They have a tendency to create tension and instigate rivalry amoung their brothers and sisters. They are intellectually creative and may open up new avenues of expression and application.

Taurus on the Fourth House Cusp

Since Aquarians admire elegant homes, much of their financial resources is channeled into creating a beautiful personal environment. Within this environment they like to be surrounded by music and art. The home is where the impersonal Aquarians' maternal or paternal instinct expresses itself in providing for their families.

Gemini on the Fifth House Cusp

Passion in love is not characteristic of Aquarians. They derive pleasure from intellectual pursuits and prefer intelligent companions with whom they can establish brother-sister relationships. Aquarians can be critical of their loved ones. They produce children of outstanding intellectual ability. Often they have twins.

Cancer on the Sixth House Cusp

Because Aquarians have the group instinct, they work where there are people and constant activity, regarding their co-workers as family members. Their work often involves civic and community life. Their health is contingent upon their emotional state. When they are emotionally upset, they may have what is commonly called "butterflies in the stomach," although this is rarely outwardly apparent.

Leo on the Seventh House Cusp

Marriage and business partners who are powerful and well established are attracted to Aquarians and occasionally dominate them. Aquarians are very independent, however, and this domination is never carried to the point of suppression. The marriage partners are generally amorous and have their own place in the sun.

Virgo on the Eighth House Cusp

Their concern for matters of health and death makes Aquarians insurance-minded. They are always alert in situations of danger where accidents could occur. Their partners help to expand the family income with practical ideas and service.

Libra on the Ninth House Cusp

Aquarians' philosophy and religion are based on the harmonious and beautiful. They like to travel for pleasure with partners or dear friends. Many Aquarians marry in foreign countries or marry people of foreign birth. They tend to marry people of education and refinement.

Scorpio on the Tenth House Cusp

Historically, many Aquarians have been revolutionaries, since they are at odds with the established regime or those who have authority over them. Aquarians do not wish to dominate or be dominated. Their opportunities for self-renewal come through their professions, and often renown follows.

Sagittarius on the Eleventh House Cusp

Aquarians enjoy famous and optimistic friends who inspire them to greater accomplishments. They usually have numerous friends. Aquarians join many large organizations which help them to expand personally.

Capricorn on the Twelfth House Cusp

Aquarians are more conservative than they like to admit. Although they are sometimes limited by unconscious fears, their hidden strength is the discipline that enables them to work hard behind the scenes. They can be trusted with secrets, and they often work on secret projects.

Pisces Overlay

Pisces on the First House Cusp

Pisceans are sympathetic, adaptable, ethereal, and visionary. Their achievements are the result of their sensitivity to the subtle currents of their surroundings. Their mystical insight allows them to penetrate the subtleties of human nature. They also have artistic and musical ability.

Aries on the Second House Cusp

Pisceans make money through starting new projects. They expend considerable energy in the monetary area and spend money impulsively, sometimes in excess. They are inclined to ignore the facts of reality. They are constantly searching for new realms of financial endeavor.

Taurus on the Third House Cusp

Being slow and deliberate in forming their ideas, Pisceans are stubborn about changing their minds once a decision has been made. Their thinking is concentrated on moneymaking or on artistic endeavors.

Gemini on the Fourth House Cusp

Pisceans travel a good deal and often change their residence. They have a tendency to establish two homes. There is usually a large library in a Piscean home. They communicate extensively with family members and give a great deal of thought to domestic affairs.

Cancer on the Fifth House Cusp

These persons are highly emotional and sentimental about their loves, enshrining them like rare paintings. Pisceans enjoy rich foods and tend to be overweight. They derive pleasure from familial contacts and are maternal toward their children. Many Piscean men attract women who remind them of their mothers.

Leo on the Sixth House Cusp

The usually meek Pisceans may be quite domineering over co-workers and subordinates; they have a feeling of authority where work and services are concerned. They glory in the sacrifices they must make in their profession and service. Their illnesses are often psychosomatic and are used to attract attention. They tend to be low in vitality because the Neptune influence on their solar First House makes them dissipate their energy.

Virgo on the Seventh House Cusp

Pisceans attract hardworking, efficient, and exacting partners who help them manage their practical affairs.

Libra on the Eighth House Cusp

The partners of Pisceans often contribute to joint resources. Pisceans enjoy the experience of working with others to devise better methods of making money. They also benefit from insurance and legacies.

Scorpio on the Ninth House Cusp

They are religious and philosophical crusaders, often engaging in arguments over religious beliefs. If they are involved in litigation of any sort, there is generally a great deal of fiery protest.

Sagittarius on the Tenth House Cusp

Pisceans can succeed as executives who have a great deal of vision, but they are not always practical. They often work in the fields of education, religion, and travel, achieving fame in these areas through their religious and spiritual accomplishments. They like to be considered philanthropists and are generous in their professional contacts.

Capricorn on the Eleventh House Cusp

Since the hopes and wishes of Pisceans are dominated by a desire for security, they choose stable, conservative, and established people as friends.   -

Aquarius on the Twelfth House Cusp

Pisceans can bring about their self-undoing by burdening their associates with their problems and alienating their friends by requiring constant sympathy and support. On the positive side, their spiritual rapport with their friends can be their hidden support. Pisceans have an unconscious desire to serve humanity and a universal awareness that enables them to tap the deeper levels of consciousness.

CHAPTER 5

The Houses: How They Relate to Man and His Environment

From an interpretative standpoint, the houses represent the various departments of life. Through them the characteristics of the individual revealed in the signs and planets are expressed in the activities and experiences of everyday life. The lines separating these departments or types of activities are called cusps.

Technically, the astrological houses indicate how the vibratory pattern established by the planets and the signs of the Zodiac relate to the auric field of the Earth itself. The Earth is the place where our lives are actually lived, and it determines the practical manifestation of the other astrological forces.

The houses are formed by coordinates in space which orient the planetary and zodiacal positions to the eastern and western horizons. On the plane of the meridian—the line going directly from north to south passing through the zenith (the point directly overhead at the time and place of birth) as well as passing through the point directly underfoot in the opposite direction from the zenith where these four directions intersect the ecliptic (the plane of the Earth's orbit around the Sun)—we have the four angular house cusps.

Where the ecliptic crosses the eastern horizon, we have the Ascendant or First House cusp. Where the ecliptic crosses the western horizon, we have the Descendant or Seventh House cusp. Where the ecliptic intersects the meridian overhead, we have the Midheaven or Tenth House cusp. Where the ecliptic intersects the plane of the meridian underfoot, we have the Nadir or Fourth House cusp.

These four angular house cusps are considered the most important and most sensitive positions in the horoscope. The other eight house cusps divide the four quadrants—the spaces between the angular house cusps—into three portions of approximately equal size called houses. These four quadrants, with three houses each, make twelve houses in all. The houses are numbered in counterclockwise order. Each is a slice of space of approximately one-twelfth of a circle, following the house cusp assigned to that house in a counterclockwise direction.

When the time of birth is not known, the Sun becomes the Ascendant or First House. This type of horoscope is known as a solar chart and indicates how the individual's affairs unfold in terms of creative self-expression, rather than in terms of environmental circumstances, as would be indicated by the regular house cusps.

The signs and planets listed here as corresponding to the individual houses are those of the natural Zodiac° and may differ in individual horoscopes. However, the sign corresponding to a house in the natural Zodiac and its rulers and exalted rulers will to some degree influence the affairs of that house, even though in most individual horoscopes a different sign will be on the cusp of that house.

The First House

(SIGN: ARIES; CO-RULERS: MARS AND PLUTO; SUN EXALTED)

The First House is called the Ascendant. Its key phrase is "I am." The sign of the Zodiac on its cusp is called the rising sign. It is the most important house cusp and the most sensitive in the horoscope. It represents the individual's basic point of reference toward life: his self-awareness, how his experiences are assimilated, and how he responds to outside stimuli.

Any planet placed in the First House, especially if it conjuncts the Ascendant, becomes highly descriptive of the individual's basic character and the quality of his consciousness. Several other influences affect the qualities of the First House: the psychological traits associated with the sign on the First House cusp; the ruler of that sign; any planet that makes a major aspect to the First House cusp; and the dispositor of the ruler of the Ascendant sign.

The First House and these ruling factors indicate the native's physical appearance and personal mannerisms. (The sign and house of the Sun and

° The natural Zodiac is a horoscope with Aries on the Ascendant, Taurus on the Second House, and the rest of the signs following in the fixed order described on page 6.

Moon are also indicators of the native's basic physical type.) The physical qualities are the manifestation of his sustaining life-force, or selfhood, and indicate the degree of his health and vitality as well as the influences affecting them.

The First House also indicates the native's early environment and conditioning by its general affinity to Aries, the sign of new beginnings.*

The Sun, which is exalted in Aries and represents the creative will and the life-giving principle, also has a strong relationship to the Ascendant and the First House. Thus someone who has the Sun conjunct the Ascendant in the First House or otherwise strongly aspecting the Ascendant is likely to be a self-aware and powerful individual with a strong will and positive direction in life.

Mars and Pluto, the ruling planets of the sign Aries, also have a strong affinity with the First House and the Ascendant. Mars is the planet of physical action based on desire, whereas Pluto is the planet of mental manipulation of energy based on will, or the determination to overcome or become. These two planets of outer and inner action exert greater force when they are in some way related to the Ascendant or First House.

The Second House

(SIGN: TAURUS; RULER: VENUS; MOON EXALTED)

The Second House deals with those material resources required by the selfhood (First House) to sustain itself. The key phrase for the Second House is "I have." Acquiring material resources generally calls for sustained and steady effort, and the Second House corresponds to the sign Taurus, the most stable of all the signs, since it is an earth sign (the most fixed element), a fixed sign, and the most stable of the quadruplicities. The resources necessary to sustain personal existence and self-expression are drawn from the earth. The Second House is concerned with the natives' ability to earn money in order to acquire the material possessions which they need or feel they need. In addition to indicating the earning and spending capacity of the natives and the manner in which

---

* The Ascendant or rising degree has a similar relationship to the vernal point or vernal equinox in the Zodiac. It is also known as 0° of Aries and is the central common node point to which all the other energy fields in the horoscope relate. The vernal point is the central common node point to which all the other energy fields of the Zodiac are geometrically and harmonically coordinated.

they meet their obligations, it also indicates how many and what kind of movable possessions the native acquires.

The sign on the cusp of the Second House, its ruler, and the planets that disposit its ruler, as well as the sign position and aspects of planets in the Second House, all contribute to determining how the natives acquire and utilize money and material resources. These factors also indicate the problems and situations that arise in the process. Aspects made to the ruling planet of the Second House cusp can likewise be of importance.

In this case then, because Venus (which rules Taurus) and the Moon (which is exalted in Taurus) relate to the Second House in the natural Zodiac, these planets can give clues to the nature of the natives' Second House affairs.

Since the acquiring of material resources requires a complex set of human cooperative factors, it is in the Second House that the natives must learn the lesson of responsibility and stewardship toward their brothers and society at large. In order for individuals to realize ultimate security and peace, they must provide a basis of security for those who are dependent on them.

Through the experience of the Second House the natives are ultimately required to learn that they must not selfishly acquire wealth for their own personal pleasure and gratification but use it, according to their capacity, for feeding, housing, clothing, and educating as many others as possible. Those they help can in turn contribute to advancing civilization.

The Third House

(SIGN: GEMINI; RULER: MERCURY)

The key phrase is "I think." The native must discriminate on the basis of accurate perception, experience, and logic what methods will be most valuable in handling the resources represented by the Second House and for what purpose these resources should be used. This procedure implies the faculty of conscious thought, the domain of the Third House. It is the conscious mind that must exercise judgment and discrimination in choosing what the attention is allowed to dwell upon and thus where the psychic energy of the individual will be directed.

We are constantly creating ourselves in the image of whatever our thoughts are focused upon. The emotional responses and action of the individual automatically follow and energize the basic pattern laid down by the thought structure. Thus by their thought patterns men create their destiny and make their own heaven or hell. Here the discriminating factor of Mercury must be exercised in choosing the course of thought and action that will lead to positive growth rather than confusion and negativity.

Because the Third House sign, Gemini, is ruled by Mercury, this house is concerned with the assimilation, processing, and circulation of information. It is the house of the practical mind, and since relationships necessarily imply the communication of ideas, this is the first of the air houses that concerns brothers and sisters, near neighbors, and people in general with whom there is daily mental exchange.

The Third House and its ruler and the planets in the Third House, as well as aspects made to them, give important clues to the natives' ability to think and communicate, their way of expressing ideas, and their intellectual reaction to their environment. The position and aspects of Mercury are highly important in this regard too.

The Third House also rules periodicals, papers, books, writing, telephone, television, radio, and speech—all things which are used in human communication.

The Third House has to do with short-distance traveling, the comings and goings which bring us into contact with people whom we influence mentally and by whom we ourselves are influenced. It indicates the mental equipment with which the native is born, although this does not necessarily represent the full scope of the matured mind, which has learned to transcend the limitations of the individual selfhood through the resources of the higher intuitive faculty linking it with the universal mind. (This intuitive faculty is linked to the individual's consciousness of the overall social order and is shown through Jupiter's rulership of Sagittarius and the Ninth House.°)

However, the Third House is only the beginning of the mind's unfolding. Here the mind is still confined to the individual's practical thoughts. This limitation by no means makes the Third House inferior to the other mental houses. Without clear logic, perception, and communication, the higher intuitive faculties degenerate into superstitious delusions and dogmas and lose their possibilities for benefiting humanity. Therefore, the development of accurate and logical practical reasoning, as represented

---

° The intuitive faculty reaches its full flowering in Pisces and the Twelfth House, where the higher intuitive faculty of Neptune, which is limitless, takes over. The mind is perfected and prepared for the influx of higher wisdom through intelligent and efficient work and service expressed through Virgo and the Sixth House, also ruled by Mercury.

by the Third House, is an essential prerequisite to all higher mental and spiritual development. It is the link between men's creative, intuitive inspirations and their ability to use these inspirations in a way that will be of practical benefit to themselves and others.

The Fourth House

(SIGN: CANCER; RULER: MOON; JUPITER AND NEPTUNE EXALTED)

The Fourth House rules the accumulated environmental conditions we have created for ourselves, primarily the domestic scene. As we appropriate resources, we build up a base of operations, which functions also as a source of security. This principle most readily expresses itself in the home, our platform for collecting, organizing, and utilizing the things with which we maintain and express ourselves. The Fourth House rules homes, foods, laundry, and household items. (It is possible to tell a great deal about the mental and emotional makeup of individuals from the environment they create for themselves. A messy environment is almost a sure indication of a confused, undisciplined, and disorderly mind.)

The Fourth House also rules the land itself—the stage upon which the drama of life is acted out. All humans appropriate a certain portion of the earth's surface for their use; they find a place to call home, where they can collect their possessions. However, in a broader sense our home can be those sets of mental and emotional conditionings within which we have come to feel comfortable.

This psychological home environment we carry with us regardless of where we may be on the earth's surface. It makes up what we call our unconscious mind and determines our unconscious response mechanisms and our emotional makeup.

The Fourth House corresponds to the sign Cancer, which is ruled by the Moon. The Moon represents the feminine reflective-reactive principle operating through the unconscious mind and the automatic emotional responses. These automatic emotional responses and habit patterns are largely established in early childhood, and the Fourth House has a great deal to do with heredity and the beginning of life, when we are subject to parental conditioning, as well as with the very end of life, when we are subject to the conditions we ourselves have created and can no longer change. In terms of the physical body, the Fourth House represents the final resting place within the earth.

The Fifth House

(SIGN: LEO; RULER: SUN; PLUTO EXALTED)

The Fifth House is the house of creative expression. It represents the next stage in an individual's development. Once there is a self to act (the First House), resources to use (the Second House), a mind to control the use of these resources (the Third House), and a base of operations (the Fourth House), the native is ready for creative self-expression and mental and physical procreation.

The Fifth House rules the children of the mind and body and has to do with all the creative arts, especially the performing arts, along with love affairs, pleasures and places of amusement, parties, social entertainment, and gambling (including stock market speculations). It also pertains to children and matters connected with their upbringing and early education, teaching, sports and all functions, whether social or otherwise, where one seeks creative self-expression and social popularity.

Since creativity requires a steady application of the will, it is natural that Leo, a fixed creative fire sign, ruled by the Sun, corresponds to the Fifth House. Here the dynamic powers of the self are expressed through the power of the Sun to create and dramatize by means of love. The individual is filled with the joy of living and reaches out to the same flow of life in the loved one. Out of this union new progeny are born and life finds its fulfillment. Thus the Fifth House is a place of power, where the universal life-force of creative power of the Sun, working through the individual selfhood of the native, finds outlet. In the Fifth House, man has the opportunity to become co-creator with God.

The Sixth House

(SIGN: VIRGO; RULER: MERCURY*)

The Sixth House concerns the hard work and detailed methodology necessary to bring to fruition that which was creatively envisioned in the Fifth House.

The Sixth House, the planets in this house, the ruler of the house, and

* The authors believe that in time the planet Vulcan will be established as the ruler or co-ruler of Virgo and the Sixth House.

their aspects will reveal much about the natives' attitude toward work and service, their ability to perform useful tasks, and their ability to use their minds in a practical way.

As Edison once said, "Invention is five percent inspiration and ninety-five percent perspiration." In the Sixth House, the natives must learn to humble themselves and forgo the grandeur of the large stage and central spotlight in order to learn the intricate details and humble tasks necessary to the theater of human life.

The key to understanding the universe is learning to understand the structure and detail of a single atom. To comprehend the subtle workings of the inner forces of the microcosm which make outer manifestation possible is a difficult and intricate task. The disciplined training of the mind (Mercury), which a comprehensive understanding of life requires, necessitates that the native learn concentration and efficiency through devotion to work and service in the handling of practical (Virgo) tasks and responsibilities. Thus, we see how essential the Sixth House is in the learning process. Obviously the work the native performs is directly related in kind, degree, and proportion to the education, formal or practical, which he has received to prepare him for his work, ruled by the Sixth House.

Part of learning responsibility for detail comes with the proper care and maintenance of a healthy body, an essential instrument for performing useful services. In this sense, the Sixth House indicates health, or the lack of it, and the native's attitude toward staying healthy. The Sixth House deals also with diet and food preparation. It rules clothes, which protect the body, and the neatness, or lack of it, of a person's appearance. A subtle communication takes place through clothing, again bringing in the Mercury significance.

The first six houses of the horoscope have a personal significance. The First House deals with selfhood, the Second with acquisition, the Third with practical thought, the Fourth with a personal base of operation, the Fifth with creative self-expression, and the Sixth with self-improvement through work and service. The greater part of our life, however, concerns relationships with other people and with human society in the larger sense. The last six houses of the horoscope are concerned with interpersonal group relationships.

The last six houses and the last six signs of the Zodiac retrace the significance of the first six houses and signs from a group or social frame of reference. They show how individuals react, function, and adapt to the human society in which they live.

The Seventh House

(SIGN: LIBRA; RULER: VENUS; SATURN EXALTED)

In the Seventh House the "I am" self makes direct contact with the non-self. The key phrase for the Seventh House is "We are." This house concerns all direct close personal relationships with others and reveals the nature of other people's reactions to our actions. This house can also be representative of the First House of individuals one is involved with and, therefore, describes the kind of partners one is likely to attract, whether in marriage or other close relationships. Venus's rulership of this house establishes the bonds of love and mutual harmony which make marriage and close friendships possible.

The Seventh House rules marriage partnerships, close personal friendships, contacts with the public, legal affairs, and the forming of contracts and agreements (the Third House having to do with the contract itself).

Because of the Saturn influence, the Seventh House is closely related to the workings of karma, or the law of compensation, as it affects the individual. What individuals do to the world, the world does back to them. The Seventh House, its ruler, and the planets placed therein reveal how this karmic pattern unfolds.

Since Venus is also related to the money sign Taurus, and since Saturn deals with business agreements, the Seventh House governs commerce. (Carrying on business requires dealing with other companies and the public. Hence the Seventh House rules business representatives and public relations people.)

The Eighth House

(SIGN: SCORPIO; CO-RULERS: MARS AND PLUTO; URANUS EXALTED)

The Eighth House is the house of joint resources, as its polar opposite, the Second House, is the house of personal property. Its key phrase is "We have." The Eighth House consequently deals with corporate money, inherited money or property, insurance and taxes, money that results from combined effort, or money belonging to the marriage or business partner. The baser selfish desires associated with Mars and Scorpio can cause conflict over jointly held wealth, generally because some individuals want the wealth of the group for their own self-aggrandizement. Throughout history, such motives and actions have led to war (Mars) and death (Scorpio, and the Eighth House, which is associated with death and destruction).

As the polar opposite of the Second House, the Eighth House deals also with the dissolution of material structures back into energy. Therefore, it concerns the death of the physical body and the practical matters connected with it: funerals, wills, and legacies. In addition it affects the release of the Indwelling Spiritual Being back into the subtle planes. Because of its concern with these subtle energy forces, which are the internal cause of physical manifestations, the Eighth House deals with the occult and such aspects of science as higher mathematics and atomic physics. Through the exaltation of Uranus in Scorpio and the Pluto rulership of Scorpio, it is also concerned with internal mystical experiences. Individuals contact planes of being which are beyond the reach of their five physical senses, and they sometimes communicate with people who are not in physical incarnations.

The Ninth House

(SIGN: SAGITTARIUS; CO-RULERS: JUPITER AND NEPTUNE)

The Seventh House involves the "We are" principle; the Eighth House, the "We have" principle; and the Ninth House, the "We think" principle (as opposed to the Third House "I think" principle). The Ninth House deals with all codified collectivistic thought structures, usually embodied in philosophy, religion and religious institutions, legal systems and laws, and institutions of higher learning. In short, the Ninth House rules all institutions in which the social concepts developed in the course of civilization are embodied and taught. It is related also to the teaching and publishing professions, through which spiritual and philosophic precepts are passed on to succeeding generations. Further, the Ninth House deals with the knowledge gained through long-distance travel, whereby a larger portion of human culture can be experienced by an individual.

Since unregulated conflict over the world's resources would lead to destruction and chaos, a collective mind as expressed through the Ninth House is essential to govern individual and communal action. By means of the higher illumination that comes through the intuitive and expansive planets Neptune and Jupiter, which embody the love principle, men can communicate with the universal consciousness and gain the spiritual inspiration to enable them to govern their conduct with their fellow men harmoniously. Through this higher inspiration, the birth of all the world's great religions occurs. The Ninth House, its ruler, planets placed in it, and aspects affecting these planets all reveal the native's ability to tap the higher levels of inspiration, unfold wisdom, and develop a social conscience.

The Tenth House

(SIGN: CAPRICORN; RULER: SATURN; MARS EXALTED)

The Tenth House deals with the individual's base of operation with respect to society (rather than his own personal sphere, ruled by the Fourth House). It deals with the carrying out of one's responsibilities before the world and concerns professional and public reputation, honor or dishonor, career, and one's relationship to political and business power structures.

While the Fourth House shows the social and economic station the natives are born into, the Tenth House shows whether they rise above, fall below, or maintain that position.

The Tenth House, the planets placed therein, and aspects made to the planets, along with the ruler of the house and the sign placed on it, govern the ability (or lack of it) to rise to a position of importance in the world. The Tenth House shows how ambitious one is and how ambition is manifested. It also indicates whether the natives will incur favor or disfavor from those in authority. It concerns the kind of employers one has and the nature of one's relationship with them.

The desire for power and status is closely related to the Mars desire principle which urges action (Mars in Capricorn). However, if this ambition degenerates into ruthless attempts to gain power, Saturn will see to it that the natives fall from their high position and the law of cause and effect takes over.

The Saturn connection also clearly indicates the degree of organization, self-discipline, hard work, and patience the native is willing to exercise to gain social or business positions. Since Saturn is exalted in Libra, which deals with public relations and justice, the native's position is secure only if his public reputation is stable and his dealings are honorable.

Politically, the Tenth House rules the executive branch of government, people in high positions of power, and official governmental power structures in general.

The Eleventh House

(SIGN: AQUARIUS; CO-RULERS: URANUS AND SATURN; MERCURY EXALTED)

The Eleventh House is concerned with group creative expression, as opposed to the individual creative expression of its polar opposite, the Fifth House.

This house, the planets placed in it, the sign on the cusp, and the aspects made to its ruler or planets in it reveal the native's capacity to form group associations, make friends, communicate, and work on ideas of universal concern. How he goes about these things is also revealed by Eleventh House factors. Such matters require the communication and thinking ability disclosed here through Mercury's exaltation in Aquarius. A certain sense of loyalty and mutual responsibility is present, along with a willingness to work for common goals, as shown by Saturn's co-rulership of Aquarius.

Real creative group expression can exist only when the members of the group are conscious of their spiritual unity and aware of the larger purposes and possibilities which can be realized through contact with the Universal Mind. When this occurs, the individual's mental aspirations can be fulfilled. The larger group resources can solve problems which are of concern to all but beyond the coping ability of one individual. Also indicated are a universality in the native's responsiveness to new ideas and innovations, a creative link with the Universal Mind, and openness to new experience as revealed by Uranus.

The Eleventh House, then, deals with friendships and humanitarian endeavors and makes possible freedom of mental expression for the individual. Personal self-expression in the Fifth House is concerned primarily with emotional self-gratification; its primary concern, directly or indirectly, is with the sex drive. Creative group expression in the Eleventh House takes place on a higher mental and intuitive level. It is freer of emotional attachment and offers the individual more real liberty.

The Eleventh House is more impersonal because the highly mental Mercury, Saturn, and Uranus principles associated with it through Aquarius are concerned with impersonal truth rather than vindication of the individual ego. If the Eleventh House matters dealt with are of real importance to humanity, they give the native a feeling of significance and fulfillment.

The Twelfth House

(SIGN: PISCES; CO-RULERS: NEPTUNE AND JUPITER; VENUS EXALTED)

The Twelfth House deals with the native's psychological health in relation to others, as well as the health and growth of society as a whole (as opposed to individual health and service, revealed in the Sixth House). The Twelfth House and the factors affecting it in the native's horoscope show a great deal about the native's characteristic emotional responses and habit patterns. The Twelfth House rules the subconscious mind— the accumulation of unconscious memories and emotional experiences and attitudes. The special pitfall of the Twelfth House is the possibility of emotional blocks, addiction to unconscious habit patterns, and automatic responses that may not be suitable to a given situation. (These patterns are based on irrational, unconscious, pleasure-seeking or pain-avoiding responses.) The backlog of past emotional experience can lead to self-pity and excuse-making, rather than attending to the duty of living in the present time and facing reality. This tendency to escape into the past is another Twelfth House pitfall and can result in an illusionary existence. Often the native's mental world and perception of reality do not correspond to physical reality (a common definition of mental illness or insanity). The Twelfth House reveals that department of life in which individuals are most likely to deceive themselves.

On the other hand, the influence of the Twelfth House can lead to great wisdom and depth of understanding. Since the planets associated with Pisces are all closely connected with the emotional love principle, and since the highest expression of the love principle is the empathy indicated through Venus's exaltation in Pisces, out of this sympathetic understanding is born the generosity toward the less fortunate indicated by Jupiter's position.

The Twelfth House can be the channel of mystical inspiration. Natives are receptive to higher states of consciousness and the wisdom received from these states by means of the image-making capacity of the mind (ruled by Neptune). This possibility of contacting the richness of the deeper levels of imagery favors artistic creativity, often associated with the Twelfth House.

On a more mundane level, the Twelfth House has to do with hospitals, mental institutions, religious retreats, and places of solitude, where the working out of karmic problems can be achieved and contact with the inner realms of being is possible.

The Twelfth House, ruling the unconscious memory, is the house most closely associated with karma. It contains the memory of all our past deeds and misdeeds and links us with all that has a similar rate of vibration, whether or not we are consciously aware of it. It rules secret enemies, because of the unconscious memory patterns and unconscious telepathy with people whom we have harmed in the past or those by whom we have been harmed.

The individual can overcome the limitations of the Twelfth House only by consciously facing the restrictions imposed on him by his karma. We can only tune in to those states of consciousness and circumstances whose seed lies within us. Thus, we are our own jailers. Only by consciously facing and accepting these conditions and correcting them in ourselves will we pass beyond the limitations of the Twelfth House.

The task of the Twelfth House is to make conscious the contents of the unconscious mind so the individual can draw upon deeper levels of inspiration and clairvoyant visualization and channelship, learning to discriminate between those unconscious impulses which are constructive and those which are not.

CHAPTER 6

Planets in the Signs and Houses

The relationship between planets, signs and the houses of the horoscope can be described in terms of a play. The planets represent the actors, indicating the major psychological drives in a person's makeup. The sign in which a planet is placed indicates the role the actor is playing: the approach or mode of expression he uses to obtain his objectives. The house in which a planet is placed, regardless of the sign, depicts the stage or setting in which the activity takes place. It indicates what department of life is affected. The aspects between the planets are indicative of the harmonious or inharmonious interaction, the type of activity it produces, and where the effects of this activity will be felt. The aspects are the plot of the play, showing how the characters interact with one another and the results of this interaction.

Since the sign positions of the planets show the manner of expression of a person's primary psychological drives, we shall deal with them first, with respect to each planet, and then go on to describe, respectively, the planets in the houses.

Sun in the Signs

For the basic Sun drives, read Chapter 3, "Sun Sign Potentials."

Sun in the Houses

The Sun in the houses represents the departments of life most strongly affected by the expression of individual power potential. It shows how and where individuals will make their mark through their creative expression and the application of their will.

Sun in the First House

The Sun in the First House, especially if it is conjunct the Ascendant, indicates a strong will, abundant vitality, and intense self-awareness. This position carries with it great initiative and powers of leadership. People with this position are not easily swayed by the opinions or desires of others; they manifest a strong determination to choose their own course in life. They have a clear view of what they want and are extremely individualistic. They have abundant energy and strong recuperative powers that help them overcome physical ailments and afflictions of every nature.

Their energy makes them ambitious for success, and they will work long and hard to achieve personal distinction and esteem in the eyes of the world. It is a paramount necessity for them to feel that they are persons of importance and distinction.

If the Sun is afflicted in the First House, there can be excessive pride, egotism, compulsiveness, false ambition, and the desire to rule others.

Sun in the Second House

The Sun in the Second House indicates natives who must learn the lesson of stewardship in the correct use of material resources. This will be in relation to the affairs ruled by the sign the Sun is in. They must learn to use money and property constructively, in ways beneficial to life, and not merely for their personal satisfaction.

The sign position gives an important clue to the way the person will acquire and utilize wealth. For instance, if the Sun is in Gemini in the Second House, the native is likely to earn money and spend it through intellectual pursuits; if the Sun is in Leo in the Second House, the native might earn money in a managerial capacity and spend it in pursuit of theater arts and romantic or social endeavors. In any event these natives will want to earn money since they have a strong will to attain financial independence.

If the Sun is afflicted in the Second House, the natives may believe they can achieve prestige merely through wealth. They also tend to impose their will on others for purposes of material self-aggrandizement. In addition, they may squander money on expensive luxuries for purposes of display and ego gratification.

Sun in the Third House

The Sun in the Third House shows a strong drive to achieve distinction through intellectual brilliance and mental accomplishments. This produces a scientific bent with an urge to attain knowledge and to understand thoroughly the inner workings of life's processes. Because of their curiosity these natives are eager to investigate new things, especially in regard to matters ruled by the sign in which the Sun is placed.

These natives also have a desire to travel and explore all the possibilities in the area in which they function. Brothers, sisters, and neighbors usually play a major part in their lives. The ability to express and communicate their ideas is important to them.

If the Sun is afflicted in the Third House, there can be intellectual arrogance and snobbery, and a tendency to force ideas on others.

Sun in the Fourth House

This position of the Sun indicates a strong interest in establishing a secure home and family. Natives with this Sun position are proud of their family heritage and may have an aristocratic outlook. They desire to make the home a showpiece of art, beauty, and opulence. The extent to which this is done, of course, and the manner of its doing, will depend on the native's wealth and social class.

The first part of life is generally an uphill struggle, with increasing prosperity and security toward the end of life.

Those with the Sun in the Fourth House often manifest a strong interest in land, houses, ecology, and natural resources.

If the Sun is afflicted in the Fourth House, there may be excessive family pride, inability to get along with the parents, and a tendency to want to dominate the domestic scene. In fact, as a rule natives with this position wish to be heads of their families or have some property that they can manage.

Sun in the Fifth House

This position of the Sun gives a love of life and a powerful will toward creative self-expression. The natives seek pleasure and want to be noticed and appreciated. They are highly competitive, with an inclination toward sports, music, theater, and other artistic pursuits. They project themselves in the most dramatic way possible, searching for pleasure and romance with others. They have sunny, happy dispositions and attract many friends. However, at times they seem to be naïvely childish and egocentric. Less-developed types may lack maturity and subtlety. Their behavior may be blatant and overly theatrical, like that of a prima donna.

These natives often take large risks because of their almost blind self-confidence. They love children and are actively interested in their development and education. However, if the Sun is in one of the fire signs—Aries, Leo, or Sagittarius—they may have few children of their own, or none at all.

Natives with this Sun position are ardent lovers; when they are involved in a love affair, it can be all-consuming. Nonetheless, they are capable of being loyal to one person in their love expression; but if the Sun happens to be in Taurus or Scorpio, there can be possessiveness and jealousy.

Sun in the Sixth House

This position of the Sun gives delicate health, requiring proper attention to dietary habits. Recuperation after illness may be lengthy.

Those having the Sun in the Sixth House seek distinction through their work and service. They are usually excellent workers because they take pride in their work. However, they demand outward gestures of appreciation, and if these are not forthcoming, they will be ill-disposed toward their employers and fellow employees and are likely to change jobs. Employers with this position of the Sun can be demanding and authoritarian toward their employees; employees with this position will demand many rights and privileges and will expect to be noticed and appreciated as equals.

If the Sun is well aspected in the Sixth House, the person intuitively knows how to care for his health and may be interested in a career related to health, such as nursing, pharmacology, or medical practice. There will be no difficulty in obtaining well-paid positions. If the Sun is afflicted, the reverse will be true, with long periods of unemployment. The self-esteem and dignity of these natives is closely linked to their work and the services they render.

Sun in the Seventh House

Those with a Seventh House Sun express their power potential through close personal relationships. If the Sun is well aspected they will attract strong, capable, and close loyal friends. Marriage is of paramount importance in their lives, and if the Sun is well aspected they will attract strong, loyal mates with enduring affection. If the Sun is afflicted, there may be danger of domination, either by the native or by his partner; the native may tend to force his will on others. In such a case this position of the Sun demands that the native learn to cooperate and to respect the individual self-expression of others.

If the Sun is not afflicted, there can be increasing success in life after marriage. This position favors popularity, dealings with superiors, and a self-confident manner. Persons with this Sun position are especially adept at public relations and can become good salesmen or promoters.

Sun in the Eighth House

The position of the Sun in the Eighth House can mean an interest in the deeper mysteries of life, such as death and the survival of consciousness after death. This may not always be evident in the early years but becomes more significant later in life.

There is an interest in self-improvement through the application of the will. The natives need to experience directly a deep level of spiritual reality that transcends outer material circumstances, rooting them in an awareness of the Eternal One God principle, which is the substratum of all manifested existence. Once this consciousness is realized, the natives become fearless in the knowledge that, as long as they adhere to principles of justice, nothing can harm their fundamental being.

The lessons that go with the Sun in the Eighth House are likely to be severe, because the realizations that must be gained are of a fundamental character. Much is required, but much can be gained with this position. Life may be a battlefield, but permeating the strife is the spirit depicted in the 23rd Psalm: "Yea, though I walk through the valley of the shadow of death, I will fear no evil." This will of course be more manifest in highly evolved types. In mundane affairs there will be concern with taxes, insurance, the goods of the dead, and corporate and business partners' finances.

If the Eighth House Sun is well aspected, it may indicate legacies or inheritances. However, if the Sun is afflicted, there may be trouble or litigation over these matters. In the case of divorce, it can indicate alimony settlements unfavorable to the natives. In a woman's horoscope it might mean that the husband will squander the resources of the family. There may also be a tendency to use unscrupulous means or have a "rule or ruin" attitude toward life.

The Sun in the Eighth House sometimes brings recognition after death, although in life the native's genius goes begging.

Sun in the Ninth House

This Sun position indicates a dynamic interest in spiritual and religious pursuits, expressed actively in the realms of higher education, religion, law, and philosophy. The intuitive mind is ordinarily highly developed, with frequent flashes of inspiration that help to solve problems, and visions of the future that border on prophecy.

There is an interest in foreign affairs and distant places and their cultures, art forms, and traditions. Often the natives are attracted to foreign travel; however, if the Sun is in one of the fixed signs—Leo, Scorpio, Taurus, or Aquarius—there may be an inclination to stay in one locale, unless travel is necessary for compelling reasons. If Leo is on the Fourth House cusp, natives can reside in a place far from their childhood homes.

The degree to which the spiritual life is expressed will depend upon the overall tenor of the chart. However, on some level there will be strong moral convictions by which the natives guide their lives, though these convictions may be narrow-minded and bigoted. Natives often desire to be authorities in some aspect of religion, education, law, or philosophy. As a rule, they are interested in the larger social order and the laws and traditions governing it.

If the Sun is afflicted in the Ninth House, the natives may seek to impose their religious or moral views on others. They can have eccentric religious beliefs, difficulties in higher education, and problems in foreign countries or with foreigners. They can also have a condescending, moralistic attitude toward others, which at times may be combined with hypocrisy.

Sun in the Tenth House

This Sun position generally indicates persons who are ambitious to attain positions of responsibility, power, and authority. Many politicians have the Sun in the Tenth House or related to the Tenth House. Individuals with this position are dignified and display a strong will to succeed. They desire honor and recognition, to which end they will work hard to acquire the necessary knowledge and skills. They generally possess strong managerial abilities.

These individuals are often born into families of high social standing or respect; thus they possess a strong moral sense and abhor anything demeaning to their dignity and moral respectability. They feel required to set a good example for others. The word *nobility* befits them.

If the Sun is afflicted in this house, there can be dictatorial attitudes, excessive love of power, and a tendency to use unscrupulous means to achieve power and position. There can be reversals, fall from high position, and public disgrace if the Sun is badly afflicted—especially if Saturn afflicts the Sun.

Sun in the Eleventh House

This Sun position gives an interest in friendships and group activities. There is an interest in occult subjects, scientific endeavors, and inventions. If the Sun is well aspected, there will be many friends and the natives will be held in high esteem. They will be helped by friends with power and influence. Often there is a strong drive to gain recognition through mental achievements and inventions, generally accomplished with the aid of friends singly or in group activity. This Sun position often gives the ambition for group leadership.

The position gives strong humanitarian feelings and a sense of brotherhood, with respect for universal human dignity. The natives like to see things in terms of universal laws that apply impartially to all. They avoid bias and favoritism.

If the Sun is afflicted in the Eleventh House, there can be a tendency to dominate friends and acquaintances, sometimes for selfish purposes. By the same token, natives can be used, let down, or led astray by their friends, usually because of the ulterior motives the natives themselves possess, which ultimately backfire, for Saturn, a karmic planet, rules this house.

Sun in the Twelfth House

This position of the Sun indicates an individual who is somewhat retiring. His will is directed toward exploring the resources of his own unconscious. If he displays leadership, it will be behind the scenes. These natives can be lonely and estranged from normal human contacts. Psychology and psychic research interest them. They may find self-expression through work in large institutions such as hospitals, asylums, or places of spiritual and physical retreat. Service to others can provide them with recognition and fulfillment.

If the Sun is afflicted in the Twelfth House, there can be neurotic tendencies and excessive shyness. There can also be a desire to control others through secret means. There can be mediumistic inclinations stemming from unconscious egotism and desire for power and recognition. The native can have powerful secret enemies and may unconsciously be his own worst enemy.

Moon in the Signs

The Moon in the signs of the Zodiac indicates the person's type of immediate emotional response to life's situations. The Moon position also shows the kind of attitudes that were instilled in the individual by the family, in childhood. It shows in what manner early experiences have colored the emotional outlook. It determines how the person is likely to react to external influences and the actions of others. It is important in determining how the person conducts his home life and the type of relationship he has with his mother and with women in general. It can indicate how the person responds to the public at large. It suggests attitudes in everyday affairs, domestic ones. The Moon position is also an indicator of eating habits and food preferences.

Moon in Aries

The Moon in the sign Aries inclines natives toward volatile, emotionally impulsive natures. People with this Moon position often behave in precipitous ways without due consideration to the consequences of their actions. They can have sudden flare-ups of temper, but these are temporary and are soon forgotten.

People with this Moon position are very independent, insisting on following their own paths of action, right or wrong, and they will not tolerate interference from others. They can have a tendency to dominate others emotionally. They are prone to take the reaction of others personally.

Moon in Taurus

The Moon in the sign Taurus indicates a need for financial and material security in order to attain emotional well-being. The Moon in Taurus is very strong because it is in the sign of its exaltation. The emotions tend to be steady and placid. There is a great deal of common sense in handling financial and domestic affairs. This is also the "green thumb" position. The position demands stimulation from other people to launch new projects, but once projects are begun there is steadfastness, and the persistence to see matters through to their end. New endeavors are usually not started until old ones have been completed.

This position of the Moon attracts wealth and the good things of life. As a rule, natives are fond of good food and seek material comforts. A stable domestic situation is important to their emotional security.

If the Moon is afflicted in Taurus, there can be unwillingness to change established emotional attitudes. Often this affliction can indicate a tendency to laziness and an excess attachment to material comforts.

Moon in Gemini

The Moon in the sign Gemini indicates an emotional nature that is likely to be vacillating, although quick-wittedness and resourcefulness are also present.

Persons with the Moon in Gemini tend to talk incessantly, sometimes to the point of annoying others; they are the type of person who never gets off the phone. They are inclined to rationalize their emotions, so that sometimes they do not know what they really feel. There is a great deal of restlessness, with frequent changes of residence and many short journeys. These people are often nervous and fidgety.

With this position there is a tendency to spread oneself too thin, to become excited momentarily by many ideas without being able to follow through on them. If the Moon is well aspected and other factors in the chart indicate practical ability, there can be resourcefulness in thinking up solutions to practical and domestic problems. If the chart is favorable, this Moon position can subject the emotions to rational analysis. However, if the Moon is afflicted, the emotions can distort reason. Heavy afflictions to this Moon position indicate excessive vacillation, superficiality, and confusion.

Moon in Cancer

The Moon in Cancer is in the sign of its rulership, indicating depth and intensity of the emotions. There can be strong ties to the mother, the family, and the home. Natives with this configuration may be good cooks and homemakers and concerned parents. Domestic security and marriage are important for their emotional well-being.

Individuals with the Moon in Cancer have a sensitivity to the moods and feelings of others that can border on the psychic; their extreme sensitivity to others' opinions and reactions may lead them to imagine slights, even when not intended. Consequently, they are inclined to withdraw and brood.

If the Moon is afflicted in Cancer, there may well be excessive emotional instability and a tendency to smother the children with love, to the point of wanting to dominate their lives.

Moon in Leo

The Moon in the sign Leo indicates an emotionally proud individual with a flair for dramatics who will often seek the spotlight. There is an unconscious need to be admired and appreciated. These people need romance and affection. They are fond of children, parties, art, sports, and entertainment in all forms. Because they may be self-centered, they can incline to stubbornness. Sometimes they act like prima donnas, out of the need to dramatize their feelings. There is a tendency to dominate others, especially those within the domestic scene. Their susceptibility to flattery sometimes appears as childish self-importance.

The tendency to self-dramatization would be unbearable if these people were not sincere in their efforts at self-improvement. Their need to love and be loved is a healthy emotional drive and makes for a sunny disposition and constructive expression in most cases. Persons with this Moon position want their children to be well groomed and their homes to be showplaces of beauty and art.

Moon in Virgo

The Moon in the sign Virgo indicates an exacting, hardworking, practical nature. There is great regard for neatness and cleanliness in personal hygiene and housekeeping. These people are particular about food and diet and concerned about health. They are good cooks, but health is as important to them as taste.

Natives with the Moon in this sign are usually shy and retiring, preferring to work quietly behind the scenes. They pay attention to detail; they wish to serve. They do not ask personal questions unless necessary; they are curious, but in relation only to their work or practical affairs.

If the Moon is afflicted in this sign, there can be excessive preoccupation with inconsequential detail and a carping and critical attitude. Perfectionism about detail can blind these people to larger issues.

Moon in Libra

The Moon in Libra indicates a strong sensitivity to the attitudes and reactions of others, especially marriage partners and close working partners. Persons with this position of the Moon find vulgarity displeasing. They are easily upset by inharmonious relationships, which have an adverse effect on their health. There is charm and elegance in their personal appearance and mannerisms. Their homes are generally places of beauty and often are gathering places for social activities. These people are courteous, gracious, and kind to everyone—because their emotional well-being depends upon the approval of others. On the negative side, there is a tendency to be easily influenced without due consideration for the value of the action or attitude that is adopted.

This Moon position can give ability in public relations. It also gives a partnership link to the parents, especially the mother. If the Moon is afflicted in Libra, dependence on others for emotional security may be indicated.

Moon in Scorpio

The Moon in the sign Scorpio indicates strong, biased emotions based on willful desire. This is not considered a favorable position for the Moon, because here it is in the sign of its fall.

There is a tendency to take personal affairs very seriously, which sometimes leads to possessiveness and extreme jealousy in some cases. When it is carried to extremes the natives can hold grudges and plan to take revenge at an opportune time; in any event, they do not easily forget personal affronts. The inclination toward brooding and revenge is a serious character defect that can go with this Moon position, and it should be avoided at all costs. These individuals sometimes desire to restructure the family and domestic situations. They may want to dominate others through subtle means. They can also be very stubborn, on account of emotional attachment to their own desires. However, if clear direction and right motivation are present, they find no sacrifice too great to achieve a worthwhile objective. They have definite motives for all their actions, though these drives may not always be apparent.

Moon in Sagittarius

The Moon in the sign Sagittarius indicates a lofty, idealistic emotional nature. Natives aspire to high goals but may lack a realistic sense of life. There can be strong attachment to traditional religious or philosophic beliefs instilled by parents in early upbringing. These people are fond of travel, move swiftly, and often take up residence in foreign countries or places far removed from the place of birth.

If the Moon is afflicted in Sagittarius, there can be narrow-minded sectarian views, combined with arrogance and an egotistical, holier-than-thou attitude. Natives also tend to identify with particular social values for personal, unconsciously motivated, emotional reasons and thus lack objectivity in their view of social issues. However, on the good side, they are optimistic and cheerful.

Moon in Capricorn

The Moon in the sign Capricorn indicates a reserved and cautious nature inclined to be cold and austere. Natives with this position take life seriously and identify emotionally with material rather than spiritual values. This is not a favorable Moon position because the Moon is in its detriment in Capricorn.

The Capricorn Moon produces ambitious, hard workers, but their ambitions have a personal bias, slanted toward status and financial security. Their active seeking of money and power, as well as status for themselves and their families, may lead to selfish vested interests when they hold positions of larger social responsibility. These people, often shy and insecure about their own worth, can be oversensitive to real or fancied slights. They seek to justify themselves by personal dignity and the ambition to succeed.

If the Moon is afflicted in Capricorn, there can be calculating tendencies to achieve power at any cost, without respect for the feelings of others.

Moon in Aquarius

The Moon in the sign Aquarius indicates a capacity to sympathize with the needs of humanity. Occasionally there are flashes of intuitive knowledge. Persons with this position are friendly to all, in an impersonal way. They seek freedom of emotional expression and demand freedom to come and go as they please within the domestic situation; thus, they are likely to have unusual family relationships. Their homes are gathering places for friends and group activities. The negative aspect of this position can give a tendency to emotional perversity and stubbornness, or an irrational need for freedom at all costs. There can also be fear of personal emotional involvements because of the threat they pose to personal freedom.

Moon in Pisces

The Moon in the sign Pisces indicates a supersensitive emotional nature which acts like a psychic sponge, soaking up the thoughts and emotions of others. This extreme impressionability on the unconscious level makes the person feel psychologically vulnerable, with the result that he withdraws into seclusion to protect himself emotionally. There are strong psychic and mediumistic tendencies, but without consideration of other factors in the chart there can be no guarantee that impressions received are reliable. People with this position have a vivid imagination which can result in poetic, musical, or artistic output. They are generally kind and sympathetic because of their sensitivity to the feelings of others. However, they can be easily hurt and may develop a persecution complex. If the Moon is afflicted in Pisces, there can be neurotic or psychotic tendencies and irrational dominance by the unconscious mind. In some cases excessive shyness is indicated.

Moon in the Houses

The Moon in the houses indicates the areas of daily activity through which a person's feelings are manifested. It is related to that part of the experiential network that is influenced by the unconscious habits of the past, since the placement of the Moon indicates the department of life in which a person reacts unconsciously both to environmental stimuli and to other people. The house position of the Moon also gives important clues to the type of activity that occurs on the domestic scene.

Moon in the First House

This position of the Moon indicates persons whose self-awareness and expression are strongly colored by their emotions, early childhood conditioning, and family affairs. Their personal identity tends to be unduly influenced by other people. Changeable and moody in their expressions and their responses to the environment, they lack long-range direction and purpose. Because of their impressionability, they may be psychic and mediumistic. Other people are likely to become involved in their personal affairs. They have an emotional need for personal recognition, which leads them to seek the approbation of others. Consequently, they are susceptible to being used.

This position gives natives a strong personal involvement with the mother. They often have round or full faces and a fondness for food which in some cases makes them corpulent.

Moon in the Second House

This Moon position has some of the qualities of the Moon's exaltation in Taurus. It indicates a strong need for monetary security in order to make possible a stable home and family situation. The natives' emotional well-being in general is dependent on material comfort. They have good business ability, especially in matters dealing with food, home, and real estate. Their ability to hold on to money will depend largely on the Moon's sign position and aspects. If the Moon is in a fixed sign or earth sign, prospects will be favorable in this respect.

Moon in the Third House

This position of the Moon indicates that the native's thought and speech will probably be influenced by emotional factors unconsciously arising from family affairs and early childhood conditioning. The natives often become emotionally involved—in some cases their reason may be distorted by emotional biases—and they identify with the ideas of others. They are prone to daydreaming and fantasy, so that their thinking is strongly influenced by their imagination. Also, their thoughts and speech may be preoccupied by trivial matters.

People with the Moon in the Third House have an incessant curiosity, tire easily of monotonous routine, and are constantly moving about. There is much activity with brothers and sisters; neighbors are regarded as part of the family.

Moon in the Fourth House

This position of the Moon is strong, and because of the relationship of this house to the sign Cancer, the Moon is accidentally dignified here. Since there is emotional identification with the home and family, people with this position cannot be happy without a meaningful home life. Family relationships will affect their whole emotional outlook. Parents, especially the mother, strongly influence them. As a rule, this position makes the natives fond of cooking and housekeeping; it is especially favorable in a woman's horoscope. In business they can excel in activities related to food, real estate, and products used in the home.

If the Moon is afflicted in this house, there can be a lack of harmony and many changes of residence. If the horoscope is favorable, financial prospects can be better in the second half of life.

Moon in the Fifth House

This position of the Moon indicates that the natives' romantic attractions and pleasures will be heavily influenced by the imagination and emotional needs. Affections may be changeable because of emotional instability. There can also be emotional dependency on the romantic partner. The family may interfere in romantic affairs, especially if the Moon is afflicted. The Moon in this house indicates fertility and the bearing of many children, especially if it is placed in a water sign.

Persons with this position are often very fond of babies and children. If the Moon is afflicted in this house, emotional impulsiveness can lead to speculation through gambling or stock market activities.

Moon in the Sixth House

This position of the Moon inclines the native to a fluctuating state of health strongly influenced by the emotions. In some cases hypochondria or psychosomatic illness results. The emotional state will affect the efficiency of the native's work and the degree of harmony he maintains with his employer and fellow employees. Employers with the Moon afflicted in this house will find it difficult to retain stable employees; and workers with this Moon position are likely to change their jobs often unless the Moon is in a fixed sign. Since the diet will be a major determining factor in the state of health, it is important that these people learn correct dietary habits. They can be skillful in food preparation; thus this position is favorable for employment in restaurants and markets.

There can be a fondness for pets and small animals.

Moon in the Seventh House

This position of the Moon indicates a tendency to marry for emotional and domestic security. The family can influence the marriage, since this position makes one emotionally sensitive to others. These natives seek emotional fulfillment through relationships and are much influenced by them. Frequently they seek a mother or father figure in the marriage partner. There can be many dealings with the public in the realm of business.

Moon in the Eighth House

This position of the Moon often gives intense emotional reactions and a strong psychic sensitivity to unseen forces. There can be an interest in spiritualism because of the desire to contact family members who have passed on.

The natives are usually concerned with inheritance, insurance, and property taxes. Financial affairs will be affected for better or worse through marriage and partnerships.

In this position the Moon is in its accidental fall; emotional desires, therefore, may lead to sensuality if the Moon is afflicted, because the

Eighth House is ruled by Pluto and related to the sign Scorpio, which rules the sex organs. Pluto is exalted in Leo, the Fifth House sign of pleasure and romantic involvements. The Eighth House also relates to Mars, the planet of desire.

Moon in the Ninth House

This position of the Moon indicates a deep emotional attachment to religious, social, and ethical values instilled in early childhood. The Ninth House is ruled by the planet Jupiter, which is exalted in Cancer, the sign ruled by the Moon; consequently, as with Jupiter in Cancer, the Moon in Sagittarius or the Ninth House gives a strong recognition of the need for spiritual and moral values in the family and domestic life.

The Moon in this house can limit the scope or depth of spiritual understanding, through emotional bias and identification with parental attitudes and experiences. If the native changes his religion, parental censure often follows. If the Moon is afflicted, a narrow, dogmatic social and religious outlook can result. Unless other factors in the horoscope counteract it, the native's convictions are based largely on feeling rather than reason; but since the Moon deals with imagination in this house of the higher mind, there can be inspired intuitive promptings.

These people are fond of travel and may well take up residence in locations far from the place of birth. They have a tendency to learn unconsciously or by osmosis.

Moon in the Tenth House

This position of the Moon indicates a need to achieve prominence and recognition. The natives often come from families with high standing in the community, and their parents are generally ambitious on their behalf; the mother especially is likely to be a dominant influence. Their careers tend to be furthered through the influence of women. This house position will bring its natives prominently before the public and, if the Moon is well aspected, is a good position for those interested in politics.

Moon in the Eleventh House

The Moon in this house gives a powerful emotional need for friendships and group activities. There can be many acquaintances, but not necessarily of a lasting or meaningful nature.

The natives' hopes, objectives, and motivations fluctuate with their moods. They can have numerous friendships with women. Their homes are often used as places for group activity. Many friendships are made through family associations.

The emotional state is influenced by the opinions and reactions of friends. These people do not like to be alone; they need companionship for their emotional well-being. However, at times they have to be alone to stabilize their feelings.

Moon in the Twelfth House

This position of the Moon indicates that the moods and emotional responses are strongly affected by the unconscious and by past experiences. Psychic and intuitive leanings can be manifest. Extreme emotional sensitivity combined with reluctance to communicate feelings can result in shyness and easily hurt feelings. If the Moon is afflicted, there can be neurotic tendencies and loneliness; if heavily afflicted, institutionalization and confinement because of mental illness. Hypnosis can be a danger with this Moon position. If the Moon rules the Fifth, Seventh, or Eighth houses or strongly aspects Venus or the ruler of the Fifth House, there may be secret love affairs.

Mercury in the Signs

Mercury in a sign of the Zodiac indicates the ways in which the characteristics of the sign influence thinking and the ability to communicate. It gives important clues to the kinds of concerns that occupy the mind of the individual.

Mercury, ruler of the thinking process, is the focusing lens through which all creative powers of the individual are directed. The sign position of Mercury is crucial because it reveals the type of psychological set determining a person's ability to make decisions and convey his ideas to others.

The sign position of Mercury tells a great deal about what information and facts a person notices and regards as important and what he chooses to ignore. For example, the thinking of Mercury in Taurus is strongly influenced by the financial significance or usefulness of particular ideas.

Mercury in Aries

Mercury placed in the sign Aries indicates a way of thinking that is inclined to be decisive and competitive. The natives are fond of debate and argument. They often have the ability to think rapidly and may produce many original ideas. However, they can be impulsive when making decisions and see things from too personal a point of view. If carried too far, this tendency can result in intellectual egotism and headstrong attitudes.

These people are impatient with opposition and delays; consequently, they will often act just to make a decision, to avoid being subjected to lengthy, frustrating decision-making processes. But their impulsiveness means they do not always follow through on ideas they initiate, unless a fixed sign emphasized in the horoscope indicates otherwise.

If Mercury is afflicted in this sign, there can be irritability and a quick temper.

Mercury in Taurus

Mercury placed in the sign Taurus indicates natives whose thinking and decision-making are determined by whatever has a practical, material, and financial application. Although perhaps lacking in brilliance or originality, they possess much in the way of practical common sense. Hence they have shrewd business minds and a natural bent for management. They are slow to form opinions, but once they do they are reluctant to change. Similarly, they dislike argument and disharmony and will fight only to protect their security and financial interests.

The ability of these natives to consider only things that are of practical concern to them gives them great powers of concentration, such that they can ignore extraneous disturbances as if they did not exist. They do not perceive that with which they do not want to be bothered. If carried too far, this attitude makes them blind to important matters that they should recognize for their own good and explains much of their stubbornness.

This position of Mercury can give mental ability in the arts. If Mercury is strongly aspected, there can be talent in mathematics and physical science, because of the Taurean-Venusian sense of form and structure which is translated into mental understanding through Mercury. If

Mercury is afflicted in this sign, there can be intellectual obstinacy, opinionated views, materialism, and avarice.

Mercury in Gemini

Mercury placed in the sign Gemini is in the sign of its rulership. If it is well aspected and strongly placed by house, pure, logical reasoning can be carried to its highest expression. The Gemini Mercury is versatile, unbiased, and impersonal in its ability to perceive truth because Mercury in Gemini is more concerned with facts than with attitudes and personal preferences. People with a well-developed Mercury in Gemini are capable of deep scientific thought. They are generally well educated, knowledgeable on many subjects, and able to communicate easily, rapidly, and accurately in speech and writing. They usually have an excellent vocabulary, which is one of the secrets of their eloquence and clarity of expression.

People with Mercury in Gemini have a highly sensitive nervous system which makes it difficult for them to shut out external stimuli; all speech and activity in their environment are registered with intensity and vividness in their awareness, and they are forced to deal with many thoughts and impressions at once. This is the basis of their agile minds, which have the capacity to register two impressions or think two thoughts almost simultaneously. However, if these people are subjected to complex, busy environments for too long a time, their nerves become frazzled; fatigue, confusion, and sometimes irritability may follow. Therefore, they need periods of solitude to become quiet, meditate, and refocus their minds.

People with this position of Mercury possess an intense curiosity; they want to know about everything. But they run the risk of spreading themselves too thin and dividing their attention too often; they may lack the continuity of purpose to complete the projects they undertake. When this tendency is carried to extremes, it produces the typical "Jack of all trades and master of none." Because it is possible for these people to see any situation from many points of view, they can experience difficulty in making up their minds and may change their minds often, thereby confusing others. In extreme cases they earn the reputation for being fickle.

Only Mercury in Aquarius can equal this position for mental originality. The inventive minds of the natives are adept at finding new and surprising solutions for problems and emergency situations. These people need to be well educated in order to make the best use of their mental capacities. This position is common among scientists, mathematicians, computer experts, secretaries, writers, reporters, teachers, and lecturers.

If Mercury is heavily afflicted in Gemini, there can be incessant talk about trivial matters which is an annoyance to others. The horoscope of an undeveloped person may reveal a tendency to get sidetracked and miss the main issue.

Mercury in Cancer

Mercury placed in the sign Cancer indicates a mind that is influenced by deep-seated emotional patterns. Unconscious desires will cause the person to look at some facts and ignore others, the results being bias and prejudice and interference with objective thinking. At times, if Mercury is badly afflicted, the natives may be untruthful without consciously realizing it.

Mercury in this sign can indicate a good memory, because of the emotional intensity that is associated with the thoughts. There is also a tendency to absorb much information subliminally or to learn by osmosis. In fact, much of the mental process occurs on an unconscious level, although it is manifested as conscious intent. Since people with this Mercury position are highly susceptible to the attitudes and opinions of those around them, their thinking can be influenced by emotional appeals, such as patriotism. They are very sensitive personally; they believe that whatever is done or spoken in their environment is especially directed toward them.

Much of the thinking centers around the home and family. There is considerable business ability in matters related to food, domestic and consumer products, and real estate.

Mercury in Leo

Mercury in the sign Leo indicates a mind that has a strong will and a fixed purpose. Natives with this position are capable of focused concentration, because here Mercury is disposited by the Sun, which bestows willpower and strength. They like to be regarded as authorities in their chosen fields, and they are aided by a dramatic and forceful manner of speech; but if carried too far, this inclination can produce excessive mental pride and arrogance.

The mental self-confidence indicated by Mercury in Leo makes for positiveness in tackling and solving problems. However, there can be a tendency to deal with things in large, general terms, thereby ignoring details. There can also be a tendency to overlook things that do not relate to the immediate focus of interest. Because Leo is a fixed sign, opinions are formed slowly and changed with reluctance.

People with Mercury in Leo do possess continuity of planning and purpose, which gives them executive ability. There is also ability in teaching and working with the mental development of children.

The theater, investments, the stock market, education, and artistic pursuits are likely to be areas of special interest. This Mercury position may well combine travel for pleasure with travel for work.

Mercury in Virgo

Mercury in Virgo is in the sign of its rulership, a position indicating an analytical mind with great practical reasoning ability. These natives insist on minute precision and accuracy to a level that can appear trivial to other people. They require orderly surroundings and efficient methods and procedures, especially in their area of work. This is the best position of Mercury for detailed scientific work and research.

These people achieve professional and financial success by acquiring a good education and specialized skills. Interest and ability in grammar can make them eloquent in speech and writing and proficient in languages. As a rule, they will insist on proper grammatical usage, spelling, and punctuation and for this reason make excellent secretaries and correspondents. Unlike Mercury in Gemini, which is concerned with ideas for their own sake, Mercury in Virgo is interested primarily in ideas having a practical application for financial success and status. The person with this position is work oriented and consequently may be shy and retiring, perferring not to waste time in idle conversation.

Medicine, diet, hygiene, mathematics, and precise detailed work of all types attract the attention of these people. In contrast to Mercury in Leo, however, they can lose sight of the main issues through overconcern with details that assume undue importance.

Mercury in Libra

Mercury in the sign Libra indicates a mind that is primarily concerned with human relations and psychology. The natives have an intense curiosity about the thinking and behavior patterns of others; they gravitate, therefore, to fields such as psychology, astrology, public relations, sociology, and law. Good communication and happiness in relationships are essential to them. They prefer to work in mental partnership with others, and they are usually easy to communicate with because of their interest in what others think. Their strong sense of justice generally makes them honest in their communication. The Venus rulership of Libra seeks harmony, and Saturn's exaltation in Libra seeks justice, making the Mercury Libra honest and balanced in all mental dealings. These people like to consider all sides of an issue before making a decision, but if this desire is used in the wrong way, it can lead to indecisiveness, and the opportunity to act is lost. When decisions are reached, however, they are generally just and well considered. If other factors in the horoscope are favorable, this Mercury position is good for the legal professions, counseling, arbitration, and other public relations work such as sales and negotiating. But unless there are some planets in fixed signs or houses, there can be impatience in these matters.

People with this Mercury position seek association with those who possess refined minds, good manners, and honest reputations. Uncouth manners and unfair motivations are distasteful and are avoided whenever possible. These people are highly sensitive to the odors, personal appearance, and mannerisms of others. They regard inappropriate dress and coarse speech as social affronts. Gentle and considerate in communication, they can be stern where principles are involved. They make the mistake of expecting the same degree of mental discipline from others that they require of themselves.

Because of Saturn's exaltation in Libra the mind can be stern and hardworking. In highly developed types this quality leads to profundity, but superficial people with this Mercury position may appear to lack the firmness of their convictions because they tend to agree with their companions in order to gain popularity and acceptance.

Mercury in Scorpio

Mercury in the sign Scorpio gives an intuitive mind capable of profound insights. The natives' perceptiveness can lead to critical examination of human motivations; they see things accurately, but not necessarily charitably. They may use sharp language, since they refuse to mince words in order to spare the feelings of others. They prefer to say exactly what they feel or else remain silent. They carry on many plans and endeavors in secret and communicate only where communication serves a definite purpose in terms of what they are trying to accomplish. However, since they can be swayed themselves by strong emotional factors, they are more objective when not personally involved.

These people have determined minds and great resourcefulness, which enables them to surmount obstacles that many would find impossible to deal with. If Mercury is afflicted in Scorpio, there can be scheming, plotting, and ulterior motives.

People with Mercury in this sign make good detectives, investigators, and researchers. In highly developed types there is scientific ability arising from their curiosity about the inner workings of the energy responsible for objective manifestation. This leads to insight into the fundamental processes of change.

If Mercury is afflicted in this sign, the mind can be preoccupied with sex. These also can be a mistrust of others.

Mercury in Sagittarius

Mercury in the sign Sagittarius indicates a mind concerned with all codifications of social thought, whether in the form of religion, philosophy, law, or other studies related to higher education. Mercury in Sagittarius is in the sign of its detriment and is manifested as a primary concern with attitudes rather than facts. The result is often constructive, in giving insight into social motivation and its subsequent events. However, natives can lose sight of the truth if they do not pay enough attention to detailed factual information, the basis of all logical thought. It must be remembered that Sagittarius opposes Gemini and squares Virgo, the signs ruled by Mercury.

People with this sign position can have prophetic insight because their concern with attitudes enables them to understand what information public opinion will regard as important. This leads to the unfolding of mass destiny and karma. These people are direct in speech and will say exactly what they think; they demand mental freedom, but their ideas seldom depart far from traditional concepts or current social morality. Hence, they are usually respected in the community. But if their social conformity is carried too far, it can lead to hypocrisy, for their moral standards may be no better than the lowest common denominator of the socially accepted norm. They need to realize that an attitude is not necessarily right merely because it is popular or prevailing.

These natives desire to entrench themselves in public institutions of higher learning or social control, such as universities, churches, and government. Their purpose is to achieve intellectual authority and status, though the price may be conformity to corrupt, stagnant institutions. They like to consider themselves paragons of truth, but whether they are or not depends on how Mercury is aspected. They may tend to moral sermonizing about the obvious, and they may become pedantic.

At times there is a preoccupation with distant goals and lofty ideals, which can make the natives oblivious to what is under their noses. Neptune's co-rulership of Sagittarius can result in woolgathering tendencies.

Mercury in Capricorn

Mercury in the sign Capricorn indicates a mind that is ambitious, shrewd, practical, organized, and concerned with attaining status through material accomplishments. People with Mercury in Capricorn are capable of extended concentration and good organization. They are methodical in thought and procedure, possessing the ability to take things a step at a time, and their reasoning process is thorough, but not necessarily original. Their patience and discipline can result in mathematical ability, which can be used in business or science. Mercury in this sign also gives good managerial ability, and it belongs to many successful executives.

People with this sign position will go through traditional educational procedures as a means of reaching professional goals and improving their financial and social status. In political and social ideas they are generally conservative and uphold the established order. They respect those beliefs that have proved their usefulness through the test of time. Since Capricorn, like Virgo, is an earth sign, Mercury in this sign regards ideas as important only if they are of practical value.

These people are realistic rather than idealistic in their approach to their goals; they see everything for what it is and are not to be deluded or taken in by false idealism. Since they have a keen sense of awareness, little of practical consequence escapes their notice. However, there is a danger that their seriousness and mental discipline will lead to a stern manner and a lack of humor.

If Mercury is afflicted in this sign, material ambition may lead to avarice and the tendency to use people to attain material goals, without regard for human values. Material status may become an end in itself, overriding human values and all other considerations.

Mercury in Aquarius

Mercury in the sign Aquarius indicates a mind that is open to new experience. The ability to see things in the light of impersonal truth gives a mind that is truthful, unbiased, and objective. To people with this position the truth must come first; they have little concern for traditional or socially acceptable ideas if these conflict with facts or first-hand experience. Here is the secret of their originality. Because of their impersonal objectivity these people are not easily surprised by anything they may see or experience. Thus they can accept things others would find unnerving or incomprehensible.

Mercury in Aquarius is in its exaltation; consequently, these individuals have the ability to know that reason exists as a patterning of the Universal Mind, of which the individual mind is but a submechanism. Thus, Mercury in Aquarius manifests its highest intuitive faculties through communication with the larger Universal Mind, transcending the individual ego. The ability of the natives to experience extends beyond the five physical senses. Because Aquarius is a fixed sign, the mental energy is stabilized and concentrated, so that it is capable of receiving ideas from the archetypal realms of consciousness. Some have the ability to perceive the mind itself as an energy field and its contents as energy patterns. People with Mercury in Aquarius are likely to be telepathic.

The direct experience of higher states of energy also gives scientific insight into the workings of material manifestations. Natives see reality as it is on the microcosmic level—a pattern of energy pulses in motion. Because Saturn co-rules Aquarius, there is good mental organization and concentration, often leading to mathematical ability, which is one reason why this position produces scientists.

The ability to see things in broad terms promotes humanitarianism and concern with the spiritual unfolding of humanity. This is an excellent position for astrology and all forms of occult study.

People with this position of Mercury like to function in conjunction with others; hence they become involved with group and organizational work. They seek mental stimulation through friendship.

Mercury in Pisces

Mercury in the sign Pisces indicates a vivid imagination and a photographic ability to visualize thoughts and memories. People with this position are highly intuitive and telepathic on the unconscious level; they are, therefore, easily influenced in their thinking through subliminal suggestion, as they tune in unconsciously to the thoughts and moods of those around them. They arrive at conclusions not through logical reasoning but rather on the basis of intuitive perceptions that float up from the unconscious mind. They learn more by osmosis than through disciplined study.

The mind can be biased by unconscious emotional patterns based on past experiences, as is Mercury in Cancer. If Mercury is afflicted in Pisces, the mind will be in danger of being trapped in memories, to the point that the perception of present reality is distorted. This can lead to neurotic conditions in extreme cases. Because of the extreme sensitivity and imagination of Mercury in Pisces, poetic and artistic abilities are often manifested. These people are sympathetic; they can imagine how it is to be in another person's situation because they have been in similar situations themselves. At times their emotions are too easily played upon.

Pisces is a mutable sign, and fluctuating emotions can cause vacillation in thinking, decision-making, and communication. There can also be a tendency to daydream and woolgather. The fact that the natives like to be secretive and keep their private thoughts to themselves can result in shyness and seclusion.

Mercury afflicted in Pisces can mean a morbid imagination and a persecution complex. The individual may be oversensitive and may sense personal criticism even when it was not intended. He needs to become more impersonal in his thinking and perception of reality; in this respect this position is similar to Mercury in Cancer.

Mercury in the Houses

Mercury in the houses gives important information about the practical affairs of life that occupy a person's mind and communication, such as speech and writing. It also shows what areas of activity will be influenced by a person's thoughts and communications.

Mercury's house position shows the type of environment and activities from which a person draws his ideas. For instance, if Mercury is in the Second House, the individual may gain information through business and financial dealings, whereas if Mercury is in the Seventh, he may learn through marriage, partnerships, and communications with the public.

Mercury in the First House

Mercury in the First House gives people an inquiring, intellectual out-look on life; very little that happens in their environment escapes them. Their actions and self-expression are based on logic and reasoning, and they often have more than average intelligence. They are talkative and in-clined to much writing because of their intense desire to express them-selves verbally.

These people come and go a great deal, because Mercury is the natural ruler of the Third House, while the First House indicates self-expression through action. Mental initiative and willpower go with this position, so that natives are generally intellectually competitive, especially if Mercury is in a fire sign.

People with Mercury in the First House make good writers, doctors, scientists, researchers, scholars, librarians, and secretaries because of their innate ability to express themselves and their high degree of intelligence. The mental self-expression—thought and communication and the degree of intellectual awareness of one's self—ordinarily relates to the affairs ruled by the planet making the closest major aspect to Mercury.

Mercury in the Second House

Mercury in the Second House indicates a preoccupation with business and monetary affairs. The value system is based on that which can pro-duce concrete, practical results. There is business ability in writing, print-ing, publishing, broadcasting, telephone interchange, teaching, and other communications media.

People with this position pursue education in order to improve their earning power. They have original ideas for ways of making money, and their financial affairs and moneymaking endeavors are always methodi-cally planned. Many professional economists, business advisers, and cor-porate planners have Mercury in the Second House. People who earn their living as secretaries, accountants, librarians, telephone operators, writers, and so forth, also may have this position of Mercury or some connection with Mercury to the Second House, through sign rulership or aspect. Business affairs are usually related to the planet that Mercury aspects most closely, and there can be financial gain through this planet.

Mercury in the Third House

Mercury in the Third House is accidentally dignified because the Third House corresponds to the sign Gemini, which Mercury rules; therefore, Mercury placed in this house tends to give superior intellectual ability in general. There is ability and interest in communication of all sorts, and people with this position make good writers and speakers, with much originality and mental agility. Short-distance traveling and frequent communication with brothers, sisters, and neighbors are characteristic, and a great deal of time is spent on the phone or in writing letters. These people are adept at finding practical solutions to problems of all sorts. They make good secretaries, telephone operators, reporters, scriptwriters, and editors.

If Mercury is afflicted in the Third House, there can be trouble due to indiscreet speech and communication or false, incomplete, or erroneous information. There can be difficulties through contracts, promises, and agreements.

Mercury in the Fourth House

Mercury in the Fourth House indicates that much mental and educational activity will go on in the home. Those with this position often have well-educated parents. They are inclined to investigate their family trees and ancestral history.

The home is likely to be used as a place of work, because Mercury rules Virgo and the Sixth House, which deals with work. People with Mercury in the Fourth House often collect large home libraries and spend much time with their families in intellectual pursuits. The home can become a neighborhood communication center, and there is much talking on the phone. These are the people who make a ritual of reading the daily newspaper at the breakfast table.

Mercury in this house can indicate an interest in real estate, agriculture, earth sciences—such as geology—and ecological and environmental problems; the native may be a writer on these subjects. People who have changeable home conditions, move often, live in trailers, or in some way pursue a nomadic life may well have Mercury in the Fourth House. If Mercury is afflicted in the Fourth House, there can be intellectual disputes and disagreements with other family members.

Mercury in the Fifth House

Mercury in the Fifth House indicates an intellectual interest in many artistic and creative endeavors. For this reason it can produce playwrights, art critics, and writers in general. Natives are attracted to the forms of art that convey information or act as media of teaching or propaganda. They have an ability to express themselves in a dramatic and forceful manner in speech and writing, and they wish to be admired for their intellectual achievements. Games of mental competition such as chess and cards attract their interest. Stock market analysts and investors who have plotted the patterns of the market often have Mercury in this house.

These people also tend to be concerned with and proud of their children's intellectual achievements. Since there is an interest in the education of children, many primary grade teachers have Mercury placed in this house. Romantic attraction is to intellectual types who are capable of providing mental excitement and stimulation.

If Mercury is afflicted in the Fifth House, there can be unwise speculation and intellectual conceit. Mercury afflicted in the Fifth House can also give an analytic, critical outlook on romance.

Mercury in the Sixth House

Mercury in the Sixth House indicates people who acquire specialized knowledge and skills applicable to the kind of work they do, such as their profession. They are methodical and efficient in handling the details of their work; they make it their business to keep up with the latest techniques and research in their field. This is, therefore, a favorable position for those involved in medicine, engineering, or science.

Mercury in the Sixth House is dignified because this house corresponds to Virgo, which Mercury rules. Like Mercury placed in the Third House, then, this position can indicate superior intellectual ability in general.

Mercury in this house indicates a concern with duty, personal hygiene, and correct dress. Keenly alert senses make disorder in the environment objectionable to the natives; they may suffer adverse psychological effects and even fall ill in conditions of chaos. Mercury in the Sixth House can indicate a tendency to overwork and to perfectionism.

If Mercury is afflicted in the Sixth House, there can be ill health, preoccupation with insignificant detail, and a generally critical nature.

Mercury in the Seventh House

Mercury placed in the Seventh House indicates people who are concerned with communication and mental cooperation with others. They prefer to work in some kind of partnership rather than individually. They are adept at communicating with the public and therefore can be successful in sales, public relations, and law.

Natives with this Mercury position are concerned about what others think. The tendency to seek mental companionship leads them to marry intellectual people who are intelligent and well educated. Other relationships also are likely to be with intellectual types.

If Mercury is well aspected in the Seventh House, natives can have ability in arbitration, mediation, and counseling. There is in general an aptitude for psychology with this position of Mercury.

If Mercury is afflicted in the Seventh House, there can be problems in communication with others, misunderstandings in marriage and partnerships, and unkept agreements. Natives must carefully consider contractual agreements before signing them. There can also be discord in marriage based on differences of opinion. If Mercury is afflicted, the partner may be untruthful and unstable, and in some cases younger than the native. With Mercury in the Seventh House, marriage has been known to take place with an employee, a co-worker, or a relative.

Mercury in the Eighth House

Mercury in the Eighth House indicates interest in the deeper phases of science and the occult. If Mercury in this house makes aspects to Uranus, Neptune, and Pluto, there can be an interest in spiritualism and communication with the dead. Interest may also center in corporate finances, taxes, insurance, and the goods of the dead, since the Eighth House is the house of death. The native's work may relate to one of these fields.

People with this house position are inclined to be secretive, especially about information they consider personal or important; they tend to make plans in secret and are ingenious at formulating strategy. They love mystery and intrigue; they enjoy reading and writing detective and mystery stories. They have the desire and ability to ferret out secrets and discover the motivations behind human behavior, for they want to get at the bottom of things.

The death of brothers, sisters, or neighbors is unusually significant to them. They are likely to travel in connection with death. They often fall heir to secret information or important documents. Mercury in the Eighth House indicates that death could be caused by disorders of the nervous system or respiratory diseases.

The natives do not easily forget the actions and slights of others. If Mercury is afflicted in the Eighth House, they may hold grudges, speak vindictively, and engage in plots for revenge.

Mercury in the Ninth House

Mercury in the Ninth House indicates an interest in philosophy, law, and higher education, leading to the acquisition of higher education and advanced degrees. It is important to people with this position to be able to understand the evolution of the fundamental ideas that govern prevailing social thought, law, philosophy, and religion. Their decisions are based on ethical and moral as well as practical considerations. Like Mercury in Sagittarius, this position is concerned with attitudes as well as facts, since attitudes govern which facts people consider important and how these facts are used. Many teachers and professors have Mercury placed in the Ninth House.

People with this Mercury position love travel and are curious about foreign countries and cultures; thus, they can be good historians and anthropologists. They go long distances to acquire knowledge that is important to them or to pursue religious teachings and the gurus that expound them.

If Mercury is afflicted in the Ninth House, there can be intellectual pride and snobbery, and dogmatic, sectarian opinions and beliefs. Mercury in the Ninth House favorably aspected, especially if it aspects Uranus, Neptune, or Pluto, can give prophetic insight into the future.

Mercury in the Tenth House

Mercury placed in the Tenth House indicates people who pursue education for reasons of professional ambition. They want to increase their knowledge in order to prepare for prestigious, lucrative careers. This Mercury position bestows upon natives good organizational ability and a capacity to plan for the future. Their careers are not accidental but result from deliberate plans designed to achieve specific goals.

Mercury in the Tenth House gives the ability to communicate with people in positions of power and leadership; consequently, many political strategists and speech writers have this position. Further, since it gives political astuteness, talent in speechmaking, executive ability, and the ability to communicate with the public, it is the position of politicians who have distinguished themselves by their brilliant ideas. People engaged in a profession concerned with communications media, printing, writing, publishing, teaching, or lecturing also may have Mercury here.

If Mercury is afflicted in the Tenth House, there can be scheming for the sake of personal ambition. This may be accompanied by a selfish, cold, and sometimes dishonest attitude in which ambition takes precedence over principles. The affairs ruled by the planet making the closest aspects to Mercury generally influence the person's career and professional education.

Mercury in the Eleventh House

Mercury in the Eleventh House indicates people who are keenly interested in communication and the exchange of ideas with friends and in groups. They especially seek out associations that will stimulate their minds and increase their knowledge; however, their thinking is strongly colored by the ideas of their friends. These people both teach and learn from their friends and can receive help from them in securing employment.

Mercury in the Eleventh House is accidentally dignified because the Eleventh House corresponds to the sign Aquarius, in which Mercury is exalted. Therefore, Mercury in this house bestows love of truth, impartiality, and the ability to think with originality and objectivity. Natives are often concerned with scientific investigation, astrology, advanced occult philosophy, and humanitarian ideals and goals; they have friends with similiar concerns. Their attitude is impersonal but friendly. They are willing to exchange ideas and communicate with anyone regardless of his background or walk of life. This openness to all humanity broadens the mind and gives compassion and profound insight into the larger social issues.

If Mercury is afflicted in the Eleventh House, the native's ideas can be eccentric and impractical. He may use his friends for personal advantage, or they in turn may misguide him for selfish motivations of their own. He may also have an inability to communicate with groups or function in them efficiently.

Mercury in the Twelfth House

Mercury in the Twelfth House indicates that the person's thinking is strongly influenced by unconscious memories and habits stemming from past experiences. Decisions are based on feeling rather than logical reasoning, since many impressions filter up from the unconscious mind to color the thinking. People with this position are likely to be secretive about their inner thoughts and ideas. Often they are shy and hesitate to say what they really think. If Mercury is well aspected, especially if aspects to Uranus, Neptune, or Pluto are present, valuable ideas and knowledge may be gained through intuitive or psychic ability. The imagination is very active with Mercury in this house.

If Mercury is afflicted in the Twelfth House, there can be neurotic tendencies, mental illness, and a fixation on past experiences that are not relevant to present circumstances. The individual may also find it hard to relate to the external environment and so experience learning difficulties. Many children with an afflicted Mercury in the Twelfth House have trouble relating during early education, which can result in reading problems or other mental blocks.

Venus in the Signs

The planet Venus in the signs of the Zodiac gives important information about how a person expresses his emotions in personal relationships, especially in love and marriage. It also gives important data about attitude toward money, personal possessions, and creature comforts, and social and aesthetic values.

Venus in Aries

Venus rules the principle of love and reaching out to others. Venus in Aries indicates those who tend to be aggressive in their emotional self-expression. Their outgoing natures lend enthusiasm and sparkle to social gatherings. They have no reticence in pursuing the object of their interests, and they can be competitive when seeking the affections of others. In a female horoscope this quality may make for an aggressive approach, in which the woman chases the man. The ability of these people to be passionate in love and romance results from Mars, the ruler of Aries, which gives energy to the affections of Venus. These affections can be impulsive and unstable, however.

Venus in Aries is in its detriment, because Aries is the opposite sign to Libra, which Venus rules. For this reason people with Venus in Aries demand a lot of personal attention and tend to be self-centered.

If Venus is afflicted in Aries, the native's manners can be coarse, lacking refinement. When Venus in Aries is well aspected, there is a positive, cheerful attitude. There is also the ability to be actively creative in artistic pursuits.

Venus in Taurus

Venus in the sign Taurus gives constant, lasting affections. Emotional security and stability in love are important for the natives. They are loyal and steadfast, although they can be possessive and jealous if their emotional security is threatened. Their sense of touch is highly developed, and they enjoy physical contact with their loved ones; but they are sensual in a passive way, seeking to attract rather than pursue the love object.

Venus in Taurus gives a love of comfort, luxury, beautiful surroundings, good food, and opulence in general. Therefore, the money that makes such things possible is important to these people. Because the Moon, which rules the domestic scene, is exalted in Taurus, they seek to make their homes beautiful and artistic. Personal beauty is important to them too, and they seek to make themselves as attractive and youthful as possible. Even hippies with this Venus position will wear beautiful jewelry or an expensive piece of clothing.

With this position of Venus there is an innate sense of the value of material objects and an ability to make purchases of beauty and long-lasting quality. Because these people tend to like material things, they may engage in businesses dealing with art and luxury goods. They can be attracted to artistic expressions in which they can directly mold the materials; painters and sculptors often have Venus placed in this sign.

Natives feel a close kinship with the earth and gain pleasure and solace from flowers, trees, and other plants. They may take up gardening or growing flowers as a hobby.

As Taurus rules the throat and larynx, and Venus confers grace and beauty, many people with Venus in Taurus have rich, melodious voices. Talented singers are likely to have this placement of Venus.

Venus in Gemini

Venus in the sign Gemini indicates people who like variety in their romantic and social lives. The desire for varied experience, coupled with curiosity about people, makes them disinclined to settle down to one permanent romantic relationship. Like Venus in Aquarius, this position makes them want to be friends with everyone, but they are nevertheless capable of sustained devotion. Because of their wit and conversational ability they are attracted to people with agile minds and keen intellects. This is a Venus that needs to be given adequate freedom.

People with this Venus position spend much time traveling in pursuit of pleasure and social activity. Literary activities—especially poetry—and jokes are favored artistic expressions, usually including some form of play on words.

As with other air signs, there is a tendency to dislike coarse behavior. The natives have a pleasing manner and maintain generally good relations with brothers, sisters, and neighbors. If Venus is afflicted in this sign, there is inconsistency and fickleness in romance. Values concerning love, marriage, and romance may be superficial.

Venus in Cancer

Venus in the sign Cancer indicates people who are deeply sensitive in their romantic feelings. Their extreme sensitivity means their feelings can be easily hurt, but they hide this vulnerability behind a dignified exterior. Since their moods can be fluctuating and unpredictable, they value both financial and domestic security. They seek marriage as the means to a stable domestic life, cherishing their families and their own homes. They want demonstrative affection because it makes them feel secure and loved. They seek to make their homes places of comfort and beauty and the focus of social activities. If unmarried they often prefer staying home with a date for dinner to going out to public places of entertainment.

Women with this Venus position are very domestic; they like to cook and keep house for those they love. They have a delicate femininity, which is eventually expressed in a maternal way. Because Cancer is the maternal sign, they are affectionate toward their children. Men with this position can mother their families and children.

Because Cancer is a cardinal sign, these people at times take the initiative when they feel bored and lonely, though they will try to do so unobtrusively.

If Venus is afflicted in Cancer, there can be maudlin sentimentality, unstable emotional reactions, and a tendency to sulk.

Venus in Leo

Venus in the sign Leo indicates those who have ardent, fixed affections. They are lovers of life and somewhat theatrical in behavior. They can have a great deal of social and personal pride, especially when in the spotlight. These are the people who throw lavish, expensive parties. Women with this position wish to be noticed by others, to be admired and appreciated. Sometimes they are prima donnas; often they compete for the center of attention at social gatherings.

Because of their ability to dramatize emotion, people with this position of Venus make good actors and actresses. They have a keen love of art, with a vivid color sense and ability in painting, sculpture, and other artistic forms.

These natives are warmhearted, outgoing, sunny, and affectionate. They are fond of children. They are born romantics and like courtships full of drama and excitement. They will be strongly loyal to those they deem worthy of their affections. The person with Venus in this position likes to show off his partner, but he can be possessive and jealous if the partner does not pay him the proper homage.

If Venus is afflicted in Leo, there can be excessive social pride, snobbishness, selfishness, and overconcern with sex.

Venus in Virgo

Venus in the sign Virgo is in its fall, since Virgo is opposite the sign Pisces, in which Venus is exalted. People with this position tend to over-analyze emotions and be too critical of those they love, making others feel self-conscious and inhibited and cutting off the spontaneous flow of affection. This analytic trait can stand in the way of a direct intuitive response to beauty. These people try to understand the beauty of a rose, for example, by dissecting it petal by petal, not realizing that the rose is beautiful because of the totality of its parts.

People with Venus in Virgo frequently seek partners with whom they can share their work and intellectual interests. But this Venus position is likely to produce more unmarried people than any other Venus sign position, because of the natives' high critical standards for what they want in a mate. When they do marry, it is often through connections with work. Unless Venus is heavily afflicted, there are congenial relationships with co-workers in general. The place of work is often made artistically pleasing by a personal contribution to the working environment.

These people are extremely fastidious about manners, personal appearance, and hygiene; they are repelled by uncouthness in any form. They have an innate sense of the beauty of order and cleanliness and hence make good cooks and dietitians. They can have ability in clothes design and dressmaking; fashion designers often have Venus in this position. In art they can have good technical ability but may lack inspiration and flow.

The extreme social propriety of these people is often a cover-up for shyness and feelings of social and sexual inferiority. Their cold exterior, especially on the part of women with this position, often stands in the way of the development of romantic relationships. A feeling of loneliness and frustration may result. In this event there is likely to be a retreat into work and intellectual pursuits and the lavishing of affection on some animal. Such confinement can in turn prevent the formation of social contacts that would help these people out of their shells. However, if Venus is well placed by house and well aspected, the difficulties can be overcome or greatly modified. Because Virgo is an earth sign, Venus placed here gives attraction to material comforts and personal possessions of quality and beauty, which, the natives feel, confer status. Often they work hard to acquire such things, sometimes using possessions and status as substitutes for personal affection.

People with Venus in Virgo are capable of sympathy and are helpful to the sick. Their ability for nurturing makes them good doctors and nurses. They can also deal with psychological problems stemming from social maladjustment, for Venus in this Mercury-ruled sign is able to combine reason with the emotions and investigate these matters in a methodical, analytic way.

Curiously, if Venus in Virgo is afflicted by Mars, Uranus, Neptune, or Pluto, there can be an overreaction against shyness and social propriety, producing loose living, promiscuity, and bohemianism. This stems from a deep fear that only thus can the natives find love and sexual fulfillment; they feel the need to make sexual conquests in order to prove their desirability. In these cases the unconscious Pisces polarity takes over. These reactionary types can become crude and slovenly in their personal appearance and mannerisms.

Venus in Libra

Venus in the sign Libra indicates a type of person to whom marriage and harmonious social relationships are of extreme importance. Venus, the planet ruling Libra, is powerful and well placed here. Since Venus usually bestows well-proportioned features and general physical beauty, people with this position are attractive to the opposite sex and have many opportunities for marriage.

These people have an innate ability to understand the feelings of others. Enjoying companionship, they seek relationships in which a harmonious and close personal bond is possible. Along with their consideration for others, they have a desire to please, which results in their being well liked. Their sense of justice and fair play in romance and social relations is well developed. Because they dislike coarseness and uncouth behavior, they have high standards for social conduct and manners. They are romantic and affectionate, but as Libra is an intellectual air sign, they seek intellectual stimulation and companionship from close personal relationships; sensuality by itself will not suffice. In this respect Venus in Libra is different from Venus in Taurus, as it is not concerned with money per se; however, natives like to be surrounded by beauty and thus usually require money. Unlike natives with Venus in Taurus, these people seek status more through their personal relationships than through possessions, but as a rule they are endowed with both because they try to establish meaningful relationships with mature individuals who have acquired wealth. Moreover, they are able to make money by their pleasing manners and aptitude in dealing with the public, which can be applied to business.

The aesthetic perceptions are highly developed with Venus in Libra. The natives often have an aptitude for some form of art, especially music. Because Libra is an air sign and sound waves travel through the medium of air, they generally have a good sense of hearing, which is the basis of their musical ability. Venus in Taurus, by contrast, is more likely to relate to painting, sculpture, and other tactile arts.

People with this Venus placement dislike disagreements and discord. If they are exposed to them too frequently, they become nervous, upset, and often ill. Consequently they avoid situations of conflict. If Venus is afflicted, they may go along with others merely to avoid argument and unpleasantness, thus appearing to lack integrity. An afflicted Venus in Libra can lead to superficial emotional and social values and produce a conformist attitude and a lack of well-defined personal values.

Women with this Venus position want to be cared for deeply; however, in public places, social propriety and a suave approach on the part of the men with whom they are seen are important to them. There is ability in giving public performances, and these natives take the limelight gracefully. Much public acclaim and popularity can accrue to those in the performing arts.

Venus in Scorpio

Venus in Scorpio is in the sign of its detriment, because Scorpio is the opposite sign to Taurus, which Venus rules. With this Venus position the emotions and sexual desires are strong and passionate, jealous and secretive, and there is much pride in sex and romance. If Venus is afflicted in this sign, sensuality and preoccupation with sex are likely. Reactions in close personal relationships tend to be emotional, and desires and intense emotions may prevent the natives from seeing other people's points of view; thus, they often lack reason and delicacy. In highly developed types of people there can be idealism and high standards in respect to close relationships and romantic and sexual involvements. These higher types will sacrifice everything for love if they feel the objects of their affection are worthy of it.

These people can take their romances too personally and too seriously, lacking a light touch and sense of humor. Because much is given in emotional expression, much is also expected, an attitude that can lead to pride and an all-or-nothing approach to love and romance. If the person with this Venus position is jilted or disillusioned, he can become very jealous, resentful, and bitter, feeling his high trust has been betrayed. Hence, the position tends toward intense love-hate relationships. If love is abused or mistreated, it can easily turn into hate or cold indifference. Once these people sever an important relationship, it can never be reinstated on the old basis; they will never again allow the person to affect them personally.

The emotional intensity of this Venus position gives a colorful personality. Artistic tastes lean toward strong dramatic contrasts. Natives are attracted to occult sciences and inner mysteries, with psychic sensitivity to the feelings of others.

If Venus is afflicted in Scorpio in a woman's horoscope, she can be the type of *femme fatale* who uses her sex appeal to gain power over people and manipulate them. There is also the danger with Venus in Scorpio that the native will want to dominate or subtly control a close personal relationship, marriage, or business partnership. This intense Venus position can lead to emotional excesses. However, even when heavily afflicted, these people never lose their personal pride and emotional dignity. Therefore, they act reserved, maintaining an air of mystery and intrigue about themselves until they are sure of their relationship.

Venus in Sagittarius

Venus in the sign Sagittarius indicates people whose emotions and responses are idealistic and spiritually oriented. They are friendly, vivacious, sociable, and outgoing. Dane Rudhyar, one of the greatest psychological astrologers, pointed out in *The Pulse of Life* that each sign of the Zodiac is a reaction against the extremes of the sign that precedes it. This observation is especially true of Venus in Sagittarius, which is frankly outspoken about inner feelings, in contrast to Venus in the preceding sign of Scorpio, which is secretive and calculating. The soul-racking emotional intensity, the jealousy and possessiveness of Venus in Scorpio leaves a bitter taste in the evolutionary experience of the soul that has Venus in Sagittarius. Consequently, people with this position seek to base emotional conduct in personal relationships on more objective, socially accepted principles founded on ethics, philosophy, and religion. Traditional moral structures make them feel more secure in their emotional conduct. They seek to be honest and open in their feelings and reactions to those they love or with whom they are romantically involved.

People with this Venus placement will often try to convert their sweethearts or spouses to their own religious beliefs or moral principles in order to have a commonly agreed-upon basis of conduct. They generally seek to marry within their own religious or philosophic milieu but are not afraid of getting involved in unusual romantic relationships.

With the Jupiter rulership of Sagittarius, their taste in art and decor tends to be lavish, and they like flamboyant displays of color and form. If they can afford it, their homes and aesthetic surroundings will display a royal, palatial atmosphere. They are attracted to classical forms of beauty such as Greek architecture and symphonic music. They are fond of art forms that have a religious or philosophic motif, and religious music can deeply affect them. Religious ceremony and pageantry appeal to them.

This sign position gains emotional satisfaction through outdoor games and sports; those who engage in horseback riding or skiing are typical examples, and dates which include these activities will appeal to them. This sign position gives a love of travel to distant places. Natives often seek to marry foreigners or people of foreign extraction or other races, those with a philosophic bent, with advanced education, or with connections to institutions of higher learning.

Women with this Venus position seek men with gallant romantic appeal. The dramatic element appeals to them.

If Venus is afflicted in Sagittarius, there can be bluntness that offends the feelings of others, impractical idealism in romance, and a tendency to impose religious and moral standards dogmatically on loved ones.

Venus in Capricorn

Venus in the sign Capricorn indicates those who need material status and wealth in order to achieve emotional security. Often they seek to improve their status by marrying above their station in life, with the attitude that one might as well fall in love with someone wealthy. In dating and courtship they are attracted to those who will take them to expensive restaurants and prestigious places of entertainment. Proud and reserved in their public behavior, they dislike overt public displays of emotion and affection, considering such conduct beneath them. Their dignified air can be based on their desire to feel superior to the common lot; sometimes this is resented by others as snobbishness.

Because of the Saturn rulership of Capricorn, people with this Venus position can repress their emotions and sexuality, as does Venus in Virgo, but they are capable of being very sensual in private. They attract sympathy through their quiet personal dignity and refinement. There is also a sense of aloneness about them, which generates a subtle mystique that appeals to others. The classical chiseled features of Greek beauty are typical of Venus in Capricorn.

People with this position of Venus, if they marry young, seek older, more mature partners. However, if they marry later in life, they choose younger mates whom they can stabilize and provide with security in return for affection. Though not openly demonstrative, they are loyal and steadfast to those they love, because they innately sense the personal responsibility in important relationships.

In art, these people have a strong sense of composition and structure; like Venus in Sagittarius, this position endows them with an attraction to classical music and other traditional art forms that have preserved their value through the test of time. Since they have business and managerial ability in matters related to art, they may become antique dealers, museum curators, and art gallery directors.

If Venus is afflicted in Capricorn, there can be emotional coldness and overconcern with property and material goods. Calculating and ulterior motives may supersede affections; marriage can be made for money and status, and love can go a-begging.

Venus in Aquarius

Venus in the sign Aquarius is reacting against the materialism and cold propriety of Venus in Capricorn. It indicates an impersonal but friendly emotional outlook. The natives want to be friendly with everyone, but not necessarily on a personal basis. They are popular and well liked, and they generally have many friends. There is a sparkling, effervescent, unusual quality in their personal manner.

The attitudes of these people toward social and sexual morality may be unusual, departing from the standard rules laid down by society. It is not that they are devoid of principles. Rather, they have their own interpretation of what is just and meaningful. As with Venus in Gemini and in Libra, they find crude behavior unattractive although they themselves do not always observe traditional concepts of social behavior.

Romantic attractions are often sudden and casual, not necessarily stable or lasting. The individual finds intellectual stimulation important in romance and marriage and is attracted to ingenious or eccentric types, as well as to those who will help him expand his social outlets. The romantic partner or spouse must be a friend as well as lover and must understand that he requires variety and mental stimulation, and dislikes boring routine. These people also dislike jealousy and possessiveness and will shy away from romantic partners who seek to curtail their social freedom. Therefore, if one wants to remain close to Venus in Aquarius people, it is necessary to allow them freedom in their relationships with others.

The eclecticism of Venus in Aquarius inclines the natives toward unusual tastes. They are attracted to art forms that are extremely modern or extremely ancient. There is a liking for electronic forms of art, because of the Uranus rulership of Aquarius. Intuition about people's social, emotional, and personal disposition can be highly developed, verging on mental telepathy of the emotional states of others.

If Venus is afflicted in Aquarius, sexual habits can be eccentric and promiscuous. These people sincerely intend to remain constant in their affections, but their emotional outlook is subject to radical sudden changes, which can result in their breaking old relationships or creating new ones—and without any apparent reason. The hidden motivation often lies in their desire for greater personal freedom or new experience. They may be unable to work within the confines of marriage or other lasting relationships. They may have stubborn emotional attitudes and so refuse to see other points of view. Because Aquarius is a fixed sign, if Venus is well aspected there can be sustained loyalty to someone they truly love and respect.

Venus in Pisces

Venus in the sign Pisces is in its exaltation. Here the love principle reaches its highest evolutionary development; the natives marry for love, no other considerations being of any consequence. Venus in this sign manifests deep compassion and sympathy verging on spirituality—the understanding of and unity with all life. The universality of Venus in Aquarius, combined with the empathy and emotional depth of Pisces—which is ruled by Neptune—produces an emotional rapport with the life of all creatures in the universe. The individual sees the Eternal Life principle flowing through all manifestation, uniting the soul with all life. These people have a high capacity to understand the feelings of others; they know what it is like to be in another person's shoes. The experience of having been through all the signs of the Zodiac gives the soul the ability to identify with all types of humanity.

People with this position of Venus are romantic and sensitive. Unless they receive clear demonstrations of love and affection from others, they feel lonely and disappointed. Sometimes the disappointment leads to a feeling of martyrdom, which may be sublimated into religious expressions. Or it may lead to neurotic tendencies or mental illness. The Neptunian rulership of Pisces gives intuitive inspiration to Venus, making these people capable of drawing on higher dimensions for resources in artistic, poetic, and musical creation; many great composers, artists, and poets have

Venus in Pisces. This Venus position probably has more innate ability for inspired artistic creativity than other placements.

Because the natives are highly sensitive to the suffering of others, people may take advantage of their sympathies unless their discrimination is well developed. Their extreme emotional sensitivity means they are often afraid of being hurt through rejection; thus they hesitate to express their feelings, suffering the pangs of love in silence. Sometimes they miss romantic opportunities. They are inclined to become emotionally dependent on others or have others become emotionally dependent on them.

If Venus is afflicted in Pisces, there can be excessive sentimentality, lack of discrimination in choosing love objects, laziness, hypersensitivity, and overdependence on others. Strong emotions can stand in the way of objective perception of reality.

Venus in the Houses

Venus in the houses gives us information about how a person expresses himself socially, romantically, and artistically in the various areas of his life. For example, someone with Venus in the Tenth House would find artistic outlet through his career and would form close relationships with people connected to his work or profession; he might marry someone he has met through his profession.

The house or department of life in which Venus is placed indicates the type of people with whom the native establishes social relationships, close friendships, and romances.

Venus in the First House

Venus in the First House indicates people who possess personal grace, a pleasing manner, and a friendly demeanor. This position is especially favorable in a woman's horoscope because it confers physical beauty. There is usually a happy childhood, which leads to a happy outlook on life. Venus in the First House also shows that the person is socially out-going and active in efforts to develop friendship and romance.

People with this position are fond of beautiful clothes and all things that will enhance their personal appearance. Their natural ability to mix socially is likely to result in business, romantic, and marital opportunities. Talent may be manifested in art, music, or some other art form.

Venus in the Second House

Venus in the Second House indicates a love of wealth, beautiful possessions, art objects, and personal adornments—in general, all the lovely things that money can buy. The natives also seek wealth in order to achieve social status. They look for romantic or marriage partners who are wealthy and can bestow on them the material comforts they desire. This position confers talent in business, especially business related to the arts. Artists with Venus well aspected here stand a good chance of making money from their art.

Women with this Venus position are usually extravagant, and men with this position are prone to spend too much money entertaining their women friends. This position of Venus receives help from friends and social contacts, leading to business arrangements and positions that bring wealth.

Venus in the Third House

Venus in the Third House indicates an intellectual interest in artistic and cultural pursuits. There is a special love for literature and poetry and an ability to communicate harmoniously, both through speech—especially on the telephone—and in writing. People with this position can make good artists, scholars, and writers.

There is much coming and going and short-distance traveling, for pleasure and social obligation. People with Venus in the Third House are inclined to analyze romantic relationships and social contacts in an intellectual manner. They usually communicate easily with their spouses and close friends; they have good relationships with brothers, sisters, and neighbors. Social and romantic contacts are made with neighbors or people met through neighborhood activities and intellectual pursuits. These are the people who write beautiful love letters and romantic poems.

Social and romantic communications carried on through newspapers and periodicals are likely to be the result of Venus in the Third House.

Venus in the Fourth House

Venus in the Fourth House indicates emotional attachment to the home and the domestic scene. Relationships with family members will be harmonious unless Venus or the Fourth House is afflicted.

The natives like to entertain their close friends and romantic partners at home, where they can cook for them and create a warm, personal environment. The home is always artistically decorated, as beautifully as the person's means will allow.

Emotional closeness to the parents is indicated, and much happiness comes through them. Inheritance can come through the parents. There is the promise of being surrounded by beauty and comfort at the end of life. There is a love of land, gardening, flowers, and beautiful vegetation, and a patriotic love of the natural beauties of the homeland.

Venus in the Fifth House

Venus in the Fifth House indicates a strong pleasure orientation and a romantic nature. There is a general love of life, with a sunny outlook. Romance is of paramount importance. If Venus and the Fifth House are well aspected, there will be happiness and pleasure through romance, and many romantic opportunities. People with this position are generally popular and well liked. They love the arts and may be very talented, especially in the performing arts. They frequent theaters and attend musical performances in their social and romantic activities.

This Venus position gives a deep love of children. It also produces loving parents, teachers, and child psychologists. The children of these natives are likely to be girls with artistic talent and physical beauty.

Venus in the Sixth House

Venus in the Sixth House indicates social activities and romantic involvements established through work. The work performed is usually connected with artistic pursuits or social doings. Love of work and harmonious, friendly relationships with co-workers, employees, and employers are typical. Working conditions can be harmonious and beautiful. People with this position often marry someone they meet through their work.

This position gives a love of beautiful clothing and an ability in dressmaking and design. Affection is often lavished on pets and small animals.

The health is good, but not robust; these people can enjoy good health if it is not abused. Health often improves after marriage.

Venus in the Seventh House

Venus in the Seventh House indicates social ability and a happy marriage if Venus or the Seventh House is not afflicted. Natives enjoy much popularity because of their pleasant manners and consideration of others. There is an ability to deal with the public, which is good for those engaged in psychology, sales, public relations, and the performing arts.

Marriage and close personal friendships are very important to these people. They seek marriage for the romantic fulfillment and happiness it provides. They usually marry early and enjoy social and financial prosperity through marriage. They express love in their personal relationships and consequently receive love in return.

These people seldom need to become involved in lawsuits, but when they do, they will try to settle out of court.

Venus in the Eighth House

Venus in the Eighth House indicates financial gain through marriage, other partnerships, and social relations. Often this position indicates an inheritance, unless Venus or the Eighth House is afflicted. If Venus is heavily afflicted here, there can be a highly sensuous nature or an overemphasis on sex. Marriage may also be motivated by the possibility of financial gain.

The Eighth House position gives overly intense emotions and sometimes jealousy and possessiveness, because here Venus is in the house of Scorpio, the sign of its detriment.

Venus in the Ninth House

Venus in the Ninth House indicates a love of philosophy, religion, and art. People with this position often take long journeys for pleasure.

Marriage partners and other important social and romantic contacts can be met through universities and churches, or during long journeys or in foreign countries. There can be strong attachments to foreigners or people of other races and religions. The natives have high ideals regarding love. They may try to convert their loved ones to their own religious or philosophic views. These people are ordinarily well educated in artistic and cultural history. In some cases they become scholars in these fields. Venus in this house often gives a love of religious music and art.

There can be profitable, harmonious relationships with the in-laws.

Venus in the Tenth House

Venus in the Tenth House indicates social and artistic ambition. The individual will probably choose a profession related to the arts, and if he has artistic talent he stands a good chance of recognition. He is likely to seek marriage with someone who will bestow status and wealth. There can be good relations and friendship with employers and those in positions of power. This position of Venus gives people success in dealing with the opposite sex, which can help further their careers.

If Venus is afflicted in the Tenth House, the native can be a social climber or one who forgets his old friends once he achieves his social ambition.

Venus in the Eleventh House

Venus in the Eleventh House indicates warm friendships and relationships established through group activities. Kindness to friends assures that kindness will be received from them. For this reason, hopes and wishes have a good chance of being achieved. With Venus in this house there will surely be many friends of the opposite sex. Friendships are also established with artists and musicians.

The marriage partner often is met through friends and group activities and consequently will share in these activities. Friends often become romantic partners, and romantic partners become friends.

Venus in the Twelfth House

Venus in the Twelfth House indicates a love of quiet and solitude. Personal and social contacts often are secretive, and there can be secret love affairs. Social shyness can lead to loneliness or romantic frustration.

There is an emotional and artistic attunement to the unconscious mind, which can give deep artistic inspiration. Much of the personal behavior is motivated from an unconscious level. People with this position are kind and sympathetic toward those in trouble; their own feelings are sensitive and easily hurt. There is a great deal of compassion with this position, because it corresponds to the sign Pisces, in which Venus is exalted.

Mars in the Signs

The position of Mars in the signs of the Zodiac gives information about the person's characteristic modes of action as influenced by the desire principle. The sign of Mars also indicates through what types of expression a person will take action. When Mars is afflicted, anger and impulsive behavior, for example, may be an inherent expression. The sign position will tell what form this impulsive emotional behavior will take. For instance, when Mars is in Gemini, there can be argumentativeness.

The sign position of Mars also indicates the person's characteristic type of ambition, which can tell a great deal about the kind of work he does. It should be remembered that desire leads to ambition, as shown by the exaltation sign, Mars in Capricorn. Since impulsive action and expressions of forceful energy often lead to danger, the position of Mars will also show how danger and violence can enter a person's life.

Mars in Aries

Mars in Aries is characterized by uncontainable energy that must find outlet. This is the basic position of the initial impulse to action and self-expression leading to evolutionary experience. Mars in this sign indicates energy, initiative, courage, and impulsiveness. The drive to get things accomplished leads to creativity and the starting of many new projects. There is leadership ability in the sense that people with Mars in Aries can take the initiative and spark enthusiasm in others. They have a great desire to be first. However, they may lack the organizational ability of Capricorn and the staying power of Leo; hence they may not sustain their interest and enthusiasm long enough to see a project through to its conclusion. Children with this position should be taught to finish useful tasks.

This Mars position makes people headstrong and independent. They will not tolerate opposition or interference. The position can lead to success if the natives can learn to think before they act; otherwise, blind action may lead to danger and mistakes.

People with this position are highly competitive; they enjoy sports and physical games in which they can pit their strength and courage against those of their opponents. The star football player or racer, for instance, is likely to have Mars in Aries. They also have an ability or liking for work involving machinery. Many sports car and hot rod enthusiasts have Mars in this sign.

These people often receive injuries to their heads. When they are ill, they run high fevers, but they are also capable of surviving fevers that would kill others.

If Mars is afflicted in Aries, there can be egotism, aggressiveness, and anger. Although these people can have violent tempers, their anger is short-lived, unlike those with Mars in Scorpio. They need to learn to express more love and patience.

Dane Rudhyar points out that the aggressiveness of Mars in Aries is a psychological reaction against an unconscious feeling of inferiority; this comes as a reaction against the muddle and confusion of Pisces, which was the previous evolutionary experience of the soul. Consequently, these people have a great need to reassure themselves of their own worth through overt expressions of strength and courage.

Mars in Taurus

Since Mars in the sign Taurus shows a strong desire for money, much energy is exerted to acquire money and material possessions. This position of Mars indicates practicality, so that the energy is channeled into useful tasks that will produce concrete results.

Mars in Taurus is the sign of its detriment, being opposite the sign Scorpio, which Mars rules. The energy and action of Mars, therefore, will be slowed down by material obstacles and limitations. As Taurus is an earth sign, the dense material plane does not respond as quickly as Mars would like to. People with this Mars position are slow to act but possess great determination and perseverance once a course of action has been chosen. Although they are not especially aggressive, if they are forced to fight, this position will make them strong and unyielding.

Mars in Taurus can produce craftsmen and skilled artisans capable of great patience and precision in the use of tools. They create objects that are lovely and durable. Often they use solid, permanent materials such as metal and stone.

If Mars in Taurus is afflicted, there can be a preoccupation with sex and sensuality and an excessive attachment to money and material goods. These people can be jealous and possessive, especially where love and sex are concerned. The violence arising from sexual jealousy with Mars in Taurus can be just as intense as with Mars in Scorpio.

Mars in Gemini

Mars in the sign Gemini indicates mental activity and aggressiveness. Those with this Mars position have active and critical minds, and as a rule engineering and mechanical skill.

This position gives a love of debate and intellectual contest. If Mars is afflicted, there can be argumentativeness and irritability. Ingenuity and resourcefulness are typical with this position, but not necessarily perseverance, unless other things in the horoscope supply it.

Reporters, critics, and journalists often have Mars placed in Gemini. Great restlessness goes with this position, leading to many changes of occupation, and these people may work at several jobs simultaneously. If Mars is afflicted in Gemini, the speech can be sarcastic and rude.

Mars in Cancer

Mars in the sign Cancer is in its fall, since Cancer is opposite Capricorn, where Mars is exalted; consequently people with this Mars position may be intensely emotional. Moodiness and emotional frustrations lead to anger, which, if expressed openly, causes discord in domestic relations. Relationships with parents can be inharmonious, raising psychological problems later in life. If the anger is suppressed, it also results in psychological problems and is likely to cause ulcers and stomach upsets.

There can be too much aggressiveness in domestic relations, which is an inappropriate area for so much forcefulness to be expressed. The energy of Mars in Cancer, however, can be usefully employed in building or improving the home through carpentry and other repair work. Many do-it-yourself repairmen have this sign position. There is also a definite desire to own and run one's home.

Mars in Leo

Mars in the sign Leo gives energy, willpower, and creativity. Since much of this ability is expressed in the arts, many dramatic actors have Mars in this sign.

Like Mars in Aries, this sign gives positive initiative, but stability and determination are greater because Leo is a fixed sign. There is a natural ability for leadership because the self-confidence of Mars in Leo people inspires confidence in others. These people want to be in the forefront of whatever is going on, and they are competitive in activities that are important to them. They have strong, undeviating beliefs and opinions, which can arouse opposition among those who disagree with them.

Mars placed here also gives fixed, passionate desires. Although people with Mars in Leo are usually ardent lovers, they are also capable of jealousy and possessiveness. The men exude strength and masculinity and are high-spirited and proud. People with this Mars position, then, are powerfully attracted to members of the opposite sex, who in turn sense their life and vitality.

As with Mars in Aries, men with this Mars position tend to lose their hair prematurely. The fiery nature of Mars burns the roots of the hair.

If Mars is afflicted in Leo, there can be egotistical leanings and an overbearing manner with a tendency to dominate others. There is an inclination to believe in one's own infallibility.

Mars in Virgo

Mars in the sign Virgo gives energy and skill wherever work is concerned. As with Mars in the other earth signs, many skilled craftsmen, such as precision machinists, have Mars in this sign. Mars rules operations and sharp instruments, and Virgo is a sign dealing with health, indicating skill also in medical work; surgeons often have Mars placed here.

People with this Mars position plan their actions carefully and execute them systematically. They are unlikely to take action without good practical reasons. Unlike Mars in Leo, who likes to dominate in large matters, Mars in Virgo wants to be the authority in exact details. There is a strong perfectionist tendency with this position, which can stand in the way of getting anything done at all. These people are fussy and highly critical, especially where detailed methodology and precision are concerned. They insist on a well-organized working environment.

If Mars is afflicted in Virgo, there can be disagreements with coworkers, employees, and employers, sometimes so pronounced as to stand in the way of job security. There can also be danger of accidents through employment. An afflicted Mars in Virgo may cause a nervous and irritable temperament.

Mars in Libra

Mars in the sign Libra gives a strong urge to action in a social context. Mars is in its detriment here because Libra is the opposite sign to Aries, which Mars rules; therefore the direct action of Mars is somewhat limited by the need for the approval and cooperation of others.

Because Libra is a cardinal sign dealing with partnerships and relations with the public, people with this Mars position are the initiators of social activity. They want to be noticed and appreciated, and they like to act in partnership with others. There is a desire for marriage and for the emotional gratification it can provide; these people seek aggressive, energetic partners. There is a tendency for them to confuse their own desires and ambitions with those of others.

Libra lends grace and refinement to the aggressive and selfish tendencies of Mars; because of such toning down, it is not an altogether unfavorable position. Of all the planets, Mars most needs softening and modification by other attributes, and in this sign it is given social grace by Venus and discipline and prudence by Saturn. People with this position can become very angry, however, when principles of justice are violated, even when they themselves are not victims. Their concern with moral principle stems from the realization that unfairness reveals a moral weakness on the part of the perpetrator that could also be turned on them.

If Mars is afflicted in Libra, there is a tendency to strictness concerning the rules of social conduct; natives can have the attitude that the game should be played according to established rules. If Mars is heavily afflicted, there can be difficulties in partnerships arising from arguments and conflicts of will.

Mars in Scorpio

Mars in the sign Scorpio indicates powerful emotions and desires. This tremendous emotional intensity gives the natives relentless courage and thoroughness in executing their intentions. It can lead to the greatest heights of spiritual achievement or to the lowest depths of moral degradation, depending on the amount of wisdom and type of motivation by which the energy is guided.

These people have resourcefulness, courage, and energy, especially in meeting difficult situations. Even the possibility of death does not frighten them, if they must face it in order to accomplish their goals. They are capable of an uncompromising fight to the end in defense of their principles. The two hundred Spartan soldiers who held off the entire invading Persian army are an example of the Mars in Scorpio principle.

The powerful sex drive that goes with Mars in Scorpio, if wrongly motivated, can result in possessiveness and intense jealousy. People with this position tend toward an all-or-nothing attitude which makes compromising with them very difficult. Since it is hard for them to be neutral or indifferent, they make either friends or enemies of those with whom they have sustained dealings. They are secretive and do not reveal their plans or actions without good reason. They need to learn greater detachment and objectivity.

There is danger of coarseness and bluntness with this position, since at times these people do not take into consideration the feelings of those less forceful than themselves.

When Mars is afflicted in Scorpio, there can be intense anger and resentment, but unlike the anger of Mars in Aries, such feelings are not forgotten easily. People with this position can hold grudges, nursing their anger like steam in a pressure cooker until the effects of its outlet are disastrous. Consequently they make the most dangerous kind of enemy. If Mars is heavily afflicted in Scorpio, there is the tendency to dominate others emotionally, forcing them into submissiveness and servitude.

Mars in Sagittarius

Mars in the sign Sagittarius gives strong religious and philosophic convictions. People with this position are crusaders for the causes they espouse. Sometimes they arouse resentment by trying to convert others to their own dogmatic beliefs. As Jupiter is exalted in Cancer—which rules the homeland—and is the planet ruling Sagittarius, there is often a strong sense of patriotism. The natives like to think of themselves as staunch defenders of God and country. They are fond of parades, military reviews, and military music.

These people are capable of acting out of idealistic motives. According to the level of their intelligence, they will seek to improve the social order in which they live. The boy scout leader is an example of this kind of person. There is a strong love of sports and outdoor games; people who enjoy hunting often have Mars in Aries or Sagittarius. These people like adventure and the excitement of distant places and travel. They seek to be leaders in law, religion, philosophy, and higher education. But they usually follow traditional lines, and they may be aggressively self-righteous in this connection. The desire for adventure in the attainment of far-reaching goals can cause them to scatter their energy and overlook the things that need attention in their immediate environment.

If Mars is afflicted in Sagittarius, there can be caustic speech, a lack of diplomacy in expressing opinions, inability to appreciate the opinions of others, querulousness, and a desire for unrestricted freedom at all costs. In some cases there is a tendency to identify with institutions that have acquired power, which can lead to the self-righteous attitude that "might is right." When carried too far this is expressed as political, philosophic, or religious fanaticism, which destroys justice.

On the positive side, these people are direct and open in their attitudes and actions. They have a sense of fair play in sports and other competitions. They will fight ferociously but usually consider underhanded tactics beneath their dignity. However, they do tend to interpret the rules of the game to their own advantage.

Mars in Capricorn

Mars in the sign Capricorn gives great energy channeled into professional ambition. This position is less sensual than Mars in Scorpio or Taurus, but it can be extremely materialistic. The desire for recognition and high status is intense; the natives' actions are well organized and carefully calculated to achieve concrete results in terms of money and professional advancement. Professional success provides the ability to supply the material needs of the self, the family, and other dependents. Hence, many business executives who have struggled to achieve high positions in their organizations have Mars in Capricorn or the Tenth House, as do politicians and others who seek recognition and fame.

Mars is exalted in Capricorn, because the organization and discipline of Saturn—the planet ruling Capricorn—makes the most efficient, practical use of the Mars energy. As with Mars in Virgo, the natives must have practical reasons for everything they do. The tendency of Mars in Aries, in contrast, is to dissipate energy in undirected action. Since Capricorn is a cardinal sign, these people are more capable of decisive action than with Mars in any other earth sign, or fixed or mutable sign. They may not expend as much energy as do those with Mars in Aries or have the emotional intensity of those with Mars in Scorpio, but the energy they do expend is more effectively used.

Generally, they have a high degree of self-control and discipline; they are able to take orders from those in power and implement them appropriately. They expect the same discipline and obedience from those under their authority. Many men who pursue military careers have Mars in Capricorn.

These people take pride in doing a job correctly, and they have a corresponding disrespect for laziness and lack of ambition. They are the ones most scornful of the hippie way of life. Parents with this position want their children to amount to something. It is very disturbing to them if the children display bohemian tendencies and live a life of inactivity.

If Mars is afflicted in Capricorn, there is a tendency to use people for the sake of status and material gain. Natives may lose sight of human values in the intensity of their material ambition. If Mars is heavily afflicted, they may totally disregard the rights of others. The dog-eat-dog atmosphere at the executive level of large corporations is typical of the negative expression of Mars in Capricorn. These people can earn a reputation for cold calculation, selfishness, and materialism. However, such negative qualities can be offset if other factors in the horoscope are well developed.

If Mars is afflicted in Capricorn, there is danger of broken bones.

Mars in Aquarius

Mars in the sign Aquarius gives the desire for independence to pursue unusual or unorthodox courses of action. The natives demand the freedom to do things their own way. Their actions may be inspired by a superior level of intelligence combined with good organizing ability, which can lead to work in mechanical, electronic, and other engineering fields. Further, if the energy is well directed there can be worthwhile accomplishment in humanitarian work concerned with inventive and scientific achievements. Much more can be achieved through teamwork than through individual efforts, if the lesson of group cooperation is learned.

This Mars position produces reformist tendencies that are translated into action. Natives devise original methods of doing things and are contemptuous of traditional views and methods, unless these conform to logic and practical experience. Tradition is respected only if it deserves respect, in contrast to the Mars in Capricorn position, with which orders are obeyed merely because they are issued by authority. Consequently, people with Mars in Aquarius do not work well under authoritarian direction. They must be allowed to do things in their own way and to learn by their own mistakes. However, they are in danger of discarding the old ways before being able to replace them with something better. Thus the outcome of their actions can be either constructive or destructive, depending on the degree of wisdom and maturity indicated by the overall horoscope pattern.

In the year 1971 Mars was in the sign Aquarius beginning on May 4 and lasting until November 6. During this period, when the planet was in a stationary position and retrograde motion, many souls came into the world who will be the spearhead of a new way of life. They will have the special abilities of Mars in Aquarius trine to Uranus in Libra, which will produce a balance between inspired social concepts and the action necessary to implement them.

If Mars is afflicted in Aquarius, there can be a desire to overthrow the established order rather than regenerate and improve it. Many revolutionaries have Mars in Aquarius. People with an afflicted Mars in this sign need to learn the art of harmonious functioning with friends and in groups.

If Mars is afflicted in Aquarius, there can be trouble with circulation of the blood.

Mars in Pisces

Mars in the sign Pisces gives strong emotions arising from the unconscious mind. Natives are in danger of harboring unconscious resentments; the repressed anger can lead to neurotic tendencies and psychosomatic symptoms. These people should learn not to brood over past resentments.

This is generally considered to be a weak position for Mars, because Pisces is a mutable water sign, indicating a lack of strength. Excess emotional sensitivity stands in the way of self-confidence and direct decisive action. These people prefer to express their disagreements or resentments in a subtle way. They tend to act in secret as a means of avoiding direct confrontation with potential opponents. They can become highly emotional and are prone to tears. They need periods of quiet or solitude to regain their energies.

People with this position work best behind the scenes in tasks that require subtlety and intuitive sensitivity. Strength will be lacking unless it is supplied by other factors in the horoscope, such as a strong Sun, Saturn, Uranus, or Pluto. This position can help artistic and musical expression, and if well aspected it can be favorable for those who work in psychology. It also favors those who work in hospitals or other large institutions.

If Mars is heavily afflicted in Pisces, there is a tendency to dominate others by requiring attention to personal problems of a psychological or physical nature.

Mars in the Houses

Mars in the houses indicates the departments of life in which a person expresses his actions and desires. It shows where he must exert energy and initiative in order to achieve results. When Mars is afflicted, the house position shows in what areas conflict is likely to arise.

Mars in the First House

Mars in the First House indicates aggressive, outgoing people who have abundant energy. The physical body is often robust and muscular, giving an appearance of strength and ruggedness. They are not content to be bystanders in life; they must be directly involved in action. They are impulsive, especially if Mars is in a cardinal sign. Since Mars in the First House has many similarities to Mars in Aries, people with this position will get better results if they learn to think before they act.

These people are ambitious and are able to work hard. Their competitive drive makes them seek recognition and public acclaim.

If Mars is afflicted, there is danger that they will be egotistical and headstrong; if they feel strong enough to get their own way, they will have no qualms about getting it. Hence an afflicted Mars here can indicate a disregard for the rights and feelings of others; combativeness and violent fits of anger can occur periodically.

This position of Mars gives a love of sports and other forms of strenuous physical exertion. The body is often robust and muscular, with an appearance of strength and ruggedness. This position is favorable for men because it makes them strong and masculine.

The physical stamina and energy of these people enables them to accomplish twice as much work as the average person, providing the energy is well directed. If the rest of the horoscope shows intelligence and a capacity for self-discipline, they often attain great heights of achievement.

This position of Mars insists on freedom in personal action and will not tolerate interference from others. The capacity for action, self-confidence, and courage produces leadership, but not necessarily organizational or managerial skills, unless these qualities are supplied by other factors in the horoscope.

If Mars is heavily afflicted, there can be a tendency to get involved in physical fights. Furthermore, rash emotional impulsiveness may lead to neglect of ordinary precautions for health and safety. Often these people acquire a scar on the head or face.

People with Mars in the First House tend to run high fevers when ill, much like those with Mars in Aries. If Mars happens to be in a fire sign, natives often have red hair. Men with this position in a fire sign are likely to lose their hair at an early age.

Mars in the Second House

Mars in the Second House indicates an actively pursued desire for financial gain and material goods. Although the business enterprise of the natives gives them good earning ability, they are impulsive in spending, often depleting their financial resources as soon as they are acquired. Consequently they must carefully examine the value and purpose of the expenditures they wish to make.

These people desire to run their own businesses and will often initiate their own enterprises rather than join existing business organizations. They are competitive in finance and business and seek to vindicate themselves by demonstrating their earning ability. They are therefore always eager to surpass their competition.

Their business may be related to mechanical concerns.

They will fight to protect their personal property. They become righteously indignant when others take what does not belong to them. On the other hand, they will give away goods in order to win favors or make good impressions.

If Mars is afflicted in the Second House, there can be excessive concern with material values. In the horoscopes of less evolved types, there can be fighting and stealing, or other dishonesty, to acquire material goods or to satisfy the desires.

Mars in the Third House

Mars in the Third House indicates an aggressive, active intellect. Mental resourcefulness assures quick thinking in emergency situations. However, there is a tendency to jump to conclusions.

People with Mars in the Third House can be direct and sometimes caustic in speech. They assert themselves aggressively in order to obtain or deliver information; many newspaper reporters and political commentators have Mars placed here. It should not be forgotten that Mars has a political connection because of its exaltation in Capricorn. People with this position often work with machinery related to communications, such as telephones, printing presses, or mail trucks. Automobile mechanics and others who work with transportation machinery are also likely to have Mars here.

There is much impulsiveness in daily movements and in short-distance traveling. If Mars is afflicted, this position can produce reckless drivers; they tend to get angry at what they consider the stupidity of other drivers, not realizing that they themselves are often guilty of the same actions.

If Mars is afflicted, sarcasm and argumentativeness can result. There may be trouble with contracts, agreements, publications, and communications with brothers, sisters, and neighbors.

Mars in the Fourth House

Mars in the Fourth House indicates that much energy is expended in the home, and there is a desire to dominate the domestic scene. This can cause family quarrels, especially if Mars is afflicted.

Vigorous efforts to improve the home environment are made; people with this Mars position are frequently do-it-yourself repairmen, like those with Mars in Cancer.

There can also be an active interest in environmental and ecological problems. If Mars is well aspected, it can produce people who work hard to improve the environment.

Mars is accidentally in its fall in the Fourth House, the house corresponding to the sign Cancer, in which Mars falls. If Mars is afflicted here, there is generally conflict with the parents. These people need to improve their emotional self-control in order to achieve domestic harmony. Often better family relations can be maintained if the natives move away from the place of birth.

These people actively seek to acquire property for their later years. They may inherit land and buildings from their parents. If Mars is afflicted, however, there can be trouble over property, and the individual's house may be endangered by fire, theft, or other disruptions. Heavy afflictions to Mars here can bring difficulties over property taxes.

This position gives a strong constitution and energy that is sustained until old age.

Mars in the Fifth House

Mars in the Fifth House indicates those who actively pursue love and pleasure. They are aggressive and emotional concerning sex and romance, and their strong sexual drive gives urgency to the finding of a sex partner.

If Mars is afflicted in this house, quarrels resulting from impatience and sexual jealousy will probably arise during courtship. If Mars is heavily afflicted, sexual passion can result in pregnancy out of wedlock.

Artists—especially those who work with tools, such as sculptors—often have Mars in the Fifth House.

There is a liking for outdoor competitive sports with this position. It is commonly found in the horoscopes of athletes.

Very often an interest in working with children and young people confers a sense of leadership, power, and authority. Coaches and physical education teachers are especially likely to have this Mars position. If Mars is well aspected, they will be skillful teachers who will arouse interest, thereby getting results from their students. But if Mars is afflicted, they may have dictatorial, authoritarian attitudes toward those in their charge.

If Mars is afflicted in the Fifth House, the native's children may be subject to accidents or death.

Mars in the Sixth House

Mars in the Sixth House indicates energy and skill expressed through work. The work generally involves the use of sharp tools, or machinery that consumes or produces large amounts of power; hence this position is found in the horoscopes of machinists, engine builders, mechanics, heavy-equipment operators, steelworkers, and mechanical engineers. Surgeons and others in the field of medicine may also have Mars placed here, as may those who use tools in the preparation of food and the manufacture of clothing.

These are hard, energetic workers. They have little patience with people who are lazy or who do not want to exert themselves to earn a living. They display skill and precision in their work, and their self-esteem comes from completing their work and doing it well.

As Mars is exalted in Capricorn—the sign indicating the employer—

those with Mars in the Sixth House can achieve security and prominence by working for a well-organized, efficient business concern.

If Mars is afflicted in the Sixth House, ill health, injuries, or irritability can result from overwork or accidents through work. There may also be involvements in labor disputes and conflict with co-workers, employers, or employees. Sometimes perfectionist tendencies appear, and an overconcern with details of work causes neglect of major issues.

Mars in the Seventh House

Mars in the Seventh House indicates a person who is aggressively involved in partnership activities or in working with the public. The marriage partner, as well as close friends and business partners, is likely to be of an aggressive, active Mars nature.

People with this position prefer to work and act in cooperation with someone else. If Mars is well aspected, much can be accomplished in this manner. However, both the native and his associates will probably engage in impulsive behavior. If Mars is afflicted in the Seventh House, there is a tendency toward disagreements with associates, and toward marital discord and divorce.

Activities often involve joint finances, which can be a matter of contention if Mars is afflicted.

Mars in the Seventh House can produce aggressive sales and public relations personnel. If Mars is afflicted, there is need to learn tact and diplomacy in dealing with others. Because Mars is accidentally in its detriment in the Seventh House, there can be an unfortunate tendency to interact with others for selfish reasons or out of a sense of competition.

Mars in the Eighth House

Mars in the Eighth House is powerfully placed because this house is ruled by Mars and corresponds to the sign Scorpio.

With this position there are strong desires and emotional intensity; energy and persistence are expended in getting things accomplished. Aggressiveness with respect to other people's money in joint or corporate finances is characteristic. This position produces a powerful sex drive. If Mars is afflicted in the Eighth House in the horoscope of a person with occult leanings, there can be an interest in sexual magic.

Highly evolved individuals—especially if Mars makes favorable aspects to Uranus, Neptune, or Pluto—may be interested in occult forces, psychic power, and the life after death.

In many cases there is an acquaintance with violent death through war or other conflict. Mars in the Eighth House may indicate the likelihood of sudden death; if Mars is afflicted, violent death is possible. If Mars is heavily afflicted in less evolved individuals, there may be criminal tendencies.

Conflict is likely over legacies, taxes, and joint finances if Mars is afflicted in this house. These people often carry on actions in secret for a variety of motives, both good and evil.

Mars in the Ninth House

Mars in the Ninth House indicates a person with an interest in travel, outdoor sports, and religious, philosophical, social, and educational causes.

Such people are crusaders who aggressively promote the ideals they espouse. If Mars is well aspected in the Ninth House and the mind is sufficiently developed to give a broad understanding of life, they can be invaluable in leading action for social reform; they work to inspire people to more ethical attitudes and behavior. They will actively support institutions of higher learning, religion, and philosophy that serve mankind. Because they express these interests in action, not just in belief, their efforts can be highly effective.

These people seek adventure and broad experience, which often leads them into foreign travel, as well as into exploration in the realms of higher philosophy and education.

Sometimes people with this position of Mars join such organizations as the Veterans of Foreign Wars. Their social militancy can express itself through organizations covering a broad political spectrum, from violently revolutionary to reactionary. This position also produces the "hellfire and damnation" kind of evangelist.

The natives can arouse resentment in others if their level of understanding causes them to be narrow-minded or fanatical in outlook. Those who aggressively promote their own beliefs and organizations and are intolerant of other approaches may well have an afflicted Mars in the Ninth House. The tendency to condemn those with whom they disagree arises out of a lack of patience for understanding the circumstances and experiences of others. Along with this, there can be a personal identification with a favorite religious, political, or philosophic belief which provides the individual with a sense of self-importance.

Mars in the Tenth House

Mars in the Tenth House indicates people who desire fame and status. Since they are energetic in pursuing a career, they have a strong competitive drive to reach the top. This often leads them into such fields as politics and corporate management; engineering and military professions also attract them.

Mars is very powerful here because of its accidental exaltation in the Tenth House, which corresponds to Capricorn. A well-aspected Mars here gives initiative and executive ability for practical achievement. It can also produce constructive, effective political leaders. The competitive professional ambition of these people usually brings them fame or notoriety.

If Mars is afflicted in the Tenth House, there is a temptation to use unfair means to gain power or position. A bad reputation and sudden reversals in fortune can result when the wrongdoings are exposed. Mars afflicted in the Tenth House can cause extreme material ambition leading to a disregard of human values, if other factors in the horoscope do not supply these values.

In extreme cases there can be a desire for power at any cost regarding career and ambition.

Mars in the Eleventh House

Mars in the Eleventh House indicates energy directed toward friendships and group activities. Friends are likely to be of a masculine, aggressive type and often help people with this position get work accomplished and achieve their business and professional ambitions. There can be good mechanical ability, which sometimes produces inventors of mechanical devices. In a mentally alert individual, energy will be expended in areas of social reform.

If Mars is afflicted in the Eleventh House, there may be discontent with the prevailing social order and revolutionary tendencies. This energy should be directed toward efforts to improve rather than overthrow existing conditions. With an afflicted Mars here, disagreements or quarrels with friends and group associations are probable. Impulsiveness in the company of friends can bring injury or death to the individual or his friends.

Mars in the Twelfth House

Mars in the Twelfth House indicates desires and actions that are strongly influenced by the unconscious mind. Work and other activities will be carried on in secret or seclusion. There can be a tendency to act in secret to avoid the open opposition of others.

Natives tend to be secretive about their desires and purposes; they may have secret sexual involvements. Often they work in large institutions where they can disguise or lose their personal identities.

If Mars is afflicted in the Twelfth House, these people can be involved in secret plots; they can bear secret enmity; they can have secret enemies. With an afflicted Mars here there is danger of incarceration in prisons, hospitals, or mental institutions. Sometimes imprisonment will be for political reasons, because of Mars's exaltation in Capricorn.

These people need to be more honest and open about their own unconscious anger.

Jupiter in the Signs

Jupiter in the signs of the Zodiac gives information concerning a person's ethical, religious, and philosophic standards and beliefs. It shows in what way he expresses his interest in philosophy and higher education. Jupiter's sign position indicates where a person expresses expansiveness, where he does things on a large scale.

The Jupiter sign position also indicates how a person shares that which has been given to him and how he reaches out in generosity to the larger social order, thus receiving help and benefit in return. This principle of social cooperation makes possible the large undertakings and expansive progress that are not possible for a person working alone.

The sign placement shows not only where one is likely to receive financial and material benefits but how he has karmically earned the goodwill of others and the right to receive spiritual protection as well. Jupiter, as co-ruler of the Twelfth House and the sign Pisces, discloses in what way a person receives the karmic rewards of past good deeds. Because of this co-rulership, it also shows how a person is compassionate and generous toward those less fortunate than he.

Jupiter in Aries

Jupiter in the sign Aries indicates the ability for leadership and innovation in philosophy, education, and other spiritual endeavors.

The highest aspect of Aries is that of pure, creative spirit from which all else comes into manifestation. Jupiter placed in this sign gives an innate understanding of spiritual creativity or at least a profound respect for it. "Behold I make all things new" is the spiritual model of people with Jupiter in Aries.

Because of the Mars and Pluto rulership of this sign—combined with the exaltation of the Sun in Aries and the natural trine Aries makes to Sagittarius, which Jupiter rules—natives exert positive action in order to improve spiritual, social, and educational conditions. They have faith in the possibility of regeneration and rebirth into a better way of life. Consequently, there is great energy and inspiration with this Jupiter sign placement.

While the positive initiative taken with this position gives the ability for religious and philosophic leadership, it also can reflect the involvement of the ego and an attitude of self-importance, which if allowed to go too far arouses suspicion and resentment in others. The manner through which this urge for social betterment is expressed will depend on the general level of understanding and evolutionary development of the individual, as revealed through the rest of the horoscope. There can be much enthusiasm and self-confidence, inspiring confidence in others and arousing them to action.

At times there is a desire to go on holy crusades that may not be holy in the eyes of others.

The faith of these people in their ability to overcome and become gives them the courage to embark on large endeavors that would not be attempted by others. They may reflect the adage "Fools rush in where angels fear to tread," but any positive effort on their part produces some good, even if it does not reach its intended goal. It can lead to evolutionary development, as Jupiter represents the principle of growth.

If Jupiter is afflicted in Aries, the natives may tend to overreach themselves foolishly. They become rash and impulsive and have an exaggerated sense of self-importance.

Carelessness and overconfidence can cause losses in business and friendship. Jupiter afflicted in this sign can cause impulsive spending of money—wasting of investment resources, for example, on a new enterprise of dubious merits. An afflicted Jupiter in Aries indicates a need to develop prudence, caution, and the habit of holding something in reserve, should not all go as expected. In order to advance, the natives must learn to prepare for the possibility of unforeseen difficulties.

Jupiter in Taurus

Jupiter in the sign Taurus indicates a capacity for the correct and beneficial use of money and material resources. If Jupiter in Taurus is well aspected in a spiritually mature person, he is aware that all resources are loaned to us by the Eternal principle of Life for our use, for the service of our fellow man, and for the general improvement of the social and physical environment. He realizes that he is only a steward of the world's goods and that he must use and share them wisely for the sustenance and development of all life, especially anyone with whom he has dealings. In this case, money and material resources are regarded as a form of energy, flowing from person to person and making expansion, evolutionary development, and maintenance of life possible in the dense material manifestation that is the physical world.

With Jupiter in Taurus the individual needs to develop the potential for the values regarding the acquisition and use of money and material resources in the context of the larger social environment. When this lesson is learned, the resources that he gives to others for their creative self-expression flow back to him manyfold because he has extended to others the opportunity to express their talents. This makes possible an even greater cycle of productive unfoldment and increase through which everyone may benefit.

It is not sufficient that people with this position learn generosity; they must also develop wisdom and discrimination in investing their money so that it can be used in the most constructive and efficient way.

Jupiter in Taurus indicates a tendency to attract wealth, which these people feel is necessary in order to enjoy material comforts and the good things of life. Often they have gourmet tastes and are fond of excellent food and luxurious surroundings. If Jupiter is afflicted in Taurus, these expensive tastes can lead to dissipation, the outcome of which can be self-indulgence, physical degeneration, and indifference to the physical needs of others. This causes resentment and jealousy in persons less fortunate, whose legitimate physical requirements are neglected.

Jupiter in Taurus gives business ability through patience and steadiness of purpose. These people can envision and carry out enterprises on a large scale and over a long period of time. But in the process of expansion, they may overreach themselves financially without sufficient collateral to meet unforeseen contingencies. This is generally the outcome when previous business sucesses make them overconfident or the habituation to wealth makes them greedy.

The religious outlook is usually quite orthodox, since the natives identify themselves with the social and moral standards of the economic class to which they belong or aspire. Unless other factors in the horoscope rule otherwise, they may not appreciate spiritual values that are not linked to financial or practical concerns. To them a religion or philosophy is worthless unless it has a direct application that they understand. The class-conscious connotation of their religious outlook gives them a feeling of expansion and self-justification.

This attitude is most typical of the average Jupiter in Taurus business-oriented person, who belongs or aspires to the upper strata of society. Such people can be resented for their smug self-righteousness by the poor, political radicals, and the younger generation. But if those with Jupiter in Taurus did not carry on their daily business enterprises, there would not be the general level of social wealth and employment to sustain those who are active in other realms of human expression. They have their necessary place in the economy of life.

If Jupiter is afflicted in Taurus, the pride that arises from financial status can lead to the downfall of these people; they are in danger of thinking that they are superior to others because they have amassed more wealth. They must learn that it is not wealth, but what is done with it, that brings honor or dishonor. The extravagant taste of Jupiter afflicted in Taurus can lead to indebtedness and trouble with creditors.

Jupiter in Gemini

Jupiter in the sign Gemini indicates a love of philosophy and the study of important ideas in the history of religion, education, law, and philosophy. The ensuing expansion of the mind opens new lines of communication and areas of social contact, which bring benefits in the course of travel, writing, study, and business connected with the development of new ideas.

Natives have an intellectual curiosity that leads to mental development, so that they are considered intellectually advanced although they may not have received a formal education. Often they do seek university training as a means of mental self-improvement.

Jupiter in Gemini can give broad intellectual comprehension spanning a number of fields. Natives tend toward mental restlessness, much traveling about, and constant dabbling in many areas of study and interest. If carried too far, this activity can produce an intellectual dilettante. However, the broad sampling of different intellectual experiences enables these people to piece together the general outline of social, political, and historical trends, giving them insights into the future and destiny of mankind. Thus this position can produce skillful social commentators and historians.

Because of the natural trine of Gemini to Libra and Aquarius, these people attract many friends, acquaintances, and partnerships and so can broaden their intellectual horizons in new and unusual directions. These social contacts also provide opportunities for creative expression of the mind.

Jupiter is in its detriment in Gemini since it is in the opposite sign to Sagittarius, which it rules. This condition can be manifested in the native as a broad but superficial knowledge, or as book knowledge unsupported by practical experience. The lesson of Mercury in Virgo shows us that the most accurate, detailed knowledge comes from direct experience through work and personal service. This position of Jupiter, in contrast, has a danger of producing an ivory-tower scholar, unless other factors in the horoscope encourage practical experience. If Jupiter in Gemini is afflicted, then, the product may be an intellectual snob.

There is ability in teaching, writing, and lecturing with Jupiter placed in Gemini. Traveling lecturers often have Jupiter in this sign. Natives can also earn money and expand their business interests through publishing, travel, personal services, importing, communication industries, and mail-order businesses.

Jupiter in Cancer

Jupiter in the sign Cancer is in its exaltation. This usually indicates a good family background—not necessarily one of wealth or social standing, but a childhood environment and parental influence that instill kindness, generosity, and religious and moral principles at an early age. Later in life these characteristics become a part of the natives' basic expression.

The parents of children with Jupiter in Cancer usually love them deeply, looking after their welfare and instilling in them a basic trust and human kindness. The Jupiter principle of morality, philosophy, and higher education has it beginnings in Cancer, because one's first teachers are one's parents, especially the mother. Those with Jupiter in Cancer seek to establish a secure, friendly, prosperous, and comfortable home environment. They are kind and generous to the family and others in the home. If Jupiter is well aspected, they will use their homes to provide for the needs of friends and acquaintances who are having trouble finding their way in life. Jupiter here often indicates a large home, with many people on the domestic scene. Natives have a strong maternal instinct, and sometimes a tendency to mother the world. The home is also used as a place for religious, philosophic, and educational activities.

Since those with Jupiter in this sign love good food, they can be good cooks. However, they may be inclined to overeat or to eat foods that are better for the palate than the digestive system.

Business interests often involve real estate, housing, farming, food produce, and articles used in the home. Jupiter in Cancer gives emotional idealism, often leading to utopian dreams that are not based on practical considerations, unless other factors in the horoscope supply them.

People with this position often receive financial help from their parents, and they may inherit money or property from parents or other family members. Often they become wealthy in the latter half of life.

If Jupiter is afflicted in Cancer, there can be maudlin sentimentality, oppressive mother love, ties that are too close to the parents, and self-indulgence in food and material comforts.

Jupiter in Leo

Jupiter in the sign Leo indicates expansive, optimistic, self-confident qualities. Natives with this position have an abundance of energy and strong constitutions. They are generous and benevolent, but they usually expect personal admiration and appreciation in return.

Their liking to do things on a lavish, ceremonious scale explains their special love of religious pageantry and drama. Parades, fraternal lodge activities, and church rituals appeal to their sense of grandeur. Similarly, they are attracted to religious art, sculpture, and music, or art forms portraying events in history. They are fond of lavish parties and social occasions. If they are wealthy, they are especially likely to engage in such activities, which give them a feeling of importance and status.

Jupiter in Leo gives leadership ability, dignity, and the ability to inspire confidence and enthusiasm in others. But if Jupiter is afflicted, these capabilities may fan the fires of conceit because the principle of expansion (ruled by Jupiter) combined with the major fault of Leo, egotism, can produce vainglory and arrogance. These people need to learn that greatness comes through service to mankind and cooperation with the impersonal, universal laws of the cosmos, not through self-importance, even with the most opulent trimmings.

If this lesson is learned, there can be great steadfastness, reliability, honesty, and generosity. Jupiter in Leo confers honor and prestige that is well deserved. Natives can radiate sunlight, warmth, genuine affection, and benevolence to others. When they become unselfish in their expression of power, they are admired and loved, and they often achieve fulfillment in romance and love.

These people have a special love of children and a benevolent interest in their growth, especially their moral development. Consequently they make excellent teachers, Sunday school leaders, and spiritual counselors to the young. If the Fifth House is not afflicted and Jupiter is well aspected, they will be fortunate in having offspring who achieve honor and distinction.

They also have an affinity for gambling and stock market activity, but if Jupiter is afflicted in this sign, unwise gambling or speculation may cause disgrace and financial ruin. There can be business involvements with entertainment industries, artistic endeavors, sports, and education.

If Jupiter is heavily afflicted in Leo, disappointments and losses in love, romance, children, and speculation may be sustained.

Jupiter in Virgo

Jupiter in Virgo is in the sign of its detriment, because it is opposite Pisces, of which Jupiter is co-ruler. This is not an unfavorable position, since natives value work and will offer practical service to others.

However, the Virgo concern with detail and precision can conflict with the Jupiterian tendency to expansiveness. It is not possible for one person to give detailed consideration to every aspect of a large project. This conflict can result either in overwork or in the improper treatment of some aspect of a project. Consequently, the individual must learn to enlist the cooperation of others and to delegate responsibilities, or else scale down the scope of his endeavors.

People with this position demand integrity in detail and are able to sift truth from error when confronted with a large amount of information. But they may have a moralistic concern for detailed perfection which many people will find difficult to deal with. If this concern is carried too far, they make mountains out of molehills; they may lose a sense of the relative importance of various factors involved in work and service, especially the human factor.

If Jupiter is well aspected in this sign, honesty and integrity characterize work and business, making for congenial relationships with co-workers, employers, and employees. These people usually enjoy pleasant working conditions and are appreciated and well paid for the services they perform.

Natives regard cleanliness and order as being of utmost importance; these values are a cornerstone of their moral integrity. They disapprove of sloppy, bohemian habits of dress or housekeeping, unless Jupiter is heavily afflicted. In that case, as a psychological reaction, there can be a reversion to the opposite behavior, similar to that of a person with an afflicted Venus in Virgo.

Their religious and moral beliefs are based on the concept of service, and they regard high ideas as of little value unless they receive practical application. This sense of realism makes them conservative and somewhat orthodox in their social and religious outlook, as with Jupiter in Taurus or Capricorn.

There can be an interest in service and charitable pursuits related to physical and mental health, in hospitals and educational institutions, for example. Wealthy people with Jupiter in Virgo often contribute to the support of such institutions, or to medical missions.

If Jupiter is afflicted in Virgo, employment may be unstable because of a tendency to drift from job to job. There may be laziness where work is concerned and dissatisfaction with working conditions, co-workers, and employers.

These people must learn that spiritual attainment calls for more than the mere expounding of beautiful ideas.

Jupiter in Libra

Jupiter in the sign Libra indicates a strong concern with justice or moral principle in marriage, partnerships, and close personal relationships. Since the native tends to marry someone interested in religious, educational, and philosophic thought, this position favors a marriage based on spiritual values and cooperation in contributing to the larger social order.

Such values go beyond sexual attraction, so that there is promise of an enduring marriage (unless Jupiter is heavily afflicted here) and of a worthwhile home life (because Jupiter is exalted in Cancer).

Religious, philosophic, educational, and social ideas are influenced by the spouse, other partners, and close friends. Natives with this position will equally influence the religious and social ideas of their close associates. Their religious concepts are centered on the love and fair play that make possible a harmonious social order.

These people are generous in their consideration of the wishes and needs of others, so that unless Jupiter is afflicted, they are popular and well liked. This consideration produces an ability for dealing with the public, which enables them to be psychologists, mediators, diplomats, peace-makers, and public relations and sales personnel.

Their talent in these capacities lies in convincing people of the merit of certain ideas or social programs. Consequently they can be efficient promoters and fund raisers for churches, charitable institutions, and other worthwhile social endeavors. On a more subtle level, they may be promoters of religious, educational, or social philosophies, depending on the overall tenor of the chart.

If Jupiter is afflicted in Libra, there is a tendency to make moral decisions for others. There can also be a desire to be all things to all people in order to avoid discord or gain approval; if carried too far this attitude may lead to double standards on many issues. The person with an afflicted Jupiter in Libra may promise more than can be delivered, in order to gain favor. In the long run he will attract the disapproval of individuals or society at large, despite his honorable intentions.

Natives with an afflicted Jupiter in Libra expect too many favors and considerations. They can initiate too many close personal ties at one time, arousing suspicions of disloyalty in those with whom they are involved. The result can be treachery from members of the opposite sex, who become jealous and vindictive when the personal consideration they expect is not forthcoming.

If Jupiter is badly afflicted in Libra, lawsuits may arise from unfulfilled legal or financial commitments related to business, property, marital, or professional matters.

Jupiter in Scorpio

Jupiter in the sign Scorpio indicates strong, large-scale involvements in matters relating to joint or corporate finances, taxes, insurance, and legacies. Business affairs are likely to relate to funerals, real estate, fund raising, taxes, and insurance.

Natives are often interested in the occult, mystical aspects of religion, in life after death, and in telepathic communication with those of the unseen realms—especially if Jupiter aspects Uranus, Neptune, or Pluto. They can be intense and uncompromising about philosophic and religious beliefs and standards, and about social conduct and principles; this kind of attitude sometimes makes for powerful, bitter enemies.

These people tend to acquire secret information regarding the private affairs of others. They can have strange friendships based on hidden motivations. They may receive inheritances because of favors they have done. If Jupiter is afflicted, however, legal battles can erupt over inheritances, alimony, corporate expenditures, insurance, and tax payments. Unwise investments in stocks or financial partnerships may bring losses. These people may dabble in such negative forms of psychic phenomena as séances and mediumship, and there may be a desire to manipulate occult forces for personal gain.

Jupiter in Sagittarius

Jupiter in the sign Sagittarius indicates a love of philosophy, religion, education, travel, and foreign cultures. Intense involvement in matters concerning the codification of social thought may lead people with this position to embrace some philosophy or system of thought by which to regulate their lives. Traditionally this means some form of religious belief; but Sagittarian, intellectual types may take up Freudian psychoanalysis, Marxian dialectics, or bohemianism. Jupiter in Sagittarius merely shows the need for a system for governing one's conduct and way of life; the form that system takes depends on the overall tenor of the chart and the social milieu of the individual, which he may be either accepting or reacting against. The desire to make personal conduct conform to an impartial set of moral principles brings these natives the respect and admiration of many, including their enemies.

These people tend to have far-reaching metaphysical thoughts. They wish to know about the nature of man's consciousness, how he can successfully adjust to society, the purpose of the individual in the universe, and what is the ultimate creative force behind physical manifestation and the evolutionary process. This questioning leads in most cases to religious belief and an acknowledgment of a Supreme Being.

Once a particular set of religious or philosophic values is adopted, satisfaction is gained from efforts to convert friends and associates to a similar way of thinking; acceptance of a system of belief confers the security to operate in a larger social context. However, these people are deep thinkers and will formulate their own standards within the context of the ethical system to which they subscribe or which has been a part of their family upbringing.

Jupiter in Sagittarius gives an interest in foreign cultures, religions, races, and social systems, often expressed both through study and through long trips to foreign countries—especially if the natives can afford it. There is also a deep interest in the social and philosophic ideas that have shaped history. This breadth of understanding produces a farsighted outlook on life and often prophetic insights into the future.

If Jupiter is afflicted in Sagittarius, these people can have narrow-minded views to which they expect all to conform; they regard those who do not as unworthy of approval. A common accompaniment is a self-righteous attitude of the type that has promulgated religious wars throughout history. Personal egotism disguised as religious, national, social, or racial chauvinism is often the motivating factor behind such an attitude.

If Jupiter in Sagittarius is not balanced by sufficient mental development and faculties of impartial discrimination, as would be indicated by a well-aspected Mercury, Saturn, and Uranus, there is danger of superstitious adherence to dogmatic religious beliefs. These beliefs are inculcated in early childhood and are used as an unconscious defense mechanism against the frightening aspects of the unknown, confrontation with which could upset the psychological security of a neatly packaged doctrine. The tendency to get enmeshed in a system applies equally to radicals and conservatives with this Jupiter position.

Jupiter in Capricorn

Jupiter in the sign Capricorn is in its fall because Capricorn is opposite the sign Cancer, in which Jupiter is exalted. This situation is manifested in an overconcern with the letter of the law rather than with its spirit. However, Jupiter in Capricorn, if well aspected, can give great integrity, especially in moral conduct, business ethics, and the responsibilities of high office.

Natives generally have conservative, traditional values concerning politics, education, and moral conduct. They support the value system of the social, economic, and political status quo, overlooking its injustices, faults, and hypocrisies. The resulting rigidity of social outlook can alienate the younger generation and those who embrace a universal point of view.

People with Jupiter in Capricorn often acquire positions of economic or political responsibility. They will exercise prudence, caution, and a mature judgment therein but may lack imagination, creativity, and the ability to innovate.

They have a strong drive for power and status, prompted either by personal ambition or by a sense of duty to society; this drive can interfere with their home life and the personal, emotional values associated with it. The corporation executive who spends all his time at the office dealing with those in power, and neglects his family, is typical of persons with Jupiter in Capricorn. These people often acquire a cold, austere personal manner in their later years, and they hide the inner feeling of emotional frustration and loneliness engendered under an attitude of dignity and importance.

With this position of Jupiter, great wealth is often attained, through ambition, patience, managerial ability, and the wise use of resources. Since these people seek the status conferred by wealth and high position, they automatically adopt the values of those with impressive status who can help them achieve prominence.

These people abhor extravagance and waste. If Jupiter is afflicted and this tendency is carried to extremes, there can be miserliness or an inclination to economize in small matters and at the same time to be extravagant in large ones.

Jupiter in Aquarius

Jupiter in the sign Aquarius indicates people who know no class, racial, or religious distinctions. They insist on social, religious, and moral values that are universal, impartial, and democratic in every respect. There is a desire spiritually to share and experience with men and women from all walks of life.

These people have great tolerance, and they understand that it is not necessary for all to live by the same life-style or have the same value system. Each person has his own place on the evolutionary spiral of life, with unique lessons to learn and valuable contributions to make to society.

Without these differences a complex, advanced civilization would be impossible.

Those with Jupiter in Aquarius realize that tolerance, respect, and co-operation are the essentials for a successful social order. They therefore attract many friends and become involved in organizational activities that are designed to uplift humanity and bring about brotherhood among men. They distrust attitudes and laws that foster social distinctions or Chauvinistic nationalism.

Jupiter in Aquarius when well aspected gives an interest in occult wisdom, such as philosophy, astrology, karmic law, and reincarnation. In advanced types one finds the pioneers of religions and social concepts of the Aquarian age. These people are broad-minded and receptive to new ideas. Many social reformers and leaders of humanitarian organizations have Jupiter in Aquarius.

If Jupiter is afflicted in Aquarius, these people can be too casual and unreliable in their relationships to friends and in group obligations. They can espouse revolutionary concepts and impractical, unrealistic causes that ignore discipline and responsibility. They often scatter their energies, thereby missing their goal.

Jupiter in Pisces

Jupiter in the sign Pisces gives emotional depth, especially in understanding and compassion. People with this position champion the underdog and those less fortunate than themselves; thus they often work in hospitals and charitable institutions. However, sometimes they are indiscriminate in their compassion and generosity, and their sympathies may be taken advantage of. They must learn to help others assume responsibility for their own lives and learn their own evolutionary lessons. These natives must come to realize that the purpose of spiritual evolution is not simply to make life easy but to make men stronger in love, wisdom, and the positive expression of the will.

Mystical tendencies and emotional religious convictions go with this position. If Jupiter aspects Uranus, Neptune, or Pluto, there can be psychic ability and intuitive perception of the spiritual realm of being. These people may have a direct, intuitive experience of the realities beyond physical manifestation. Their spiritual understanding can be more universal than the orthodox Jupiter in Sagittarius person. However, their intuitive perception is not necessarily free of astral illusion, egotism, or desire for glamour.

Needing periodic seclusion, intuitive search, meditation, and spiritual renewal, they often associate with spiritual retreats, ashrams, churches, and monasteries.

If Jupiter is afflicted in Pisces, there can be guru worship and cultism because of the emotional drive to belong to something that confers spiritual status. These people also feel the need for a human figure or personification of the Deity to whom they can express their religious devotion. In this they are often unconsciously seeking a father figure who can assume responsibility for the direction of their life, especially if Jupiter is afflicted by Neptune. The identification with a guru or cult also provides a vehicle through which they are able to express service in order to feel that they are uplifting humanity. When they attain greater spiritual maturity, they grow in the understanding that their allegiance must be only to a universal, infinite spiritual power which is the ultimate reality. It is in this power that all time, space, form, and personality manifestation are contained.

If Jupiter is afflicted in Pisces, it can produce social parasites who throw themselves on the kindness of friends or religious and charitable institutions, instead of exercising discipline to make their own way in the world.

Jupiter in the Houses

Jupiter in the houses gives information about the departments of life and the types of activity through which a person expresses his religious, philosophic, and educational ideas. This is the area in which he will be expansive in working with the larger social order and in sharing his material and spiritual abundance, thereby receiving good fortune in return. In other words, Jupiter in the houses represents the departments from which an individual will reap the rewards of bread cast upon the waters.

The house position of Jupiter shows where a person thinks positively and optimistically. There is an easy flow in the affairs ruled by the house in which Jupiter is placed. The greater the flow to others of the good things of life, the greater the return will be to the sender.

Jupiter in the First House

Jupiter in the First House indicates an optimistic, sociable personality. Those with Jupiter in this position tend to focus on the brighter side of life. They are generally honest and trustworthy, friendly and benevolent—

and thus popular and well liked. Their optimism and self-confidence inspire confidence in others. They have a dignified personal manner, especially in their later years.

Jupiter in the First House, if it is well aspected, can give an ability for social, educational, and religious leadership; people with this position like to be regarded as authorities in some field of religion, philosophy, or education. They pursue higher studies in these fields as a means to outfit themselves in their search for a role. Being generally fortunate throughout their lives, they seem to have a type of divine protection, as if Providence were always looking after them. Help, however, may not come until the last hour.

Jupiter in the First House usually gives strong religious or moral convictions. If it is well placed by sign and has strong aspects to Uranus, Neptune, or Pluto, there can be prophetic insight into spiritual law and the destiny of mankind. This placement often produces spiritual leaders.

If Jupiter is afflicted in this house, there will be a tendency to grow fat, particularly in the later years. Also, there can be self-indulgence and an exaggerated sense of self-importance.

An afflicted Jupiter in the First House produces exaggeration. These people tend to promise more than they can deliver.

Jupiter in the Second House

Jupiter in the Second House indicates substantial business ability and expansiveness, giving good fortune regarding money and property. However, if Jupiter is badly afflicted, the money is likely to disappear as fast as it comes in, or the gains may be only on paper.

People with this position often engage in businesses related to real estate, domestic products, food, hospitals and other institutions, psychology, education, fund raising, travel, and publishing.

If Jupiter is afflicted in the Second House, the natives have a tendency to take too much for granted and to overreach themselves. They can also be oblivious to unforeseen contingencies in business enterprises. If Jupiter is heavily afflicted, there should be caution in incurring debts.

Jupiter in the Third House

Jupiter in the Third House gives a mentality that is optimistic, philosophic, and spiritually oriented. There is an interest in mental expansion in education, philosophy, teaching, publishing, religion, communications, and travel. The thinking is usually compatible with the prevailing beliefs and modes of communication of the culture.

This position makes people fond of travel, so that much time is given to long and short journeys, unless Jupiter is in a fixed sign. There is much curiosity concerning trends in social thought and modes of communication as expressed through all forms of writing and speech. These people can be good analysts, as well as perceptive social and political commentators.

This position confers congenial relationships with brothers, sisters, and neighbors, unless Jupiter is afflicted. If Jupiter is afflicted, there is danger of accidents while traveling, due to overconfidence or recklessness. In most cases, however, the person is not harmed physically. The propensity to accidents while traveling is especially likely if Jupiter afflicts Mars or Uranus.

Jupiter in the Fourth House

Jupiter in the Fourth House is accidentally exalted, because this house corresponds to Cancer, in which Jupiter is exalted. This position of Jupiter gives congenial family relationships and safety, comfort, and security in the home and all domestic matters. Since the natives generally belong to financially secure families with good standing in the community, they enjoy many social and educational benefits. This position also gives good fortune in general in the second half of life. These people often inherit land and property from parents or other family members. If Jupiter is well aspected in the Fourth House, there will be harmony in the family with respect to religion and moral standards. As with Jupiter in Cancer, the parents provide good religious and moral training in the early lives of these natives.

Usually a large home and family circle are indicated. The home may well be used as a center for religious, social, philosophic, and educational activities.

If Jupiter is well aspected, material and spiritual benefits will come within the locale of birth. However, if Jupiter is afflicted, it is a good idea to leave the place of birth and settle elsewhere.

If Jupiter is badly afflicted in this house, family members may be a burden on the natives because of heavy expenses incurred in supporting them according to their accustomed style. An afflicted Jupiter here can also bring limitations through outmoded religious beliefs imposed by family members.

Jupiter in the Fifth House

Jupiter in the Fifth House indicates people who are creative in the arts, education, sports, and all things pertaining to children. Being especially fond of children, they make inspiring teachers, counselors, and spiritual advisers of the young.

Their own offspring usually are fortunate, achieving honor and distinction. The children are likely to show interest in philosophy and religion, and as a rule they do well and go far in their education.

Unless Jupiter is badly afflicted, this position indicates happiness in romance and the possibility of romance with a person of means or status.

Those with Jupiter in the Fifth House often engage in businesses related to the stock market, investments, education, the arts, or places of entertainment. If Jupiter is afflicted here, there can be large financial losses as a result of unwise speculation or investment. As with Jupiter in the Second House, the natives tend to overextend themselves, thus inviting financial downfall. This is due to Jupiter's co-rulership of Pisces, the karmic sign.

Jupiter in the Sixth House

Jupiter in the Sixth House indicates an active interest in service and constructive work. People with this position want to do something practical in order to serve others and contribute to the social order.

There is an interest in healing the body and the mind, which often leads to the work of spiritual healing. There can be an innate understanding that a person's mental and emotional states have a great deal to do with his physical health. Since work, especially in healing, is often linked with religion, these people will become interested in medical missions, spiritual healing, massage, homeopathy, and other forms of natural medicine. Christian Science and similar disciplines are prevalent with this position.

These people are usually well liked and respected in their work. Unless Jupiter is badly afflicted, they will have congenial relations with co-workers, employers, and employees because they are conscientious about their work and seek to do it well.

If Jupiter is badly afflicted, laziness and a tendency to push one's work onto others will be evident. A sanctimonious attitude in relation to work and what is expected from others derives from the fact that Jupiter is accidentally in its detriment in this house, the opposite of the sign Pisces, of which Jupiter is co-ruler. An afflicted Jupiter here can cause health problems due to overindulgence, which often results in liver complaints.

Jupiter in the Seventh House

Jupiter in the Seventh House indicates openness, benevolence, and friendliness to others, which brings good fortune through marriage and partnerships. A strong sense of justice makes people with this position honest and fair in their dealings; they expect honesty and fairness from others. Sound moral and spiritual values concerning relationships usually result in a fortunate and lasting marriage. These people often marry someone of wealth or high social standing. Business partnerships will also prosper because there is good judgment in choosing associates and honesty in dealing with them.

If Jupiter is well aspected in the Seventh House, selfless love is openly expressed; the natives desire the greatest spiritual and material well-being for others. This sincere concern brings trust and friendship in return.

There is ability in the fields of law, public relations, sales, negotiating, and mediating.

If Jupiter is afflicted in the Seventh House, there can be a tendency to take too much for granted and to expect too much from others. If Jupiter is badly afflicted here, there can be naïveté in partnerships and business dealings, making these natives susceptible to charlatans and people who have grandiose ideas without sufficient backing.

Jupiter in the Eighth House

Jupiter in the Eighth House indicates benefit through inheritances, insurance, and joint finances. However, if Jupiter is afflicted, there can be litigation over heavy taxation of inheritances.

Often the natives are attracted to such businesses as funeral homes, insurance, tax accounting, and corporate fund raising.

In religious matters, there is a strong interest in the life after death, and if Jupiter aspects Uranus, Neptune, or Pluto, these people are likely to become interested in spiritualism. Some may even have telepathic communication with those in other realms.

Unless Jupiter is badly afflicted, in later life death is usually peaceful and due to natural causes.

Jupiter in the Ninth House

Jupiter in the Ninth House gives a deep love for philosophy, religion, and higher education. People with this position formulate a definite moral standard and system of philosophy by which they regulate their lives. They also have a keen interest in all codifications of thought including law, religion, philosophy, and higher education. They therefore make good teachers and often associate themselves with institutions of higher learning.

Generally they seek to acquire as much education as possible, unless Jupiter is afflicted. In that case they may not have the opportunity for advanced education, or they may waste it out of either laziness or indifference to the discipline that education requires.

They often become ministers or occupy positions of importance within a church hierarchy, since they are usually broad-minded and tolerant in their understanding of people. If Jupiter is afflicted, however, extremist religious beliefs can cause narrow-mindedness.

These people are fond of travel and seek to study foreign countries and visit them in order to learn about other cultures.

Business activities may relate to publishing, lecturing, teaching, and travel.

Jupiter in the Tenth House

Jupiter in the Tenth House indicates prominence and high standing in the profession, manifested mostly in the later part of life. Religious and ethical principles are applied to business dealings and public responsibilities. Benevolent actions lead to positions of influence, but these good deeds may not be apparent to the casual observer.

With this placement of Jupiter there is considerable professional ambition, as well as honesty and reliability concerning professional duties or public office. People with Jupiter in the Tenth House usually acquire good reputations and are regarded as pillars of society. It is a favorable position for those who seek public office or who engage in politics. It also confers organizational and executive ability and therefore is a favorable position for managers and business executives.

In the realm of higher education, these natives strive to equip themselves in order to be worthy of greater trust and responsibility, so that they will be rewarded with additional recognition.

These people have a dignified personal manner, especially in the later years. If Jupiter is in an earth sign, they also have excellent business ability and acquire wealth at this later time.

As with Jupiter in Capricorn, neglect of domestic affairs while career ambitions are pursued can cause unsatisfactory relations in the home.

If Jupiter is afflicted in the Tenth House, there may be hypocrisy and vainglory, leading to disgrace and reversals of fortunes.

Jupiter in the Eleventh House

Jupiter in the Eleventh House indicates people who achieve their goals through friendships and group activities. These people are kind to their friends and concerned about the welfare of humanity at large. Hence they are well liked, and they attract friends who are generous and helpful to them.

If Jupiter is well aspected in this house, much substantial, inspiring moral and spiritual advice is received from and given to friends. But if Jupiter is afflicted, the advice is not always sound or practical.

There is a spirit of cooperation and mutual consideration with friends, making it possible to carry through large, constructive endeavors successfully. With this position, group activities often have charitable or humanitarian goals, and they often take place through religious, educational, or fraternal organizations.

Business activities may relate to inventions, science, or organizational endeavors.

If Jupiter is afflicted in the Eleventh House, there can be a tendency to sponge off friends and take them for granted, while neglecting responsibilities toward them. Friendships are sometimes built on the ulterior motive of personal gain.

Jupiter in the Twelfth House

Jupiter in the Twelfth House shows an interest in an inner spiritual search through seclusion, meditation, and introspective study. Mysticism and intuition may be prevalent, especially if Jupiter aspects Uranus, Neptune, or Pluto.

Deep sympathy for those in need is incorporated in this position of Jupiter. If the planet is well aspected, the natives aid those in need by lavish donations to charity. They derive emotional satisfaction from helping others, and they often work behind the scenes in large institutions, such as hospitals, asylums, universities, and churches.

With this position of Jupiter also comes the ability to make friends out of enemies, if the planet is well aspected. Sincerity and humility are the rule if Jupiter is not afflicted. When it is afflicted, there may be neurotic tendencies, a martyr complex, and an impractical idealism. These people can become wards of charitable or religious institutions or parasites on those who take pity on them. In this way they neglect the responsibility of developing their own capacities for creative work and productivity. There is likewise a tendency to escape into fantasy, as with an afflicted Neptune in the Twelfth House.

If Jupiter is well aspected, these people receive hidden support and sustenance in times of crisis, which they merited by their past good deeds.

Saturn in the Signs

Saturn takes twenty-nine years to complete one cycle of the Zodiac. The sign position of Saturn shows the ways a person must shoulder responsibility and develop maturity and discipline.

Through its natural rulership of Capricorn, Saturn is an important factor in determining a person's career. Its position in the signs can give important clues to the kind of work for which a person is suited and the kind of career he is likely to pursue. People with weak Saturns often do not have well-developed careers.

Saturn's position also indicates the kind of responsibilities a person is obliged to face and the type of lessons he must learn. The affairs ruled by the sign in which Saturn is placed are especially serious matters for the individual, for with Saturn he learns, by dint of hard work and discipline, to cope with many difficulties in various areas of his life. It is in this way that he finds order and security.

Saturn in the signs shows how a person seeks status and recognition—the areas in which he tries to accomplish something of lasting value in the eyes of the world. In overcoming and becoming, he climbs one more hill; Saturn sees to it that he carries his own load.

With Saturn we come to grips with the harsh realities of dense physical manifestation; thus, Saturn's sign position indicates where we are likely to experience difficulties and limitations. We learn that Rome was not built in a day, that it takes time and hard work to bring an idea into practical reality. Through the concentration and application involved in this process, we develop discrimination, willpower, and patience. These are some of the essentials for the development of true spirituality.

Saturn in Aries

Saturn in the sign Aries indicates a person who is forced by circumstances to acquire initiative, patience, and self-reliance in providing the practical necessities of life. By the obligation to develop his own resources, he comes to develop his will and strength of character.

Saturn is in its fall in Aries because Aries is the opposite sign of Libra, in which Saturn is exalted. Aries represents the initial impulse of action, while Saturn represents the law of cause and effect that brings back the consequences of an action. Saturn in Aries is in its fall because there has not been sufficient time for these consequences to take effect. Thus it is difficult for people with this position to see themselves as others see them; they are initiating a new cycle of experience, and so they have not had time to learn the consequences of their actions. They may, therefore, lack awareness of the principles of social justice and the rights of others.

This position of Saturn gives resourcefulness; natives are capable of evolving new methods in their work. In the case of highly developed people, discipline combined with initiative leads to mental creativity, which enables them to produce new concepts in their chosen fields. Einstein, who had Mercury conjunct Saturn in Aries, is a good example of this characteristic.

If Saturn is afflicted in Aries, natives can be very defensive, always expecting opposition from others; this quality makes it difficult for them to understand, communicate, and cooperate with others.

An afflicted Saturn in Aries also indicates self-centeredness and an impulse to self-justification. Since these people are concerned with their own ambition and security, they may overlook the needs and aspirations of others. Their tendency to pursue exclusively personal aims can hinder them from cooperating with others and thus can place limitations on their success.

With this position of Saturn, therefore, one can be short on diplomacy. Natives tend to do things alone, taking care of their own needs without giving or requesting help. They prefer to be in business for themselves, but it is not always possible with this position.

Saturn in Aries can cause headaches and a tendency to worry because of a restriction of the normal flow of blood to the head.

Saturn in Taurus

Saturn in the sign Taurus indicates people who need discipline and hard work if they are to acquire material possessions; they come to feel a strong need for financial and emotional security. They cannot be at peace if their practical affairs are not in order. If Saturn is well aspected in Taurus, enduring patience, steadfast adherence to principle, and practical management ability in business affairs will be characteristics.

When they are about twenty-nine years old these people seek stable career positions that will ensure financial and domestic security, which they require for their well-being. They are likely to be reliable and persistent in their careers. Often they enter professions in banking, investments, insurance, or business management. Since they tend to be frugal, they usually make purchases of lasting value, with primary consideration for their utilitarian qualities. They save money for future emergencies and for security in old age. They must develop a well-balanced sense of the value of material resources.

If Saturn is afflicted in Taurus, there can be obstinacy and excessive materialism. In extreme cases the result is either miserliness or—conversely —a burdening of oneself with material possessions, instead of allowing things to flow from one so that new things can flow in as needed.

Saturn in Gemini

Saturn in the sign Gemini indicates a practical, well-disciplined, systematic, and logical mind. There is a capacity for discipline in thinking, reasoning, and writing, and in solving problems of all sorts. Ideas are judged on the basis of their practical usefulness and on whether they have been proved out through direct experience.

Discipline in all forms of mental work, especially mathematics, science, and the concrete implementation of ideas, usually enables the natives to carry through in formal courses of study. These people like things to be well defined, organized in detail, and set down on paper. They are particularly concerned about clarity in contracts and agreements.

Honesty in communication and dependability are of paramount importance; hence these people generally end up with something substantial to show for their efforts.

Saturn functions well in all the air signs because it adds discipline, justice, and practicality to the intellectual functions. Saturn's exaltation in Libra and co-rulership of Aquarius give strength to its position in Gemini, through the double trine in the air triplicity of the natural Zodiac.

Many secretaries, stenographers, bookkeepers, accountants, writers, teachers, and researchers have this position. It also favors those engaged in engineering, the physical sciences, and mathematics.

If Saturn is afflicted in Gemini, there can be a tendency to experience and display excessive doubt, suspicion, shyness, and a critical attitude. However, the natives are flexible in adapting to the practical needs of any situation, being resourceful in finding the solutions to problems; they view life with a practical objectivity.

Saturn in Cancer

Saturn in the sign Cancer is in its detriment, because Cancer is the opposite sign to Capricorn, which is ruled by Saturn.

Saturn in Cancer may cause inhibition of the expression of emotion, which is likely to result in estrangement from family members; such emotional isolation in the domestic scene can lead to neurotic reactions. The early family environment and parental relationships are sometimes cold, austere, or beset by problems, and the natives may be left with emotional scars and inhibitions. People who have Saturn in Cancer nevertheless take family responsibilities very seriously.

The need for respect for the individual and his family is deeply felt. These people hide their inner feelings from public view in order to preserve their dignity. Emotional sensitivity and the need for approval sometimes force them to build a shell around themselves, which can inhibit the expression of true warmth in personal relationships.

Saturn in Cancer often indicates difficulties in stability and security in the home life. While these people strive to have their own home and property, they may well incur financial struggle and domestic strain.

In some cases poor or sluggish digestion and body metabolism lead to overweight and excessive water retention in the tissues. In others there may be undernourishment, resulting in a bony appearance.

If Saturn is afflicted in Cancer, there can be emotional hypersensitivity, defensiveness, and unusually strong attachments to material possessions.

Saturn in Leo

Saturn in the sign Leo gives natives a need for importance and recognition and a compulsive drive for personal control of their environment; thus they seek to attain positions of power and leadership. If Saturn is afflicted, there is the danger of developing dictatorial or dogmatic attitudes. The need of these people to defend their ego can result in stubbornness and rigidity. Seeking security by means of autocratic personal authority, they require a great deal of attention and respect from others. Parents with this Saturn position are generally severe and strictly disciplinarian with their children.

Saturn rules the sense of practicality and the appreciation of universal laws and principles of justice. Since these laws are of an impersonal, cosmic nature, as indicated by the sign Aquarius, which Saturn co-rules, the interpretation of them must be free of personal considerations if an accurate view of reality and successful relationships with people are to result. However, Saturn is in its detriment in Leo, because Leo is the opposite sign to Aquarius; consequently, the laws that Saturn governs are distorted here by egotism and the desire for power. Thus this position can indicate people who must develop a proper set of values in dealing with love, romance, children, and matters of creative self-expression.

Saturn in Leo gives professional interest in education, and in management in the fields of entertainment, business, and speculative investments. Physical ailments usually take the form of stiffness in the back and heart trouble.

An afflicted Saturn in Leo can bring disappointments in love or problems through children, as well as losses through financial speculation.

Saturn in Virgo

Saturn in the sign Virgo indicates people who are practical, exacting, and hardworking. They are concerned with detail, accuracy, precision, and efficiency, especially in work.

If Saturn is afflicted in Virgo, perfectionism may be manifested in relations with co-workers, employers, and employees. Since these natives are punctilious about rules and regulations, it is difficult for others to get along with them. They tend to drive themselves and others to overwork, while ignoring major issues through their excessive concern for detail.

They often work in such fields as medicine, health research, and science, or in record-keeping activities—bookkeeping or library work. They exercise patience and precision in scientific experimentation and analysis of experimental results.

This position often makes people austere, gloomy, and depressed because of the excessive weight of work and detailed responsibility. They need to take a break once in a while, and to develop a sense of humor. Worry and overwork can lead them to ill health, and they can have problems with nervousness and digestion.

Saturn in Libra

Saturn in the sign Libra brings the realization that to accomplish anything of lasting value, or even to make life possible, human cooperation is necessary—and it must be enduring if it is to be effective. But enduring cooperation is feasible only when all parties in a project are dealt with justly, and justice requires mutually accepted rules of conduct and commitment. Each person must strive to complete his work and must be responsible to the whole. Most discipline and responsibility grow out of the understanding that human relationships entail mutual commitment, as in marriage, business partnerships, and close friendships. The reason is that Saturn is exalted in Libra, the sign ruling relationships.

Because Saturn in Libra deals with responsibilities in relationships, it also rules the laws that formally regulate such affairs. Thus people with this Saturn position often become lawyers, judges, and mediators.

To a large extent Saturn in Libra rules contracts, including marriage contracts. These Saturn agreements often are of a karmic nature, arising as they do out of interactions with people who have incurred past responsibilities and moral debts.

Because Libra is an intellectual air sign and a cardinal sign of activitiy, people with Saturn in Libra deal extensively with business arrangements: organizational planning, formulation of legal contracts, cooperative division of work responsibilities among people. The ability to plan and organize group endeavors is seen with this position.

Saturn in Libra can indicate marriage in later life or marriage to a serious person with heavy business or professional obligations. The marriage itself often incurs burdens, hard work, and the need for patience.

This is a powerful position for Saturn; it gives much social awareness and social responsibility. If Saturn is well aspected, these people often attain positions of great wealth and social honor 'through their ability to work with others—an ability that implies receptiveness, tact, reliability, and good organization.

If Saturn is afflicted in Libra, there can be exacting attitudes toward people and a tendency to drive them at work. Natives can lack love, forgiveness, and a sense of responsibility in their relationships. They are inclined to apply the letter of the law strictly instead of understanding the justice implied by the spirit of the law. The concept of justice that they enforce so strictly is colored by their personal outlook. An afflicted Saturn in Libra can indicate a false ambition leading the natives into too many commitments, which they can fulfill only at the price of overwork. In some cases they cannot meet their commitments, and the consequent resentment they arouse in others results in their own loss of status.

Saturn in Scorpio

Saturn in the sign Scorpio indicates responsibility in financial affairs, such as corporate resources, partner's finances, taxes, inheritances, insurance, and matters concerning the property of others. Business activity is likely to deal with corporate financing, insurance, and tax accounting. If Saturn is afflicted in Scorpio, there can be conflict over inheritances, taxes, and joint finances, which often incurs legal battles and losses through litigation.

The natives are usually perfectionists in their work. They are always trying to improve the structure of the status quo. If this proclivity is carried too far, they can earn a reputation as hard taskmasters. Having little patience with attitudes that reflect laziness or unwillingness to work, they are sensitive to lack of diligence in others as well as in themselves. They exert much energy and willpower on practical accomplishments.

These people accept responsibilities with a serious emotional intensity that often burdens them; they must learn to deal calmly and efficiently with them as they arise. Thoroughness, persistence, and determination are the rule with Saturn in Scorpio, giving a drive for success that is equaled by only a few other positions. These people desire authority and will struggle hard to attain their ambitions; whether they use fair means or foul depends on Saturn's aspects.

These people are capable of harboring deep resentment when they feel they have been dealt with unjustly. They can also have an almost fanatic adherence to principle.

If Saturn is afflicted in this sign, there can be a tendency to scheme and plot. A desire for revenge and an inability to forget past emotional injuries may also be present.

In health matters there can be problems with constipation or calcification.

Saturn in Sagittarius

Saturn in the sign Sagittarius indicates people who are serious in their pursuit of philosophy, religion, and higher education. They generally develop strict moral codes or a strict adherence to religious and philosophic systems. They will defend moral precepts and conduct themselves according to principles of justice; they search for truth and constructive values in personal conduct.

Saturn gives the Saggitarian person intellectuality, additional discipline, thoroughness, and depth of concentration. What these people learn is absorbed thoroughly and can be put to practical use. When they achieve honor or distinction, they feel they have earned it through diligent effort.

A desire for power and leadership manifests itself in the wish to be regarded as an authority in some phase of higher education, religion, law, or philosophy. There is a deep need for some intellectual, philosophical, or spiritual achievement which will bring distinction.

This position gives intense intellectual pride; natives fear disapproval or censure and feel resentful if they have been thought of or spoken about unjustly. Their personal reputations are of extreme importance to them.

If Saturn is afflicted, these people are likely to be self-righteous in trying to impose their philosophic and religious systems on others. If carried too far, this practice results in an intellectual and spiritual self-righteousness.

Saturn in Capricorn

Saturn in the sign Capricorn indicates strong ambitions for worldly power, status, and authority, usually manifested through business, science, or politics. Natives feel great need to make significant achievements in their careers, and they undertake no endeavors without having practical purposes in mind. They are good organizers; they alternate between favoring their ambitions and protecting their security, thus attaining prominence without risks to either. They have an aura of dignity and seriousness which can make them appear austere and cold.

They are able to accept orders from those in authority, and when they achieve their own positions of authority, they expect similar obedience from others. Hence they are conservative in business and politics. They feel that the traditional power structure exists for necessary reasons, which should not be questioned by those who lack the practical experience of dealing with the responsibilities of power.

Their struggle in early life to attain security and self-sufficiency helps form such practical, conservative attitudes later on. They feel that until a person can manage his own affairs successfully he is in no position to give advice to others, or to handle larger political or economic responsibilities.

People with this position of Saturn know that everything has its price and that everyone must contribute to the work of the world. They feel that everyone should earn what he gets through his own efforts. Thus, when they reach the top, they seek to help others help themselves. In later years, however, they tend to forget the hard struggles of youth and the difficulties of getting started without money, tools, or resources—despite sincerity and a willingness to work. If Saturn is afflicted, these people may use their acquired wealth and material goods to control others.

How and when power and authority are attained will depend on the level of understanding and the degree of spirituality as revealed through the rest of the horoscope.

These people generally have a strong sense of family pride and honor; they often come from families respected in the community. However, those born into wealthy and socially prominent families are in danger of being extremely callous about human values, because they lack the experience of personal struggle without resources. Such people are likely to regard social and economic inferiors as manipulable commodities rather than as sensitive human beings. This tendency can be offset if the horoscope shows spiritual understanding and compassion inherited from a past incarnation. As in Scorpio, those with Saturn in Capricorn can reach either the heights of spirituality or the depths of materialism and selfishness.

If there is a childhood of poverty and family disgrace, this position gives the necessary drive to overcome difficulties and achieve prominence and power. For these people, life is always a serious business and a struggle. Sometimes they are lacking in aesthetic sensitivity, judging things solely according to their price or reputation. They need to develop a sense of humor and an understanding of other values besides materialism and status. If desire for status is carried too far, it can become an end in itself, rather than a means of contributing to the social order.

If Saturn is well aspected in Capricorn, there will be honesty and integrity in all business, political, and professional dealings. If Saturn is afflicted, unscrupulous means may be used to achieve wealth and power, the result being dictator types in extreme cases; there can be a tendency to use literal interpretations of the law for unfair advantage. When unscrupulous means are resorted to, however, they often bring about reversals of fortune, public disgrace, and a fall from power.

These people should avoid becoming rigid in their attitudes and beliefs.

Saturn in Aquarius

Saturn in the sign Aquarius indicates a capacity for well-organized mental concentration. The mind is impersonal and scientific; the concern for impartial truth is paramount. Highly evolved types are able to set aside the ego and see all issues—social or scientific—in the light of impartial, universal law.

The ability to quiet the mind and steady the attention is the necessary prerequisite for the development of the Uranian intuitive faculties of the sign Aquarius. Saturn here gives the steadiness of attention necessary for this development.

People with this sign position are mentally ambitious, often working hard to make original scientific discoveries or new applications of scientific knowledge that will bring them status and distinction. Saturn in Aquarius gives an ability to visualize form and structure, often of a geometric nature, and it confers mathematical ability.

Like Saturn in Libra, Saturn in Aquarius, if well aspected, gives a sense of justice and responsibility in relationships. People with this position are loyal and responsible to friends and to groups with which they work; they often become involved in highly structured fraternal organizations, such as the Freemasons. They are generally level-headed, offering good advice based on universal laws.

Social relations are very important, but if Saturn is afflicted, these people may be selfish and domineering. They expect others to play the game by their rules and to serve their personal interests.

If Saturn is afflicted in Aquarius, there may be a tendency to coldness and emotional insensitivity in personal relationships. The individual's manner can be formal, exclusive, and intellectual, and lacking in feeling. There is also danger of intellectual pride.

Saturn in Pisces

Saturn in the sign Pisces is a difficult position because here the karmic planet is in the karmic sign. The natives have a tendency to become trapped in their memories of the past. An overactive, fearful imagination generates all types of anxieties and neuroses. Consequently, it is difficult for these people to deal effectively with the demands of the present. In extreme cases the imagination creates personal slights and problems that do not really exist.

On the positive side, Saturn in Pisces can give these people emotional understanding, humility, and the willingness to work hard on behalf of those less fortunate than themselves. If the rest of the horoscope indicates mental clarity, there also can be psychological insight into others.

If Saturn is well aspected, these people are capable of deep meditation. This steadies the psyche and makes possible profound spiritual understanding.

An afflicted Saturn in Pisces can result in paranoia, excessive worry, fretfulness, and regret over past mistakes and misfortunes. When carried too far, these reactions can result in neurotic or psychotic tendencies leading to incarceration in mental institutions or other places of confinement. In some cases the neurotic problems are manifested in physical illness and hospital confinement, especially with oppositions to Saturn in Pisces from Virgo, the sign of health.

These people need a certain amount of quiet and solitude in order to tap their inner resources. They should also spend some time actively participating in the affairs of the world, to avoid moroseness and excessive introversion. If Saturn is afflicted in Pisces, they should make strong efforts to avoid self-pity.

Vain regretting of the past can become a cancerous growth on the soul, destroying happiness, creativity, and usefulness to self and others. This position demands objective, critical self-analysis so that the natives can discover their personal worth and abilities—as well as defects—and thus find a way out of their difficulties. They must learn to let go of the past and take constructive action in the present.

This position of Saturn often indicates that work will be done behind the scenes in large institutions—hospitals, asylums, universities, or government agencies.

Saturn in the Houses

Saturn in the houses indicates the areas of life in which a person must learn to act with discipline. It shows what practical circumstances require responsibility from the individual, thus forcing him to mature. It shows how he must build structure into the areas of his life that lack it, and how he will express practical ambition.

Saturn in the First House

Saturn in the First House indicates an austere, dignified personal manner. The natives accept responsibility and are serious-minded and hardworking. They do not speak or act without a definite purpose in mind. They may seem cold and unfriendly to the superficial observer, but if Saturn is well aspected they can be loyal friends who will offer practical help when it is most needed.

People with this position have good reasoning ability and a sense of justice. The feeling that they must shoulder heavy responsibilities can lead them to believe that fun is frivolous and that they have no time for it. They need to become more outgoing and to develop a sense of humor.

If Saturn is afflicted in the First House, limitations and hardships in childhood are common. Many obstacles have to be overcome before these people can achieve self-sufficiency, independence, and freedom. If Saturn is badly afflicted, there can be selfish, materialistic ambition, a psychological result of the suffering experienced in early life. Such suffering leads to mistrust of others and the attitude that they must protect their own interests, for no one else will. In such cases, they build an emotional wall around themselves that is difficult for others to penetrate. They may thus alienate people even more, in a vicious circle bringing further defensiveness and loneliness.

These people work hard and long to achieve prominence through their own merit, because they wish to vindicate themselves by accomplishments leading to power and status. Limitations on the fulfillment of personal ambition can cause frustrations, and hence hostility. This does not take the form of overt violence but can be manifested as scheming to get even with or take advantage of others.

Saturn in the First House is accidentally in its fall because this house corresponds to Aries, where Saturn is in its fall. Consequently, these people often must learn to love and cooperate with others before they can achieve personal fulfillment and happiness. Only when they have acquired some of the attributes of Libra and the Seventh House will they escape from their self-limitation.

At times an afflicted Saturn in the First House results in physical hardship or disability. Saturn placed here is likely to produce a bony appearance. Two distinct physical types go with this position: one is short and swarthy with dark eyes, the other tall and large boned.

Saturn in the Second House

Saturn in the Second House indicates ambition and hard work to acquire money, material possessions, and the status that these confer. Natives generally have to work hard for a living. They are shrewd in business and can get their money's worth in whatever they buy. They conserve their money, saving it for security in old age. If this frugality is exaggerated, it can result in stinginess, so that the person is overly cautious with money and unwilling to make even necessary expenditures. This sometimes stands in the way of business expansion, by which more money could be made.

These people need to realize that if they are to achieve financial growth money must be fluid; it has to flow out in order for more to flow in. In many cases, their cautiousness arises from a deep fear of poverty, and often they work hard and amass great wealth because of this fear.

If Saturn is afflicted, there can be much hard work for little gain. If Saturn is well aspected, there can be financial security and an easy acquisition of money and property, especially in the later years. A well-aspected Saturn here often makes for prudence and farsightedness in business affairs. In general, people with this position acquire land and property of lasting value.

Material gain through the father, employer, or people in positions of power is often indicated. Money can be made through government contracts, business management, mining, and construction.

If Saturn is afflicted in the Second House, there can be selfishness and possessiveness concerning money and material resources.

Saturn in the Third House

Saturn in the Third House indicates mental discipline and practicality; ideas are judged according to their usefulness. Speech is deliberate. Mathematical and scientific ability are evident, because of the patience and methodicalness Saturn gives to the thinking process.

People with this position often work in publishing, printing, and the communications media. They make good accountants, secretaries, researchers, librarians, writers, and teachers. They are careful where contracts are concerned, and they exercise caution when signing papers or making agreements.

They are not inclined to travel, except for business purposes. Business activities may require much telephoning and writing.

If Saturn is afflicted, there can be difficult relations with brothers, sisters, and neighbors. An afflicted Saturn in the Third House can also cause worry and negative thinking, which may result in complaining and fault-finding. Difficulties and disappointments may arise in obtaining education or career training.

If Saturn is well aspected, much hard work is put into acquiring training for career purposes.

Saturn in the Fourth House

Saturn in the Fourth House indicates heavy responsibilities incurred through the home and family. The parents of the natives are generally strict and conservative and may be a burden in later years.

Since Saturn is accidentally in its detriment in the Fourth House, there can be emotional isolation from the family. These people often have to struggle to achieve domestic security and to provide for their families. There can also be limitations in later years if Saturn is afflicted in this house.

Professional and business activities are likely to center around real estate, building, contracting, or farming, or the manufacture of domestic products.

This position of Saturn indicates care in managing home, property, and inheritance. Natives seek to preserve these things for later years in order to provide security for themselves.

In the last years of their lives they often become recluses or shut-ins, or they may be tied to their domiciles by the force of necessity.

Saturn in the Fifth House

Saturn in the Fifth House indicates heavy responsibilities concerning children or difficulties in giving birth.

If Saturn is well aspected, there can be organization and a sense of structure in art and music. Business or career may deal with speculation, schools, or places of entertainment. People with this position make good investors and stockbrokers of a conservative type. Often Saturn placed in the Fifth House gives ambition for power and leadership through artistic self-expression; politics and business management can serve as creative outlets.

If Saturn is afflicted, there can be financial loss through speculative investments.

These people often become romantically involved with an older, mature person. Romantic involvements in general are likely to entail weighty obligations.

If Saturn is afflicted, romantic opportunity may be lacking, or there may be disappointment in love. These people are too reserved in their creative self-expression, and in their attitudes toward art and pleasure. Self-consciousness stands in the way of their attaining happiness and the love of others. They must learn to give themselves, to reach out with love to others. Only when they discover how to express themselves openly and warmly will they be able to find happiness.

If Saturn is heavily afflicted here, there can be an inability to relate to children, or an excessive strictness and severity toward them. Often there is emotional coldness and an inability to love. Saturn afflicted in the Fifth House can cause sexual inhibition and frigidity because of emotional blocks.

Saturn in the Sixth House

Saturn in the Sixth House indicates an ability for hard work and efficiency in one's job. Work is taken seriously and much specialized skill and knowledge are acquired. Heavy responsibilities are usually incurred through work or service, and there is a serious attitude toward the care of health.

Natives enter careers in medicine, dietary work, food processing, clothing, science, engineering, and other mechanical fields requiring skill and precision. This position of Saturn gives a careful, analytic mind because of Mercury's natural rulership of the Sixth House. These people can achieve financial security by use of their abilities and specialized skills.

If Saturn is afflicted in the Sixth House, there can be chronic health problems and low vitality, often as a result of worry and overwork. Employment may be hindered by ill health or lack of opportunity.

If Saturn is well aspected, the natives are respected by their co-workers, employers, and employees. However, if Saturn is afflicted, relations with these persons are unsatisfactory.

Saturn in the Seventh House

Saturn in the Seventh House is accidentally exalted, because the Seventh House corresponds to the sign Libra, in which Saturn is exalted. Thus there is a strong sense of responsibility and justice in all important relationships and public dealings. The natives either marry late in life or marry a serious, mature, career-oriented individual. If Saturn is well aspected, the marriage will be stable and enduring. If Saturn is afflicted, marriage and partnerships will entail problems.

People with Saturn in this house will work hard and conscientiously in cooperation with others, and will uphold their share of responsibility. If Saturn is well accepted, they will be reliable workers and may be depended on in agreements. They can be interested in law and have an ability for business organization and management, or for formulating contracts. They can establish their future welfare and improve their careers by working with others.

If Saturn is afflicted in the Seventh House, there is a tendency to be inhibited, critical, and negative in relationships. The marriage partner can be cold, unloving, uncooperative, critical, and obstructive. An afflicted Saturn in this house also can indicate treachery from enemies and lawsuits.

People with Saturn in the Seventh House are in some way forced into relationships that entail responsibilities.

Saturn in the Eighth House

Saturn in the Eighth House indicates involvement with partners' finances, corporate money, insurance, taxes, and inheritance. Such involvement always brings responsibilities. The natives must develop a sense of justice in the use of material resources because they are accountable for other people's property as well as their own.

If Saturn is afflicted in the Eighth House, there can be litigation or other trouble over money, inheritances, or goods belonging to others. These people may be denied their rightful inheritance; in the case of divorce they may suffer losses through alimony settlements. They will probably be burdened by heavy taxes, and they should pay all their taxes on time in order to prevent legal difficulties. An afflicted Saturn also means that death can be caused by long-term illness.

The native may marry a poor person, and the marriage can be a financial burden. There can also be restrictions on career ambitions due to lack of capital. However, if Saturn is well aspected, money can be made through the skillful management of other people's money and resources placed in the native's jurisdiction.

Saturn in the Eighth House can cause fear of death if the individual is lacking in spiritual values. Distressing dreams and psychic experiences that have a disturbing psychological effect are common.

If Saturn is well aspected to Uranus, Neptune, or Pluto, there can be deep spiritual insight into life's mysteries.

Saturn in the Ninth House

Saturn in the Ninth House indicates a serious interest in religion, philosophy, and higher education. Systems of belief are judged according to their practical value and their contribution to social stability, especially in the native's later years.

People with this position generally seek education at traditional institutions of higher learning, as the gateway to status and professional advancement. As with Saturn in Sagittarius, they desire personal distinction through some achievement in education, philosophy, or religion. They seek positions of power and authority within important educational or religious institutions; hence many professors and university officials can have Saturn placed here. They are also concerned about their moral reputations. Their religious standards are conservative and traditional, unless other factors in the horoscope indicate otherwise.

Business and professional activities are likely to deal with law, teaching, publishing, religion, and travel. People with this position of Saturn take long journeys more for business purposes or as a means of obtaining status than for reasons of pleasure.

If Saturn is afflicted in the Ninth House, there can be narrow-minded authoritarian attitudes toward religion and morality.

Saturn in the Tenth House

Saturn in the Tenth House is powerfully placed because this house corresponds to the sign Capricorn, which Saturn rules. Saturn also holds the most elevated position in the chart when found in this house. Therefore, it indicates strong career ambitions; the drive to achieve status through the profession is paramount, especially after age twenty-nine and in the later years.

If Saturn is well aspected, moral integrity and hard work result in the attainment of authority, high position, wealth, and leadership. If Saturn is afflicted, however, the tendency to compromise principles for the sake of ambition leads eventually to reversals in fortune, public disgrace, and a fall from high position. Those with Saturn in this house must exercise extreme caution concerning principles, or disgrace and heavy karmic debts may be incurred. A great price must be paid for the infraction of universal law.

It is important that ambition and success not become ends in themselves but rather be the means to serve the larger social order. To this end a careful examination of the motives for power is required. It is far better that positions of leadership never be obtained if they are to be abused and cause suffering to others; the ensuing mistakes may be correctable only under difficult and unfavorable circumstances.

Saturn in the Tenth House gives farsighted organizational and managerial ability. Hence it favors business executives and politicians.

If Saturn is afflicted, there can be obstacles, disappointments, and lack of opportunity or security in the career.

Saturn in the Eleventh House

Saturn in the Eleventh House indicates a sense of responsibility concerning friendships and group associations. Saturn here makes one seek to know important and influential people as a means of advancing one's own status and career.

If Saturn is afflicted in the Eleventh House, the person and his friends may use each other for reasons of personal gain or ambition. If Saturn is well aspected, loyalty and good advice are exchanged among friends, who can also provide the native with opportunities for knowledge and intellectual growth. A well-aspected Saturn here gives the native a sense of justice, which is manifested as a recognition of the need to help others advance their interests equally with his own.

If the principle of equal justice for all—represented by Saturn exalted in Libra—is brought into play in friendships and group associations, everybody will receive equal benefit from group cooperation and organizational structure.

People with this position are likely to establish friendships with older, serious, career-oriented people who will have a maturing influence on them. Natives can have karmic associations with those they have dealt with in the past.

Saturn in the Twelfth House

Saturn in the Twelfth House indicates that much time will be spent in seclusion or working behind the scenes in such large institutions as hospitals, universities, corporations, and government agencies. Work may be carried out in psychology or in charitable institutions. This position makes it hard to obtain recognition, unless Saturn makes favorable aspects to the Tenth House or to the ruler of that house.

Saturn afflicted in the Twelfth House means loneliness and depression. If it is badly afflicted, there can be mental illness and confinement in hospitals, prisons, or other places of detention. An afflicted Saturn here often gives secret enemies who contribute to the native's downfall. However, in many cases these enemies are more imaginary than real.

People with this position need to get away from their own psychological problems by serving others and by energizing themselves in practical, constructive work.

Uranus in the Signs

Uranus in the signs indicates the ways in which a person's urge for freedom and individuality are manifested. It shows how he establishes an intuitive link with the Universal Mind, whereby he is enabled to receive original ideas and the inspiration for understanding life and solving its problems.

The sign position of Uranus indicates the motivations behind a person's wishes, hopes, and goals, especially the goals set by the mind. It points to the type of friends a person is likely to seek, and the purpose and style of activity of the groups to which he belongs.

Since Uranus takes seven years to go through one sign of the Zodiac, everyone born during a given seven-year period has Uranus in the same sign. (The house position of Uranus will vary within this period.) Consequently, the sign position of Uranus is important in indicating generational differences—the common destiny of a large group of people who are born at the same time. As with the other outer planets, Uranus's sign position is less important than its house position in demarcating individual differences in the affairs ruled by the planet. The sign position has more historical than personal importance.

The sign and house positions of Uranus also tell something about the unique work or purpose of the soul in the present incarnation. It shows where one is given opportunity and freedom from the karmic limitations of the past so that he may express himself creatively.

Uranus in Aries (1928–1934)

Uranus in the sign Aries indicates people whose mission it is to blaze new trails in science and social reform. Freedom to act in their own way is of paramount importance to them. They have courage, daring, initiative, and resourcefulness. When Uranus is afflicted in Aries, however, they can be explosively impulsive, politically fanatic, violent, and indiscriminate in their rejection of the past.

This sign position makes its natives blunt and outspoken. As a generation they demand change and refuse to live in the style of their parents or preceding generations. Their spirit of adventure is strong, and they need constant new experiences in order to remain happy.

Impulsiveness and temper are the pitfalls of this sign position. Natives must learn to develop more consideration for others and a greater ability to cooperate. When individualism is carried to extremes, it blinds people to the social structure upon which large endeavors depend.

Many people who were born in the late 1920s or early 1930s have Uranus in Aries square Pluto in Cancer. Their lives and destinies were torn apart by World War II.

Uranus in Taurus

Uranus in the sign Taurus indicates a generation with new ideas concerning the use of money and resources. These people are likely to seek reforms in business and the economy, in which areas they desire the application of humanitarian principles. They wish to be practical, in a unique and original way. They can have tremendous determination and fixity of purpose; but if Uranus is afflicted, there can be unyielding stubbornness.

Uranus is in its fall in the sign Taurus; therefore, the urge to freedom and the expression of intuitive ideas are limited by an attachment to material objects, or by difficulties incurred in the attempt to change material conditions too quickly. Attachment to home and family can also dampen individual expression. Spiritual impulses, too, may be frustrated by subservience to conservative institutions in business and government that reflect the materialism of the prevailing social order.

Uranus in Taurus can give unusual artistic and musical talents if it is well aspected. Natives are often interested in using modern electronics techniques in management, accounting, and other businesses.

Uranus in Gemini

Uranus in the sign Gemini indicates a generation of people who are destined to be the progenitors of a new way of thinking. They have brilliant, original, intuitive minds; they will pioneer new concepts in science, literature, education, electronics, and communications media.

People with this position have a tendency toward extreme restlessness, which can make it difficult for them to follow an idea through to completion; they need to exert self-discipline in order to bring their ideas to fruition. Because of their restlessness they generally travel about a great deal, seeking new social contacts and an exposure to new ideas. This position indicates great freedom in thinking and—since we create our destinies with our minds—gives the ability to break habitual living patterns as a result of the awareness of alternative modes of activity.

If Uranus is afflicted in Gemini, the thinking can be disjointed, eccentric, and impractical. There can be confusion and the danger of accidents while traveling, as well as unreliable relationships with brothers, sisters, and neighbors.

Uranus in Cancer

Uranus in the sign Cancer indicates a generation of people who seek freedom and excitement through emotional expression. They will have untraditional ideas about home and family life, and they seek independence and freedom from a too strict parental authority; they prefer to be friends with their parents. However, when they leave home they make certain that they can return if the new territory they are exploring is untenable. Most of the young people today born between June 1949 and June 1956, with Uranus in Cancer, have been known to leave their homes in order to have more freedom than family life allows.

Those with Uranus in Cancer run their homes in an unusual way. They have a taste for modern architecture or uniquely styled buildings, and they will fill their homes with electronic gadgets and striking decor. They like to use their homes as meeting places for friends and group activities. They may also be interested in communal living or in other family arrangements besides the traditional nuclear family. In many cases their friends become members of the family.

There is considerable psychic sensitivity with Uranus in Cancer. Occult activities are likely to be part of the domestic scene.

If Uranus is afflicted in Cancer, there can be an erratic temperament and sudden changes in mood.

Uranus in Leo

Uranus in the sign Leo indicates a generation of people who seek freedom in love and romance. Their ideas about courtship and sex may depart from traditional moral standards, and they are likely to believe in free love.

Uranus in Leo can give strong willpower and creativity in the arts and sciences, as well as the potential for original kinds of leadership. People with this position seek to create a unique type of expression in order to be outstanding in their endeavors. They can develop new concepts in art, music, and the theater. Rather than conform to the standards of the society they live in, they prefer to create their own standards. However, there is danger of egotism with this position, as Uranus is in its detriment in Leo; hence they should get involved in matters of social or universal—rather than personal—concern.

These people can be stubborn, and they have difficulty compromising or cooperating with others. If Uranus is afflicted in this sign, they will insist on having their own way, to the extent that they will completely refuse to cooperate.

Uranus in Virgo

Uranus in the sign Virgo indicates people who have original yet practical ideas in regard to work methods, especially in such fields as health, science, and technology.

While Uranus was in Virgo—the sign ruled by Mercury, the mental, scientific planet—many electronic inventions were produced, including the computers that have revolutionized business and industry. The same time period has brought about the development of miniature solid state circuitry (Virgo is an earth sign) in the form of transistors and similar devices.

Since the generation that is still in childhood has Uranus in Virgo, it will display unique and ingenious approaches to industry, science, technology, labor relations, ecology, and health care. Children born between 1964 and 1968, having Uranus conjunct Pluto in Virgo, will be of especially revolutionary influence in these fields. That generation will bear the brunt of the practical hard work needed to regenerate human civilization in preparation for the new Aquarian age ruled by Uranus.

These people have an unusual talent for business and a tremendous practical resourcefulness in work. However, they are likely to suffer many changes and disruptions in employment.

Uranus afflicted here can cause erratic health problems. Natives may be interested in the healing effects of correct diet and in mental control of the bodily functions.

Uranus in Libra

Uranus in Libra indicates a generation of people with new ideas about marriage, partnerships, and social conduct. They seek freedom in the marriage relationship and regard the relationship as more important than the legal contract. With Uranus in Libra there is likely to be experimentation with new living arrangements, such as communal living, as well as with other forms of social innovation. People of this generation—babies being born at the time of this writing—will in the future enact laws that will make it difficult to get married and easy to get divorced. In general, they will have new concepts of justice and will seek to change and modernize the existing legal codes.

These people will have keen insight into all kinds of human relationships, which will take the form of intuitive or telepathic knowledge of other people's motivations.

Uranus in Libra is also likely to produce new and unusual forms of music, probably incorporating electronic techniques.

If Uranus is afflicted in this sign, natives may have difficulty getting along in marriage or partnerships, and they may be unreliable in relationships requiring mutual responsibility.

Uranus in Scorpio

Uranus in the sign Scorpio is in its exaltation. As Uranus is the planet of drastic change, it is most potent in Scorpio, the sign of death and regeneration. Those born with this Uranus position must learn to adjust to the destruction during their lifetime of old forms of civilization, which is the necessary prerequisite to the birth of a new form of civilization. At this writing those in their late seventies and early eighties have Uranus in Scorpio. In their youth many of them lived through World War I, a war that brought the Victorian era to a drastic end and initiated a time of rapid change.

The next period of Uranus in Scorpio, which starts in 1975, will mark the beginning of the final destruction of the Piscean age in preparation for the Aquarian age, which starts about the year 2000. People born during this period will experience the greatest upheaval of human civilization in recorded history.

Those with Uranus in Scorpio have powerfully charged emotions. They believe in decisive action and cannot tolerate inactivity or laziness in any form. If Uranus is afflicted in Scorpio, they are likely to have violent tempers and a fierce determination to bring about change, no matter how destructive.

These people can be highly resourceful; they can possess great mechanical and scientific ingenuity. They can have strong occult tendencies, with knowledge of the afterlife and an awareness of the supraphysical dimensions of energy.

Uranus in Sagittarius

Uranus in the sign Sagittarius brings about new concepts in religion, philosophy, and education. Natives of this position of Uranus can pioneer new religious and educational forms. They have a strong desire to incor-

porate into religion the principles of science and the occult, such as reincarnation, astrology, and mental telepathy.

If Uranus is afflicted in Sagittarius, there can be dogmatic adherence
to eccentric religions and social philosophies, or a desire to negate all
religious concepts, producing skeptics and agnostics.

Uranus in Sagittarius gives natives a great deal of curiosity about foreign cultures. They will travel suddenly, taking long journeys out of the
spirit of adventure. They will have many unique experiences in foreign
countries or with foreigners, and they tend to adopt foreign religions and
philosophies.

Uranus in Capricorn

Uranus in the sign Capricorn indicates a generation of people who will
effect important changes in the governmental and business power structures. They wish to change the status quo in order to ensure greater
security for the future, but they must be careful to do so in a practical
way, building the new on the foundations of the old. They seek constructive change, yet are reluctant to release the past completely.

These people have strong ambitions and a desire to succeed. They
have original ideas in science and business, which they use to advance
their careers or improve their status. They are also able to develop old
ideas in new or unusual ways.

If Uranus in Capricorn is afflicted, they are likely to be overambitious
and tend to overextend themselves in pursuit of professional advancement.

Uranus in Aquarius

Uranus in Aquarius is in its own sign and is therefore very powerful.
People with this position have a penetrating, intuitive insight into scientific and occult truth. In highly developed types there is the capacity to
understand spiritual energies and religious concepts in a scientific context. These people have great scientific and inventive talents.

This position of Uranus gives strong will and mental independence.
Natives insist on making their own decisions and drawing their own conclusions. Their independent, intellectual minds are bent on discovering
the impartial truth; they will discard yesterday's ideas and methods if
they cannot be proved scientifically or if they fail to conform to fact.

Direct experience is their final test for determining the truth of any matter. Their capacity for direct experience and observation can be extended in higher dimensions through the unfolding of their clairvoyant faculties.

They are concerned with what is good for humanity as a whole; they believe in human brotherhood and the dignity of man. Their openness to new ideas is a manifestation of their humanitarian tendencies. They seek to reform society, and they like to work through groups and organizations.

If Uranus is afflicted in Aquarius, there can be license instead of freedom, producing unreasoning stubbornness and impractical eccentricity. Uranus heavily afflicted here can make the native unwilling to follow any system of routine or discipline.

Uranus in Pisces

Uranus in the sign Pisces indicates intuitive abilities and a scientific curiosity about the workings of the unconscious. Natives have religious leanings colored by mysticism, which can take the form of interest in meditation, Eastern philosophies, or systems of yoga, for example. They receive ideas through intuition and dreams.

The fundamental motivating factor of Uranus in Pisces is to seek liberation from the mental and emotional influence of the past. There is a spiritual struggle to overcome past materialistic tendencies, combined with a seeking for higher spiritual identity.

If Uranus is afflicted in Pisces, there can be impractical idealism, as well as unreliability and deceptiveness toward friends. There can also be an inclination to avoid facing unpleasant situations.

Uranus in the Houses

The position of Uranus in the houses indicates the type of activity through which a person expresses his urge toward individuality and freedom. It shows through what circumstances sudden, unusual, and exciting events will enter his life. It indicates the type of friends a person chooses and the type of activity he enjoys with friends and in groups. The manner in which he expresses his intuitive faculties and occult interests is also shown by the house position of Uranus.

Uranus in the First House

Uranus in the First House indicates people with a strong drive for freedom in their personal behavior. They often possess unusual scientific and intuitive talents. They are generally regarded as eccentric, unusual, or advanced in some way, since they have little concern for conventional behavior. They seek unusual friendships and activities.

If Uranus is afflicted in this house, there can be unreasonable obstinacy, as well as a pursuit of personal freedom without regard for common sense or the rights of others. Sometimes, when Uranus is afflicted in this house, eccentricity becomes an end in itself rather than the means to an end.

This position of Uranus encourages restlessness and a desire for constant change and excitement. These people find it hard to accept a routine existence, often preferring excitement and adventure to security.

There is a desire for leadership in groups and organizations, especially the type that promotes reforms, new ideas, and advanced spiritual concepts. These people seek to become involved with the new, the untried, the inventive. They are subject to many changes of attitude and purpose; they tend to vacillate between extreme viewpoints, especially if Uranus is afflicted; they are not inclined toward moderation. For these reasons their personal behavior is unpredictable.

If Uranus is well aspected and the rest of the horoscope indicates superior intelligence or intuitive insight, Uranus in the First House can produce people of genius, who will make important discoveries in their chosen fields.

These people tend to be tall in stature.

Uranus in the Second House

Uranus in the Second House indicates people who have unsettled finances. They are impulsive with money, earning and losing it with equal abruptness. They can have unusual talents and methods for making money if Uranus is well aspected. However, if Uranus is afflicted, they may become involved in impractical financial ventures. They can make money through businesses related to inventions, electronics, or other scientific fields. They tend to borrow from or loan money to friends. If Uranus is afflicted, there is often conflict over unpaid debts. If Uranus is well aspected, however, money can be used for worthwhile humanitarian and scientific purposes.

The values of these people concerning the use of natural resources differ from those of the ordinary person. They may regard conventional values as worthless, or, conversely, their own values may be scorned by others.

Uranus in the Third House

Uranus in the Third House indicates people with unusual, intuitive minds. They are freethinkers and form their opinions on the basis of direct experience and scientific fact; their thinking is not influenced by the opinions of others. Impersonal and impartial in their evaluations of ideas, they are always investigating unusual fields of interest. This exploration entails much sudden coming and going and traveling about within their locales. They are open to new ideas, which they often receive through sudden insights. Consequently, many inventors and creative scientists have Uranus in the Third House. These people are inclined to expound revolutionary ideas, but unless Mars aspects Uranus, they will limit themselves to the written and spoken word.

People with this position seek friendships and group activities with intellectuals who will provide mental stimulation and educational advancement. Even relationships with brothers, sisters, and neighbors are often unusual and stimulating.

If Uranus is afflicted in the Third House, the mind can be restless, impractical, and flighty. There is much jumping to conclusions and frequent changing of opinion.

Often this position produces writers on occult, astrological, or scientific subjects. Natives may also be involved with the communications media, especially radio and television.

Uranus in the Fourth House

Uranus in the Fourth House indicates an unusual home life and family connections. In certain cases one of the parents is exceptional in some way. In their homes people with this position seek freedom to come and go as they please. The house itself may be of uncommon architecture; it may contain many gadgets or electronic devices.

Close friends are accepted as members of the family. The home is often used as a meeting place for group activities and occult endeavors.

There are likely to be sudden changes of residence, especially if Uranus is afflicted or in a mutable sign. There can be many changes in family and domestic situations. Unusual circumstances arise in the later years.

If Uranus is afflicted, there can be difficulty with family members and upsets in the home. The parents and family do not have a binding effect on these individuals.

Uranus in the Fifth House

Uranus in the Fifth House indicates sudden and unusual romantic involvements. Romances blossom suddenly but break off just as suddenly. Romantic partners may be eccentric, ingenious, or otherwise remarkable. Natives are unlikely to follow conventional sexual morality, since they tend to seek excitement through pleasurable pursuits. If Uranus is afflicted, there can be bohemianism and promiscuity.

Stock market activities could bring precipitous changes in fortune, for better or worse.

The children of these natives can be extraordinarily gifted if Uranus is well aspected. If Uranus is afflicted, the children will be prone to peculiar problems and psychological difficulties or abnormalities. These people may be interested in new techniques of education and child-rearing. They generally give their children a lot of freedom. However, if Uranus is afflicted in this house, the children may be given too much freedom or may be neglected.

In some cases Uranus in the Fifth House can produce inspired artistic creativity. Or there is an interest in the electronic forms of art. Many movie actors, rock musicians, recording artists, and radio and television personalities have Uranus in the Fifth House.

If Uranus is afflicted in the Fifth House, there can be a tendency toward antisocial behavior and a taste for pleasure through unhealthy forms of excitement. An afflicted Uranus in the Fifth House can indicate extramarital love affairs; in female charts, there may be pregnancies out of wedlock. In general, unless Uranus is well aspected, the romantic life is unstable.

Uranus in the Sixth House

Uranus in the Sixth House indicates strange and advanced methods used in work and service. There can be an interest in unusual forms of healing, such as sound therapy, homeopathic medicine, or spiritual healing. Those who experiment with different forms of diet may have Uranus placed here.

Electronic engineers and technicians, computer programmers, and others whose work involves advanced technology often have Uranus in the Sixth House. Originality in developing new techniques will help expedite work.

Uranus well aspected in this house can indicate mathematical and scientific ability and an inventiveness applied to practical problems.

These people make friends and engage in group activities through their work. If Uranus is well aspected, there will be friendly, mentally stimulating relationships with co-workers, employers, and employees. If Uranus is afflicted, however, these relationships may be explosive and discordant. Uranus in this house can also indicate political involvement with labor unions.

These people are sensitive to working conditions and relationships with co-workers, employers, and employees. They are likely to terminate a job if such relationships are not satisfactory. People with this Uranus position want freedom to do their job in their own way. They balk at close or rigid supervision.

An afflicted Uranus in the Sixth House can indicate inability to accept routine. It can also mean many changes of job and unstable employment situations; employment will often be ended suddenly. An afflicted Uranus in the Sixth House can indicate nervousness and irritability resulting in ill health.

Uranus in the Seventh House

Uranus in the Seventh House shows a desire for freedom in marriage and partnerships. People with this position are prone to divorce if Uranus is afflicted. The extreme need for independence stands in the way of long-term commitment to a marriage partner.

Marriage ordinarily occurs suddenly and under novel circumstances. The marriage partner can be either unusually brilliant or eccentric, depending on how Uranus is aspected. At times natives resent their spouses because the latter outshine them.

Other relationships involve either extremely close friends or impersonal, superficial acquaintances subject to rapid turnover. There can be telepathic awareness of other people's moods and feelings.

If Uranus is afflicted, there is danger of loss through lawsuits and bad public relations arising from the person's unwillingness or inability to cooperate. Sudden changes of mood, opinion, and attitude can leave others confused and disgruntled. In some cases, however, the person is disoriented himself because of the unpredictable actions of the partner.

If Uranus is afflicted, its unpredictability does not favor those engaged in politics, law, or relations with the public. Too many unforeseen factors cause difficulties for which these people will be held responsible. In general, unusual experiences are produced by marriage, partnerships, and relations with the public.

Uranus in the Eighth House

Uranus in the Eighth House indicates a concern with the mysteries of life beyond mere physical appearance. Uranus being accidentally exalted in the eighth house, there is interest in the occult, telepathy, life after death, and scientific fields such as atomic and fourth-dimensional physics. If Uranus is well aspected, there can be a profound insight into the inner workings of nature and the universe.

The natives often have sudden changes in fortune, through inheritance, marriage, business partnerships, insurance, taxes, and corporate finances. These changes will be either favorable or unfavorable depending on how Uranus is aspected. Death will probably occur suddenly and, if Uranus is afflicted, through accident. Sometimes there is foreknowledge of the conditions and time of death.

These people need to exercise emotional detachment toward sex and material wealth. This position is designed to bring about the realization that spiritual values are the only things of lasting importance. Life must be seen as a dynamic process: The only thing certain in the material realm is change.

Uranus in the Ninth House

Uranus in the Ninth House indicates advanced ideas in regard to philosophy, religion, and higher education. People with this position often depart from orthodox religious views and become interested in astrology, telepathy, occult sciences, or the idea of reincarnation, for example. Their notions about education will be progressive, with an interest in new methods of teaching, such as the use of audio-visual and electronic techniques. Often they have utopian ideas, which can vary in practicality depending on the aspects of Uranus.

These people are inclined to travel suddenly, in search of stimulation and adventure. The mystery of the remote past, far distances, or the utopian future fascinates them; hence their interest in such subjects as astronomy and archeology. If Uranus in this house is afflicted, it can produce fanatical adherence to esoteric cults and political or social philosophies. Or the native can be an "armchair philosopher," whose pat answers for the world's ills are not based on any practical experience. If Uranus is well aspected, however, there will be inspired insight into the changes needed to bring about a more humane social order.

Occult and astrological writers and philosophers often have Uranus in this house.

Uranus in the Tenth House

Uranus in the Tenth House indicates an unusual profession and reputation. This position can produce leaders in scientific, humanitarian, and occult fields; electronics, mathematics, and astrology are typical professions. Whatever the career chosen, there will be innovations in methods and techniques.

Natives are generally liberal or radical in their politics; they have no tendency toward conservatism. If Uranus is afflicted, revolutionary inclinations can be manifested.

These people are strong-willed and have a driving ambition to achieve prominence through their unique contributions to their profession. Many executives in science and electronics have Uranus placed here. However, changes in fortune and status can be sudden. There may be many different jobs and an inability to get along with those in positions of authority. A sudden rise to prominence can be followed by an equally sudden fall to obscurity, if Uranus is afflicted. There may also be an unwillingness to submit to routine responsibility. These people demand and need freedom where they work, and they are happiest when they can regulate their own career activities.

Uranus in the Eleventh House

Uranus in the Eleventh House is accidentally dignified. This position indicates open-minded people who are concerned with truth and facts and have no consideration for tradition or approval. They have a definite humanitarian bent and a sense of brotherhood with people from all walks of life.

People with Uranus placed here possess an intuitive ability to perceive universal laws and principles. This is ordinarily manifested as an interest in science or occultism, or sometimes in both. They generally have many unusual friendships which are mentally and spiritually stimulating. They are fond of group activities that have a humanitarian or scientific purpose.

Their impersonal approach to marriage and romantic relationships leads them to unconventional or bohemian attitudes regarding such relationships. Their desire for stimulation can make them unwilling to be tied down to a single relationship. Their sense of equality makes them tolerant of similar ideas and behavior in others. In this respect they are very democratic.

If Uranus is afflicted, friendships can be unstable and at times treacherous. The native can be unreliable in regard to friends and group commitments, and his selfish motivations are likely to boomerang, since no one wants to be used. With Uranus afflicted in this house, there may also be irresponsible and impractical social ideals.

Uranus in the Twelfth House

Uranus in the Twelfth House indicates an occult search into the unconscious. The quest for a higher spiritual identity in the inner reaches of the mind can be manifested as an interest in yoga, meditation, and other forms of mysticism.

If Uranus is heavily aspected, intuitive abilities and clairvoyance may be highly developed. Often people with this position become repositories for the secrets of their friends; often they join secret organizations. They have an ability to work behind the scenes in pursuit of humanitarian and scientific goals if Uranus is well aspected.

If Uranus is afflicted, however, there can be illusionary mediumistic tendencies based on neurotic motivations. Dabbling in negative psychic phenomena, instead of allowing the intuition to develop naturally, can produce much confusion and delusion in the lives of these individuals.

Neptune in the Signs

Neptune takes approximately 164 years to make a complete cycle of the Zodiac, spending about thirteen years in each sign. Consequently, the sign position of Neptune has more generational and historical significance than personal significance.

Neptune's sign position indicates the kind of cultural expression manifested by the imaginative and creative faculties of mankind in a given thirteen-year period. The generation that has Neptune in a given sign shares a common spiritual destiny. The intuitive and creative faculties of such a generation will take on the qualities of whichever sign Neptune occupies.

Neptune in Aries (1861/62–1874/75)

Neptune in Aries indicates a generation in which important advances are made in the pioneering of mystical religious concepts. It is a generation that shows considerable initiative and drive for spiritual creativity and regeneration. The negative side of this expression, however, is spiritual pride and egotism.

Neptune in Taurus (1874/75–1887/89)

Neptune in Taurus indicates a period in history of much idealism regarding the uses of money and resources. This generation seeks practical applications for visionary insights. The negative side of the expression is preoccupation with money and material values.

Neptune in Gemini (1887/89–1901/2)

Neptune in Gemini indicates a generation of people who do much to develop the creative and intuitive faculties of the mind, through literature and poetry. These people have active, versatile imaginations and the ability to channel ideas from higher realms of consciousness through the image-making faculties of the mind. The negative side of this expression is a preoccupation with a dream world and its superficial values. There can also be confusion in practical thinking and communication.

Neptune in Cancer (1901/2–1914/16)

Neptune in Cancer indicates a generation of people with strong psychic ties to the home, family, and the earth. They are highly sympathetic and emotionally sensitive. They tend to be religious but in an emotional way.

If Neptune is strongly placed and aspected, psychic and mediumistic tendencies are in evidence. Many clairvoyants are born with Neptune in Cancer. The negative side of this expression is maudlin sentimentality and an exclusive, emotional attachment to one's family and country. There can also be misguided mediumistic tendencies, which can attract low-grade astral influences.

Neptune in Leo (1914/16–1928/29)

Neptune in Leo indicates a generation of people with strong musical and artistic talents. They are especially interested in the theater and other performing arts. Much of their creativity is inspired from higher levels of consciousness. This position of Neptune inclines toward romanticism and idealism in love and courtship.

The negative side of this expression can be self-delusion regarding love and courtship. Extravagant expenditures in pursuit of pleasure, and impracticality in dealing with children are pitfalls of this position.

Neptune was in Leo in the Roaring Twenties, during which period unwise stock market speculations led to financial ruin and the Great Depression.

Neptune in Virgo (1928/29–1942/43)

Neptune in Virgo is in its detriment, indicating a generation whose creative, imaginative faculties are thwarted by adverse material circumstances. Neptune in Virgo encompasses much of the generation that grew up during the Great Depression of the 1930s. This was a time of chaos throughout the economic system resulting in scarcity of employment, which is ruled by Virgo.

The negative side of Neptune in Virgo can manifest itself as a tendency to psychosomatic illness and excessive emotional preoccupation with inconsequential detail. Also there is likely to be doubt or negativity toward intuitive impulses, which is manifested as materialism. Unwise dietary habits are typical of Neptune in Virgo if it is afflicted. Much of the chemical adulteration of our food began during this period.

Neptune in Libra (1942/43–1955/57)

Neptune in the sign Libra is the sign position of the present postwar generation. During the war the institution of marriage was subject to much confusion and an increasing divorce rate. The resulting broken homes led to uncertainty of values regarding relationship obligations among the younger generation. There is an instinct for emotional and social conformity with Neptune in Libra, which in its negative expression results in the blind leading the blind. This is manifested in such contemporary phenomena as drug abuse, rock music, and the psychedelic culture.

On the positive side, Neptune in Libra gives the present younger generation an intuitive awareness of social relationships. The concept of mutual social responsibility is based more upon the spirit of the law and less upon literal interpretation.

This sign position has brought about the development of the new forms of art.

Neptune in Scorpio (1955/57–1970)

Neptune in the sign Scorpio indicates a period of exploitation of man's natural desires. A few people have experienced spiritual regeneration and initiated a search into life's inner mysteries, but many are marked by the exploitation of sex for commercial purposes. Scorpio is the sex sign, and Neptune rules drugs. Loose sexual morality at this time has led to widespread venereal disease, and the use of drugs as a psychological escape has spread. There is much emotional intensity and confusion, causing the turmoil in the unconscious to break out in such chaotic artistic phenomena as rock music.

Many of the children born with Neptune in this sign will have clairvoyant abilities and will be forced to acknowledge the need for spiritual regeneration when Uranus and Pluto conjunct their natal Neptune position.

Neptune in Sagittarius (1970–1984)

Neptune in the sign Sagittarius has brought us into a period when the need for higher religious and spiritual values will find positive expression: There will be a return to God and a desire to spiritualize the larger social order. Even music and art forms will be spiritually oriented. There will be much foreign travel and exchange of ideas and religion with foreign cultures.

Mystical and occult subjects will be gradually introduced into the university curriculum. Religions will put more stress on man's personal contact with God through his inner being, which will result in the increased practice of meditation and the use of the intuitive faculties of the higher mind. The mystery and the power of the mind will be explored and developed as mystical experiences become more common. –

The negative expressions of Neptune in Sagittarius are likely to be aimless wandering, as among the hippie generation, and fanatical adherence to misguided, impractical religious cults, false prophets, and gurus. However, Neptune in Sagittarius will bring to many the realization of the presence of the One God in Everything.

Neptune in Capricorn (1984–2000)

Neptune in Capricorn indicates a period to come in which world governments will be in chaos and economic and political structures will be brought to their knees. Out of this chaos and suffering will come true spiritual responsibility and discipline, which will be expressed in practical dealings.

People will no longer have the luxury of abstract Sagittarian spirituality. In order to survive they will be forced to incorporate spirituality into their practical lives. Through these experiences of the karmic summing-up of the Piscean age, many of those who survive will reach new heights of spiritual attainment.

New forms of government and political concepts will be brought into being out of necessity. The end of this period will produce the beginning of world government.

Neptune in Aquarius

Neptune will enter the sign Aquarius along with Uranus about the year 2000, which marks the real beginning of the Aquarian age. At that time a new civilization will be born, based on enlightened humanitarianism and on a science using new technology and new forms of energy. This will mark the beginning of a thousand years of peace, which was spoken of in the biblical Book of Revelation. The intuitive, clairvoyant faculties of humanity will be highly developed, and universal brotherhood will be established in practical reality.

Neptune in Pisces

Neptune in Pisces will be a time of peace following the beginning of the Aquarian age. This period will provide an opportunity for the unfolding of spiritual faculties and the development of exalted forms of music and art; healing will make great strides. The highest form of Aquarian culture will begin, making use of all the highest creative attainments of the past Piscean age. Many great mystics, artists, and spiritual leaders will be born during this period.

Neptune in the Houses

The position of Neptune in the houses indicates the way a person expresses his mystical potential. It also shows through which practical circumstances a person will be used as a channel by the higher spiritual forces. Whenever Neptune is found, one must serve unselfishly, with an impersonal love.

Neptune's position shows how a person uses the image-making faculties of his mind—that is, his ability to visualize. It indicates which circumstances of life will be affected by premonitions, dreams, clairvoyance, and deeper intuitive insights. Neptune's position also reveals much of the meaning of the karma produced by past actions. When Neptune is afflicted, its house position shows the areas in which a person is likely to be unrealistic and prone to self-delusion.

Neptune in the First House

Neptune in the First House indicates a sensitive, intuitive awareness of self and environment. If Neptune is strongly aspected, there can be a conscious positive use of clairvoyant faculties, leading to awareness of the motivating factors behind human actions and events.

People with Neptune in the First House are highly impressionable and subject to subliminal influences. They can have inspired mystical vision if Neptune is well aspected; but if Neptune is afflicted, they may be in danger of being used by negative psychic forces, which in extreme cases can even mean possession by astral entities. They should avoid the use of alcohol and drugs, as these can open the door to negative psychic influences.

This position can bestow highly developed artistic and musical talents, which use intuition as a source of inspiration. In their physical appearance the natives often have an air of mystery about them; their eyes in some cases radiate a magnetic quality.

This position of Neptune attracts peculiar relationships, many of which have roots in the past.

If Neptune is afflicted, there can be self-delusion, unreliability, and confusion in personal goals. Neptune afflicted in this house can result in alcoholism, use of drugs, loose living, and a tendency to drift aimlessly through life.

Neptune in the Second House

Neptune in the Second House indicates people who are idealistic about money and the use of material resources. If Neptune is well aspected, they will generously donate their funds to humanitarian and spiritual causes and will be liberal with material resources. If Neptune is well aspected in the horoscope of an astute person, he may have intuitive insights into ways of making money and acquire great wealth. However, money may come and go through mysterious and unusual circumstances; and as this position often makes one extravagant, these people may have trouble holding on to their funds. These tendencies need to be balanced by a discriminate use of money if Neptune is at all afflicted.

An afflicted Neptune can also indicate impracticality, financial muddle, and laziness in earning a living. The natives may be taken advantage of financially. People with an afflicted Neptune here often depend on others for financial support; they therefore need to develop greater practicality.

Neptune in the Third House

Neptune in the Third House indicates those who have intuitive minds and who are able to receive ideas from higher planes of energy by means of the image-making faculties of the mind. The capacity for visualization is often highly developed, especially if Neptune aspects Mercury. Telepathic communication is frequently indicated by Neptune in the Third House.

This position makes people inclined to study occult and mystical subjects; writers on these subjects may well have Neptune placed here. Often they can have some connection with the mass media. Those with Neptune in this house must share knowledge impartially and act as a channel for information.

This position calls for practicality in thinking and discipline in study. If Neptune is well aspected, intuitions can be put to practical use, especially when Neptune is in an earth sign. If Neptune is afflicted, there may be learning difficulties, absentmindedness, fantasizing, and daydreaming. There also may be misunderstandings or other troubles with brothers, sisters, and neighbors. Those with an afflicted Neptune here should be careful about signing contracts and making agreements. They can experience confusion in communication or while traveling.

Neptune in the Third House often means the natives will have nicknames and pseudonyms.

Neptune in the Fourth House

Those with Neptune in the Fourth House have strong unconscious emotional ties with the home and family, often of a karmic origin. One of the parents may be psychic or in some way peculiar. Often people with this position live near the water or would like to. They can have intuitive feelings for the land and all of nature.

Neptune afflicted in the Fourth House can give confused family relations and a chaotic domestic environment. Since there is a desire to mother the world, people with this position often take strangers or outsiders into their homes. Family secrets and mysteries regarding the home life are common.

If Neptune is afflicted, strange nervous disorders may develop in later years that are difficult to diagnose and that have emotional causes. The end of life is usually spent in quiet meditation or seclusion.

Neptune heavily afflicted here can produce neurotic problems arising out of difficulties with parents or other members of the family.

Neptune in the Fifth House

Neptune in the Fifth House indicates an unconscious desire for love and appreciation through romance and creative self-expression. Artistic and musical talent may be inspired from intuitive levels. The ability to play roles gives talent in the performing arts; there is in general a love of the theater.

Peculiar circumstances may surround romantic attachments and the sex life. If Neptune is afflicted, secret love affairs and disappointments in love are likely.

If Neptune is well aspected, there can be intuitive insight into stock market activities, but natives with this position must be careful with investments and speculations.

This position of Neptune indicates that the native's children will be sensitive and intuitive. If Neptune is afflicted, the children will probably have psychological problems that are difficult to deal with. The natives may even severely neglect their children; and they may adopt children, or bear them out of wedlock. Sometimes this position indicates broken families, creating for the native's child a situation similar to one in which the parents have never been married.

Neptune in the Sixth House

Neptune in the Sixth House puts emphasis on work and services performed in a spiritual way. Neptune is accidentally in its detriment in the Sixth House, indicating that the lessons of work and health will be difficult to learn. Many sacrifices are demanded of the natives. If Neptune is well aspected, however, they can have intuitive understanding of the various methods of making work effective and efficient.

Neptune in this house gives a tendency to care for pets and other animals, and sometimes the ability to communicate with animals psychically.

If Neptune is well aspected, natives will be interested in spiritual healing, homeopathic medicine, health foods, and other related forms of healing. If Neptune is afflicted, they will be subject to psychosomatic ailments and to infections that are difficult to cure; there can also be mental illness and hypochondria. With an afflicted Neptune drugs, alcohol, and unnatural forms of medication should be avoided. Care should be taken with the diet, and illness should be treated with natural foods and remedies.

If Neptune is afflicted in this house, unemployment, a tendency to be unreliable about work, and unsatisfactory working conditions and relationships are likely. In contrast, if Neptune is well aspected, there can be harmonious working conditions and close emotional ties with co-workers, employers, and employees. Natives usually work in hospitals and large institutions; their work may be related to psychotherapy.

Neptune in the Seventh House

Neptune in the Seventh House indicates karmic ties in marriage or partnerships. Often there is a strong psychic link with the marriage partner, and in general a strong intuitive awareness of other people. People with this position can be easily affected by the moods and feelings of others. If Neptune is well aspected, spiritual values are applied in relations with others, manifested as unselfish love and understanding. The ability to understand others may be intuitive. A well-aspected Neptune can indicate an ideal spiritual marriage.

Neptune in the Seventh House indicates artistic and musical talent, or at least an appreciation of the arts.

If Neptune is afflicted, there can be difficulties in marriage, often caused by emotional confusion. Natives can be confused and misled by other people, and they should be careful of the company they keep. They may also tend to be unreliable or vague concerning partnerships and social responsibilities. If Neptune is badly afflicted, natives may deliberately deceive others, or their partners may be deceptive, unreliable, or psychologically deformed. An afflicted Neptune here also indicates the possibility of public scandal and lawsuits.

Neptune in the Eighth House

Neptune in the Eighth House gives psychic tendencies, often manifested in spiritualism or a desire to communicate with the dead. Unusual, secret or deceptive circumstances may surround partners' money, insurance, taxes, and inheritances.

An interest in occult subjects and the ability to obtain information from higher realms through clairvoyance are shown by a well-aspected Neptune in this house. If Neptune is afflicted, the individual may be tempted to manipulate occult forces for personal gain. In extreme cases, this aptitude can be manifested as a practice of black magic.

An afflicted Neptune here can indicate losses and bizarre difficulties with partners' finances or corporate money, through deception by either the natives or others. There can also be attempts at tax evasion or falsifying insurance, surrounding death.

Neptune in the Ninth House

Neptune in the Ninth House indicates an interest in mystical forms of religion. Natives may be involved in mystical cults, systems of yoga, meditation, and mystical oriental religions. If Neptune is well aspected, there can be spirituality and prophetic vision.

This position shows a highly impressionable intuitive mind. If Neptune is well aspected, much valuable knowledge can be gained through intuitive sources. If Neptune is afflicted, there can be fanatical adherence to impractical cults and worship of spiritual leaders. The individual may believe that he is the chosen pupil of a great prophet or spiritual teacher. Care must be taken to distinguish the real spiritual teachers from the false by the lack of spiritual pride and egotism a truly spiritual person displays.

The person with an afflicted Neptune here is often impractical about education, neglecting to acquire the training necessary for obtaining a job. He will probably have problems with relatives through marriage.

Neptune in the Tenth House

Neptune in the Tenth House indicates that intuitive factors play an important part in the career. This is a good position for ministers, psychologists and psychiatrists, astrologers, and clairvoyants. The career of these natives may involve activities carried on secretly or behind the scenes or under security. This position can signify a capacity for spiritual leadership.

One of the parents may be unusual in some way; the profession is always unusual and has bizarre circumstances surrounding it. Many actors, musicians, and artists have Neptune in the Tenth House.

A well-aspected Neptune in the Tenth House can confer honor as a result of unique personal achievements or sacrifices. An afflicted Neptune in the Tenth House causes impracticality in the profession, often resulting in an inability to get along with employers or to hold a job. If Neptune is afflicted, there can be scandal or loss of reputation due to the native's unreliability or dishonesty on the job. The person often deserves the misfortunes he encounters because of the selfish motivation of his ambitions.

Neptune in the Eleventh House

Neptune in the Eleventh House indicates unusual, idealistic friendships and group associations. If Neptune is well aspected, generosity will be extended to friends; spiritual guidance and help in the realization of goals will be received from them, because these natives have earned such help in the past. There will be a close spiritual link with friends and group associates. People with this position are sensitive to the needs of humanity and join groups that have a humanitarian or spiritual purpose; they often are attracted also to secret or mystical organizations.

If Neptune is afflicted in the Eleventh House, there can be unreliability and deception in friendships. Friends often become secret enemies. Unsavory associations lead to self-undoing, often through alcoholism or drug abuse. These people should develop discrimination in their choice of friends. An afflicted Neptune can also indicate an impractical, misguided idealism; bohemian tendencies may be manifested.

Neptune in the Twelfth House

Neptune in the Twelfth House indicates an intuitive link with the unconscious mind. Strong mystical religious tendencies are manifested. Privacy and seclusion are sought, being necessary for inner spiritual search. Often there are memories of previous incarnations, and much depth of spiritual wisdom is brought over from the past.

If Neptune is well aspected, there is ability with clairvoyance, psychology, and healing. Poetic, musical, and artistic sensitivity and ability are also present. If Neptune is afflicted, there is neurotic preoccupation with the problems of the past, since the natives are open to negative, misleading psychic influences. This often results in mental confusion, woolgathering, and withdrawal from the practical affairs of life. These people are prey to fears and neurotic problems arising from the unconscious.

Pluto in the Signs

Pluto, the slowest moving of the planets, takes approximately 248 years to make one complete round of the Zodiac. Since it has an eccentric orbit, the number of years it spends in each sign varies from twelve to thirty-two. As with Uranus and Neptune, the significance of the sign position of Pluto is more historical and generational than personal.

The sign positions of Pluto have great historical importance, as they reveal fundamental upheavals and bring about drastic transformations in the areas of human life and civilization that they rule. These changes may be either regenerative or degenerative, but usually both effects are felt, resulting in extremes of good and evil in the area ruled by a given sign. Pluto in the signs always produces a permanent change.

Pluto in Aries (1823–1852)

Aries is a new sign of experience, initiating a new cycle of action. Pluto in Aries was the golden age of the American pioneer, when self-reliant people of dauntless courage carved a vast nation out of a virgin wilderness. These people overcame many obstacles and dealt with many hardships in order to establish freedom and a new way of life. An accompaniment was the violent struggle that has come down to us in the folklore of the Wild West.

Simultaneously in Europe many revolutionary movements were afoot, in which men asserted their freedom and began the overthrow of ancient monarchies.

Pluto in Taurus (1852–1884)

Taurus is a sign of material production and monetary concerns. Pluto in Taurus marked a period of great economic expansion, during which such concepts as standardized parts became prevalent and the industrial revolution reached its peak with the broad-scale establishment of factories and cotton mills in the United States and Europe. Forms of corporate organization—typified by the railroad industry—began to appear at this time.

Pluto in Gemini (1884–1914)

Gemini is a sign of ideas and inventions. Pluto in Gemini marked a period of important inventions and scientific discoveries. Nikola Tesla, Thomas Edison, Alexander Graham Bell, and others discovered the uses of electricity and laid the groundwork for modern electrical technology and communications. The automobile was developed, and the Wright brothers flew the first airplane. This era saw breakthroughs in the practical application of scientific knowledge and technology.

Pluto in Cancer (1914–1939)

Cancer is a sign dealing with personal emotional expression, domestic concerns, the land, the environment, and food production. Pluto in Cancer marked a time of economic struggle and the development of strong nationalist sentiments all over the world, which led to World War II. There was a revolution in agricultural techniques, with the introduction of chemical fertilizers and insecticides and the damming of waterways for irrigation and production of electric power.

By reflex to Capricorn, in response to the economic and social pressures threatening family and national security, new concepts of government came into being: the New Deal in the United States, Fascism in Europe, and Communism in the Soviet Union.

Pluto in Leo (1939–1957)

Leo is a sign of leadership and of expression of energy and power. Pluto in Leo marked an era in which atomic energy—which is ruled by Pluto, expressed through its sign of exaltation—was discovered and the first atomic bombs were exploded. For the first time in history humanity was faced with the awesome alternative of the total destruction of civilization or undreamed-of heights in technological achievement. This period began with the intense conflict of World War II. In subsequent years many new sovereign nations were born out of the former colonial empires of European nations. A worldwide power struggle took place between capitalism, represented by the United States, and Communism, represented by the Soviet Union, a struggle that affected the destiny of all mankind.

Pluto in Virgo (1957–1972)

Virgo is a sign dealing with work, health, and the practical application of technology. Pluto in Virgo has marked a period of revolutionary changes in employment, medicine, and industrial production. Computers have revolutionized science, business, and industry; labor unions have become powerful political forces; widespread prepackaging of food has been developed. Automation in industry has replaced many human workers. Medical science has made startling strides and new discoveries.

The introduction of psychedelic drugs in the early 1960s opened formerly unknown realms of consciousness to the masses and brought about social upheaval among the younger generation. As Pluto rules Scorpio, the sign of sex, and Virgo is the sign of health, this period has seen the development of methods of birth control and a new sexual morality. A drastic increase in chemical adulteration and pollution of food has become a major concern, causing a movement toward natural foods.

Pluto in Libra (1972–1984)

Libra is a sign of justice, human relations, social expression, and psychology. While Pluto is in Libra, man must renew his consciousness of responsibility for his fellows if world destruction is to be avoided. As part of this awakening, new concepts of marriage, law, and justice will be developed.

If the necessary regeneration in personal, national, and international relations does not occur at this time, worldwide chaos and war will ensue during Pluto's transit through Scorpio. During this period we must learn to settle domestic and foreign disputes by law and arbitration rather than by armed conflict if civilization is to survive.

Pluto in Scorpio (1984–2000)

With Pluto in Scorpio worldwide conflict is likely to reach a peak of intensity. "Regenerate or die" will be the order of the day, because Pluto rules Scorpio, the sign of death and regeneration. There is no other planetary sign position of such potency. This period marks the final death-gasp of the Piscean age; time will have run out on human folly, and there will be no choice but to face the consequences.

Pluto has its fastest orbital motion while going through Libra and Scorpio. As the biblical Book of Revelation says, "Unless these times were shortened there would be no flesh saved." The greatest danger of plague, famine, and atomic and biological warfare will occur during the last twenty-five years of the twentieth century. From 1975 to 2000 Uranus is in Scorpio, and from 1984 until the end of the century Pluto is in Scorpio. In this period the human race will be forced by dire necessity to regenerate itself in preparation for the Aquarian age and the year 2000.

Pluto in Sagittarius (2000–   )

Sagittarius is a sign of religion, law, philosophy, higher education, and travel. Pluto will enter Sagittarius around the year 2000, marking a period of spiritual regeneration at the beginning of the Aquarian age. At this time there will be a fundamental understanding of deeper spiritual values among all people. Religions as they are known at present will be completely transformed. There will be one world religion based on man's direct intuitive communion with the One Creator. New spiritual leaders will arise to teach the fundamental laws governing all life in the universe. The new world religion will combine all the highest expressions of the great religions of the past, with a more comprehensive scientific understanding of the underlying forces of life.

Pluto in Capricorn (1762–1777)

Capricorn is a sign dealing with political and economic power structures, profession, status, ambition, and leadership. During the years in which Pluto was in Capricorn, new concepts of government were born. Their most notable manifestation was in the American Declaration of Independence in 1776. The birth of democratic forms of government at this time began the displacement of aristocratic power structures.

When Pluto again enters Capricorn, a world government based on the best interests of all mankind will begin. This government will be founded on new social, legal, educational, and religious concepts, which will be developed during Pluto's stay in Sagittarius.

The generation that will be born with Pluto in Capricorn will manifest dynamic, practical will in organization, business, and government. This will be based on the concept that all human beings must be given a chance to develop their own potential according to their ability and self-discipline.

Pluto in Aquarius (1777–1799)

Aquarius is the sign of group activity, intuitive mental development, science, and humanitarianism. The period in which Pluto was in Aquarius witnessed the American Revolutionary War and saw the formulation of the United States Constitution and Bill of Rights and the presidency of Thomas Jefferson. The United States had its real birth as a democratic nation, being the first to demonstrate that rule by the people in a well-organized democracy was possible.

This period also marked the French Revolution, the major European experiment in political freedom, representing the revolt of the common people—ruled by Aquarius—against outmoded dictatorial forms of government.

The next transit of Pluto through Aquarius will be a time of tremendous scientific discovery and worldwide brotherhood. The Aquarian age will come into its full flower then.

Pluto in Pisces (1799–1823)

The sign Pisces represents the deep levels of the unconscious, mystical experience, and intuitive artistic creativity. Pluto in Pisces marked a time of great cultural change. Many works of art with a universal message and lasting value were created during this period.

The next generation to be born with Pluto in Pisces will bring forth notable advances in art and culture. Its members will manifest spiritual insights into the inner mysteries of life.

Pluto in the Houses

The house position of Pluto shows in which department of life a person must exercise conscious creative willpower to regenerate himself and his surroundings. Since Pluto deals with forces of mass destiny, its house position shows how these changes will affect each person individually—that is, how mass karma is linked to individual karma. The house position of Pluto also indicates in what way a person will manifest occult tendencies and otherwise use the subtler faculties of the mind and will.

Pluto in the First House

Pluto in the First House indicates an individual with intense self-awareness and the potential for developing a powerful will. If Pluto is conjunct the Ascendant and heavily aspected, clairvoyant faculties can be manifested. Understanding life in terms of its energy substratum, the individual may be interested in advanced forms of technology.

The early environment is often filled with extreme hardships, as a result of which the person becomes acquainted with struggle for survival at a tender age. This leaves its mark in later years, when he tends to be a loner and holds his innermost self aloof from those around him.

In physical appearance he may have a robust build and an intensely penetrating gaze. He can be difficult to know; there is much more to his being than is manifested on the surface.

People with this position display considerable initiative but at times find it difficult to cooperate with others or to conform to traditional conduct. They have the capacity and need to regenerate themselves through a deep occult understanding of life and consciousness. They are aware of health, but they must learn that the body serves the mind and not the other way round.

Pluto is accidentally dignified in the First House, which corresponds to the sign Aries, also ruled by Pluto. Thus a highly developed sense of personal power and will is indicated, arising out of the realization of one's innermost being as spiritual being, as a consciousness that observes the mind and emotions. The nonconformity and individualism of this position often makes it difficult to get along in home, marriage, and profession.

Pluto in the Second House

Pluto in the Second House indicates a driving ambition to acquire money and material resources. Because Pluto rules Scorpio and the Eighth House, which is opposite Taurus and the Second House, one's personal financial ambitions here are likely to involve other people's money.

Pluto well aspected in the Second House indicates great resourcefulness in making money, through the ability to perceive hidden financial possibilities, by insight or by obtaining inside information.

An afflicted Pluto in the Second House means that the person may become greedy and selfish, thus losing friends and becoming involved in lawsuits and other legal difficulties. In such cases problems with taxes, inheritances, and insurance may arise, and financial reverses may result from speculation.

The basic lesson of Pluto in the Second House is to learn the purification of financial motives by realizing that we are merely stewards of material resources, which must be used unselfishly for the benefit of all.

Pluto in the Third House

Pluto in the Third House indicates a penetrating mind able to comprehend the fundamental causes of life's experiences and manifestations. People with this position generally have strong opinions, which if they cannot express forcefully they will not express at all. In any event they will not compromise their beliefs unless factual evidence shows them they are wrong. Their original ideas will attract friends and partners who will help in the utilization and improvement of their ideas.

This position gives mental resourcefulness and scientific ability. There can also be interest in the study of occult subjects.

Through various circumstances these people are often responsible for exclusive or secret information pertaining to matters of great importance. What they communicate and think may have serious consequences. They also tend to travel in secret for mysterious reasons, encountering strange experiences, such as accidents, in the course of travel.

If Pluto is afflicted, scheming and plotting can cause difficulties with brothers, sisters, and neighbors. This difficulty can also occur with co-workers, institutions representing the values of the social order, and secret enemies.

Pluto in the Fourth House

Pluto in the Fourth House indicates a desire to be the master of one's own home and domestic scene. A dominating attitude can alienate other family members if Pluto is afflicted. However, deep resourcefulness in the roots of being make it possible to provide for and improve the domestic situation.

A strong occult tie with the earth can be manifested as a love of nature, an interest in ecology or conservation, or an ability to know the secrets of the earth through dousing, study of geology, or other means. Sometimes there is an involvement in mining.

If Pluto is afflicted, one of the parents may die in early years. Occult interests are likely to develop in later years. There may be mysterious or occult circumstances in regard to home and family. There is also danger of a power struggle with members of the family or other residents in the home.

Pluto in the Fifth House

Pluto in the Fifth House indicates creative power, which is expressed in many ways through art, intense love involvements, or talented children. When Pluto is well aspected in this house, profound works of art can be inspired from higher levels of consciousness. Spiritual regeneration takes place through love, and the individual's children can manifest willpower, talent, and genius.

If Pluto is afflicted in the Fifth House, there is danger of self-degradation through sexual excess. The individual tends to dominate or be dominated by the romantic partner and may take an overly severe or dominating attitude toward children. Severe losses through speculation are possible if Pluto is afflicted.

Pluto in the Sixth House

Pluto in the Sixth House gives the ability to improve existing employment and methods of work. The work may be secretarial. Junkyard owners, people involved in salvage industries, and those who work on government atomic energy projects are also likely to have Pluto placed in this house.

These people must apply their will in order to better their health, which can be accomplished through positive thinking and correct habits of diet and hygiene. Occult healing powers may be present; hence spiritual healers often have Pluto placed here.

Pluto badly afflicted in the Sixth House requires serious work on improving the health. It can also indicate a need to change attitudes about work and service in order to achieve job security, since there is a tendency to be overbearing or uncooperative toward co-workers, employers, and employees. Inability to get along in work could cause mental disorientation; dishonesty at work could bring legal retribution. Conscientious regenerative work will bring financial gain, status, and recognition with this placement of Pluto.

Pluto in the Seventh House

Pluto in the Seventh House indicates people whose lives are drastically altered by marriage, partnerships, and dealings with others. The native attracts a partner who is strong-willed and even domineering, and who may manifest occult tendencies. This person has an urgent sense of justice and intense reactions against any wrongdoing by others.

He must develop conscious spiritual awareness of the need for constructive cooperation with others. Positive efforts must then be made to achieve this cooperation.

If Pluto is well aspected, a profound intuitive ability enables these people to gain insight into others, to understand their motives. This is therefore a good position for psychologists, lawyers, and judges. Pluto is accidentally in its detriment in the Seventh House, indicating a tendency to dominate or be dominated by others whose will is respectively weaker or stronger than that of the native. People with this position must learn to share initiative and responsibility equally.

Pluto in the Eighth House

Pluto in the Eighth House is a powerful occult influence that deals with understanding the continuity of life and consciousness after destruction of the physical body. The need to know the immortal can be manifested as an interest in reincarnation, karma, astrology, yoga, meditation, and other occult subjects. The awareness of subtle planes of energy gives profound insight into physics, a subject dealing with energy and the fundamental constituents of matter.

If Pluto is well aspected, the individual is able to overcome evil by reliance on higher spiritual powers. He also has the ability to regenerate the discarded resources of others.

This position gives natives a powerful will, sometimes combined with clairvoyant ability. Often an extreme do-or-die attitude is present; life to these people is a serious business, and they usually concern themselves only with really important matters, having little patience for trivialities. Hence they are prone to getting involved in drastic life-and-death situations which sometimes cause them to reverse their way of life or their moral outlook. If Pluto is well aspected, they possess great strength and resourcefulness in crises. Many of their activities are carried on in secret and appear only in the final stages of development.

If Pluto is afflicted, serious problems with partners' money, insurance, taxes, and inheritances may arise. There can also be the temptation to use occult forces selfishly in order to gain the resources of others.

Pluto in the Ninth House

Pluto in the Ninth House indicates an interest in the regeneration of legal, educational, moral, and philosophic systems. This is manifested in an ability to perceive the fundamental causes of problems connected with the larger social order. The intuition regarding such matters is highly developed, giving profound insight into the future of humanity and its institutions. A capacity for spiritual leadership is evident if Pluto is strong and well aspected.

Ambition to achieve distinction through higher education, travel, or spiritual attainments, when carried too far, can result in spiritual pride and competitiveness. Significant achievements are made through higher education when Pluto is well aspected. This can be a good position for Pluto, because here the will is guided by a moral standard.

People with this position have little tolerance for hypocrisy and social injustice. Sometimes they become revolutionaries, if they feel that existing institutions are unworthy of their respect.

An afflicted Pluto in the Ninth House can produce an overbearing religious fanatic, bent on imposing his view of life on others. If Pluto is badly afflicted, there can be antisocial philosophies and atheistic beliefs. However, the native may eventually undergo profound experiences that force him to change his religious outlook.

Pluto in the Tenth House

Pluto in the Tenth House indicates a highly developed willpower and a strong drive to succeed. People with this position can be spiritual leaders in the reform of existing power structures. They are likely also to be leaders in science and the occult, and their special bent for healing, clairvoyance, or prophecy can bring them renown. Since they are adept at dealing with those in positions of power and at understanding their motives, this is a favorable position for being involved in politics and other forms of public work. Farsightedness leads to wise leadership when Pluto is well aspected.

The desire to reform and rehabilitate the world produces powerful friends and enemies. These people tend to be misunderstood and can become controversial figures. Crises in their careers may force them to alter drastically their professional activities.

When Pluto is afflicted in this house, dictatorial tendencies and selfish personal ambitions may come to the fore. At times this position makes the natives feel alienated from others because of their own oppressive responsibilities.

Pluto in the Eleventh House

Pluto in the Eleventh House indicates reformist tendencies expressed in friendships and group associations. The nature of the individual's motivations is all-important with this position of Pluto, since it will determine whether associates feel that he is helping them or using them. If Pluto is well aspected and the motivations are good, the individual attracts powerful friends and group associations that will help him achieve scientific and humanitarian advances. Pluto is accidentally in its fall in the Eleventh House, and natives must be careful to respect the rights of others, to use their own willpower cooperatively in order to function creatively within the group. If motivations and dealings with friends are selfish, financial losses, disappointments in love, and trouble over taxes and joint resources will follow. There can be instability in health, in employment, and in the domestic situation. On the other hand, cooperation with others will make possible successful partnerships and great increase in personal knowledge.

Those with a well-aspected Pluto in the Eleventh House have a capacity for successful, dynamic group leadership. They tend to join occult organizations and have occult friends. They have a penetrating intuitive insight, which, if the rest of the horoscope indicates intelligence, can be manifested as scientific genius.

An afflicted Pluto in the Eleventh House indicates abruptly terminated friendships and financial losses caused by extravagant spending on friends and pleasurable activities.

Pluto in the Twelfth House

Pluto in the Twelfth House indicates a need to regenerate the unconscious mind by bringing its contents into consciousness. This can be manifested as an interest in psychology, occultism, or mysticism.

When Pluto is well aspected in this house, there can be profound insight and clairvoyant ability. A well-aspected Pluto here can give sympathy and a capacity to improve the circumstances of the unfortunate. People with this position are capable of deep meditation and of understanding occult mysteries, an ability that is evidenced in highly developed intuitive powers. They have an unconscious telepathic sensitivity to the thoughts, feelings, and motives of others, but it may cause them to withdraw into privacy and seclusion, or to take secretive action against those they dislike. Mental preoccupation with their own problems, causing them to ignore the ideas and moral viewpoints of others, often results in an inability to get along at work.

An afflicted Pluto in this house can indicate treacherous secret enemies, neurotic problems, and danger of involvement with destructive psychic forces. These people should avoid contact with séances, drugs, and other circumstances that are likely to involve them with lower astral phenomena.

CHAPTER 7

Dispositors of the Planets

The dispositor of any given planet is the planet ruling the sign in which the given planet is found. A planet placed in the sign of its rulership—for instance, Mars in Aries—has no dispositor or disposits itself.

A dispositing planet will have some effect upon the affairs governed by the sign and house in which the disposited planet is placed. In other words, there is a subtle influence on a planet and sign and the house it is in by the planet it is disposited by. The house placements and sign placements of the disposited and dispositing planets are also subtly linked.

If two planets disposit each other—that is, if they are in each other's sign, such as Uranus in Gemini or Mercury in Aquarius—they are said to be in mutual reception. Mutual reception gives added positive strength and dignity as well as special talent or ability to both planets. They see eye to eye, as it were, and support each other's function.

Indirect dispositors are a sort of chain of command created by a dispositing planet, which is in turn disposited by another planet, and so on. For example, if Mars is in Gemini, it is disposited by Mercury, the ruler of Gemini. If Mercury is found in Sagittarius, it in turn is disposited by Jupiter, the ruler of Sagittarius. If Jupiter is found in Leo, then Jupiter is disposited by the Sun, which rules Leo. If the Sun is in Capricorn, Saturn disposits the Sun, and if Saturn is also in Capricorn, Saturn is the final dispositor of Mercury, Mars, Jupiter, and the Sun. This is an example of the chain of indirect dispositors. The final dispositing planet is found in the sign of its own rulership, which gives it special power and dignity and makes it the final dispositor of other planets.

If, as is sometimes the case, a single planet is found in the sign of its rulership and is the final dispositor of all the other planets in the horoscope, this planet is given tremendous importance, the equivalent to its being the ruler of the horoscope.

If no planet is a final dispositor, the native will be a person who has a hard time making up his mind or choosing a decisive path of action. This case can occur only in a horoscope in which no planet is found in the sign of its rulership.

Sometimes we get a circle of dispositors, as in the following example: Mars in Virgo disposited by Mercury, Mercury in Libra disposited by Venus, Venus in Sagittarius disposited by Jupiter, and Jupiter in Aries disposited by Mars, completing the circle that started with Mars in Virgo disposited by Mercury. This pattern is a circular chain and has no final dispositor; it represents a person who tends to go around in circles and is unable to arrive at conclusive decisions.

If two or more planets in a horoscope are found in the signs of their rulership and disposit one or more planets of the horoscope, they share ruling positions of power which act as autonomous or individual sets of behavior in the life of the individual. If the dispositing planets are in aspect to each other, these sets of behavior patterns are linked in a larger pattern of harmonizing or conflicting psychological tendencies.

Another special case occurs when two planets in mutual reception are paired as the final dispositors of the other planets. In this case the two planets act in partnership as the deciding influence on the person's course of action. Jupiter in Capricorn and Saturn in Sagittarius are an example. If Jupiter and Saturn are together the final dispositors of all or most of the planets in the horoscope, they would together be the final determinant in decision-making. However, other factors, such as exaltation, detriment, or fall, often make one of the two stronger than the other. An example is a mutual reception of Mars in Capricorn and Saturn in Aries. Here Mars is in the sign of its exaltation while Saturn is in the sign of its fall. Thus Mars will dominate Saturn, and desire and ambition will rule over the Saturnian principle of caution and reserve. These two signs are also in square aspect to each other, indicating that Mars and Saturn have a tendency to fight each other here. Sometimes both planets are weak, as when Venus is in Scorpio and Mars in Libra. Since both planets are in the signs of their detriment and are basically of opposite nature, they will tend either to neutralize each other or to mutually saddle each other with their unwanted burdens.

If both planets in mutual reception are in compatible signs, such as the Moon in Taurus and Venus in Cancer, one can still be stronger, since the Moon is exalted in Taurus and may be given added strength by house placement. An example is the Moon in the Tenth House and Venus in the Twelfth.

If two planets in mutual reception aspect each other, the aspect they make is also more powerful than it would be otherwise. For example, if Mars is in 10° of Leo and the Sun is in 12° of Aries, even though this trine is separating, the fact that the Sun and Mars are in mutual reception gives the aspect added power. Thus the native receives tremendous courage and energy. However, the solar principle of power and rulership will somewhat dominate the Mars principle of action, since the Sun is in its sign of exaltation (if all the other factors are equal—Mars having more aspects than the Sun, for instance).

If the Sun is the final dispositor of all the planets in a horoscope, the drive for significance, power, and rulership is the principle that dominates all the other abilities of the native, which are made to serve this basic drive for power. This is the sign of the super Leo, which most strongly and dramatically expresses the basic qualities of this luminary. The way in which solar Leo tendencies express themselves will depend on the house placement of the Sun and the aspects made to the Sun. The natives can be self-centered, believing that life ought to revolve around them. However, they have tremendous gifts for leadership and organization and often become famous as a result of their energy, courage, and self-confidence. At times their childlike innocence can be completely disarming, but it is only a scene in a play, and their Leo quality will change once again.

If the Moon is the final dispositor of all the planets in a horoscope, considerations of home, family, and often the stomach are uppermost in the native's mind and feelings. He arrives at decisions and major courses of action more on the basis of emotions than after rational deliberation. Often he is dominated by inherited behavior patterns, received from the family. Emotionally very sensitive, he takes on the coloring of people and events around him. Women often play a dominant role in the lives of the natives. How they are affected depends on the aspects to the Moon, since the Moon assumes the attributes of whatever planets aspect it strongly. Since the Moon has no life of its own, it acts as a step-down transformer for the influence of other planets. These individuals tend to allow themselves to be led passively by the potent influences around them—represented by the nature of the planets most strongly aspecting the Moon. They often, therefore, become involved in dealing with the public, although they are followers rather than leaders. Sometimes they are shy, as a protection against their vulnerability to outside influences; then the Cancer crab withdraws into its shell or retreats until it is expedient to move forward again.

If Mercury is the final dispositor of all the planets in the horoscope, individuals are indicated who choose their courses of action and make their major decisions on the basis of rational thought. These natives will not act without practical reasons for doing so; for them, to act without knowing why would be intolerable stupidity and blindness. Sometimes, however, they lose decisiveness and fail to act promptly because they insist on understanding every single detail. They can get so bogged down in reasoning everything out that they forget that all knowledge, if it is to be accurate, must stem from experience and empirical observation. Yet they are noted for their intelligence and scientific approach to life; they succeed by using the key of knowledge, where others fail because they act with brute force. They can put reason and love of truth above personal bias and emotional considerations and thus avoid much of the emotional turmoil that other people get mired in. They sort out experience and come to rational conclusions based on the best information they can obtain. These natives make excellent writers, teachers, researchers, and scientists and are able to communicate clearly concerning every aspect of life. On the negative side, at times they appear cold and aloof; they tend to live in an ivory tower detached from real experience.

If Venus is the final dispositor of all the planets in the horoscope, the native makes his final decision and chooses his course of action by considering what will bring the most love, beauty, and harmony into his life. Social considerations are uppermost in the minds of such people. They make excellent artists and musicians; they are also skilled in public relations and like to work in partnership with others. They can always be counted on where social grace and diplomacy are called for. In its highest expression this position represents the person who by his very nature is a peacemaker. He has the power to bring joy and happiness to others; he makes the world a more beautiful place to live in. He is romantic and seeks fulfillment in love and marriage. The Venus principle of attraction operates so strongly here that the natives may be inundated by the many people passing through their lives; they do not have time to cope with them all and must retire in order to reestablish their own harmony and balance.

If Mars is the final dispositor of all the planets in a horoscope, the natives choose their course of action and make their final decisions on the basis of what will produce the most immediate and decisive results through action. These people make strong leaders and are capable of acting effectively in any sphere of life. They excel in any task that requires the expenditure of large amounts of energy; as a rule, they have abundant vitality, willpower, and courage. They can turn ideas into reality through work or service, for action is one of the attributes of Mars. If Mars is favorably aspected to one of the higher active planets (Uranus, Neptune, and Pluto), they are good healers. However, they are prone to strong likes and dislikes and can make dangerous enemies.

If Jupiter is the final dispositor of all the planets in a horoscope, the native is permanently disposed to social, philosophical, moral, and religious considerations as the final basis for his decisions and course of action. He wants to act in the interests of the greatest good for the greatest number of people, hence tends to associate with institutions with a humanitarian purpose. He believes in thinking positively, so that often he succeeds by dint of confidence, optimism, and goodwill. He has the ability to instill faith in others, thus gaining their support and inspiring them to cooperate. This is Jupiter's great secret of success. The native's insights and ability to see the potentials of the future give him a head start on the road to success.

If Saturn is the final dispositor of all the planets in the horoscope, the native achieves success through tremendous discipline and ability to organize the affairs of his life efficiently. He makes decisions and chooses his final course of action on the basis of what will in the long run lead to the greatest security and stability. Considerations of safety and practicality are foremost in his mind. He proceeds deliberately and systematically, completing each task thoroughly and well before going on to the next. He achieves success through reliability and hard work and gains a reputation for being a solid and dependable citizen in his community. Everything he does is done with a definite goal in mind. Thus he builds up his career and public standing through patient, methodical effort.

If Uranus is the final dispositor of all the planets in the horoscope, the native can be counted upon for brilliant originality. He often taps superconscious levels of the mind as a means of gaining creative inspiration. He is a leader especially in scientific and spiritual fields. His final course of action and major decisions are often arrived at by sudden flashes of insight. He has a telepathic ability to know what is happening in all areas of life and what to do about it, since his faculties of perception extend into realms of consciousness which other people are not able to tap so easily. Thus he may often do the unexpected for seemingly inexplicable reasons. Such people demand a great deal of latitude in personal expression, caring little if they are regarded as eccentric, for their desire to be free and original supersedes any consideration of what others think of them.

If Neptune is the final dispositor of all the planets in the horoscope, the native will be inclined to make major decisions and choose his final course of action on the basis of something that is intangible to others. He is often difficult to understand because he seems to lack practical reasons for his decisions; he is motivated by a subtle spiritual inclination. Such people do not occur in every generation, since it takes Neptune an average of fifteen years to go through one sign, and it would have to be in Sagittarius or Pisces in order to be the final dispositor. Neptune will be in Sagittarius until February 1984.

If Pluto is the final dispositor of all the planets in the horoscope, the natives are dominated by an inner spiritual compulsion. They are capable of choosing a path of action that requires tremendous willpower and inner strength in order to achieve their goals. As in the case of Neptune, these natives do not occur in each generation, since Pluto is a slower-moving planet than Neptune and must be in either Aries or Scorpio in order to be the final dispositor.

CHAPTER 8

Exaltations of the Planets

Planets are strongest in those signs in which they are in their exaltation or rulership. A planet is said to be exalted in that sign in which the
principle of the planet involved gains its power from the principle of the
sign involved. That is to say, the planet in its sign of exaltation is in the
environment which according to natural law generates the basic principle
of that planet. Therefore, a planet in the sign of its exaltation is in its
most powerful sign position for volume or intensity of energy.

The sign of a planet's rulership is the sign providing the conditions in
which a planet can most easily express itself; these are not necessarily
the conditions that generate the planet's power.

The sign of a planet's fall, always the opposite sign to the one of a
planet's exaltation, is the sign in which a planet is weakest and most
debilitated.

The sign of a planet's detriment is always the opposite to the sign of
its rulership. It is the sign in which the planet is most limited in the
expression of its basic characteristics; it is not necessarily the one in which
it is the weakest, as that is the sign of the planet's fall. In other words,
the fall is much worse than the detriment. For example, Mars is in its
detriment in Libra but is not in a totally undesirable position there, since
the Saturnian and Venusian influences of Libra add restraint and refinement to the basic Mars quality of aggressiveness. On the other hand,
Mars in its fall in Cancer is watered down, emasculated, and confined to
the home, which is the most inappropriate place for the aggressiveness
of Mars to express itself.

Signs of the Zodiac should be interpreted not merely on the basis of
their ruling planets but also on the basis of their exalted planets. The
planet that is exalted in a given sign, such as Venus in Pisces, is said to
be the exalted ruler of that sign. To ignore the exalted ruler is to under-

stand only half the basic meaning of the sign. Exalted rulers become increasingly important in influencing signs when we are dealing with more highly evolved types of people. These people are working their way back on the evolutionary arc of existence to the primary causal principles of life's manifestations, which astrologically are represented by the exalted rulers of the signs. For instance, since Libra has Saturn as its exalted ruler, the more highly developed Libra people are as much influenced by Saturn as they are by Venus. Hence their sense of justice, love of balance and proportion, organizational powers, ambitious tendencies, and discipline. The Uranus-Saturn-Aquarius-ruled middle decan of Libra is particularly susceptible; this decan has an additional Saturn influence because Saturn is co-ruler of Aquarius.

The Sun Is Exalted in Aries

There is an obvious reason why the Sun, giver of life and origin of energy for our solar system, should be exalted in Aries, the sign of new beginnings and of the start of a new cycle of experience. The Sun, representing the principle of power, must be the causal principle behind all manifestation. Highly evolved Aries people will be far more subject to the creative solar influences than to the combative Mars tendencies; they are not marked by the competitiveness of the less evolved Mars Arians, who are motivated by emotional desires instead of spiritual inspiration. The solar-influenced Arian knows that the power of the Eternal Creator is within him as his own "I am" principle or pure faculty of attention. He is not compelled to prove himself through aggressive Mars action but can allow the solar divine energy to be expressed through him. Arians of the more developed type often demonstrate powerful Mercurial mental tendencies, since all new things have their birth in the world of thought, the direct creative manifestation of solar energy (just as Mercury is the closest planet to the Sun and receives the solar energy more directly than the other planets). According to Alice Baily, Mercury is the esoteric ruler of Aries.

The Moon Is Exalted in Taurus

The Moon is the ruler of the etheric plane of manifestation, which is comprised of the four higher subplanes of the physical plane. The Moon is responsible for conveying form and physical manifestation to all living organisms on Earth; it must have physical substance to work with to fulfill its function. Since Taurus is the first of the earth signs, it provides the etheric and physical substance for the lunar influences to work in. Hence the Moon gains its power and is exalted in Taurus. The Moon also is related to the seventh or physical subplane of every plane and is therefore esoterically said to be a step-down transformer or blind for Uranus. Uranus is the planet that harmonically resonates to the seventh subplane of all the seven planes of our solar system. In other words, there is a harmonic overtone relationship between the Moon and Uranus, whereby the Moon gives form manifestation to Uranian power.

The polar opposite of Taurus is Scorpio, where Uranus is exalted. This fact must be considered when one evaluates the vibrational interaction of the Moon exalted in Taurus. It will be noticed that Moon-Uranus aspects can be counted upon to bring drastic changes into the practical affairs of people's lives. Since Uranus precipitates ideas into form manifestation, it is said to be the significator of sudden change. The Moon exalted in Taurus confers the ability to steady the feelings and generate the vital energy needed to give ideas physical manifestation. We would like to pose the thought that the Moon is often the trigger influence in earthquake horoscopes; it can set off stress conditions created by eclipse and other configurations that strongly involve Uranus. The Moon acts as the harmonic vibration link between the higher-plane stresses generated by Uranus and the gross physical substance of the Earth itself. People with the Moon in Taurus often attract special possessions to which they become strongly attached; these possessions do not necessarily have monetary value. The Moon in Taurus, because of the powerful etheric body it generates, produces natives who are known for their robust health and great stamina. They are determined to obtain practical results in any project they undertake.

Mercury Is Exalted in Aquarius

The superconscious mind, or cosmic consciousness, is related to the sign Aquarius. Without the existence of this superconscious mind and its lower-overtone harmonic manifestation of individual consciousness, there could be no expression of the mental principle of Mercury. Mercury therefore gains its power in Aquarius or is exalted in Aquarius.

Individual reasoning power, ruled by Mercury, is but one of the creations of the all-pervasive superconscious mind. Hence all of man's great creative mental achievements are the workings of God as a super-conscious mind, functioning in and through individual human intelligence by the reflection of divine ideas in the individual minds of men. Our creative thoughts emanate from the Universal Superconscious Mind and are things we harmonically tune in to. In reality there is but one God, one Mind and one Consciousness inherent in all creation. Individual consciousness is only a submechanism of the universal creative intelligence that we call God or the Absolute.

People who have Mercury in Aquarius are inspired intuitively by their higher selves or by the mental expression of the "I am" principle within them—that is, pure self-awareness. They often receive the answers to problems in sudden flashes of insight. They are highly scientific and can solve problems by their understanding of the basic laws of the universe. They think independently and are more likely than others to examine everything and not to follow accepted concepts blindly. They communicate well and are a mental inspiration to their friends and group associations.

Venus Is Exalted in Pisces

To mature to its full fruition, Venus, which rules the principle of love and attraction, must go through the entire cycle of experience in the Zodiac. Only when we can put ourselves in another person's shoes and feel with him what he feels can we be sympathetically attuned to him and capable of loving him. Love in the true sense requires that we be attuned to all creation. Only in Pisces, where Venus works with the transcendental vibrations of Neptune and the goodwill of Jupiter, does such a high goal reach fulfillment. Love is the most transcendent and exalted product of the evolutionary process; only one who has lived through all the experience of humanity—as represented by Pisces, the last sign of the Zodiac—can fully experience the meaning of it. Even this is limited, since Pisces is but the end of one turn on the spiral of evolution, the next spiral holding a greater promise of the expansion of consciousness and the unfolding of new creative powers.

In Pisces the earthy love of Venus, as expressed through the attraction of the sexes, is tinged with the divine and rendered more mystical and altruistic. People with Venus in Pisces are frequently endowed with musical talent of a higher order. The music of the spheres plays through their souls. The music they create can bring peace, harmony, and divine emotion to those who listen. People with this position are also fine dancers, since Pisces rules the feet. The voice is rendered soft, expressive, and melodious; the singer has an angelic quality. Painters and other artists with this position will display a soft, glowing quality in their work. These natives love and are inspired by the highest teachings of Christianity and often do much to live up to it.

Mars Is Exalted in Capricorn

The aggressive energy of Mars is best utilized when it is applied to useful work. Likewise, the desires that Mars rules are best used when channeled into constructive ambition with a high goal. Just as an explosion of gasoline is worthless until it is confined in a cylinder chamber to run a gasoline engine, so the desire energy of Mars is worthless until it is harnessed and directed by Saturnian restraint. It is in the professions and in the world at large that the aggressive Mars energy can best be used for the good of the individual and society.

People with Mars in Capricorn are practical and ambitious; they make good, efficient workers. Their desire to achieve importance and prove their powers drives them to work steadily and hard to attain high standing in their careers and respect from the world at large.

Jupiter Is Exalted in Cancer

Cancer rules the home and family relationships. The Fourth House of Cancer is one of the parental houses, representing the mother. Jupiter is the principle of social and religious thought and ethics. Through expansion of consciousness, it gains its power in the sign which rules the home, since our mother is our first teacher and makes the deepest imprint on us while we are growing and formulating our basic outlook on life. Just as the Fourth House rules the earth or the land and provides the nutriments for all growth, so our mother is essential to our early growth. Only by nourishment from Mother Earth, the mother of all that lives, can the abundance represented by Jupiter exist and increase.

Jupiter also rules the principle of social conduct based upon mutual goodwill among the members of society. The family is the basic unit of society. Out of the love of the members of the family for one another grows the larger social conscience which Jupiter represents. Since Jupiter rules the Ninth House, representing foreign peoples, religion, philosophy, and higher education, it is only through love, spiritual awareness, and mutual generosity that a family fulfills its potential of raising children to be the citizens and leaders of tomorrow: Jupiter also represents the future, and the destiny that will make us whole. Those with Jupiter in Cancer are emotionally sympathetic to people around them and will treat them as members of their own family. They will enjoy cooking and beautiful home surroundings. They often live in large homes and are members of large families. Their homes are likely to be used as places for social and religious activities.

Saturn Is Exalted in Libra

Saturn rules karmic law, which can operate only in terms of relationships. Saturn gains its power in Libra, which is the sign of relationships and deals with the reaction of the not-self to the self. If one had just himself to deal with, there would be no necessity to make laws governing one's conduct; but since in reality we are dependent upon each other and must be in partnership with the rest of humanity, laws are essential in order to make cooperative effort possible. In the last analysis laws are concerned with time and space, which are ruled by Saturn; if we are to cooperate with others, we must meet them in specified places at specified times to perform specified tasks, and we must avoid encounters that would cause injury to person or property. This rather obvious statement is of supreme importance because of the basic fact that all relationship is governed by time and space.

Saturn is the great teacher; only by learning to cooperate with others do we learn the fundamental lessons of life. Since Libra rules marriage, this discipline is brought into play in the responsibilities of marriage and child-rearing. If the relationship is merely a Fifth House love relationship, the same legal and moral obligations are not incurred. Since Saturn is in its detriment in Leo and rules Aquarius, these obligations are implicit if children are produced, forcing the Fifth House relationship to become a Seventh House one even when this is not required by human law.

The Seventh House and the Tenth House are related because Saturn is the natural ruler of the Tenth House and the exalted ruler of the Seventh House sign, Libra. Thus marriage generally leads to increased status in the community, entailing as it does greater professional stability in order to meet the responsibilities of supporting a family. This also is the effect of a square aspect, which likewise indicates increased professional status resulting from the need to undertake increased family obligations.

Saturn rules mathematics and geometry; through its Libra connection it governs even the geometrical relationships between atomic particles, as well as those of the Sun and the planets. The reason is that Saturn is the vehicle of the structure-building principle of the solar system.

People who have Saturn exalted in Libra make good lawyers, judges, mathematicians, and engineers, since they understand relationships on human and scientific levels. They possess well-organized minds which can perceive the overall pattern inherent in all phases of life. They can give form to beauty and create gracefulness through proper balance and proportion. They make good organizers and public relations people because they know how to do the right thing at the right time and place. Their conception of justice contains spiritual understanding, which can make them more compassionate than one who follows man-made laws literally.

Uranus Is Exalted in Scorpio

Uranus, the planet of sudden change and release of energy, is exalted in Scorpio, the sign of death and rebirth. When old forms outlive their usefulness and are an obstacle to progress, Uranus, which gains its power in Scorpio, sees to it that they are annihilated so that new forms appropriate to the use of evolving consciousness or energy may be born. Death and rebirth take place through revolutionary change. It takes courage and daring combined with fixed willpower to bring about significant advances in civilization.

Scorpio is the sign that provides these characteristics necessary for progress. Uranus rules change and releases energy into the material aspect of manifestation, which causes drastic reorganization in the material realm. To the superficial observer this appears as catastrophe and destruction, but to the wise observer it is the process of evolution, which is expressed as death and rebirth in the realm of physical manifestation.

People with Uranus exalted in Scorpio have unusual courage and daring and will even stake their lives on adventures into the unknown. They are fearless and have powerful, decisive wills. There are few people with Uranus in Scorpio alive today, but a fresh crop of them will be born in the late 1970s and the early 1980s. These people learn how to regenerate themselves and conditions around them through insights into the hidden forces in nature.

Neptune Is Exalted in Cancer

Neptune (a sixth-ray planet ruling the sixth subplane of every plane and the astral plane in general—the sixth major plane) deals predominantly with the emotions, which find their highest expression in universal love. Again, it is at the hands of the mother in early childhood that emotional habits and attitudes of life are formed. Neptune, which is god of the sea and ruler of Pisces, is at home in the watery sign of Cancer. Neptune can also be said to be a higher harmonic of Jupiter, which is likewise exalted in Cancer. Both of these planets are expansive religiously and mystically inclined; they have much in common with each other. Neptune rules the subtle and the illusive; as is well known, the real emotional bases of our past habits are difficult to pin down. Habit has a strong hold on the emotions, and the Moon, which rules Cancer, also rules our habits.

Jupiter and Neptune are co-rulers of Pisces, where Venus too is exalted. These three planets are closely linked, representing different harmonics of the basic love principle. Venus rules love at the level of personal and sexual attraction between individuals. Jupiter is expressed in the family, social, religious, and ethical spheres. Neptune deals with love in the transcendental union with God and all life. Therefore it is logical that Neptune and Jupiter are linked in the exaltation in Cancer as well.

Those with Neptune in Cancer have highly developed psychic abilities and are keenly attuned to the feelings of those around them. They may be likened to photographic film, which records everything impinging on it. They are finely attuned to the astral plane and easily influenced by impulses emanating from it.

Pluto Is Exalted in Leo

Pluto (a first-ray planet dealing with the principle of focalized energy or power) gains its power in the sign Leo, which is a sign of intense consciousness or self-awareness. Pluto is like a solar seed and is attuned to the inter-dimensional node points in the auric field or sparks sent out from the central solar fire. These sparks can be fanned into divine flames when nurtured by spiritual virtues. In the human body, Pluto rules the seed or reproductive principle, as is borne out in its rulership of Scorpio, which rules the sexual organs. This seed is utilized and gains its power through the Fifth House sign, Leo, which rules love and sexual relations. When the seed is raised to higher planes, it stimulates the head or brain, awakening the spiritual consciousness. According to Eastern yogis, the Kundalini fire emanates from the root chakra at the base of the spine, rising through the central spinal channel until it activates the highest head chakra or "thousand-petal lotus." This is represented by the sign Aries, which with Pluto co-rules the head.

People with Pluto in Leo, represented by our present younger generation, have the power to bring about fundamental changes through their dynamic leadership and concentrated self-awareness.

Pluto also rules atomic energy, discovered when Pluto was in Leo, and which when developed drastically changed the destiny of humanity and the nature of our world. The present Pluto-in-Leo generation is the first one to grow up in an atomic age. The ever-present danger that man will destroy himself and his civilization has necessitated a new outlook; hence this generation is sharply different from its parents. The social and sexual mores of its members also differ radically from those of previous generations. These are the people who must spiritually regenerate themselves or perish. Thus we see in operation the strong influence of Pluto in Leo.

Part II
INTERPRETING
THE ASPECTS

CHAPTER 9

General Rules for Interpreting and Integrating Aspects

Integrating and interpreting aspects is a step-by-step process which follows a logical and systematic pattern:

1. Consider the meanings of the aspect. For example, a square aspect represents obstacles to be overcome; a quintile aspect represents special talent.

2. Then consider the nature and combined meaning of the two planets involved in the aspect. For example, a combination of Mars and Saturn represents the controlled (Saturn) use of energies (Mars). Whether this is constructive or destructive will depend on the nature of the aspect formed between the two planets.

3. Consider other aspects made to the two planets involved. Those aspects show forces which can ameliorate or worsen the effects of stress aspects and determine the constructive possibilities of the positive aspects.

4. Next, make note of the signs in which the aspects are found, especially in the cases of the square, trine, opposition, and conjunct aspects. The signs in which the two planets forming a particular aspect are found color the basic expression of the planets involved and influence the operation of the aspect. For example, a sextile formed between Taurus and Cancer indicates opportunities for gain in financial and domestic affairs, whereas the same sextile between Aries and Gemini provides opportunities for the formation of new and original ideas relating to the affairs of the two planets involved. Simultaneously, note the quadruplicities and triplicities in which the signs are found. A square between two fixed signs indicates a tendency toward stubbornness; a trine in an air sign indicates intellectual ability.

5. Consider the houses occupied by the two planets involved in the aspect. These indicate which practical affairs the aspect influences. For example, a trine aspect between the First and Fifth houses gives good

fortune for self-expression in creative endeavors, whereas the same trine between the Second and Tenth houses indicates financial gain from professional affairs related to the nature of the two planets involved.

6. Then consider the houses which are ruled by the two planets forming the aspect. For example, if Mars rules the Fifth House when Aries is on the cusp of the Fifth House and a square aspect is formed between Mars and Venus, emotional upsets related to the square of Mars and Venus will affect the romances of the native. Men's charts will show disappointment in the love life due to impulsiveness and crudeness in dealing with women.

To continue with the same example: Aries concerns the self and self-expression, and the Fifth House cusp, where it is found here, deals with pleasure and romance. Venus (ruler of Libra, which deals with relationships) represents the principles of attraction, love, and harmony. So squares to Venus in males' horoscopes indicate stress conditions in their relationships with women.

When Aries is on the cusp of the Sixth House, which relates to work, service, and health, the same Mars-to-Venus square occurs, indicating conflicts in work relationships with women. Male natives tend to antagonize women co-workers by an abrupt and aggressive attitude. (In general, this condition indicates inharmonious relationships with co-workers.)

7. Consider the planets dispositing the two planets involved in the aspect. For example, if there is a sextile aspect between Mars in Aquarius and Mercury in Sagittarius, Uranus (which rules Aquarius) will disposit Mercury, bringing an influence of originality (Uranus) and philosophy (Jupiter) into the otherwise pragmatic mental abilities indicated by this sextile. If Jupiter is in the Second House and Uranus in the First, the Mars-sextile-to-Mercury mental energy is expressed in originality (Uranus in the First House influence) in making money (Jupiter in the Second House influence). In addition, the sign positions and aspects of the dispositing planets will exert some influence. This would indicate intercepted signs.

8. Then consider the decan rulers and house rulerships of the two planets involved in the aspect: for instance, an opposition between the Sun and Uranus from the third decan of Taurus to the third decan of Scorpio with the Sun in 25° of Scorpio and Uranus in 26° of Taurus. Here the Sun is in the Moon-ruled Cancer decan of Scorpio, so the effect of the Moon, as subdispositor, blends with Mars and Pluto, the main dispositors, to indicate emotional sensitivity. Uranus in the Capricorn, Saturn-ruled decan of Taurus indicates a certain caution and reserve. Thus

the aspect of the Sun in opposition to Uranus usually points to difficulties in adjusting the desire for free expression and independence to the need to cooperate with other people. In this case, these personal idiosyncrasies would be compounded by the Scorpio, Cancer-decan hypersensitivity and the Taurus, Capricorn-decan pride and stubbornness, making the aspect unusually difficult.

Suppose further that in this horoscope the third Uranus, Aquarius decan of Gemini is on the M.C. (the Midheaven) and the third, Sun-ruled Leo decan of Sagittarius is on the Fourth House cusp. In addition to affecting the houses which the Sun and Uranus rule (those houses having Capricorn and Aquarius on their cusps), this aspect would also bring stresses into the Tenth House professional career affairs and the Fourth House domestic affairs.

9. Finally, consider the overall aspect pattern of which the aspect being considered is a part. A square that is part of a T-square will have a different interpretation from a square in isolation; a trine that is part of a grand trine will have a different interpretation from an isolated trine. For example, an isolated square puts stress on both planets involved in the aspect, with perhaps greater emphasis placed on the planet in dignity or exaltation or otherwise heavily aspected. A T-square places primary emphasis on the planet in square aspect to the two planets in opposition. This planet is then said to be in "point focus," and its sign and house position will provide the key to the problem. The T-square also involves problems of relationship because of the opposition incorporated in it, as well as indicating obstacles to overcome (the usual meaning of a square aspect).

As a further example, where there is a grand square created by two opposition aspects 90° apart, an entirely different situation exists. Whereas the T-square represents a high degree of energy focused through the planet in point focus, the grand square represents the opposite condition—dissipation of energy. This situation occurs because all planets involved in the grand square aspect can be said to be in point focus, so that any attempt to solve the problems by working with one of the planets will irritate the conditions ruled by the other three, or by the signs and houses affected and the houses which these planets rule. Thus, a dynamic condition of perpetually rotating crisis is set up, preventing the native from working on a method of solution for any substantial length of time. The only way to work with this configuration is to focus on the planet or planets in the configuration that have the greatest number of good aspects.

CHAPTER 10

Interpreting the Aspects

Sun Aspects

All aspects of the Sun in some way affect the basic selfhood and the nature and use of willpower. The Sun represents the principle of potential and unfolding power.

No matter how good the rest of the horoscope may be, if the Sun is weak, the natives are not likely to go far in life. They will lack the basic energy and courage to make use of the opportunities life offers.

Moon Aspects

Aspects of the Moon deal with the unconscious mind, habit patterns of the past, and automatic reactions. The Moon represents the feminine, passive principle, that aspect of the consciousness which is receptive to outside stimuli. It indicates to a large extent how the native reacts to the influence of other people. The Moon is also connected with the faculty of memory, especially where emotional experiences are concerned. Thus, aspects made to the Moon can give clues to the natives' ability to retain information.

In the horoscope of a male, lunar aspects indicate the way the natives react toward women, especially as it relates to attitude patterns established in early childhood. In a woman's horoscope, the Moon represents the way basic femininity and maternal qualities are expressed. It is also an important factor in health, since it deals with the biological cycle of menses. (This cycle and its glandular effects also bear upon the emotional cycles.) The aspects to the Moon, as well as house rulership, sign, and house placement, indicate what kind of mother a woman will be. In both male and female horoscopes the Moon represents the influence of the mother.

Mercury Aspects

Aspects of Mercury, as well as sign, house position, and the houses it rules, are the key to the way the natives think and the kinds of minds they have. Their predominant manner of thinking and their primary area of mental interest are indicated by the dominating aspects made to Mercury. Mercury is neutral as far as mental communication, perception, memory, and reasoning are concerned. It therefore takes on the coloring of the planets which most closely aspect it, and of the sign and house in which it is placed.

No one can achieve a high position without having a reasonably well-developed Mercury, for the mind is a coordinating factor or lens through which all other abilities must be focused and filtered.

Aspects of Venus

Aspects of Venus, as well as the sign position and houses Venus rules, indicate the areas of life most strongly influenced by the desire for companionship, how love is expressed on a person-to-person basis, and the aesthetic or artistically creative tendencies. They also indicate the areas in which there is either ability or difficulty in closely relating to others; how and in what areas the social, romantic, and sexual urges are expressed; and where the natives serve or give with love, joy, and harmony.

The strength of Venus in a horoscope indicates the capacity to create beauty, harmony, and material prosperity, as well as the ability to attract the people and things which the natives love and desire to have. Where Venus is afflicted, there are problems to be worked out in social behavior and in the natives' desires for gratifications.

In male horoscopes, Venus and factors affecting it indicate the kind of woman the native wishes to attract. In a female horoscope, they signify what a woman will do for a man.

Aspects of Mars

Aspects of Mars, as well as the sign, house position, and houses ruled by Mars, indicate ability for self-expression through dynamic action, whether the action will be constructive or destructive, and the areas of life affected by the action.

If Mars has stress aspects, the natives tend to act rashly and precipitously without considering the consequences.

Afflicted, Mars signifies ill temper and possible outbursts of anger and violence. Therefore, the Mars energy needs to be constructively and purposefully channeled. Favorable aspects from Mercury, Jupiter, and Saturn will help in this regard. Mercury gives mental insight, Saturn gives discipline, and Jupiter gives altruistic motivations.

In a woman's horoscope Mars indicates the type of man she wishes to attract. In a man's horoscope, it represents the way he expresses his masculinity in attracting a woman.

Mars has much to do with the desire nature of the individual. Most people are motivated by what they want to have. Only in the highly developed individual is mentally based willpower the prime determinant for action.

Aspects of Jupiter

Aspects of Jupiter, as well as the house and sign position and houses it rules, are major factors in determining how natives expand the framework of the process of self-actualization. This expansion takes place by means of a collective principle: The natives gain the cooperation of others. Such cooperation is based on shared social, philosophic, and religious attitudes with the purpose of providing for the collective needs of the community.

Cooperation implies the need for a standard of ethics and philosophy, and aspects of Jupiter deal with the moral and philosophic nature of the individual and determine the channels through which it will function.

This Jupiterian principle is a two-way process. The individual cannot expect to receive from society without contributing in equal measure. A community, by combining resources and abilities, can accomplish tasks of greater scope and finer intricacy then the individual alone is capable of. Jupiter indicates how a native can serve this general welfare.

If Jupiter is afflicted, the natives have difficulty in cooperating with commonly accepted modes of social behavior or they are hypocritical in their motives for doing so. The planets which aspect Jupiter indicate how the natives cooperate with the larger purposes of the social structures to which they belong.

Aspects of Saturn

Aspects of Saturn, as well as the house, sign position, and houses it rules, indicate how the natives express capacity for self-discipline, and where and how they build structure into their lives. Without a well-developed Saturn, an individual cannot go far in life, because the discipline and experience necessary to accomplishment are lacking.

The placement of Saturn and its aspects to other planets shows where the native is forced to fulfill himself and correct the mistakes of the past, thus acquiring valuable experience and redeeming the deficiencies of his nature.

If Saturn is heavily afflicted, the natives can be selfish and rigid in their attitudes. This weakness blocks normal life processes and social interactions and leads to misfortune and personal limitation.

Natives who have a strong Saturn in their horoscopes are ambitious. They want to build something of importance and lasting value in the areas which relate to the sign and house Saturn occupies, to the planets Saturn aspects and their houses, and to the signs they rule.

Aspects of Uranus

Aspects of Uranus, as well as the house and sign position, are indicators of the natives' originality and of their departures from the normal modes of expression and behavior as a result of drawing on a higher source of inspiration. Uranus expresses a quality of originality and genius through all its affects in the horoscope. This is often manifested in scientific abilities which lead to new discoveries.

The affairs ruled by the planets which aspect Uranus are subject to sudden and dramatic changes, favorable or unfavorable according to the aspect. Intuition or insight based on extrasensory abilities plays an important part in bringing about these changes and creating an unusual lifestyle. If Uranus is afflicted, the natives are likely to be eccentric, erratic, undependable, and foolishly precipitous in the departments affected by Uranus.

The true freedom which Uranus offers can be had only after the lesson of Saturn has been learned: that self-discipline is a prerequisite of freedom and that freedom which is not based on self-discipline is short-lived and destructive.

Uranus also emphasizes humanitarian tendencies, very often expressed as cooperation in group endeavors. A strong, well-aspected Uranus gives occult abilities, expressed through such fields as astrology.

Aspects of Neptune

Aspects of Neptune, as well as the house and sign position, indicate the areas in which transcendental or psychic influences can touch the lives of the natives. When well aspected, it gives the natives transcendental-emotional experiences, often expressed through art and music, or drama, photography, and cinematography. Highly developed natives may have the capacity to act as a channel for spiritual inspiration emanating from a higher level of consciousness. This often manifests itself through a talent for imagery. Very often the natives are clairvoyant and able telepathically to send and receive mental images.

If Neptune is afflicted, self-deception and unrealistic desires will affect the natives through the affairs ruled by those planets afflicting it, as well as the signs and houses which Neptune and those planets occupy and rule.

Aspects of Pluto

Aspects of Pluto, as well as its house and sign position, indicate the areas in which the natives are able to regenerate their self-expression.

Pluto signifies a principle of fundamental will or energy that is capable either of raising the level of expression of any basic pattern in the natives' lives or of completely altering the quality of life for good or evil. (The outcome depends upon whether the motivation behind the use of Pluto's power is constructive or destructive.) This power can degrade or regenerate any of the affairs ruled by the planets which Pluto aspects, as well as the signs and houses that Pluto and these planets occupy and rule.

Pluto also gives the capacity to work with the superphysical forces of nature through the application of the will. Pluto can be expressed in its highest form only when the natives are developed enough to focus the will through the mind impartially, without the desires which would distort mental clarity.

Pluto indicates, moreover, how the lives of the natives are altered by vast impersonal forces beyond the natives' control.

Aspects of the North and South Nodes

Aspects of the North Node determine the natives' relationships to prevailing social trends and attitudes and their use of the opportunities afforded by history in the making. The North Node, because it brings occasions for increase, has a Jupiterian connotation.

Aspects of the South Node indicate in what ways the habit tendencies arising out of the natives' past experience influence their present attitudes and behavior. Also the South Node shows the karmic influence of the natives' past conduct. Thus it has a Saturnian connotation.

CHAPTER 11

General Remarks Concerning Conjunctions, Sextiles, Squares, Trines, and Oppositions

Aspects of the Sun

Conjunctions

Sun conjunctions emphasize willpower, creative ability, and initiative, especially in regard to the affairs ruled by the planet or planets which form the conjunction and the affairs of the signs and houses in which the conjunction is found. Whether this expression is constructive or destructive will depend upon the other aspects made to the conjunction and whether the conjunction involves malefic or benefic planets.

Sextiles

Sextiles of the Sun indicate opportunities for self-expression, mental development, and the unfolding of creative potentials in regard to the affairs ruled by the Sun in its house and sign position, by the planet or planets making the sextile, and by the houses and signs they occupy and rule.

Squares

Sun squares indicate difficulty in using will and power potential harmoniously and wisely. Past misuse of power often thwarts the natives' self-expression in the affairs ruled by the planet involved in the square and in the houses and signs which these planets occupy and rule. Difficulties and frustrations will come from these quarters.

How the square is ultimately resolved depends heavily upon the overall abilities. It acts as a spur to greater achievement for some, while it causes discouragement and resignation in others.

Trines

Trines of the Sun indicate good fortune and an easy flow of creative self-expression and leadership in the affairs ruled by the Sun and the planet or planets which make the trine and the signs and houses they occupy and rule.

These trines, in general, favor happy love relationships. The natives will benefit through education, working with children, and all things related to the Sun, such as the creative arts.

Oppositions

Oppositions to the Sun usually indicate a conflict of will between the natives and those ruled by the planet or planets which oppose the Sun. Sometimes the natives' egotism and tendency to be domineering cause resentment in others and lead to frustration for themselves.

The natives should consider all viewpoints impartially. One result of this opposition is that conflicts force the natives to recognize the not-self as well as the self. However, they may also, when faced with strife, take up a partisan point of view and pick sides. The nature of the conflicts will be determined by the signs and houses which the Sun and the opposing planet or planets occupy and rule.

Aspects of the Moon

Conjunctions

Moon conjunctions indicate intense feelings and a dominant emotional influence in the affairs ruled by the planets involved in the conjunction and the signs and houses which they occupy and rule.

Domestic affairs, food, and parental considerations will also strongly influence the affairs ruled by the planets involved in this conjunction. In such matters the native is inclined to act out of unconscious impulses, hereditary patterns, and early conditioning.

Women are likely to exert a decided influence on the native in the affairs affected by this conjunction.

Sextiles

Moon sextiles indicate an opportunity for emotional and domestic growth and for general development in the affairs ruled by the planets making the sextiles and the signs and houses which the Moon and these planets occupy and rule. Very often women play an important part in furthering the natives' progress. Mothers, or the home relationships in general, can be of considerable help. The configuration aids friendship and good emotional communication with both women friends and the mother.

Squares

Squares of the Moon indicate emotional blockage and frustrations arising out of early childhood and heredity, often in the form of racial and social prejudices. These are especially likely to hamper the natives' ability to act as emotionally free agents. Unconscious resentment toward women occasionally occurs here, often the result of conflicts with the mother. Especially when Saturn is squaring the Moon, these crystallized emotional habit patterns are an obstacle to the natives' happiness.

Trines

Trines of the Moon indicate habit patterns and unconscious conditioning which further the natives' progress socially, particularly in their relations with women. These trines usually favor a happy childhood and a successful family life.

The natives are able to make use of their creative imaginations and the automatic responses that stem from the unconscious. They are also sensitive to the moods of others.

These benefits will come through the affairs ruled by the planet or planets which make the trine, through the house and signs occupied and ruled by the Moon, and through the planets forming the trine.

Oppositions

Oppositions of the Moon indicate emotional problems in relationships. Often there is a psychological mirror effect, whereby the natives project their own emotional problems onto others and blame them for their own unrecognized faults.

These natives must learn emotional detachment and objectivity, especially in the affairs ruled by the planet or planets which make the opposition and in the affairs ruled by the signs and houses occupied and ruled by the opposing planets.

Aspects of Mercury

Conjunctions

Mercury conjunctions indicate that the mind is given power and understanding in its reasoning and communicating ability in all areas ruled by the planet or planets which make the conjunction, the house and sign the conjunction occupies, and the houses and signs ruled by Mercury and the planet it conjuncts.

Sextiles

Mercury sextiles indicate opportunity for mental growth in the affairs influenced by the planets involved in the sextile, and by the signs and houses which Mercury and these planets occupy and rule. Natives have good thinking and reasoning ability in these areas. They are especially skilled in writing, in communicating, and in forming new friendships. They have many opportunities for expressing ideas through groups and associations.

Squares

Mercury squares indicate difficulties and mental blocks in learning and communication. Natives can be intelligent and mentally active with Mercury squares, but they are inclined to be opinionated and one-sided in their viewpoints and to use their abilities fruitlessly or destructively.

There can be an overemphasis on skepticism, argumentativeness, and intellectual pride. These difficulties will be most in evidence in those matters ruled by the planet or planets which make the square and by the signs and houses they occupy and rule.

Trines

Mercury trines indicate a creative and inspired use of the mind. The natives are able to think and communicate rapidly and harmoniously; their ideas frequently gain acceptance, and proper use of their minds brings them success in life.

These natives benefit from education, which makes possible social and professional advancement. They will do well in areas ruled by the planet or planets involved in the trine with Mercury and the signs and houses which these planets occupy and rule. They comprehend clearly what is involved in these areas.

Oppositions

Mercury oppositions indicate difficulties in relationships, arising out of differences of opinion and outlook. There is also trouble in communicating with others. The natives have a tendency to argue and confuse—they must learn to see the other person's point of view as easily as they see their own.

These problems will show themselves as differences in mental outlook relating to the planet or planets which oppose Mercury and the signs and houses occupied and ruled by Mercury and these planets.

Aspects of Venus

Conjunctions

Venus conjunctions indicate a heightened expression of the natives' social, romantic, and aesthetic proclivities. Their gentleness and grace in expressing their emotions attract others to them, especially the opposite sex. They have a great deal of emotional empathy. Their ease and sensitivity in expression extend to all the affairs ruled by the planet or planets that Venus conjuncts in the houses and signs in which the conjunction occurs and in the houses and signs which Venus rules.

Sextiles

Venus sextiles indicate opportunity for the development of aesthetic and social qualities related to the affairs ruled by the planets, houses, and signs involved. Aesthetic and emotional expression can be refined and affections developed in the areas ruled by the signs and houses which Venus and the conjuncting planet occupy and rule.

Squares

Venus squares indicate difficulties in social relationships and emotional fulfillment. Natives tend to have unhappy or unfulfilled experiences in love and romance. They frequently lack refinement and good taste in matters of aesthetics.

They can either be self-indulgent and sensual or block their emotions—especially if Saturn makes the square.

All the affairs ruled by the planets which square Venus and the signs and houses occupied and ruled by these planets will be affected by some form of emotional or social difficulty.

Trines

Venus trines indicate joyous, creative, romantic, and artistic expression. They favor happiness in love and romance and general popularity. They indicate beauty and grace of manner.

The natives attract people who will benefit them, and these people are of the type ruled by the planet or planets making the trine. In turn, the natives often have a soothing and pacifying effect on others.

These aspects are strong indicators of musical or artistic talent.

The planets involved in the trine indicate areas which are affected. Areas of benefit will also be shown by the signs and houses which the planets and Venus occupy and rule.

Oppositions

Venus oppositions indicate relationship problems in emotional, marital, and romantic spheres. The natives are likely to be overly sensitive and to demand too much emotional gratification while neglecting to give others the same consideration. Since this attitude leads to disappointment and unhappiness, there is a great need for the natives to consider others as well as themselves.

The areas which are involved are indicated by the signs and houses occupied and ruled by Venus and the opposing planets and by the affairs naturally ruled by the planets which oppose Venus.

Aspects of Mars

Conjunctions

Mars conjunctions indicate a tendency to take direct action in the affairs ruled by the planet or planets making the conjunction, and this action affects the departments of life ruled by the signs and houses which Mars and the planets conjuncting it occupy and rule.

Mars conjunctions give ample energy for work. This can be the basis of much constructive accomplishment since it is accompanied by leadership and courage. If the conjunction is afflicted, there can be a tendency toward rash, ill-considered action. People affected by this should cultivate an attitude of peace and love and should think carefully before taking any action. Thus much destructive misuse of energy can be avoided.

Sextiles

Mars sextiles indicate that the Mars energy and willpower give constructive expression through action and work, with intelligent direction provided by the basic mental nature of the sextile, as indicated by Gemini and the Third House, and by Aquarius and the Eleventh House. The natives are afforded many opportunities for constructive action, which leads to experience—the basis of all wisdom. They possess the courage and initiative to overcome obstacles and are thus able to make great progress in life.

Squares

Mars squares indicate frustration in the desire for action: The basic Saturnian and lunar nature of the square aspect, which relates to the Fourth and Tenth houses, often causes the natives to lash out in rash ways. This reaction can be destructive for the natives as well as for those around them.

People with Mars squares must learn the lesson of patience and must consider the rights and needs of others as well as their own. If they are able to channel their energy intelligently, they can accomplish much, since a driving ambition often accompanies a Mars square. The Saturnian restriction on the Mars energy, which the square aspect represents, can be utilized as one way of organizing this energy to produce useful results.

The primary areas of the natives' lives which will be affected by Mars squares are those ruled by the planet or planets making the square and those affairs ruled by the signs and houses in which the square is found.

Trines

Mars trines indicate an easy flow of the Mars energy into constructive channels. The natives have a passionate love of life, which finds expression through affairs ruled by the planet or planets that trine Mars and the houses and signs occupied and ruled by Mars.

The Ninth House Sagittarius and Fifth House Leo connotation of the trine aspect links the Mars energy with the creative power potential of the Sun and the growth-producing, philosophic, and benefic power of Jupiter. Natives will naturally possess a strong source of practical accomplishment and will fulfill the higher, spiritual ideals of life.

Oppositions

Mars oppositions indicate relationship problems arising out of the natives' tendency to be rash and aggressive in their actions toward others. They must learn to love and must try to view any issue from the other person's point of view as well as their own.

With Mars oppositions there can be an unfortunate inclination toward competitiveness, fighting, and anger. Whether such expression is mere verbal bickering or something more serious will depend on other factors in the horoscope.

Used properly, the opposition of Mars gives firm and energetic action in partnerships. Natives are forced to become aware of the presence of the not-self and the necessity of cooperating with it. Refusal to cooperate can lead to violent conflicts with other people.

Aspects of Jupiter

Conjunctions

Jupiter conjunctions indicate a general attitude of optimism, goodwill, and awareness of constructive possibilities. Natives with this conjunction are generous and benevolent, thereby gaining the confidence and willing cooperation of others.

The affairs ruled by the planets involved in this conjunction and the houses and signs which these planets occupy and rule are areas of good fortune and increase in the natives' lives.

Sextiles

Jupiter sextiles indicate the opportunity for rapid mental growth in regard to affairs of the planets involved in the sextile, as well as the signs and houses which Jupiter and the sextiling planets occupy and rule.

The Eleventh House and Third House connotations of the sextile aspect indicate that the natives will have many friends and will profit through education, writing, travel, and communication. They will work well with groups and will get along well with brothers, sisters, and neighbors.

Squares

Jupiter squares indicate that the natives are overly ambitious and likely to hinder their progress in life by attempting more than they can accomplish. When they fall short of their goals, their careers and reputations suffer.

They should learn to use moderation and careful forethought in the affairs ruled by Jupiter and the squaring planets as well as the signs and houses which they occupy and rule. Although their optimism is good, they must make certain to have a solid foundation on which to build and expand.

Trines

Jupiter trines indicate good fortune and easy progress in life. They signify that past actions are being rewarded. However, such good fortune can also be dangerous by making the natives careless.

The natives have marvelous talents and resources to draw upon if they choose. Their assets are in the departments of life ruled by the trining planets and the signs and houses which Jupiter and the trining planets occupy and rule.

Oppositions

Jupiter oppositions indicate that the natives will have relationship problems arising from their tendency to demand too much from others and to take too much for granted. Their hail-fellow-well-met attitude will not always be appreciated, nor will their tendency to promote grandiose schemes at the expense of others.

These difficulties will emerge in relationships involving the planet or planets which oppose Jupiter and the signs and houses which Jupiter and these opposing planets occupy and rule.

Aspects of Saturn

Conjunctions

Saturn conjunctions indicate ambition and hard work. However, many obstacles and limitations must be overcome.

Natives are generally conservative and serious and are respected for their self-discipline, although a certain austerity about them discourages warm relationships.

These characteristics will be manifested most strongly in the affairs ruled by the planet or planets which conjunct Saturn and the signs and houses which Saturn and these planets occupy and rule.

Sextiles

Saturn sextiles indicate progress and mental development through serious hard work and good organization. The natives will be loyal to friends, brothers and sisters, neighbors, and organizations.

These stabilizing influences will be most noticeable in the affairs ruled by the signs and houses which Saturn and the sextiling planets occupy and rule.

Squares

Saturn squares are among the most difficult of all aspects because they usually indicate severe obstacles and limitations that frustrate natives' ambitions and desires for happiness. The natives must work twice as hard to achieve the same results that someone else may attain with ease. These difficulties tend to affect their careers and homes.

Natives must learn to overcome negative thinking and acquire a more positive attitude. Although Saturn squares indicate major life problems to overcome, they also spur the native to greater achievement.

These difficulties will affect the affairs ruled by the squaring planet or planets and the signs and houses which Saturn and these squaring planets occupy and rule.

Trines

Trines of Saturn indicate good fortune and lasting success through disciplined creativity and a serious philosophic outlook. The natives' high moral conduct inspires confidence and trust in others. Thus, they are often given positions of responsibility. They make good teachers, organizers, and managers.

These abilities will affect the affairs ruled by the planet or planets which trine Saturn and the affairs ruled by the signs and houses which Saturn and these planets occupy and rule.

Oppositions

Oppositions of Saturn indicate that the natives will have relationship problems arising out of negative, restrictive, and selfish attitudes. Being much too serious and austere, the natives appear unfriendly and unapproachable. Such attitudes generally result in loneliness and frustration. They must learn to correct these characteristics and not become embittered and isolated, thereby aggravating the situation.

These difficulties will affect the affairs ruled by the planet or planets opposing Saturn and the signs and houses which Saturn and these planets occupy and rule.

Aspects of Neptune

Conjunctions

Neptune conjunctions indicate actions that are often difficult or impossible to understand. The natives usually possess some psychic faculty, being influenced by an unconscious and sometimes intuitively superconscious aspect of the mind. They are often mystical and appear otherworldly to the ordinary person.

If the conjunction is well-aspected, there is great depth of emotional understanding and spiritual compassion. If the conjunction is afflicted, natives can be self-deluding and tend to ignore reality.

These characteristics will be manifested in the affairs ruled by the planet or planets which conjunct Neptune and the signs and houses occupied and ruled by Neptune and these planets.

Sextiles

Neptune sextiles indicate an opportunity for mental and spiritual growth through the use of the imagination and intuitive faculties. Natives may have a creative ability which is expressed through writing, communications, friendship, and group associations.

They are likely to work for idealistic causes. These tendencies will be most noticeable in the affairs ruled by the planet or planets which sextile Neptune and the signs and houses which Neptune and the sextiling planets occupy and rule.

Squares

Neptune squares indicate a great deal of confusion, disorganization, and destructiveness, arising out of neuroses or unconscious negative conditionings. Often the natives evade responsibility and refuse to face up to reality. At times this attitude is manifested in drink and drug abuse. The natives are often subject to negative psychic influences.

These characteristics are manifested mainly in affairs ruled by the planet or planets which square Neptune and the signs and houses which Neptune and these planets occupy and rule.

Trines

Neptune trines indicate good fortune and gain through creative use of the intuitive, imaginative faculties. Natives are often clairvoyant and possess inspired creative abilities in the fields of art and religion. They may have a marked degree of spiritual insight.

These characteristics will be manifested most strongly in affairs ruled by the planet or planets which trine Neptune and the signs and houses which Neptune and these planets occupy and rule.

Oppositions

Neptune oppositions indicate relationship problems due to the natives' deceptiveness and unreliability. These people confuse others because of their unconscious emotional hangups and are consequently undependable in relationships.

They can also have the tendency either to project their own psychological difficulties onto other people or to assume the burden of the psychic problems of others. The result is misunderstanding and confusion so that other people never know where they stand with these natives.

The problems will be most noticeable in the affairs ruled by the planet or planets opposing Neptune and the signs and houses which Neptune and these planets occupy and rule.

Aspects of Uranus

Conjunctions

Uranus conjunctions indicate original, creative, and dynamic tendencies. The natives will always be unusual in some way. Often they will be interested in the occult or in new areas of scientific discovery.

They are never bound by tradition and possess a strong spirit of independence. They are friendly and humanitarian. They have a strong willpower and the capacity for dynamic action. Sudden changes often occur in their lives.

These attributes will be most noticeable in the affairs ruled by the planet or planets which conjunct Uranus and the signs and houses which Uranus and these planets occupy and rule.

Sextiles

Uranus sextiles indicate sudden opportunities for mental growth and progress, which arise out of the natives' interest in and receptivity to new ideas. Natives communicate well, make friends easily, and are interested in groups and organizations, especially of an occult nature. They are scientifically inclined and often intuitive and clever.

These abilities will be manifested mostly in the affairs ruled by the planet or planets which sextile Uranus and the signs and houses occupied and ruled by Uranus and these planets.

Squares

Uranus squares indicate that the natives are likely to block their own progress and success because of instability, impulsiveness, and rash actions. They tend to be unreasonable, willful, and obstinate.

They change their minds often. Because they refuse good advice, they often blunder into serious mistakes. A great deal of work may be brought to naught through some foolish action.

These characteristics will be most noticeable in the affairs ruled by the planet or planets which square Uranus and the signs and houses which Uranus and these planets occupy and rule.

Trines

Uranus trines indicate sudden and unexpected good fortune. The natives are intuitively creative and have original ways of doing things. Being generally happy, they have many friends and exciting adventures.

These benefits will be most noticeable in the affairs ruled by the planet or planets which trine Uranus and the signs and houses which Uranus and these planets occupy and rule.

Oppositions

Uranus oppositions indicate relationship problems arising out of an unpredictable, demanding, unreasonable attitude toward others. Natives are undependable, erratic, and willful, and therefore exasperating to deal with and difficult to work with. They are likely to damage relationships through their unwillingness to sacrifice their personal desires and freedom.

These difficult tendencies will be most in evidence in the affairs ruled by the planet or planets which oppose Uranus and the signs and houses which Uranus and these planets occupy and rule.

Aspects of Pluto

Conjunctions

Pluto conjunctions indicate that the natives have the power to transform, for better or for worse, their own natures and their modes of self-expression. They have powerful wills and penetrating insight into the underlying forces of life. Their great power of concentration often results in clairvoyance and occult abilities. At times they are interested in science, especially in the field of atomic energy.

These characteristics will be most noticeable in the affairs ruled by the planet or planets which conjunct Pluto and the signs and houses occupied and ruled by Pluto and these planets.

Sextiles

Pluto sextiles indicate opportunity for self-transformation and mental growth through the dynamic use of willpower. Often there is interest in science and the occult.

The natives may have a marked effect upon the world through writing, communication, friendships, and group endeavors. They sometimes travel for reasons that others cannot fathom.

These effects will be most noticeable in the affairs ruled by the planet or planets which sextile Pluto and the signs and houses which Pluto and these planets occupy and rule.

Squares

Pluto squares indicate that the natives create difficulties for themselves by being ruthless in getting what they want. They are so impatient and overbearing that they often defeat their own purpose. At times they attempt the impossible. In extreme cases dictatorial qualities may appear.

These characteristics will be most noticeable in the affairs ruled by the planet or planets which square Pluto and the signs and houses which Pluto and these planets occupy and rule.

Trines

Pluto trines indicate good fortune and spiritual development brought about by the creative use of the will and the occult power of concentration and transformation. The natives have the ability to improve, reform, and transform their environments. They make good spiritual leaders. Many healers, clairvoyants, and prophets have this aspect in their horoscopes.

These abilities will manifest themselves in the affairs ruled by the planet or planets which trine Pluto and the signs and houses which Pluto and these planets occupy and rule.

Oppositions

Pluto oppositions indicate relationship problems stemming from demanding, dictatorial, and domineering attitudes. Natives wish to reform others according to their designs, without consideration for the wishes, desires, and rights of others. Naturally such an attitude generates resentment, often alienating the natives from warm human contact.

These characteristics can lead to arguments and impasses which will affect relationships involved in the affairs ruled by the planet or planets opposing Pluto and the signs and houses which Pluto and these planets occupy and rule.

CHAPTER 12

The Conjunctions

Conjunctions of the Sun

Sun Conjunct Moon (☉ ☌ ☽)

Sun conjunct Moon represents identification of the feelings with the will. Emotional impulsiveness is combined with the tendency to concentrate all of one's forces in one area of expression.

Health problems result when the solar energy overpowers the nurturing lunar principle that rules the etheric body, the force field around which the physical body is organized. Physical vitality is burned out by overactivity and overstimulation.

This conjunction also indicates a new cycle of experience dealing with those houses ruled by the Sun and Moon and the house in which they are placed. There is a tendency to alternate between masculine and feminine roles—passive action can suddenly become aggressive and vice versa. People with this conjunction are active and creative where their selfhood ties in with home, spouse, and children.

Sun Conjunct Mercury (☉ ☌ ☿)

Sun conjunct Mercury confers creativity and the ability to act in all things denoted by Mercury, especially in ideas, work, and friendships.

This aspect shows a tendency to enforce ideas and decisions with willpower. However, it also hinders objectivity in self-analysis by contributing to a very close identification of mind and ego. This makes it difficult for natives to view themselves impartially, or as others see them.

These natives are endowed with mental stamina and have a great deal of mental energy. If Mercury is conjunct the Sun within an orb of ½° to 4°,

Mercury is said to be "combust," creating a condition in which the lines of thought communication are overloaded with solar energy. Then a breakdown of communication and thought processes occurs, which can be compared to the way fine wires in an electronic computer are destroyed if they are subjected to an overload of electricity. When this excess energy overheats the mental processes, a more or less momentary mental blind spot results.

When Mercury is conjunct the Sun within less than ½° or 30′, Mercury is said to be "casimi." This position, while having some of the same difficulties of the "combust," is also a "dignity"; when the alignment of wave patterns is so perfect, the solar energy is modulated by Mercury and becomes a perfect carrier-frequency for the mind. In other words, the will becomes a vehicle for mental expression. This confers high powers of intellect, especially when the conjunction is in Gemini, Virgo, Aquarius, and Libra.

Sun Conjunct Venus (☉ ☌ ♀)

This conjunction gives power and energy to the emotions and makes the natives lovers of life. They are generally cheerful and optimistic, although they can be somewhat narcissistic. Often this conjunction makes them fond of fun and social activities. It confers beauty and ease in self-expression. These individuals have talent in music and art. If there are no afflictions to the Fifth and Second houses, people with this conjunction often gain through speculation. They also have the ability to bring happiness to others, because of their strong affections and romantic drives. They get along especially well with children.

Sun Conjunct Mars (☉ ☌ ♂)

This conjunction confers willpower, expressed in actions that require strength and courage. It is decidedly a masculine aspect. The houses ruled by the Sun and Mars will be areas of intense activity and power potential, as will the house in which the conjunction is found.

Individuals tend to be aggressive and self-assertive, since there is a natural tendency to express the power principle of the Sun through the action principle of Mars. How the aggressiveness is expressed depends on the sign and the house in which the conjunction is found, the house ruled by the planets involved, and the aspect made to the conjunction.

Sun Conjunct Jupiter (☉ ☌ ♃)

The solar principle of power and will is expressed through the Jupiterian principle of expansion. Natives with this conjunction are able to increase their own social influence and accomplish their aims.

They attract good luck by their pleasing personalities and generous, optimistic natures. Their positive outlook enables them to take advantage of their environments. Through enthusiasm and concern for the good of all, they are able to win others to their purposes, thus accomplishing more than they could do alone. The reason is that Jupiter (the natural Ninth House planet and the ruler of Sagittarius) rules philosophy, religion, and all codifications of group thought. Therefore, people with this conjunction are able to gain power by initiating projects that subsequently gain popularity or by utilizing commonly held ideas and goals. They use the social aspirations of others as a vehicle for their own ambition and self-expression.

Sun Conjunct Saturn (☉ ☌ ♄)

Saturn, which rules the principle of limitation, inhibits self-expression and ambition. Natives are not free to express themselves until they have completely mastered the sphere of limitation in which they find themselves.

Anything they achieve is gained through extremely hard work; they earn whatever they gain. Often they are sad and self-depreciating because of the continual frustrations they encounter. They should take advantage of all available opportunities.

However, since Saturn also represents the principle of fulfillment, natives can gain a significant degree of power through their organizational ability. Ultimately, their self-discipline will lead to personal fulfillment.

Sun Conjunct Uranus (☉ ☌ ♅)

The power potential of the Sun is expressed in this conjunction by venture into untried realms of experience, often scientific investigation at the frontier of human knowledge where the high-frequency, high-potency forces of nature are being discovered and used for the first time. The natives have the ability to delve into the higher-frequency planes of mind by applying their wills. Thus they can experience, understand, and work with what are generally termed "occult forces," forces expressed primarily through new and untried ways of doing things. They will act powerfully, suddenly, and decisively. In the eyes of people who do not understand their purpose, they seem unpredictable and eccentric.

Individuals with this conjunction are not necessarily subject to ordinary limitations. The means they use are based on a higher law or, more correctly, on a more advanced understanding of the One Universal Law. Thus, they are often called geniuses.

Sun Conjunct Neptune (☉ ☌ ♆)

Natives often seem to be transfixed by celestial music which only they can hear. They are subject to desires and emotions emanating from a subtle and high source which can lead them either into confusion and self-deception or to divine inspiration. Their power potential is expressed through the ability to merge on the emotional level with the universal life-force, to which their deeper levels of consciousness are attuned. This intuitive awareness often finds expression in the arts. These people therefore become mystics, psychics, clairvoyants, and, in the case of highly evolved natives, channels of divine guidance for humanity.

Whether they are pure channels depends on (1) the sign and house position of the conjunction, (2) the houses ruled by the Sun and Neptune, and (3) the other aspects made to the conjunction. Above all, it depends on the general evolutionary stature of the individual as revealed by the overall horoscope pattern.

These natives need well-developed minds (revealed through Mercury, Saturn, and Uranus) that can act as a rational check upon their psychic impressions, for with this conjunction it is sometimes difficult to distinguish between genuine inspiration and the projection of one's own ego or desire for importance, dressed in the symbolic garb of a confused unconscious. Neptune, through its association with the astral (or desire) body, is subtly linked with Mars (the desire nature) and often brings peculiar yearnings which, in the case of this conjunction with the Sun, can cause a subtle form of ambition or wish for self-importance.

On the negative side, these people can be self-deluded victims of their own imaginations to the point where they lose touch with the realities of life, becoming useless to themselves and to others.

Sun Conjunct Pluto (☉ ♂ ♇)

Natives having this conjunction express their power potential through their ability to regenerate and change themselves and the things around them by focusing their wills. Since tremendous energy is at their disposal, they can penetrate to prime causes.

Pluto rules the ability to penetrate dimensions and tap the fundamental dynamic energy of the universe responsible for all form manifestation and evolution. In the human organism, this primal energy is manifested as sexual potency, which can be expressed through the mind or through the body. When it is expressed through the mind, higher universal states of consciousness are revealed, and the individual can become an instrument of the Divine Will. Through the mind, the transforming power of Pluto is able to re-create individuals into spiritual beings with universal power for good.

It is important that these natives learn to bring their wills into harmony with the Divine Will. If they fail to do so, their efforts will backfire and cause their own destruction. People with this conjunction can have a power complex and, if allowed to go too far, can become dictatorial. They must realize they are not the only power in the universe, that each person's will and power are borrowed from a universal source of energy and must maintain harmony with it.

Sun Conjunct North Node (☉ ♂ ☊)

This conjunction indicates birth near the time of a solar or lunar eclipse. It also shows that this is a major event in the natural world, which causes major events and sets of circumstances in the natives' world and provides them greater scope for their self-expression as well as opportunities for expansion of their power and leadership potential. The conjunction suggests an inherited karmic tendency toward good luck as a result of previous use of the life energies for the benefit of the individual's larger environment. When carried too far, however, this influence can dissipate the individual's energies, causing exhaustion and a depletion of the life-force.

Sun Conjunct South Node (☉ ♂ ☋)

This conjunction refers to a condition in which major circumstances in the native's environment deny him opportunities and resources for self-expression, limiting especially his leadership and power potential. Obstacles are thrown in his path, making it difficult to achieve what he desires, even to the extent that he is denied the fruits of his efforts.

Natives are not swept along in the mainstream of events, as in the case of the Sun conjunct North Node. This conjunction indicates a karmic situation in which individuals in previous incarnations selfishly promoted their own ambitions at the expense of the self-expression of others. This time around, they experience what it is like to be thwarted by the actions of others. However, this aspect can bring a thorough mastery of that which the native is able to command.

Sun Conjunct Ascendant (☉ ☌ Asc.)

This conjunction indicates powerful individuals whose basic consciousness and mode of self-expression are united with the life-force. They can master their environments and themselves because their action springs directly from the solar fountainhead of life. (In this position the Sun is dignified by being in the house of Aries, the sign and house of its exaltation.)

These people possess strong bodies and constitutions. They are rarely ill or tired unless their horoscopes and the Sun are heavily afflicted. They have tremendous recuperative powers, even if they become very ill.

They are in tune with that consciousness which encompasses the past, present, and future in the exact present moment or the Eternal Now. Thus, as spiritual beings they can exert tremendous influence for good, especially those whose overall horoscope patterns show them to be highly evolved (a highly integrated, overall pattern of aspects involving most or all of the planets with strong aspects to Uranus, Neptune, Pluto, Sun, M.C., and Asc.).

Afflictions involving the Sixth and Twelfth houses show the energy of the solar constitution to be out of harmony with itself and thus used to its own detriment.

Sun Conjunct Midheaven (☉ ☌ M.C.)

Natives with this conjunction have tremendous influence through their careers, professions, and reputations. They are often found in politics and public life and usually achieve fame or notoriety in some way as indicated by the nature of other aspects made to (1) the Sun and M.C., (2) the sign in which the Sun and M.C. are placed, and (3) the sign and house position of the ruler of the Sun sign and aspects to this ruler.

Sun Conjunct Descendant (☉ ☌ Desc.)

Natives with this conjunction express their power potential through partnerships.

Unless the Sun and the Seventh House are both afflicted, these natives have powerful and magnanimous marriage partners and close friends who aid them in fulfilling their power potential. They are skilled in public relations and make good salesmen because of their ability to influence individuals as well as the public in general.

Sun Conjunct Nadir (☉ ☌ Nadir)

The natives express their will and power potential through home and family. They like to entertain important people.

Since the Sun's influence must pass through the entire body of the Earth, they have to overcome many material obstacles to achieve full self-expression. Unless the Sun in the Fourth House is heavily afflicted, the latter part of their lives is a period of security and fulfillment.

Conjunctions of the Moon

Moon Conjunct Mercury (☽ ☌ ☿)

This aspect represents a direct linking of the unconscious mind and the conscious reasoning mind. The native is intellectually aware of his emotional nature and responses—especially to other people—and his conscious thoughts and interpersonal communications have an immediate effect upon his emotional responses. (He is particularly sensitive to what other people think of him.)

However, if the conjunction is badly afflicted by other aspects, there is a tendency for the feelings to overrule the reason, giving the thoughts an emotional coloration. The native is likely to be hypersensitive to personal remarks and criticisms.

On the positive side, this conjunction gives an unusual access to information stored in the unconscious mind, especially to experiences of an emotional nature.

The native is likely to devote much thought to domestic and family affairs, in particular in the area of food and health, for this aspect links the dietary concerns of Virgo with the nutritive Cancer concerns of the Moon.

Moon Conjunct Venus (☽ ☌ ♀)

This aspect indicates a highly emotional response to beauty and harmony which is often manifested in artistic ability. Women will reveal creativity in choosing clothing and preparing food. Their talent for decorating will produce beautiful environments. They have a great deal of charm in dealing with other women.

This conjunction confers sensitivity, tact, and the tendency to be affectionate, and natives find success in romance and courtship unless other factors in the horoscope militate against it. Their sensitivity to others makes them good diplomats.

If the conjunction is afflicted, natives tend to be self-indulgent and can easily be taken advantage of by a play upon their feelings.

Moon Conjunct Mars (☽ ☌ ♂)

This conjunction generates strong feelings, which on the negative side can result in outbursts of anger and other emotional outbreaks. Children with this aspect are prone to temper tantrums. If the conjunction is well-aspected, such strong emotions can lead to energetic action and accomplishment. But they may result in jealousy, anger, and emotional frustration if the conjunction is afflicted by other aspects. In any event, the natives feel and act with great intensity.

Unless a prominent Mercury is involved in the horoscope, or Saturnian discipline is definitely indicated, these natives can make dangerous and vindictive enemies, because their actions are likely to be based upon emotion rather than reason. Their feelings can blind them to caution and common sense. They will often bravely crusade for a cause and accomplish much if they guide their energies with wisdom.

Moon Conjunct Jupiter (☽ ☌ ♃)

This aspect confers sympathy and generosity. The natives wish to bring good to others. Their concern with social welfare, if put into political action, yields a return of good karma; consequently, they are usually trusted —especially by women—and receive the cooperation and help of others.

If the conjunction is afflicted, waste and self-indulgence can ensue. These people also have a tendency to be gluttonous. If well aspected, the conjunction confers honesty, integrity, and business ability.

There is an inclination to good health because of a generous supply of energy to the Moon-ruled etheric body. The natives tend to identify with and work for religious and educational causes. But messiah complexes can result if the conjunction is afflicted.

Contrary to what might be expected, this aspect does not necessarily incline to world travel. Emotional attachments to home, family, and friends, as well as to material possessions, inhibit travel, especially if the conjunction is found in a fixed sign.

Moon Conjunct Saturn (☽ ☌ ♄)

This aspect creates a tendency to identify emotionally with material things and the memories attached to them. The native's emotions are chained to past memories. His attention should be directed to constructive activities and goals and diverted from the well-worn emotional grooves of past experiences.

The personality is somewhat somber. Unless other factors in the horoscope contradict this, there is an inclination to emotional depression and lack of joy in life. In the eyes of many, the natives are wet blankets.

The aspect does bestow practical realism and common sense. Natives are self-disciplined and can devote themselves to hard work. Whether the constructive or depressive qualities of this aspect are dominant depends to a large extent upon other aspects made to the conjunction.

Moon Conjunct Uranus (☽ ☌ ♅)

This aspect indicates intuitive ability, original imagination, and erratic emotional impulses. The native is subject to peculiar and sudden changes in mood and will often behave unexpectedly and impulsively.

Domestic and family life may be unusual. The home is often used for entertaining friends or as a meeting place for group activities.

If the conjunction is afflicted, natives may be cranky, erratic, irritable, and not always reliable. But if it is well aspected, resourcefulness and unusual creative abilities are evident.

People with this aspect seek the strange and unusual. Their emotional life requires excitement and novelty. If the aspect is afflicted, extremes of emotional behavior may be seen.

Moon Conjunct Neptune (☽ ☌ ♆)

Natives with this aspect are highly impressionable and tend to be psychically attuned to the emotional reactions of others. Vulnerability where their feelings are concerned makes them sympathetic and under-standing. On the other hand, they can be too easily influenced by the emotional tenor of their surroundings.

Mediumistic and psychic inclinations are in evidence, but whether these can be relied upon or whether they are fantasies picked up through the unconscious mind depends on the rest of the chart. Natives often have powerful and sometimes prophetic dreams.

Vivid imagination is indicated and, if correctly used, can enhance musical and artistic ability.

If the chart is afflicted, strong unconscious influences may cause the native to live in a dream world, building castles in the air and seemingly unable to relate to reality.

In a good horoscope this conjunction can give religious and spiritual tendencies.

Moon Conjunct Pluto (☽ ☌ ♀)

Natives with this conjunction have intense feelings and are strong-willed where their emotions are concerned. They may display psychic and occult tendencies and a leaning toward a subtle emotional domination of the surroundings. They can have a compelling influence over other people. They are open to superphysical realms of manifestation, but in a more positive manner than those with Moon conjunct Neptune. Their in-terest in spiritualism or matters pertaining to life after death can make them aware of those who are discarnate.

There is also a tendency to let the past die and to create entirely new bases for emotional experience. Natives are fearless and willing to take risks, and Pluto, ruling the principle of elimination, death, and rebirth, causes them to seek extreme and drastic changes in their lives. They may deal drastically with their families, bringing about sudden changes in the domestic sphere. Sometimes they alienate women by their brusqueness and tendency to be overbearing.

Whether this conjunction is expressed in creative genius or in destructive emotionality will depend on the aspects made to it and the horoscope as a whole.

Moon Conjunct North Node (☽ ☌ ☊)

This conjunction brings good fortune through the natives' ability to sense and to flow in harmony with the prevailing current of events. In other words, they are instinctively capable of taking advantage of current trends. Carried too far, this attribute leads them to jump on whatever bandwagon happens to be passing, without due concern for the consequences.

Natives' enthusiasm brings them popularity. Good fortune in dealing with women or the public is also indicated. Thus, the aspect is beneficial to those in public relations, selling, entertainment, and politics.

If the chart as a whole bears out this tendency, natives will be generous and interested in religion.

This is a favorable karmic influence, created by generosity and helpfulness to others in the native's past.

Moon Conjunct South Node (☽ ☌ ☋)

This is a difficult aspect because circumstances in the natives' lives make it hard for them to synchronize their activities with current trends. In other words, the natives are plagued with bad timing due to their own circumstantially imposed inability to be in the right place at the right time, doing the right thing in the right way.

Thus they are constantly forced to draw upon their own personal resources. They cannot depend upon the cooperation of others. They are emotionally alone against the world.

This isolation leads to depression and a negative emotional outlook which further alienates others. ("Laugh and the world laughs with you; cry, and you cry alone.")

Natives are capable of disciplined, well-planned, concentrated effort. Their ingenuity in making the most of meager resources brings solid accomplishments and a strength of character which meets adversity with courage and determination.

According to some writers on the subject, this is a karmic condition, created by previous misuse of wealth, position, and popularity.

Moon Conjunct Ascendant (☽ ☌ Asc.)

This conjunction causes the natives to identify their basic consciousness with their emotions. On the positive side, it can lead to a good memory and to an awareness of the workings of the unconscious mind.

Natives have a lively imagination and much emotional stamina. They can empathize with others. This is a more favorable conjunction for women than for men, because it tends to femininity in manners and appearance.

Natives often have a full round face with a soulful expression. They are impressionable, and the experiences of life touch them deeply in an emotional, personal way. Their early childhood experiences have more than ordinary effect upon their later personalities. They seem to identify strongly with home and family. If the rest of the map is corroborative, psychic tendencies are indicated.

If the conjunction is afflicted, reactions to life are overly subjective and personal.

Moon Conjunct Midheaven (☽ ☌ M.C.)

This conjunction, unless afflicted, indicates popularity and life in the public eye. It favors actors, entertainers, and politicians. If the conjunction is well aspected, the natives gain through women of wealth and high social standing who aid them in achieving status.

Very often, professional activities are carried on in partnerships, or positions of responsibility are bestowed by someone in authority.

Sometimes this conjunction indicates that the native will inherit the family business, or that the career is linked with the family life.

This lunar position is advantageous to people in businesses connected with food and articles of domestic use. Also favored are those in real estate and other businesses which deal with homes.

Moon Conjunct Descendant (☽ ☌ Desc.)

This conjunction creates close emotional ties with the spouse, other partners, and close friends. It also is good for emotional sensitivity in public relations. It favors salesmen, especially those dealing with food and domestic articles.

Emotional attitudes are strongly influenced by other people. The natives can be romantic and idealistic concerning marriage.

This conjunction is favorable for building up family life and the domestic environment through a good marriage. It is more propitious in the horoscope of women because it enhances the feminine attributes in relationship to the husband. However, in a man's horoscope it gives emotional understanding of the wife and of women in general.

The attitudes of others can have more than the usual effect upon these natives, making them somewhat vulnerable emotionally. Often, the mother comes into the home and is either a part of the marriage environment or a big influence on it.

Moon Conjunct Nadir (☽ ☌ Nadir)

In this position the Moon is strong because it conjuncts the house cusp which it naturally rules, creating domestic tendencies and emotional ties to family and parents.

The natives delight in preparing and eating food. Firm maternal or paternal bonds are indicated: The natives feel unhappy and incomplete without home and family.

They like to be near lakes, rivers, or other bodies of water. Sometimes they wander from place to place seeking new emotional experiences. The feelings run deep when this aspect is in the chart.

There is also skill in gardening and farming and an emotional identification with Mother Earth.

Sometimes this aspect brings the mother into the home or creates an emotional reliance on the mother.

Conjunctions of Mercury

Mercury Conjunct Venus (☿ ☌ ♀)

This conjunction confers grace of expression in speech and writing. The voice is often soft and has a musical quality. The aspect produces literary talent and poetic ability. Money can be made through writing and communication. Natives possess diplomacy in communicating with others, as their actions are based on a consideration of what will produce the most beauty, balance, and harmony. Often their mental endeavors are carried on in partnerships. This conjunction can also produce scientific and mathematical ability because of the talent it gives for understanding relationships.

The natives enjoy others and are able to improve health through the beauty and balance which they generate. The mind is turned toward thoughts of love, and these persons, if the rest of the horoscope concurs, bear goodwill toward their fellows. This aspect gives a practical turn of mind, especially in earth signs.

If the conjunction is afflicted, the fickleness of mind that produces the social butterfly can be in evidence.

Mercury Conjunct Mars (☿ ☌ ♂)

The native with this conjunction has a sharp mind and abundant mental energy. There is a tendency to take sides and become involved in partisan causes. This is a good aspect for reporters or investigators, of whom action for gaining information is required. The native is mentally aggressive and will say exactly what he thinks, letting the chips fall where they may. He is decisive and acts upon his decisions.

Often there is an interest in politics and speechmaking. Individuals having this aspect love to debate and bring up controversial issues. They are competitive and like to show that they possess more knowledge or are intellectually superior to others in a given field. They tend to express themselves vehemently and with extraordinary directness where things of the mind are concerned.

When the conjunction is afflicted, they tend to become involved in heated arguments, and desires can overpower their minds, blinding them temporarily to reason.

Mercury Conjunct Jupiter (☿ ☌ ♃)

This aspect broadens the mind and gives an interest in philosophy, religion, law, and higher education. The natives are confident of their mental abilities and skillful in influencing others through their fluent speech. The conjunction favors teachers, ministers, lecturers, and politicians—those whose careers require verbal ability to win the support of others.

The natives' mental work frequently brings them into institutions as teachers, advisers, or counselors. They possess intellectual integrity and use their mind for the advancement of humanity. This, in turn, often brings respect and recognition.

They are also fond of travel, usually making a long journey at some time in their lives. They generally acquire good educations, which then lead to social, professional, and financial advancement. Highly respected, they gain reputations for being authorities in their professions.

Mercury Conjunct Saturn (☿ ☌ ♄)

Although natives with Mercury conjunct Saturn are not as fluent and expressive as those with the Mercury conjunct Jupiter aspect, they are more exact, painstaking, logical, and scientific in their thinking. This conjunction bestows strong mathematical and scientific ability. Foresightedness and careful planning are among its good qualities. The overall quality of the horoscope and the other aspects found in it will determine how this type of mental ability is used.

Natives are hardworking and thorough in learning and in study. When they write and speak, no steps are omitted. The conjunction produces notable powers of visualization, since the natives understand form and structure. They are, therefore, excellent in geometry and make good designers, draftsmen, architects, and engineers. They tend to be mentally ambitious, but they can encounter periodic difficulties in gaining recognition.

On the negative side, this conjunction can signify people who are critical, worry too much, and are subject to depressions. Often skeptical and doubting, they are not likely to accept ideas which are not traditional or which they cannot readily assimilate.

Mercury Conjunct Uranus (☿ ☌ ♅)

This aspect confers mental genius and originality. Natives possess lightning-quick minds. They are able to gain insight through intuitive flashes and frequently are interested in mental telepathy or other forms of occultism. Their ability to tune in to the Universal Mind and receive guidance from it especially favors those who study astrology.

The conjunction creates an interest in science, particularly where electronics and the use of microcosmic forces are concerned. Natives often become professionally involved in electronic forms of communication. Mentally, they are independent and will not accept ideas simply on the basis of tradition. They must understand and prove everything for themselves, constantly seeking the new or the unusual. Hence their ability to arrive at original solutions to problems which those who think along more traditional lines overlook.

Natives with this aspect should receive a good education, especially in scientific fields, in order to make the best use of their mental talents.

If the horoscope or the conjunction is afflicted, these people can be eccentric, harebrained, conceited, hard to get along with, and too independent for their own good.

Mercury Conjunct Neptune (☿ ♂ ♆)

Natives with this conjunction have vivid imaginations and an awareness of their unconscious minds. Their interests center in mysticism, psychic phenomena, and psychology—they both read and write books on these subjects.

If the overall horoscope and other aspects made to the conjunction bear it out, they can possess unusual clairvoyance and act as channels for ideas emanating from higher planes of consciousness. Telepathic ability and prophetic ability can go with this conjunction in a favorable map.

The natives tend to be dreamers and often like to be alone in order to drift off into psychic realms of consciousness. The aspect can confer poetic and literary or other creative talents that result from a lively imagination. Photography is a good profession for the natives to pursue if the rest of the map concurs.

Natives can be elusive and deceptive and, if the conjunction is afflicted, downright untruthful or at best hard to pin down. They are not likely to argue but will quietly proceed to do what they intend, regardless of advice to the contrary. Thus, this conjunction can make one secretive.

If the conjunction is afflicted, the native may live in his own dream world and lose touch with reality. Mental aberrations leading to psychosis are possible if the general horoscope is afflicted as well.

Mercury Conjunct Pluto (☿ ♂ ♀)

This aspect produces penetrating and resourceful minds. The natives have the ability to see through others and to ferret out secrets—they are determined to get to the bottom of what they wish to understand. A strong willpower combines with real genius and resourcefulness. This aspect tends to make the native disinterested, and able to see things as they really are. To him, truth is more important than comfort.

There is a special aptitude for understanding reality in terms of energy rather than in terms of material objects; therefore, the native is able to comprehend the forces that can generate fundamental changes in his environment. Interest in science, especially in atomic physics, is indicated.

The aspect also shows that the natives make good investigators and detectives since much of their mental work is concerned with secret information. There can be a definite interest in the occult and in working with the superphysical forces of nature, inasmuch as people with this conjunction study and communicate about these forces.

When the conjunction is afflicted, these natives can be mentally overbearing or even deceitful in order to serve their personal ends. There is also a tendency to want to remake others' thoughts and mental perceptions.

Mercury Conjunct North Node (☿ ☌ ☊)

Natives with this aspect are able to express ideas acceptable to the culture in which they live at a time when they will receive recognition. (There is nothing so urgent as "an idea whose time has come.") Thus they are popular and are considered intellectual leaders. If other factors in the horoscope give a capacity for original thought, the native can be an effective force in bringing important new concepts into acceptance.

On the negative side, there is a tendency for the natives to be swept along in the current of popularly held views and to do little original thinking. They are then merely mental children of their time, subject to all its limitations and errors.

Mercury Conjunct South Node (☿ ☌ ☋)

This aspect produces a condition in which the natives' ideas are either behind or ahead of their times. On the positive side, the conjunction can bestow mental originality and independence. Then natives escape the pitfalls of popular opinion. In the long run, if the rest of the map indicates good mental capacity, the native will prove to be correct.

On the negative side, the native is forced to proceed alone with his ideas since he cannot gain support for them. He does not speak out at the right time in the right place, and when he does speak, he is not listened to. Consequently he is sometimes frustrated and feels mentally alone.

Mercury Conjunct Ascendant (☿ ☌ Asc.)

This aspect produces exceptional intelligence. The natives think before they act and express themselves in clear logical terms. Their basic consciousness is closely linked with their logical thinking ability.

The native is likely to have a somewhat nervous appearance and a frail but agile body. His primary interests are in education, speech, and writing. If he is educated to use his intelligence, his exceptional mental abilities will help him achieve prominence.

As a rule, the natives are inclined toward verbosity, which can be an annoyance if Mercury is afflicted.

Mercury Conjunct Midheaven (☿ ☌ M.C.)

Natives with this aspect can impress their superiors with their original thinking and speak and write well. Occupations involved with communication, or the means of communication, such as newspaper work and printing, are favorable for people with this conjunction.

Education is their key to professional success. They make good writers, teachers, researchers, scientists, librarians, secretaries, clerks, and telephone operators.

Mercury Conjunct Descendant (☿ ☌ Desc.)

This aspect gives skill in communicating with the public. It is favorable for public relations men, salesmen, messengers, and representatives. The natives are noted for their social wit and conversational ability. They make good diplomats because they can understand the other person's point of view. Many become interested in the study of law and matters relating to contracts.

Here, Mercury attracts an intelligent spouse and partner. Close friends are also intellectual.

Mercury Conjunct Nadir (☿ ☌ Nadir)

This position of Mercury indicates that natives who come from an intellectual environment usually have intelligent and well-educated parents.

There is also a tendency for the natives to live in the same house with a brother, sister, or former neighbor. Often the home is a center for communication, service, and study. Natives usually have large libraries in their homes.

Conjunctions of Venus

Venus Conjunct Mars (♀ ☌ ♂)

Although this aspect is considered one of the primary aspects concerned with sex, the natives incline toward passionate involvements of all types.

The desire nature of Mars joined with the attraction principle of Venus must manifest itself in some form of creativity. Whether it is expressed through sex or through social and artistic activities depends on the rest of the horoscope and other aspects made to the conjunction.

This conjunction gives vitality to the emotional nature, and the natives have an intense love of life and emotional warmth. The result can be excessive aggressiveness if other factors in the horoscope permit, but even their aggressiveness is coupled with a certain charm by the Venusian influence.

The love nature of Venus is rendered more physical in nature by this aspect—to what degree will depend on whether Mars or Venus is the stronger, as well as on their sign placement and aspects to other planets. Natives should have some outlet for their powerful creative energies.

These people are somewhat impulsive in spending their own and other people's money. They are generous and outgoing but must avoid prodigality in their financial affairs.

Venus Conjunct Jupiter (♀ ☌ ♃)

This aspect gives a generous and optimistic disposition. Unless there are strong factors in the horoscope to indicate otherwise, the natives are cheerful and friendly toward their fellow beings, sociable, and open-handed to those who need help.

They are inclined to donate money for religious causes and to help people who are less fortunate. They can bring joy to others. Artistic ability, often related to religious expression, is also indicated. Highly evolved natives may be talented as peacemakers.

On the negative side, the aspect can lead to too much ease and comfort for the natives' own benefit and may create a tendency toward indolence. A strong Saturn in the horoscope negates this danger and allows the positive qualities of the aspect to be taken advantage of.

Venus Conjunct Saturn (♀ ☌ ♄)

This aspect is often found in the horoscope of talented artists. Saturn gives form, structure, and concrete practical expression to the artistic tendencies of Venus, as well as the patience necessary for attention to detail. Since Saturn rules time as well as space, musicians can be favored by a good sense of rhythm, harmony, and melody.

This conjunction, especially when combined with a harmonious Mercury, also confers mathematical ability. The tendency toward harmony and balance constitutes the mental side of Venus, which, when combined with Saturn and Mercury, provides insight into the harmonious workings of the laws of nature.

Many of the attributes of this aspect are related to the sign of Libra, which is ruled by Venus and in which Saturn is exalted. Thus a sense of justice, fair play, and loyalty is engendered. Although the natives may not be as socially outgoing as other people, they form lasting and meaningful partnerships and make loyal friends. If other factors indicate a generous disposition, these natives, because of their down-to-earth approach in dealing with problems, are of more practical help to those they serve than are many other people.

Ambition for money can be present, as well as a desire to improve social and financial status through marriage and partnerships. When the desire is pursued with a sense of fair play, all parties concerned can benefit. However, used negatively, it leads natives to marry for financial consideration only. They must be wary of the tendency to use others to gratify their own emotional needs. Much will depend upon the rest of the horoscope as to how this aspect will be used.

On the negative side, the aspect can lead to depression and an inclination to feel unloved and unappreciated.

Venus Conjunct Uranus (♀ ☌ ♅)

Natives having this aspect are inclined to sudden attractions. Their effervescent, sparkling personalities make them quite popular. They love social activity, amusement, parties, and stimulating experiences in general. Artists with this aspect have an original, individualistic style.

Natives have strong social inclinations, since the aspect has the combined influences of Libra, the Seventh House, and Aquarius, the Eleventh House. There is a tendency to confuse friendship and love, so that their love life tends to be erratic, with powerful, immediate attractions that break off suddenly.

Since these natives want to bestow their affections universally, it is hard for them to remain romantically tied to one person. They should never marry in haste, even though they may have an extraordinary urge to do so. A long engagement will determine whether a given relationship will last.

If there are other indications in the horoscope, such as emphasis on earth signs or a well-aspected Saturn—indicating that the natives can keep their feet on the ground—they can bring happiness to others through original means of service.

Venus Conjunct Neptune (♀ ☌ ♆)

This aspect has qualities similar to those engendered by the sign of Pisces, which is ruled by Neptune and in which Venus is exalted.

On the positive side, it can indicate the highest and purest form of spiritual love. Highly developed natives can possess healing ability and spiritual understanding of a transcendental nature. Aesthetically sensitive and perceptive, they can bring joy and peace to others through their presence. In general, the natives are impressionable and have a deep and far-reaching capacity for emotional rapport.

An almost hypnotic power of attraction can be exerted by these persons, which operates for good or bad depending on the motivation behind its use. In any case, a vivid imagination and fertile unconscious mind are indicated. The aspect inclines the natives toward music and mystically inspired art. They are fond of soothing music and all that is soft and fine in texture. Photography and art forms that make use of transcendental or unseen forces are favored (such as those perceived in visions).

On the negative side, this powerful aspect can indicate impractical, romantic dreamers who are a burden to those around them. Undeveloped natives may be deceptive and unreliable where love is concerned.

Venus Conjunct Pluto (♀ ☌ ♇)

This aspect is one of passionate and often karmic emotional involvement. In horoscopes of highly developed individuals it can indicate the capacity for a regenerating, redeeming spiritual love, capable of uplifting all who come in contact with it.

In such cases love is combined with spiritual power and the will is manifested at a very elevated level. Usually there is an ardent love of life, often involving fervent attractions to members of the opposite sex. Natives tend to experience emotional death and rebirth. Ultimately a valuable spiritual lesson is learned: that love must be directed toward the spiritual source of all of life's manifestations, and that the Eternal, as the Inner Essence of all creation, must be worshiped, rather than the material manifestations of this power.

This aspect, like all strong Venus contacts, can give artistic talent, expressed in this case through drama as well as drama-music combinations, such as opera, operetta, and serious musicals.

The negative side of the conjunction is just as perverted as the positive side is exalted. There is inordinate involvement in sexual passion and indulgence. In any event, the natives are creatively potent in whatever ways they choose to express this powerful energy.

Venus Conjunct North Node (♀ ☌ ☊)

This aspect indicates good timing in social contacts and in forming relationships favorable for money, romance, partnerships, marriage, and friendship. Through an innate ability to be in the right place at the right time, the natives attract those things necessary for happiness. According to some authorities, this ability represents the good karma coming from friendliness and generosity in the past.

On the negative side, this aspect can lead to a frivolous involvement with every passing pleasure so that time is wasted on useless social activity.

Venus Conjunct South Node (♀ ☌ ☋)

Natives with this aspect tend to loneliness and personal isolation where their feelings are concerned. They are inept in timing social and romantic advances, approaching others when they are preoccupied or indisposed. Consequently they suffer frequent brush-offs and develop inferiority complexes.

On the positive side, love takes on a serious and profound meaning. There is a desire to help and relate to those who really need love and friendship. In the long run, this brings spiritual rewards.

Some people believe that the conjunction is the karmic result of a previous lack of appreciation for the love and help of other people. The natives have to learn the true meaning of love and help by being deprived of them.

Venus Conjunct Ascendant (♀ ♂ Asc.)

This aspect often confers physical beauty, especially on women. Natives' personal mannerisms and appearance are pleasing and harmonious. They are able to bring harmony and beauty into their surroundings through their ability to express these qualities.

In less highly developed natives this conjunction could lead to narcissistic tendencies and infatuation with their own beauty. The rest of the horoscope would have to be very weak for this to be the case, however, since the aspect indicates an intense awareness of the laws of harmony and beauty as a means of self-expression.

These natives can sometimes be socially aggressive because of the Mars/Aries connotation of the First House.

Venus Conjunct Midheaven (♀ ♂ M.C.)

This aspect favors people in artistic professions, public relations work, and diplomacy. Females are often able to promote their careers by charming their bosses or those in authority.

Natives are prone to social ambition. Their status can be improved through marriage, and marriage is sometimes contracted in order to achieve this, especially if Venus is in Taurus or in Capricorn. They also have the ability to attract money through social prominence or by forming partnerships with those in positions of power.

Venus Conjunct Descendant (♀ ♂ Desc.)

Natives with this aspect, unless there are afflictions in the horoscope to indicate otherwise, are blessed with a harmonious married life. They marry for love and are devoted to their spouses and partners. Grace and ease in dealing with the public are indicated. Those in diplomacy, public relations, and entertainment are especially favored, since they are popular with the public.

These natives consider the happiness of others and therefore attract happiness. Since success depends upon interlocking human relationships, they achieve success through their ability to get along with other people. Tact and diplomacy are their particular talent.

Venus Conjunct Nadir (♀ ♂ Nadir)

This aspect indicates a love of domestic harmony. Therefore, the natives' home will be artistic and beautiful, even if on a simple scale. Since the relationship of home to marriage is important to this person, much of his money is spent on improvements in the home. Thus, there is likely to be a deep love for family and parents, along with a tendency to marry for the sake of having a beautiful family and domestic life. Fondness of good cooking is also indicated.

Conjunctions of Mars

Mars Conjunct Jupiter (♂ ♂ ♃)

This aspect gives an abundance of energy and enthusiasm. The natives are zealous in the pursuit of what they consider to be worthwhile—knowledge, religion, or efforts on behalf of those less fortunate. The conjunction gives self-confidence in action—natives will not accept "No" for an answer and feel it to be within their capacity to accomplish what they set out to do.

This aspect favors those in businesses in which enterprise and financial gain are important. Their wholehearted involvement in their cause verges sometimes on fanaticism.

A military career, or business connected with the military, characterizes many natives. If the conjunction is afflicted, there can be an avaricious, bellicose tendency, with the attitude that might makes right. This conjunction can also lead to a misplaced chauvinistic patriotism. There is a love of parade and the show of strength through pomp and ceremony.

Mars Conjunct Saturn (♂ ♂ ♄)

On the positive side, this aspect gives a capacity for hard work, enduring strength, resourcefulness, and courage in situations of danger and great difficulty. The strong Spartan qualities favor military careers or situations in which the natives must use caution and prudence in the face of danger. Very often, however, they resent people who lead easier lives.

Unless it is well aspected and in a good horoscope, this conjunction signifies a tendency toward anger, hard feelings, and malice. Negative attitudes combined with resentment and violence can result. The anger is due to the Saturnian frustration of action and self-expression. Often natives suppress their anger until it suddenly erupts. In a heavily afflicted horoscope with many stress aspects to this conjunction, organized, deliberate destruction could follow. There can also be an ambition for power that leads to oppressive and dictatorial attitudes.

When the conjunction is afflicted, natives are prone to broken bones or inflammation and other diseases of the skin. There is a tendency to be rigid and musclebound.

Mars Conjunct Uranus (♂ ☌ ♅)

With this aspect the natives are likely to evidence impulsiveness and precipitate action. There is a tendency to rebel against constraint. Typical is the natural revolutionary or the leader of any organized movement whose purpose is to bring about drastic and sudden social change. The natives cannot bear a dull life and constantly seek excitement through danger and unusual action. Courage and decisiveness are prominent, but unless factors in the horoscope indicate otherwise, prudence is lacking. Since this aspect puts a strain on the nervous system, the natives should learn to relax in order to recharge their vitality.

Natives gain emotional satisfaction from dramatic manifestations of energy: sport car racing, jet planes, rockets, firearms, or the explosive human situations found in large crowds.

Mechanical and scientific bents are indicated. Natives like to experiment with machinery and electrical apparatus. If the conjunction is afflicted, these preoccupations can be a source of danger through accidents. The thrill of excitement can sometimes lead to reckless driving. People with this conjunction, especially if it is afflicted, should avoid carelessness in driving and mechanical experimentation.

Interest in aviation characterizes this conjunction, especially if found in air signs. Yet it is more of a technician's than a scientist's aspect, unless both a strong Mercury and a strong Saturn are in the horoscope. There is involvement with hardware but not necessarily with theory, unless the conjunction is aspected by Mercury, Venus, or Saturn.

Mars Conjunct Neptune (♂ ☌ ♆)

This aspect gives the natives strong psychic magnetism. If the conjunction is well aspected, they may have healing abilities, since an abundance of psychic energy is available to them. They may also be interested in magical forces or the use of occult power. Their desires and ambitions can lead to lofty spiritual achievement, but their goals can also tend toward the impractical, the unrealistic or the overly romantic and lead them into misguided activities. Quite often these activities are determined almost entirely by unconscious impulses, and they sometimes result in disaster.

The natives have a tendency to act through subterfuge and secrecy, and their movements are often surrounded with mystery. Romantic involvement and exotic or peculiar emotional desires are often present. Sometimes there is treachery on the part of the natives or treachery directed against them. Usually, this comes through the affairs of the house in which the conjunction is found.

These natives can be susceptible to bad drug reactions, poisoning, or infectious diseases.

Mars Conjunct Pluto (♂ ☌ ♇)

With this aspect the natives have tremendous energy and power in action. Through their spiritual reserves they are able to tap the energy of universal power. Having more than normal endurance, they can accomplish things beyond the scope of the ordinary person. Their immense courage and willpower give them the ability to face danger, and even death, unflinchingly. Whether this energy is used constructively or destructively depends on other aspects and the general tenor of the horoscope.

Much depends on whether the desire principle of Mars or the will principle of Pluto is the determining factor. If Mars is the stronger, the conjunction will serve only to intensify personal lust, greed, and egotism, making the natives potentially dangerous and destructive. It requires highly developed individuals to make the Plutonian principle of will control the desires. If such control is achieved, great powers of regeneration will make possible a spiritual leadership in improving the affairs of humanity.

In the horoscopes of less developed people, this conjunction can produce violent natures, and occasionally criminal tendencies.

Mars Conjunct North Node (♂ ☌ ☊)

Natives with Mars conjunct North Node tend to act in harmony with
the people in their environment, thus gaining both cooperation and approval.

However, as the saying goes, "Nobody is right if everybody is wrong."
The desires of the natives and their resultant actions can be swept
along in a chain of mass passions that ends in self-destruction. For
example, individuals caught up in a flood of misdirected patriotism can
find themselves the agents or victims of war.

Mars Conjunct South Node (♂ ☌ ☋)

On the positive side, this aspect can cause the natives to question
the militaristic values or group actions of their society. They may step
aside if they feel that the trend is to no good. They sometimes become
loners, acting upon their own decisions and disregarding what others
think or do.

On the negative side, their actions and desires tend to be out of
harmony with the standards of society. They may act at the wrong time
and in the wrong place, antagonizing others and causing opposition.
They are likely then to lash out in anger and frustration.

Mars Conjunct Ascendant (♂ ☌ Asc.)

This aspect confers aggressive and forceful personalities. The natives
unfailingly make themselves noticed and markedly affect their environment. Their desire to be leaders is combined with a competitive spirit.

The aspect confers muscular strength and a rugged constitution.
Unless Mercury and Saturn are strong, the natives tend to precipitate
action and to plunge boldly into things before considering the consequences. Since they are naturally aggressive, they dominate others unless
they are held in check. They often want to change the people and situations around them. They are inclined to act for themselves to achieve
their personal ends. Sometimes other people resent what they consider
the natives' unwarranted interference and bossiness, and the upshot is

friction and personal isolation. If these natives can learn diplomacy, they can accomplish a great deal.

Mars Conjunct Midheaven (♂ ♂ M.C.)

This aspect makes the natives highly ambitious. They desire importance and prominence in the world and in their professional lives. Their energy is directed toward definite purposes that will further their long-range goals. They are highly competitive where position is concerned and will fight to get to the top.

They are often found in politics, whether in a corporate structure or in government. The conjunction favors those in industrial professions and jobs connected with machinery and engineering. It also disposes the natives toward a military career.

Mars Conjunct Descendant (♂ ♂ Desc.)

This aspect tends to make the natives aggressive in dealing with the public and with their partners. It can also work the other way, making the partners or the public aggressive toward the natives. Thus a great expenditure of energy is required in cooperating with others. The conjunction can also create disagreement with others if the horoscope is afflicted. Conditions of competition dominate conditions of active cooperation.

Relationships, especially in marriage, are likely to be emotionally packed; conflict can result from strong desires (often unrecognized) on the part of one or both parties.

Mars Conjunct Nadir (♂ ♂ Nadir)

With this aspect vehement actions and desires manifest themselves in the domestic life of the native. Since the conjunction partakes somewhat of Mars in its fall in Cancer, it tends to create a situation of disharmony in the home unless it is very well aspected. The forceful combative nature of Mars does not harmonize well with family life, in which sensitivity and mutual love are needed. The home, which should be a place of beauty and harmony, can become a battlefield generating emotional tension and upset. Mars conjunct Nadir is something like a bull in a china closet.

This conjunction is favorable for people connected with industrial occupations having to do with the earth itself, such as mining or building construction. The Mars energy can also be used to make do-it-yourself improvements in the home.

Conjunctions of Jupiter

Jupiter Conjunct Saturn (♃ ☌ ♄)

This aspect gives a serious outlook on life and an involvement in heavy responsibilities unless other factors in the horoscope contradict it. The natives are conservative and practical.

Since they have to overcome severe obstacles in order to expand their business and financial affairs, there are often problems connected with money. To achieve a goal or to make any substantial increase requires endless patience. If the natives have resources to work with, they can build things or institutions that will have lasting value. Endless toil combined with hard work and danger are common to this conjunction.

Sustained disappointments over a long period of time can drain the natives' optimism. Sometimes the effect of Jupiter operating on Saturn is a protection to them in their darkest hours, but there is a conflict between the Jupiter expansion and the Saturn contraction principles to the extent that the two planets can nullify each other's effects. There is a tendency for the natives' destiny to be at the mercy of larger social issues. For instance, factors affecting industry, business, and economics in a nation can create extreme difficulties.

This aspect is more difficult if Jupiter precedes Saturn because endeavors beginning in optimistic expansion soon run into snags and disappointments. This sequence occurs every time a transiting or progressing planet aspects first Jupiter and then Saturn. Saturn preceding Jupiter is more favorable: Once the structural basis has been erected by Saturn, disciplined, hard work can be rewarded.

Jupiter Conjunct Uranus (♃ ☌ ♅)

This aspect creates unusual opportunities and breakthroughs in expansion and growth for the natives. Such advantages come through the introduction of new methods and from unexpected sources, very often from friends.

The natives are likely to travel suddenly. They are given opportunities for training and education that open new possibilities for business and profit, frequently in scientific fields.

Many of the natives are interested in new, progressive, and occult forms of religion such as New Thought, "power of positive thinking," yoga, or astrology. They do not follow ordinary business procedures, educational endeavors or religious beliefs, but think and act for themselves with originality and ingenuity.

This conjunction makes the natives generous toward their friends. They encourage other people who are also interested in doing worthwhile, unusual things. In politics they tend to be reformers and advocates of new political philosophies. They are generally in opposition to the established way of doing things.

Jupiter Conjunct Neptune (♃ ☌ ♆)

This aspect confers a fertile imagination which can find an outlet in art, music, philosophy, and religion (if other factors in the horoscope provide the necessary practical application to put it to use). This conjunction inclines the natives to extreme sensitivity where emotional and psychic proclivities are concerned. Flights of religious ecstasy and mystical absorptions into the astral realms are characteristic, often giving rise to involvement in mystical cults and psychic forms of religion. The tendency is for extreme idealism, which, unless the rest of the horoscope indicates otherwise, does not result in much practical common sense or self-discipline.

If this conjunction is afflicted by other planets, the natives may lose contact with reality and live in a world of private fantasy. Although they are well-meaning, they are not necessarily practical or reliable—they often promise more than they can deliver.

Jupiter Conjunct Pluto (♃ ☌ ♇)

This aspect confers the determination to achieve goals that will bring about improvement for both the self and others. The natives have the intense concentration to draw upon the power and inspiration of higher planes of consciousness and will often find themselves involved in Yoga, systems of meditation, spiritual healing, clairvoyance, and prophecy. The purity and accuracy of their abilities and perceptions will, of course, depend upon other aspects made to the conjunction as well as upon the general tenor of the horoscope.

The capacity for spiritual regeneration given by this conjunction provides leadership qualities and the ability to channel constructive forces in times of crisis. The conjunction favors judges and administrators, who need penetrating insight into the motives and actions of people in society.

Jupiter Conjunct North Node (♃ ☌ ☊)

This aspect gives the natives unusual ability to harmonize with prevailing social, cultural, and religious attitudes. Popularity and good fortune are likely to follow.

At the same time, there is a tendency unquestioningly to accept traditional values without subjecting them to critical analysis. There is also the danger of fast and too easy expansion that creates the possibility of a future fall or collapse. That which is attained too easily is not always valued or properly used. These natives tend to take too much for granted.

Jupiter Conjunct South Node (♃ ☌ ☋)

This conjunction is similar to the Jupiter-Saturn conjunction. The endeavors of the natives may be blocked because of bad timing. Their social and ethical aims may clash with prevailing societal customs, creating conflicts of interest. At the same time, the natives can give a detailed and honest appraisal of commonly accepted values.

They can encounter obstacles in obtaining higher education and find themselves in disagreement with prevailing religious institutions. There can be difficulties and delays in foreign lands and problems connected with all these matters.

Jupiter Conjunct Ascendant (♃ ☌ Asc.)

This aspect gives rise to optimism and self-confidence, which, properly used, can inspire the confidence and goodwill of others.

The natives are inclined toward religious and philosophic interests. Sometimes they attempt to take on the role of religious leader or to start a religious group. There may be outlets for self-expression through religion, law, teaching, and philosophy.

The natives are fond of travel, unless Jupiter is in a fixed sign.

If the conjunction is afflicted, it can sometimes cause delusions of grandeur. The native's tendency to have a large body may lead to overweight in later years.

Jupiter Conjunct Midheaven (♃ ☌ M.C.)

This aspect is favorable for attaining prominence. The fact that the natives are usually honest and benevolent in their dealings often leads to promotion, public confidence, and a good reputation.

If the natives were born in lowly circumstances, they usually rise to a position of importance. Often a profession in the ministry, law, education, or business is indicated, since this conjunction favors people who are in the public eye or who pursue a career in politics.

If the conjunction is afflicted, ambition and desire for importance for its own sake are indicated.

Jupiter Conjunct Descendant (♃ ☌ Desc.)

This aspect indicates good fortune through marriage and partnership. It gives the natives ability in public relations, especially selling, entertainment, and diplomacy. It also favors those in the legal profession and persons who act as representatives for religious and educational organizations.

People generally respond in a positive manner toward these natives, because the natives are sincerely interested in the well-being of others. If the conjunction is afflicted, however, this interest is hypocritical, masking a selfish motive.

Jupiter Conjunct Nadir (♃ ☌ Nadir)

This aspect is favorable for people dealing in real estate or in businesses related to the construction and improvement of homes. It also favors farming or those businesses related to the growing of food.

The natives usually live in large homes with large families, and unless other factors contradict, parental relationships are good. The home is often the site of religious and educational activity. In the last half of their lives natives are prosperous, comfortable, even opulent.

Conjunctions of Saturn

Saturn Conjunct Uranus (♄ ☌ ♅)

This aspect bestows ability for concrete practical expression of original genius ideas arrived at intuitively.

The natives do not form useless habit patterns, because the tendency of Uranus toward freedom and originality overcomes the negative Saturnian crystallization. At the same time, the realism and practicality of Saturn keeps Uranus from making the natives eccentric and overhasty in bringing about change. Usually, they have learned the lesson of self-discipline and thus are able to express the true freedom that comes from the voluntary acceptance of responsibility.

There is also the ability to make creative use of established ideas and conditions. The new is built upon the solid foundation of that which has stood the test of time.

If the overall horoscope is well balanced and this conjunction is well aspected, the natives are highly developed and have much to offer the world. Their creativity stems partly from the richness of their past experiences. The conjunction is conducive to the serious study of mathematics and science as well as astrology and other occult matters. It confers the ability to use systematic, mathematically oriented methods to make new discoveries and breakthroughs.

When afflicted, the conjunction gives rise to stubborn obstinacy and autocratic attitudes. There is a danger of sudden accidents and of threats to the natives' security. Natives tend to be somewhat abrupt and to vacillate between pessimism and unrealistic optimism. They should be careful to work with the good aspects to either planet in the conjunction.

Saturn Conjunct Neptune (♄ ☌ ♆)

If it is well aspected and in harmony with the overall horoscope, this conjunction gives steadiness and powers of concentration in meditation and in the use of clairvoyant faculties. It also confers, when well aspected, maturity of spiritual insight and compassion based on practical experience.

The natives are able to use the Neptune inspiration practically, so that it is more than just a beautiful dream. Because Saturn gives this inspiration form and brings it into concrete expression, the conjunction favors artists and musicians. It can also indicate a professional engagement in secret or behind-the-scenes activities. If the conjunction is afflicted, foul play may be involved. If well aspected, the natives walk softly and go far.

Saturn conjunct Neptune afflicted can give rise to depression, anxiety, a morbid imagination, and subjection to destructive psychic influences, probably indicating a previous abuse of the psychic or imaginative faculties. Natives may be institutionalized, especially if the Twelfth House is involved. When this conjunction is afflicted, the natives should avoid drugs and entanglement with psychic phenomena dealing with emotional, or astral, forces.

Saturn Conjunct Pluto (♄ ♂ ♀)

This aspect is sometimes called the aspect of the magician because of the ability it gives to channel occult powers through structured systems. The power urge of Pluto combined with the power nature of the conjunction and the status urge of Saturn leads to strong ambitions in the areas ruled by Pluto.

The natives' ideas and projects can have a transforming effect upon the world. They use their scientific knowledge to find better or more efficient ways of using the resources and powers in their environment.

They are usually serious and secretive in their plans and projects. If the conjunction is afflicted, they are subject to secret enemies, intrigue, selfish motives, and desire for power.

For good or ill, these natives have far-reaching and long-lasting effects on their environments, although their efforts may require patience, toil, and hard work.

Saturn Conjunct North Node (♄ ♂ ☊)

This aspect makes the natives conservative and careful to conform to prevailing social, religious, and ethical values. They generally adhere to protocol as to the proper time and place for approaching those in well-established positions of authority. Thus they may further their personal ambitions, but at the expense of enslavement to the lowest common denominator of culturally accepted standards.

Saturn Conjunct South Node (♄ ♂ ☋)

This aspect tends to be extremely limiting; the natives' rigid personal habits and ambitions put them out of harmony with prevailing cultural attitudes. In order to overcome the isolation thus created, they must learn to cooperate with the ideas and methods of their society.

On the positive side, the natives may achieve things which put them in a class by themselves by their individualistic and painstaking approach to work, in which all external influences are disregarded. This is especially the case with experts in obscure fields of endeavor.

Saturn Conjunct Ascendant (♄ ♂ Asc.)

This aspect shows the natives to be reliable and to have a strong sense of responsibility. They may be counted on where serious work needs to be done.

They project an image of austerity, self-absorption, seriousness, Spartanism, and reservation, which makes them appear formidable and often leads to unpopularity. Their tendency toward personal reserve is frequently misinterpreted as haughtiness or unfriendliness. Often people do not realize that they are shy or that their sense of responsibility does not incline them toward idle social discourse.

This conjunction creates difficulties and hardship in early life. The natives are likely to be either bony and tall or so reduced in stature as to have a dwarflike appearance.

Saturn Conjunct Midheaven (♄ ♂ M.C.)

The Saturn conjunct Midheaven aspect characterizes those who rise to high stations through hard work and steady ambition. If the conjunction is well aspected, they are honest, responsible, and foresighted in their dealings. They make good executives and administrators. In politics they tend to be conservative, seeking policies which lead to stability and to the expansion of existing institutions along traditional lines.

If this conjunction is afflicted, disgrace and fall from a high position are possibilities.

Saturn Conjunct Descendant (♄ ♂ Desc.)

This aspect favors the creation of lasting and stable partnerships.

The natives, often interested in the legal profession, are just in their dealings with others, although they are reserved and may even appear calculating. Very often they are public representatives for governmental or other organizations dealing with the public.

If this conjunction is afflicted, the natives are subject to unhappy marriages, or to marrying simply for status and position. Marriage can take place late in life.

Saturn Conjunct Nadir (♄ ♂ Nadir)

Since this aspect partakes of Saturn's detriment in Cancer, the natives may show coldness and formality where the home life is concerned. Home problems may impose heavy responsibility on them. One parent may become a burden, or there can be a lack of warmth in the parent-child relationship.

This conjunction often creates conflict between professional and domestic obligations.

Conjunctions of Uranus

Uranus Conjunct Neptune (♅ ♂ ♆)

This conjunction, which takes place about every 171 years, corresponds to a period of major spiritual and scientific progress for humanity. Its occurrence is marked by the incarnation of a whole group of highly developed souls who introduce new philosophies and political and social systems and thus further man's evolution.

The generation which has this conjunction as part of its horoscope is attuned to the subtle forces of nature and the unfolding of intuitive potentials. Natives are influenced by superphysical forces related to the sign and more particularly the house in which the conjunction is found. These factors will also have bearing on the affairs ruled by planets aspecting the conjunction favorably or unfavorably.

These people have keen imaginations, a touch of originality and insight, and emotional and mental sensitivity, especially in regard to the affairs ruled by the planets, signs, and houses affected by the conjunction.

The conjunction creates a tendency to become involved in secret spiritual societies and religious organizations. It results from a combined Ninth, Tenth, Eleventh, and Twelfth House connotation.

Notes: Uranus, the co-ruler of Capricorn, is found in the Tenth House of many large business concerns and of people who have become successful because of some unique discovery. Many scientists are Capricorns have Saturnian discipline combined with Uranian originality.

Most great religions begin with the Neptunian mystical experiences of an inspired teacher or prophet and later become codified in religious creeds or systems of ethics in the Jupiterian-Sagittarian sense. (This religious connection can be explained by Neptune's co-rulership with Jupiter of the sign Sagittarius.) Business enterprises of these natives are often related to secrecy (Neptune, ruler of Twelfth House), and work is a group endeavor (Uranus, ruler of Eleventh House). Often they are inspired by an occult mystical philosophy.

In its highest expression this conjunction is manifested as the synthesis of Divine Wisdom and Divine Love.

Uranus Conjunct Pluto (♅ ☌ ♇)

This conjunction occurs approximately every 115 years. The generation in whose horoscope it appears is often considered revolutionary—its destiny is to overthrow or regenerate outmoded social institutions. The conjunction represents an interaction between the personal will of the individual and the Universal Will of the Creator. If the individuals are highly developed, they become channels for expression of ideas which will better the human environment. They can use the conjunction's power to bring about a more precise understanding of the laws that govern conditions needing improvement in civilization. (This can be manifested in the fields of science, psychology, and metaphysics.)

Such breakthroughs draw man closer to his origin in spirit and facilitate his evolutionary destiny: to return with full self-consciousness to the source from which he emanated.

This conjunction has many of the qualities of the sign Scorpio, in which Uranus is exalted and which Pluto rules. It is, therefore, highly occult in its significance and deals with death and regeneration (or the process of destruction of form manifestations and the release of the life imprisoned in the form to seek a more constructive embodiment).

If the natives are undisciplined or uneducated and the conjunction is under stress, they may be tempted to use collective power for selfish purposes.

Uranus Conjunct North Node (♅ ☌ ☊)

Natives with this conjunction are likely to profit from sudden changes in surrounding social conditions. For example, if the conjunction is found in the Tenth House, they can benefit by jobs created by the introduction of new electronic technology.

Natives are attuned to the changing times but are subject to being swept away by unexpected social changes without giving consideration to the ultimate consequences of impulsive group enthusiasm.

Uranus Conjunct South Node (♅ ☌ ☋)

The lives of natives with this conjunction are upset by changing social and technological conditions. For example, if the conjunction were found in the fourth house in Gemini, a native might be forced to move his home to make way for highway construction, probably at a financial loss.

This conjunction often occurs in the horoscope of individuals whose lives are disrupted by war and revolution. Afflictions made to the conjunction by other planets can cause additional complications.

On the positive side, these are determined and individualistic in preserving traditional worthwhile values against the onslaught of fads and new social movements.

Uranus Conjunct Ascendant (♅ ☌ Asc.)

The natives are likely to be unusual in physique—frequently they are quite tall. They are alert and quick in their responses and extremely individualistic, with strong interests in the unusual, either scientific or occult. Their intuitive faculties are highly developed and they are able to tap a superconscious level of knowledge, gaining insights beyond the capacity of the average individual. If well aspected by other planets, this conjunction often leads one into the study of astrology.

These natives lead adventuresome, unusual lives. However, they may suffer a great deal of nervous tension, especially if the conjunction is afflicted.

Sometimes Uranus gives a certain personal arrogance. Natives tend to feel automatically that other people should bow before what they feel to be their superior intelligence. They demand personal freedom and will not tolerate interference in their chosen way of life.

They are often leaders in revolutionary activities, social philosophies, and new scientific ideas.

If Uranus is afflicted, natives are inclined to hang obstinately onto eccentric and "crank" notions but are subject to sudden—and periodic—

switch-abouts. However, as a rule, these people are progressive in their attitudes, broad-minded, and tolerant.

Uranus Conjunct Midheaven (♅ ♂ M.C.)

This conjunction indicates unusual conditions where work and public reputation are concerned. If the conjunction is well aspected, the natives can gain fame and high positions by originating scientifically advanced methods in their professions. The conjunction favors jobs related to science, electronics, physics, and occult work such as astrology.

Other aspects made to Uranus can cause sudden changes in reputation and professional standing.

· If the conjunction is afflicted, the natives may become impatient with professional routines and rebellious toward their superiors—often for foolish reasons—so that a change in positions is likely. They are happier if they are their own bosses or at least have a free hand in the work they do.

In politics, this conjunction may lead to revolutionary views. Unless other factors in the horoscope contradict it, the natives will be known at least for their liberalism.

Uranus Conjunct Descendant (♅ ♂ Desc.)

This conjunction is conducive to extreme individualism and a desire for freedom in marriage and other close relationships. It is generally not favorable for stability in marriage—many astrologers have observed its frequent appearance in the horoscope of divorced people. Marriages of the natives require a great deal of mutual understanding and tolerance in order to succeed. There is a tendency to meet people suddenly, become infatuated for a short time, and then break off the relationship.

Popularity and contacts with the public are erratic and unstable. Much will depend upon other aspects made to Uranus. Attraction to people of occult or scientific bent is a strong likelihood. There is an inclination to regard the husband or wife more as a friend than as a spouse.

Uranus Conjunct Nadir (♅ ♂ Nadir)

This conjunction creates an unusual and constantly changing domestic situation. The parents or the home itself may be out of the ordinary in some way. Natives may be forced to change residence suddenly. Their homes are filled with modern conveniences and electrical gadgets or else with artifacts of ancient or unusual origin.

Often the home is used for group activities such as clubs or occult organizations. Electronic or scientific hobbies are characteristic, with basement workshops or gadget rooms to accommodate them.

If the conjunction is afflicted, it can cause sudden disputes and separations in the family life, such as estrangements from parents. If it is well aspected, the natives are friendly with their families and share interests with their parents.

Conjunctions of Neptune

Neptune Conjunct Pluto (♆ ☌ ♀)

This conjunction is probably the most subtle of all aspects. It relates to changes in fundamental attitudes in human society, attitudes concerning religion, philosophy, and man's understanding of his own consciousness and ultimate purpose in the universe.

This aspect can also represent major turning points in the rise and· fall of nations, cultures, and social institutions. Its occurrence coincides with a general testing of philosophies and cultural institutions, which must either meet the challenge of expanding needs or collapse and be replaced by new and better structures.

However, the death of old concepts heralded by this conjunction can also have a disintegrative effect on society, and disquiet and confuse the generation that experiences it.

In the horoscope of exceptionally developed individuals, the conjunction can represent the spiritual mission of bringing a new and higher level of consciousness to humanity. It also furthers the regeneration of mankind through service motivated by the awareness of the unity of all life, which can be defined as Universal Love.

Properly to express this aspect, individuals must forget themselves and dedicate their wills to the service of humanity. How this conjunction affects them depends upon the house position of the aspect and the houses ruled by Neptune and Pluto. It also exerts an influence through the planets that aspect the conjunction and through the affairs of life on which they have bearing (through dispositorships, etc.).

Note: Uranus, Neptune, and Pluto, especially when they form aspects among themselves, represent the high-frequency carrier waves which are modulated by emanations from other planets. They indicate how the individual karma is integrated into the group and mass karma of religions, nations, and cultures.

Neptune Conjunct North Node (♆ ☌ ☊)

This conjunction tunes natives to what is socially popular and acceptable. They have an intuitive ability to be in the right place at the right time.

On the negative side, there is a tendency to be mindlessly swept along with current social conditions, wherever they may lead. Going along with the crowd can be the easy way out and end ultimately in disaster. For example, a native involved in the cocktail party circuit may overindulge in drinking simply because it is the socially acceptable thing to do and end up as an alcoholic. It is important for these natives to exercise discrimination.

Misused, this aspect can be highly seductive. It can sweep the natives along without their being aware of it.

Neptune Conjunct South Node (♆ ☌ ☋)

This conjunction does not make for popularity. The natives' unconscious habits and intuitive promptings are out of harmony with current social trends, and their timing is likely to be off when they have an opportunity for good fortune. However, they are often individualistic and discriminating in relation to popular social trends and can sidestep the folly of the masses through superior intuitive wisdom.

There is a danger that things on which the natives have worked hard will be stolen or taken from them through intrigue or unfortunate circumstances which are beyond the natives' control.

Natives may have the responsibility of acting as channels for working out spiritual purposes under difficult conditions.

Neptune Conjunct Ascendant (♆ ☌ Asc.)

This conjunction gives the natives a definite intuitive or psychic quality. Very often they appear to be living in another world, and depending on how Neptune is aspected, they can live in their fantasies, away from worldly reality. Their actions may be difficult for people to fathom, since they are based on unconscious promptings and intuitive perceptions.

However, if Neptune is well aspected, and Saturn and Mercury are strong, they can have a superior grasp of reality through their sensitivity to the many subtle factors affecting a given situation, factors which other people cannot understand.

Frequently these natives have a subtle magnetism that bestows an air of fascination. Their eyes may have a mysterious hypnotic quality ("bedroom eyes"). Their highly developed imaginations may be accompanied by artistic talent.

Neptune Conjunct Midheaven (♆ ♂ M.C.)

Natives with this conjunction tend to be anything but the average employer's ideal of stable employees. The dreams and mystical qualities of Neptune do not combine well with the routine discipline required by the average job. These natives do better in professions that make use of their creative imaginations and ascetic traits.

The conjunction favors musicians, actors, painters, photographers, moviemakers, psychologists, and persons interested in the occult. Professions may be related to the occult in some way. Even though these natives may be in the public eye, they feel spiritually isolated—alone in a crowd, and in fact most people do not understand their inner motivations.

If the horoscope is that of an exceptionally developed person, he may be destined to perform a mission in the world that will lift many people around him to greater attainment and spirituality.

If this conjunction is heavily afflicted, scandal or public disgrace is a danger. This can come through the natives' unreliability or because of alcoholism, drugs, or other forms of addiction.

The natives should be careful not to get involved in secret intrigues, especially when they cannot know all the factors involved. Private secrets are not so private when Neptune is found in this position.

Neptune Conjunct Descendant (♆ ♂ Desc.)

This conjunction can denote peculiar circumstances where marriage and partnership are concerned. Depending on aspects made to the conjunction, marriage and partnerships may be either ideal and spiritually based relationships or confused situations in which one party deceives the other or the deception is mutual.

This aspect is unfavorable for contracts or legal procedures: It introduces many loopholes, unforeseen contingencies, and factors which do not appear on the surface. Only if there is mutual goodwill can such situations have a satisfactory outcome.

The natives can confuse or be confused by other people. However, in good horoscopes this conjunction can give intuitive sensitivity to the intentions, desires, and motivations of partners or the public at large. This sensitivity sometimes confers a subtle and disarming charm; whether it is used for selfish or altruistic purposes will depend on the horoscope viewed as a whole and on other aspects made to Neptune.

Neptune Conjunct Nadir (♆ ☌ Nadir)

This conjunction partakes of the same qualities as Neptune exalted in Cancer. It helps to bring spirituality into the home life. Often it signifies a mystical attunement to Mother Earth and the forces of nature.

If Neptune is afflicted, the home environment can be affected by peculiar conditions. The house may seem to be haunted, for example, or give the native an uneasy feeling. Whether this is the product of the native's own imagination does not matter as far as its effect upon him is concerned. The native may shut himself up in his home, or use it as a place for séances or psychic activities of some kind. In any event, the home is likely to have something unusual connected with it, even if not the proverbial skeleton in the closet.

Natives tend to live near the ocean or other large body of water. Those with afflicted horoscopes may live in institutions or spend the end of their lives in nursing homes or hospitals.

Conjunctions of Pluto

Pluto Conjunct North Node (♇ ☌ ☊)

This conjunction gives the native a special knack for seeing through prevailing social trends and provides the necessary drive and willpower to take advantage of them.

As is the case with Neptune conjunct North Node, there is an intuitive ability to understand the forces shaping present trends. However, in the case of Pluto, the native is much more deliberate and calculated in taking advantage of this ability. Whether it is used for selfish or for altruistic purposes depends upon the aspects of Pluto and the overall tenor of the horoscope.

On the negative side, this conjunction gives a dangerous tendency to try to manipulate social forces too large to be handled with safety. The natives may become entrapped or crushed by the weight of circumstances in which they have involved themselves. The affairs of their lives can get out of hand, with subsequent danger of collapse. (This is the tiger-by-the-tail aspect.) In what department of life this condition arises depends on the house position and house rulership of Pluto.

Pluto Conjunct South Node (♀ ♂ ☋)

This conjunction creates a condition in which the native's will is out of harmony with prevailing social trends. The tendency to initiate things at the wrong time and place generates resentment and misunderstanding.

The natives are forced to regenerate their lives without the help of others. Very often large social events which are beyond their personal control endanger or destroy their work and personal security.

On the positive side, this conjunction fosters self-reliance, resourcefulness, and the ability to survive under hardships.

According to some astrological philosophers, this conjunction indicates a past condition in which the natives initiated large-scale changes without regard to their effect on others' lives. Now they must learn how it feels to be the victim of circumstances beyond their control.

Pluto Conjunct Ascendant (♀ ♂ Asc.)

This conjunction in its highest aspect bestows the ability to see reality as energy. It gives a kind of X-ray vision that enables the natives to perceive the workings of the subtle forces of the universe, unknown to other people. These intuitive abilities are at least equal to those produced by Uranus or Neptune conjunct the Ascendant, but they are more consciously and deliberately used.

The conjunction signifies willpower and stamina, which come from an ability to tap the subtle forces of nature for self-regeneration. The natives are usually aware of the need to redeem themselves by applying the will to spiritual development.

At times they appear to be remote and unreachable because they are focusing their attention on a higher dimension of being. They tend to try to remake the circumstances in which they find themselves, and through the forces they can control, are able to exert a subtle and far-reaching influence upon their environments. They are aggressive, but not in the usual Mars sense, for they use secretive, and even superphysical, means of accomplishing their purposes.

If Pluto is afflicted, this conjunction results in obstinacy and self-will. However, even then, the natives' high level of consciousness produces a kind of spiritual detachment that helps prevent their being motivated by selfish personal gain.

It is important for these natives that Saturn and Mercury be well placed and strongly aspected. They will thus be provided with the necessary discipline and the mental capacity to make constructive use of the powers available to them.

The natives tend to have a very impersonal and universal attitude toward life and even toward themselves. However, these spiritual qualities will be manifested only in exceptional people whose overall level of development makes it possible for them to respond constructively to the high-frequency influence of this conjunction.

The major factor in determining whether the powers bestowed by the conjunction will be used for unselfish, spiritual purposes or for selfish, destructive ones is this overall evolutionary development as revealed by the underlying tenor of the horoscope. Many natives will simply be unable to respond to the possibilities offered them by this conjunction.

Those who have Pluto conjunct the Ascendant must continually regenerate the image they project to the world, especially in relationship to the affairs ruled by the house which has Scorpio on its cusp.

Pluto Conjunct Midheaven (♀ ♂ M.C.)

This conjunction bestows the tendency constantly to remake one's profession and public standing. Unless the overall horoscope is weak, this position will produce natives who achieve either fame or notoriety. Very often they will use highly sophisticated techniques to accomplish their professional tasks.

A scientific or occult profession may be indicated—perhaps magic, astrology, physics, or atomic physics. There is the ability to use intuitive and occult forces to influence people in positions of power. This is good if used with unselfish motives but can lead to underworld types of political activity if used selfishly.

Exceptionally developed natives can have an important spiritual mission to perform in some sphere of activity for the regeneration of the forces controlling society. This sphere is determined by Pluto's house rulership and by other aspects.

Some of the same perceptions of the workings of subtle forces of the universe which Pluto conjunct the Ascendant gives are found with this configuration. It provides the necessary spiritual impetus and insight for the natives to fulfill the roles of spiritual leaders. Their actions have subtle but far-reaching influences upon the world in which they move.

Pluto Conjunct Descendant (♀ ♂ Desc.)

This conjunction indicates the natives' tendency to dominate or remake a partnership or to have a partner who attempts to do the same. If carried too far, this tendency can lead to friction. Natives often have penetrating insight into the motives and characters of other people. And others may have the same insight in regard to them.

Natives are likely to make strong demands on their spouses. This conjunction necessitates the continual regeneration of close personal relationships, including marriage and partnerships. Such relationships can also undergo fundamental changes. Former friends can become envious or vice versa.

If its possibilities are properly expressed, this conjunction can raise close relationships to a higher spiritual plane. How the aspect will work depends upon the houses which have Scorpio, Aries, and Leo on the cusp, and the signs of Pluto's rulership, Scorpio, Aries, and the exaltation in Leo.

Pluto Conjunct Nadir (♀ ♂ Nadir)

This conjunction indicates a need for regeneration in the domestic life. How it should take place is designated by the houses where Scorpio, Aries, Leo are found, plus other aspects made to the conjunction. This regeneration applies especially to family relationships and, even more specifically, to relationships with parents. Conditions at the end of the native's life will indicate whether the Plutonian energy has been correctly used, as the flowering of higher spiritual faculties will take place in the later years.

In this conjunction, as with Neptune conjunct Nadir, the home can be a place of occult activity or have peculiar conditions connected with it. There is often an occult attunement to nature and to the resources found in the bowels of the earth. Persons who mine uranium ore will undoubtedly have Pluto in the Fourth House. The conjunction favors those whose profession is geology. Many dowsers have this aspect.

Conjunctions of the North Node

North Node Conjunct Ascendant (☊ ☌ Asc.)

This conjunction gives natives the ability to shape their personalities according to prevailing social trends. Although this favors popularity, it can also lead to superficiality. The natives are other-directed and base their actions not on any fundamental convictions but on the lowest common denominator of popularly accepted behavior.

In appearance, natives are likely to be tall and lanky. Their nature is cheerful, optimistic, jovial.

North Node Conjunct Midheaven (☊ ☌ M.C.)

This conjunction gives natives the ability to further their professional ambitions and public standing through their aptitude for harmonizing with present social trends. They are fortunate in meeting and gaining the assistance of people in prominent positions who will help to further their careers; they have the ability to be in the right place at the right time.

If the rest of the chart is weak, the natives' lives can become unbalanced —they may attain more power and responsibility than they have the knowledge or integrity to handle. This can be dangerous for the natives as well as for those whom their power affects.

The conjunction brings good fortune and, even in a heavily afflicted chart, will protect the natives from ruin and disaster.

North Node Conjunct Descendant (☊ ☌ Desc.)

This conjunction indicates good fortune through partnerships and public relations, and, if well aspected, through marriage. Although natives are personally detached from the prevailing social trends by virtue of having the South Node conjunct their Ascendant, they are able to view objectively the workings of these popular attitudes in their partners and the public at large and use this understanding to advantage in relating to them. On the negative side, there can be deliberate manipulation by others, who play upon their social conditionings.

North Node Conjunct Nadir (☊ ♂ Nadir)

This conjunction tends to bring success and increase through the natives' domestic lives. They are never without a roof over their heads, though it may be only temporary. They will benefit from parents and other members of the family unless other factors in the horoscope dictate otherwise.

The timing of events in the natives' lives with current social events will bring about good fortune, especially in the later years.

Conjunctions of the South Node

South Node Conjunct Ascendant (☋ ♂ Asc.)

The natives do not go out of their way to conform to accepted modes of social behavior. This attribute makes for strong individualism but not for popularity. At times these people are very serious in manner and can make anyone who expects overt signs of sociability feel uneasy. They are also subject to periodic moods of personal inhibition.

The natives tend to be short in stature and somewhat dwarfish in appearance. They occasionally have speech peculiarities as well.

South Node Conjunct Midheaven (☋ ♂ M.C.)

This conjunction often brings misfortune into natives' lives by thwarting their careers—the timing of events denies them the recognition they sometimes deserve. This is especially likely to be the case when Saturn transits in conjunction or in adverse aspect to this configuration.

In addition, the natives' long-held habits tend to put them out of harmony with the current trends of thinking that lead to public recognition, and often poor timing prevents their meeting people of influence who could further their careers.

On the positive side, the conjunction gives the capacity for hard work which leads to success in the long run. But often others reap the benefit of the natives' hard work.

South Node Conjunct Descendant (☋ ☌ Desc.)

This conjunction is unfavorable for the forming of partnerships and close personal relations—other people tend to be somewhat inhibited where the natives are concerned because of the latter's effusive outgoing qualities resulting from the North Node conjunct Ascendant. People suspect a lack of sincerity and feel the natives are merely trying to play a popularity game.

Natives can also be serious and calculating when dealing with partners and the public. Sometimes the partner is a burden or the public makes demands on the native's resources.

South Node Conjunct Nadir (☋ ☌ Nadir)

This conjunction brings heavy responsibilities into the natives' lives where their homes and families are concerned. Sometimes parents are a burden. The domestic sphere will limit the natives' expressions.

CHAPTER 13

The Sextiles

Sextiles of the Sun

Sun Sextile Moon (☉ ✳ ☽)

This aspect indicates the opportunity and the ability to establish friendship and communication with the opposite sex. It is favorable for harmony in marriage and friendship, for popularity, and for good relations with the public.

Unless other factors in the horoscope are contradictory, the natives understand how to be good parents. They have close ties of love and friendship with their families or partners' families. This feeling can also be extended to embrace love of the homeland, or patriotism.

The health and vitality of the natives are strengthened by this configuration. They tend to be at peace with themselves because of the harmonious flow of communication among the unconscious mind, the memory, and the conscious will. The harmony of emotions and will makes possible self-expression without internal conflicts.

Note: Mercury's orbit is so close to the Sun that it cannot form any aspect with it except a conjunction or parallel. Since Venus and Mercury are never more than 76° apart, they can form only conjunctions, sextiles, and parallels with each other. (This book deals solely with major aspects.)

Sun Sextile Mars (☉ ✳ ♂)

This sextile confers courage and energy, which, combined with its mental nature, produce intelligent and constructive enterprise. The natives have the ability to initiate projects. They can be good leaders and cooperate and communicate well with friends, associates, and groups.

Creativity, expressed in a positive manner, will work through the houses and signs occupied and ruled by Mars and the Sun. Opportunities will arise for constructive action in these departments whenever transits and progressions reinforce the sextile.

Strong willpower is characteristic of these natives, and they are champions of justice. They are decisive and energetic in accomplishing worthwhile objectives. Nothing is too much trouble for them.

If other factors in the horoscope are confirmatory, especially if the sextile is found in air or mutable signs, the natives possess clear, profound insights. They are courageous in the face of danger and show endurance in bearing pain or hardships.

Sun Sextile Jupiter (☉ ✳ ♃)

This sextile confers a generous and optimistic nature. The lives of the natives are protected; serious harm rarely comes to them—should it come, there is always a mitigating factor. Insight into constructive ways to overcome difficulties is characteristic.

The natives act in a way that benefits others as well as themselves. They generally have religious temperaments and engage in spiritual and philosophical pursuits. Because of their optimism and self-confidence, they never lose sight of their goals, generally accomplishing what they set out to do.

These people are charitable. They give a helping hand to those in need or to those less fortunate than themselves. As parents, they are kind and benevolent toward the family and are good providers.

The sextile confers excellent mental abilities which enable the natives to enjoy contemplative lives. They may prefer simple wholesome conditions to extreme wealth.

Persons with this aspect are fond of travel. As a rule, they do not travel just to change their environments but to gain knowledge of foreign peoples and cultures. They enjoy friendship and sharing with people from other countries.

Sun Sextile Saturn (☉ ✳ ♄)

This sextile confers patience and self-discipline, along with clarity and precision of thought. The natives are practical and methodical, with leadership ability along organizational and executive lines. They work hard to achieve their ambitions and are down-to-earth and honest in business dealings. They are loyal friends although they may be somewhat stern.

Often they have political ambitions and the desire, as well as the ability, to shoulder responsibilities. Their prudence and circumspection will preserve their health and secure their hard-won gains.

Sun Sextile Uranus (☉ ⚹ ♅)

This sextile confers originality and intuitiveness. The natives' strong willpower and perceptive mentality enables them to accomplish many things others cannot do. They are leaders of movements, inventors, thinkers, and reformers. Their magnetic quality inspires confidence and enthusiasm; their sense of the dramatic makes them accepted and obeyed.

They are broad-minded and humanitarian, with a stability and strength of character that brings them great popularity. Often they show interest in occult subjects in general and astrology in particular. They may be prominent members of occult or humanitarian organizations.

Sun Sextile Neptune (☉ ⚹ ♆)

This sextile promotes creativity and inspiration which can be manifested through art, religion, and mysticism. The natives have the ability to form vivid mental images and to translate these images into reality. Writers, artists, and musicians are likely to have this aspect.

The visions and imagination of the natives sometimes focus on practical areas such as empire building or acquiring wealth and power. Keen sensitivity to the joys and suffering of others, combined with mystical insights, provides them with a humanitarian outlook. There is also a love of animals.

Sun Sextile Pluto (☉ ⚹ ♀)

This sextile gives resourcefulness, strength of will, and the capacity to regenerate self and surroundings through the application of the will.

A subtle but powerful emanation of energy comes from people with this aspect, giving them more than ordinary endurance. Even when they are totally exhausted, they can recharge themselves, unconsciously perhaps, by drawing upon the high-frequency energies or prana of the universe. They may be interested in yoga, meditation, or the understanding and control of occult forces.

Sun Sextile North Node Trine South Node (☉ ✳ ☊ △ ☋)

This sextile to the Sun includes a trine of the South Node to the Sun. Any interpretation of the aspect must take this factor into consideration.

The natives have opportunities to work in harmony with the prevailing tide of social events. They have the ability to make constructive use of the existing moral and social traditions of their culture. Often this is manifested as social leadership, because they know how to win the support of other people by appealing to their social and ethical standards.

They may make valuable artistic commentaries, through drama, music, and art, on cultural conditions.

Sun Sextile South Node Trine North Node (☉ ✳ ☋ △ ☊)

This sextile to the Sun includes a trine of the North Node to the Sun. Interpretation of the aspect must take that factor into consideration.

This aspect has almost the same meaning as Sun sextile North Node trine South Node, except that a different house is emphasized. However, these natives are more intellectually directed.

There will be dramatic creativity, expressed within the bounds of the traditional social customs and patterns.

Sun Sextile Ascendant Trine Descendant (☉ ✳ Asc. △ Desc.)

A harmonious blend of basic consciousness and self-expression is indicated. The will is highly developed, especially along intellectual lines. The natives have an abundance of creative energy, harmoniously expressed.

These natives are enthusiastic, creative, and dramatic in their personal relationships, marriages, partnerships, and in their relations with the public. This aspect favors good fortune in marriage.

Sun Sextile Midheaven Trine Nadir (☉ ✳ M.C. △ Nadir)

The natives are skillful in expressing their ideas, especially where career and profession are concerned. They are enthusiastic, dramatic, and creative in their domestic life and family relationships.

They are also skillful in politics and possess executive ability and leadership potential.

Sextiles of the Moon

Moon Sextile Mercury (☽ ✳ ☿)

This sextile confers a good memory and practical mental ability. Mind and feeling are in accord. Thus, the natives are motivated to put their thoughts into action.

Matters relating to health and diet are planned and sensibly carried out. Since the natives are careful with personal hygiene, they are the epitome of neatness and cleanliness.

The domestic sphere is well organized, and family communications are good. Ideas are put to practical and profitable use; a good business sense accompanies this aspect. The natives are efficient in handling the small details of life and do not waste time.

There is conscious awareness of the thoughts and feelings of others. Thus, the natives instinctively know when to be tactful. In general, their emotions are well-regulated. Their ability to convey ideas simply and directly enables them to communicate easily with others. They make good lecturers and writers.

Moon Sextile Venus (☽ ✳ ♀)

This sextile is favorable for all matters pertaining to marriage and home life. Unless other factors in the horoscope are contradictory, the natives have happy and successful marriages.

Men with this aspect can empathize with women. Women possess the traditional feminine virtues of love, grace, sweetness, and domesticity.

Natives have productive imaginations, along with artistic ability. They are often good cooks and excellent housekeepers.

The intelligent awareness conferred by this sextile gives these natives ease in their social relations and communications with friends, neighbors, and groups. They are likely to have close ties with their families, especially with brothers and sisters. An affectionate nature goes with this aspect along with a charm that makes them popular with the opposite sex and with people in general.

Moon Sextile Mars (☽ ✳ ♂)

This sextile gives natives an abundance of energy and the emotional force necessary to carry actions through to completion.

They go into moneymaking enterprises or direct their energy to improving the home and domestic conditions. These natives will fight, if necessary, to protect their family and domestic sphere. Women natives have excellent health.

Moon Sextile Jupiter (☽ ✳ ♃)

This sextile produces generosity and emotional sympathy. The natives are charitable, especially where the family is concerned. Money and resources will be used in the home to make it a place of beauty and comfort.

There may be strong religious emotions which will make the natives devout and idealistic in their religious practices.

Contentment, optimism, and a cheerful disposition frequently accompany this aspect and contribute to the natives' success and sometimes to the accumulation of wealth. Their honesty, integrity, and genuine fondness for people also contribute to their business success. Often the business will involve real estate, food, housing, or products used in the home. Their instinctive knowledge of what brings comfort and contentment gives them the ability to choose products that will sell.

Because of their strong emotional ties to the home, these natives travel only when necessary. However, when they do travel to foreign countries, they are especially favored.

They possess strong imaginations, which, when combined with other aspects conferring mental capability, give creativity and insight into how to take advantage of the good things of life. This is a "green thumb" aspect, especially when it appears in fruitful signs.

Moon Sextile Saturn (☽ ✳ ♄)

This sextile gives patience and practicality in professional and domestic matters. It also indicates good organization, frugality, and integrity in these areas.

The natives always keep their financial affairs in order. Since they are level-headed rather than inspired, this is a better aspect for maintaining the status quo than for empire building. Sometimes wealth and position are inherited.

Even with the generally favorable nature of this aspect, unless other factors are evident in the horoscope, natives may lack "sparkle" and be subject to depression.

Moon Sextile Uranus (☽ ✶ ♅)

The natives are able to let go of the past.

This aspect gives quick emotional responses and intuitive rapport with others. The natives are able instinctively to take advantage of new opportunities that arise in daily life and respond to them in original ways. They possess a magnetic quality that infuses excitement and fun into everyday conditions. They have unique imaginations.

The home is often used as a place to entertain and carry on group activities, a situation that makes for friendly relations with family and parents. Sometimes the mother is an unusual person. Out-of-the-ordinary opportunities for advancement come through association with women. In any event, there will be friendships with the feminine sex.

Moon Sextile Neptune (☽ ✶ ♆)

This sextile is definitely an aspect of psychic potentialities. Often intuition plays a role in creating opportunity for financial and domestic progress. These mystic inclinations lead the natives to join fraternities and organizations of an occult nature. The aspect expands the imagination into the realms of the transcendental.

Unconscious promptings play a part in the natives' decision-making. Unconscious storing of knowledge from the distant past enables them to bring unusual information to light.

Keen emotional sensitivity is characteristic, facilitating empathy with other people. Often there are close ties to the family, although the individuals may not be conscious of them.

Moon Sextile Pluto (☽ ✶ ♀)

This sextile applies to the concept that "thoughts are things." The natives use their wills constructively to guide their imagination and in this way bring about the regeneration of both their practical affairs and their emotional lives. The added ability to renew vitality improves

stamina and health. The aspect also provides the talent to improve business methods and domestic life.

Being able to unclutter their lives, these natives can relinquish old emotional habits and initiate new ones, as well as find new uses for, or rid
themselves of, useless possessions.

Moon Sextile North Node Trine South Node (☽ ✶ ☊ △ ☋)

This combination is favorable for the effective timing of day-to-day
events and the handling of small matters in a way that is harmonious with
contemporary society. The natives' socially acceptable habit patterns make
them popular. Family background may bring them good fortune.

Moon Sextile Ascendant Trine Descendant (☽ ✶ Asc. △ Desc.)

This combination gives harmony between the natives' conscious self-
awareness and unconscious habit patterns, feelings, and emotions. It
bestows emotional balance.

In a man's horoscope, it indicates harmonious relationships with women
and therefore favors marriage. It also enables the native to work in harmony with other individuals or with the general public.

Moon Sextile Midheaven Trine Nadir (☽ ✶ M.C. △ Nadir)

This pattern is favorable for harmonious home life and family relationships. Natives are able to cooperate in professional matters and to get
along with employers or superiors. They can adjust to and accept routine
responsibility.

Sextiles of Mercury

Mercury Sextile Venus (☿ ✶ ♀)

This sextile gives grace and skill to thoughts, speech, and writing.
Literary talent, often in poetry, may be present. The aspect is also favorable for art and scholarship relating to art. The natives are skillful in
diplomacy because of their ability to communicate in a way which is
pleasing to others. They are likely to have calm dispositions, although this
attribute is more than ordinarily dependent on the rest of the horoscope.
The aspect lends a pleasing quality to the voice, which has a soothing

tone and is therefore good for singing. Many composers and songwriters have this configuration.

Mercury Sextile Mars (☿ ✳ ♂)

This sextile gives mental energy and a sharp intellect. Decisiveness is a prime virtue of the aspect. The natives say what they mean and mean what they say. They are able to plan their actions and are therefore effective and productive. Likewise, their ideas are put to use in practical action. In short, this is a good aspect for getting things done well.

The natives are skilled in making points understood, and they speak clearly and directly. Besides having scientific abilities and engineering talent, they are good strategists and are able to win games such as chess and bridge.

Mercury Sextile Jupiter (☿ ✳ ♃)

This sextile is favorable for all intellectual pursuits, especially those dealing with philosophy, religion, higher education, and law. The intuitive mind is well developed; the person is at home with abstract ideas.

Natives enjoy study and therefore generally do well in school and college. They are fond of travel—their curiosity and desire for breadth of experience makes them want to learn about foreign lands and cultures.

Very often they are writers, especially on religious and philosophic subjects. Being able to express themselves eloquently, they are good authors, lecturers, teachers. Their homes are usually places of intellectual activity. They can inspire and help those who are ill or in need through encouragement and sound suggestions.

Their optimistic outlook serves as the basis for a constructive way of life. Man brings into his life those conditions which he allows his mind to dwell upon, and emotional desires and actions generally follow thought patterns. This is the reason these natives attract so much good to themselves.

Mercury Sextile Saturn (☿ ✳ ♄)

This sextile generally indicates a disciplined mind. The capacity for organization applies to matters of job and profession since both the Sixth and the Tenth houses are involved.

The natives are inclined to use prudence and forethought in decision-making, communication, speech, and writing. They make good lecturers, writers, and teachers. Their exactness and discipline extend to the areas of health and hygiene. Often they have a talent for mathematics. When combined with other factors, this aspect can indicate scientific ability.

The natives tend to leave as little as possible to chance. They have a purpose behind every move and thought.

Mercury Sextile Uranus (☿ ✳ ♅)

This sextile indicates a quick, intuitive, inventive mind, together with a good memory. While it gives astrological and occult interests and abilities, it may also produce scientific leanings. People who work with electronics, physics, atomic energy, or other advanced areas of science often have this aspect. For full expression in these fields, favorable aspects to Saturn are helpful.

The natives always think for themselves and are very independent. Solutions to problems come to them in sudden flashes of inspiration: Logical reasoning has taken place in the unconscious mind, which then presents its conclusions to the conscious mind. These people often express themselves in an original, dramatic manner.

Mercury Sextile Neptune (☿ ✳ ♆)

This sextile gives intuitive insight and a fertile imagination. There is harmony and good communication between the conscious reasoning mind and the unconscious mind. The perceptions are keen and delicate and sometimes are manifested through clairvoyant faculties. Mental telepathy and the ability in general to sense the thoughts and motives of others are often found.

Photographers and people whose work requires imagination and creative inspiration benefit from this sextile. It also favors creative writers.

This is a good aspect for financial or military strategy, because the native can anticipate the opponent's moves. Natives may plan and work in secret, carrying out their intentions in such a way as to bypass all interference and opposition.

Mercury Sextile Pluto (☿ ✳ ♀)

The natives' keen mental penetration can manifest itself as an ability to understand causes and the energy behind the outward structure of things. This ability occurs in various fields, depending on other factors in the horoscope, but most often in science, physics, occultism, or areas related to the Eighth House such as insurance, inheritances, and taxes.

These people express themselves powerfully and effectively. An abundance of willpower allows the intellect to probe deeply into any field of interest. Also characteristic are creativity and intellectual originality.

Mercury Sextile North Node Trine South Node (☿ ✶ ☊ △ ☋)

This configuration gives the ability to plan and communicate in a way that is harmonious with prevailing cultural standards. The natives have a good understanding of the traditions and trends of their society. This gives them an advantage in gaining acceptance of their ideas.

Mercury Sextile Ascendant Trine Descendant (☿ ✶ Asc. △ Desc.)

This configuration gives facility of mental self-expression. The natives can make others understand them and their way of perceiving reality.

Harmony in communication minimizes misunderstanding and conflict and makes possible intelligent cooperation with friends, brothers, sisters, and partners. The natives are able to accomplish mutually agreed upon objectives.

Mercury Sextile Midheaven Trine Nadir (☿ ✶ M.C. △ Nadir)

This configuration is favorable for the intelligent planning of professional and domestic activities. The natives communicate successfully with people in high positions—their employers or others in authority. Thus, they are able to get people of importance in the world to accept their ideas. At the same time, they are able to communicate with members of their families and to intelligently work toward domestic comfort and harmony. Thus they can work out the proper balance between professional and domestic responsibilities.

Sextiles of Venus

Venus Sextile Mars (♀ ✶ ♂)

This sextile confers a happy, energetic disposition. It is favorable for harmony between the sexes, as well as emotional compatibility in marriage. The natives are socially inclined, vivacious, and lively.

This aspect favors artists, especially those who work in sculpture or other media requiring the use of tools. It also favors business enterprises concerned with artistic creations or merchandise. The popularity of the natives can be an asset in financial and professional dealings. These natives may become wealthy. They often gain emotionally and sometimes financially through marriage.

The muscular activity characteristic of Mars is given artistic expression (dancing, sports) by the influence of Venus.

Often the natives are impulsively generous, giving of themselves as well as of their possessions.

Venus Sextile Jupiter (♀ ✳ ♃)

This sextile indicates a happy disposition with strong social tendencies. It generally brings good fortune, ease, and comfort.

Artistic abilities and grace of expression often go with this aspect. The natives may be interested in religious forms of art. Business dealings in art and home furnishings are favored. Success can come through good taste and an understanding of what items are attractive to others.

The natives may gain emotionally, socially, and financially through marriage and partnerships. Their liking of people—and knowing how to get along with them—usually results in popularity and many friends. Although they frequently are kind and generous, this sextile does not necessarily confer profound understanding, but may do so when coupled with favorable Saturn and Neptune aspects.

Venus Sextile Saturn (♀ ✳ ♄)

This sextile figures prominently in the horoscopes of artists who have exceptional skill. (The same thing of course is true of the trine and the conjunction of these planets.) Saturn gives concrete expression to the Venusian aesthetic tendencies.

The natives are loyal to their friends and loved ones and serious and constant in the expression of their emotions. The aspect is favorable for an enduring marriage, provided other aspects involving the Seventh House do not contradict it.

Many of the positive aspects of Libra are to be found in this sextile because Saturn is exalted in Libra and Venus is its ruler.

There is the capacity to sacrifice personal happiness for the sake of duty or the happiness of others. In some cases grace, refinement, and good breeding are evident. The natives tend to be polite but formal in social conduct.

These people have the ability to make money through their professions and are generally skillful in business affairs. Since they are frugal and use good judgment in the field of finance, they always get their money's worth.

Venus Sextile Uranus (♀ ✷ ♅)

This sextile bestows scintillating, vivacious emotional expression. It is likely that the natives will be popular and have many friends.

Artistic and musical ability of highly original character is also likely; the natives are at least fond of music and art. Interest in some of the newer forms of electronic art is highly probable. Natives make money in unusual ways, often through cooperative or group endeavors. Often their businesses are unusual, involving art, electronics, or science. People who work for radio, television, or recording companies may have this aspect.

Very often the natives fall in love suddenly and are likely also to marry suddenly. They require a great deal of emotional freedom, resisting conventional patterns of romance. They are usually fortunate in matters of friendship, love, marriage.

Venus Sextile Neptune (♀ ✷ ♆)

This sextile gives keen artistic imagination, often expressed through music and art of a spiritually uplifting nature. It embodies many of the positive attributes of the sign Pisces, where Venus is exalted and Neptune the ruler. The emotions and sympathies have a religious trend, giving the natives compassion and understanding.

A sense of the sublime is evident; it manifests itself in a craving for ethereal beauty. There is gentleness in social expression, conveying grace. The natives tend to form alliances, friendships, or marriages with those of a mystical, psychic character. They seek an ideal love relationship.

In a weak horoscope the natives can be indolent, relying too heavily on the kindness or help of others.

Venus Sextile Pluto (♀ ✷ ♇)

This sextile gives strong feeling and keen perception. The natives understand the transforming power of love. They also can help others in understanding how to raise relationships to a higher level. Dynamic, original creativity goes with this sextile, especially in art or music.

Often with this aspect the native feels that his marriage was ordained from the beginning of time.

An understanding of the laws of harmony and balance as they relate to creative prinicples is felt and sometimes clearly articulated by these natives. In some cases, when Mercury, Saturn, and Uranus are strong, this aspect can contribute to scientific ability.

Venus Sextile North Node Trine South Node (♀ ⚹ ☊ △ ☋)

This configuration bestows social grace and good manners according to the native's culture. Generally the natives know how to use their charm to gain the approval of their society and of the established institutions with which they must deal.

Often they possess good timing in relation to financial affairs, public relations, partnerships, social activities, and marriage. This aspect especially favors business because of the natives' ability to keep in step with current vogues and economic trends.

Venus Sextile Ascendant Trine Descendant (♀ ⚹ Asc. △ Desc.)

This configuration gives harmony to the native's personal self-expression, and the social graces needed to gain public favor and to make a fortunate marriage and good partnerships.

The natives are natural diplomats and are sometimes called peacemakers. Their cheerful disposition generates a joyous response in others. If other factors in the horoscope confirm it, artistic and musical talent can be present.

Venus Sextile Midheaven Trine Nadir (♀ ⚹ M.C. △ Nadir)

This configuration gives diplomatic abilities in professional matters. It brings harmony and love into the native's family life. There is contentment in marital, home, and professional affairs. The relationship with the parents is likely to be a close one.

Love of beauty in nature characterizes the aspect. These people often grow roses and other flowers in an effort to make their surroundings more pleasant. The home is usually tastefully and artistically decorated. In some cases, the career will be related to artistic pursuits.

Sextiles of Mars

Mars Sextile Jupiter (♂ ✳ ♃)

This sextile bestows enthusiasm and energy in work, self-expression, and self-improvement.

The natives are optimistic when carrying on their activities and do not acknowledge defeat. They can be generous in a practical way. Their religious inclinations are also practical. They will work strenuously on behalf of those who are underprivileged or unfortunate; they often engage in missionary endeavors and are especially good at working with young people. Seldom does one find a lazy person with this aspect. The natives usually achieve some degree of success and material comfort.

Mars Sextile Saturn (♂ ✳ ♄)

This sextile manifests its best qualities where strenuous work and physical discipline are required. Endurance and fortitude are the prime virtues of this aspect. Precision in workmanship is favored.

Mechanical abilities are often part of the general capacity for careful work.

The natives use their energy in the most practical and efficient way. Saturn controls the impulsiveness of Mars while Mars overcomes the fearfulness characteristic of Saturn, producing courage. The sextile between these two planets does not make for a charming personality; the natives have a Spartan attitude toward life and often give the impression of coldness and austerity.

Mars Sextile Uranus (♂ ✳ ♅)

This sextile signifies capacity for rapid, decisive action and bestows willpower and courage. Many of the positive qualities of the sign Scorpio, where Mars rules and Uranus is exalted, are evident. Unique accomplishments may bring the natives fame and high position. Sometimes there is a do-or-die attitude, even to the extent that the will is too powerful for the body that must house it. In any event, the natives have forceful dispositions and know exactly what they want. Having a great deal of nervous energy, they are inclined to work hard and to accomplish their tasks with originality.

Often mechanical abilities and electronic and scientific interests accompany this aspect. It especially favors those who are involved with aviation.

Mars Sextile Neptune (♂ ✳ ♆)

This sextile gives a superphysical energy that can be used for healing or occult work. Sometimes there are clairvoyant faculties or strong personal magnetism.

The natives are skilled in carrying out endeavors in secret or behind the scenes, thus bypassing obstacles and opposition. Like Mercury sextile Neptune, this aspect favors strategists, especially those who plan military maneuvers. It also favors performing artists such as dancers and actors, who must use their bodies in subtle, imaginative ways, as well as film makers and photographers.

The natives are usually honest and in good control of their emotions. They can detect insincerity in others and are not easily fooled.

Often this aspect encourages systems of exercise or some more inclusive kind of physical culture, such as hatha-yoga.

Mars Sextile Pluto (♂ ✳ ♀)

This sextile gives tremendous energy, courage, and willpower. The natives have a way of consciously or unconsciously using natural forces to bring about changes that will benefit them.

The sextile provides the opportunity to raise the affairs of whatever house Pluto rules to a higher level of expression.

All Pluto sextiles cause regenerative changes that heighten the natives' awareness. Since Mars rules the muscular system, there is often an interest in physical culture, notably in hatha-yoga as a means of regeneration.

Mars Sextile North Node Trine South Node (♂ ✳ ☊ △ ☋)

This configuration gives the natives the ability to act at the right time to further their well-being and improve their relationship to society. Their activities gain the cooperation and approval of their social order, and they are able to find support for their endeavors to bring about constructive change.

Mars Sextile Ascendant Trine Descendant (♂ ⚹ Asc. △ Desc.)

This configuration is favorable for initiating actions that inspire cooperation, especially in the contexts of marriage partnerships and public dealings. At times other people will create opportunities for constructive action by the natives or vice versa.

The natives are usually frank, direct, and forceful in their self-expression and in dealings with others. This attribute brings them approval and respect.

Mars Sextile Midheaven Trine Nadir (♂ ⚹ M.C. △ Nadir)

This configuration is favorable for constructive action in professional and domestic affairs. There are opportunities for career advancement, which in turn leads to fulfillment in the home. Sometimes the home is used as a base for carrying on professional activities.

Sextiles of Jupiter

Jupiter Sextile Saturn (♃ ⚹ ♄)

This sextile gives an intelligent balance between expansion and consolidation in the natives' affairs. In business they will use Saturnian caution, prudence, and good organization combined with Jupiterian optimism, enthusiasm, and expansion. They are thus able to carry through plans and fulfill their obligations, earning respect in their business and profession. They are usually honest and possess integrity in their dealings.

There is often an interest in philosophy and religion along traditional lines.

The natives will help people in need. There is generally wisdom and discrimination where the help is given. However, in turn, they expect the recipients to help themselves.

The natives desire a stable home life and are often "pillars of the community."

These natives are likely to be prominent in politics. They take a long-range view of life, and work toward a goal. They make good lawyers if other factors in their chart are not contradictory.

Jupiter Sextile Uranus (♃ ✳ ♅)

This sextile gives the ability to make constructive use of new conditions. Often there is an interest in new forms of religious expression or in the religious application of occult sciences in general. Prophetic vision and extraordinary insight into the future may be evidenced if the rest of the horoscope is similarly inclined. The natives make good astrologers because of the foresight bestowed by the aspect.

People with this aspect are usually optimistic and kindly disposed toward their fellow men. Therefore, they have many friends and are well liked. They like to entertain in the home. They tend to be altruistic, being active in humanitarian organizations. They may belong to groups of an unusual nature. They realize hopes and wishes through being open-minded and optimistic and are lucky in sudden, unexpected ways.

There is an ability to profit financially through new industries and opportunities that are created by scientific advancement.

Jupiter Sextile Neptune (♃ ✳ ♆)

This sextile gives a mystical, expansive, and kind—but not necessarily practical—disposition.

There can be an active imagination which expresses itself best through religion, philosophy, and art. However, the highly emotional nature of this aspect is such that the affairs of the houses that Jupiter and Neptune rule may be dominated by emotional considerations. For this reason, the natives will probably lack the discipline and common sense to make use of their altruistic inspirations, unless a good Mercury and Saturn bestow these qualities. There is often a good deal of sentimentality or plain gush.

The positive expression of this aspect is the natives' ability to raise their emotional nature to a level of universal altruism, reaching out to those who are unfortunate or in need. They often obtain help from their friends and relatives even when they do not appear to merit it.

In extreme cases they will seek seclusion in a religious retreat, such as a monastery.

Jupiter Sextile Pluto (♃ ⚹ ♇)

This sextile gives the opportunity for spiritual regeneration through philosophy, higher education, religious practices, and constructive efforts aimed at bettering human conditions. The natives can tap powerful spiritual forces through prayer and meditation. Divine Providence opens the way for creative self-expression when the cause is for the good of all.

This aspect gives wisdom and insight if other factors in the horoscope are confirmatory. It also signifies ability for action and creative self-expression in religious, philosophic, and philanthropic endeavors. Pluto gives power to all the beneficent qualities of Jupiter, rendering them effective and far-reaching.

Jupiter Sextile North Node Trine South Node (♃ ⚹ ☊ △ ☋)

This configuration is favorable for all expansive endeavors requiring the cooperation and approval of prevailing social attitudes and institutions. The natives are often closely involved in religious activities which tend to be along conventional lines. There is generally a good sense of timing in business and promotional matters.

Jupiter Sextile Ascendant Trine Descendant (♃ ⚹ Asc. △ Desc.)

This configuration favors grace of personal self-expression and popularity with the public. The natives are able to gain the support and cooperation of others because of their generous, optimistic outlook on life. They are usually fortunate in marriage partnerships and dealings with the public. Since they are capable of arousing enthusiasm in others, they may be good promoters.

Jupiter Sextile Midheaven Trine Nadir (♃ ⚹ M.C. △ Nadir)

This configuration favors professional success and an excellent reputation, as well as good fortune in domestic and family affairs. Career preferment and public standing will make possible an opulent home environment.

The natives are generally honest and generous in their professional dealings, thus attracting popularity especially with those in power.

They will have an expansive, religious attitude toward their family responsibilities.

Sextiles of Saturn

Saturn Sextile Uranus (♄ ✳ ♅)

This sextile is favorable for endeavors that require the ability to apply original ideas in a practical way. It represents the true freedom and opportunities that result from self-discipline and from conscientiously discharging one's responsibilities.

The natives make loyal, dependable friends who can be relied upon for truthfulness as well as good advice in finding constructive solutions to problems.

Activity in groups and organizations is due to the strong Eleventh House connotation of the aspect, expressing, as it does, many of the positive qualities of Aquarius, which Uranus and Saturn rule. This sextile often gives considerable mathematical and scientific aptitude and confers the ability to combine advanced ideas with system and discipline. Sometimes political ability in government or business is evidenced.

Saturn Sextile Neptune (♄ ✳ ♆)

This sextile bestows the capacity to discipline and focus the imaginative faculties—to give practical form to inspiration. It is also favorable for meditation, because Saturn confers the ability to concentrate so that the inspiration of Neptune is unobstructed. There is efficient organization and practicality in occult or metaphysical group endeavors.

This aspect affords excellent tactical and strategic talents because of the insight it confers. Natives are especially good at making career plans and carrying them out in secrecy. Often they work behind the scenes in some manner. They have a gift for getting to the bottom of mysteries and ferreting out secret information.

The natives are idealistic, and their high standards enable them to be honest in handling responsibilities and discharging duties. They demand the same of others. They are compassionate, particularly toward those in need, giving help in practical and discriminating ways.

Saturn Sextile Pluto (♄ ✳ ♀)

This sextile gives the ability to organize and control the power of the will.

The natives have opportunities to regenerate themselves through discipline and hard work. Highly developed people may be interested in the systematic, organized use of occult forces, as in magic. This aspect can confer scientific talents in physics and mathematics. The natives are often ambitious and can use power wisely and decisively.

The effect of this aspect is not strong unless the rest of the horoscope is of a similar tenor.

Saturn Sextile North Node Trine South Node (♄ ✳ ☊ △ ☋)

This configuration is favorable for those whose professional goals require the approval of traditional social customs and institutions. The natives are able to win support for their endeavors, especially from established conservative members of society and the institutions they represent.

Saturn Sextile Ascendant Trine Descendant (♄ ✳ Asc. △ Desc.)

This configuration gives the natives serious dispositions. Generally they have the respect and support of their partners and the public because of their integrity, reliability, and sense of responsibility. A great deal of discipline and good organization goes with this configuration. The natives possess the virtues of adherence to principle and a strong sense of justice. Even when they are considered somewhat cold and impersonal, they are respected for the above reasons.

Saturn Sextile Midheaven Trine Nadir (♄ ✳ M.C. △ Nadir)

This configuration gives the natives the ability to stabilize their domestic lives and steadily improve their professional standing through forethought, discipline, and sustained effort.

A steady climb through the ranks of an established organization characterizes the configuration. The natives' ability to systematize and work hard gains the confidence of their superiors, making it possible for them to advance their careers and at the same time secure their home life. These natives often carry on the traditions of their parents and ancestors.

Sextiles of Uranus

Uranus Sextile Neptune (♅ ✳ ♆)

This sextile indicates a propensity for idealism. Since it remains in orb for a long period of time and affects a whole generation, it indicates an opportunity for the people of this generation to develop and expand spiritual consciousness and create a more utopian way of life.

The effects of this aspect will not be pronounced unless Uranus and Neptune are angular or heavily aspected. Should Uranus or Neptune be conjunct on one of the angular house cusps, then real talent, and in some cases genius, can be found.

In general, this sextile gives interest in occult and mystical pursuits. There is a tendency to join fraternal groups. Because of the mental connotation of sextile aspects, the native is likely to write or study books on occult or mystical subjects.

Artistic ability may be evidenced—of a type that reflects a highly developed imagination. Often there is love of music and all experiences that expand the consciousness.

Uranus Sextile Pluto (♅ ✳ ♇)

People with this aspect have the opportunity to advance scientifically and spiritually through the discovery and application of laws pertaining to the subtle electrical, atomic, and psychic forces of nature.

They receive sudden intuitions on how to expand and utilize their present knowledge to improve the status quo and bring about constructive revolutionary changes in their environment. They make discoveries in science and metaphysics, actively seeking higher knowledge and an understanding of intuitive revelations.

Uranus Sextile North Node Trine South Node (♅ ✳ ☊ △ ☋)

This configuration indicates an intuitive ability to anticipate and take advantage of sudden changes in public opinions. In other words, the person has a finger on the public pulse.

The natives make good social reformers—they have both their desire

and the ability to change social attitudes and the institutions that reflect
them. They can capture the public imagination by surprise effects and
unusual methods.

Uranus Sextile Ascendant Trine Descendant (♅ ✳ Asc. △ Desc.)

This aspect produces natives who can express themselves and relate
to others in unusual ways. Because of their original style of self-expression they stand out from the crowd and are sought after as persons of
interest. They have intuitive ability in dealing with others and evoking
their cooperation. They can be relied upon to do and say out of the ordinary things. Sometimes marriage and other partnerships occur suddenly
in unique ways.

Uranus Sextile Midheaven Trine Nadir (♅ ✳ M.C. △ Nadir)

This configuration gives exceptional talent in the native's chosen profession and in capturing the support of people in prominent positions.
Friends help further his professional advancement. When combined with
other favorable influences, this configuration signifies a successful political
career.

It also helps the natives create their own distinctive domestic environment. They often entertain their friends at home. One or both of the
parents may be unusual.

Sextiles of Neptune

Neptune Sextile Pluto (♆ ✳ ♀)

This aspect is of extremely long duration, especially at the present
time in history, because of a peculiar timing of the eccentric orb of Pluto
with reference to the orbit of Neptune. These two planets have been
more or less continuously in sextile aspect for at least thirty years as
of this date—April, 1973. Therefore, this aspect affects world karma and
mass destiny far more than it influences individual natives. It indicates a
tremendous opportunity for spiritual advancement in world civilization.

We are fortunate to have this aspect at such a critical juncture of
history. The present atomic age can bring about world utopia with

prosperity and happiness for the entire human race, or it can mean the nearly total destruction of civilization. Humanity must take the occasion to express universal love (Neptune) with power and to utilize fully and creatively the awesome Plutonian potentials which science has made available. Our future depends on how many of the human family can constructively respond to the high-frequency vibrations of these two outermost planets.

In individual horoscopes, should Neptune or Pluto be angular and heavily aspected by other planets, this configuration will indicate unusual occult, intuitive, scientific, and aesthetic abilities.

Neptune Sextile North Node Trine South Node (Ψ ✳ ☊ △ ☋)

This configuration indicates the intuitive ability to harmonize with and subtly influence existing social customs and institutions. The natives instinctively ride the currents of public mood, opinion, and action. Their understanding of cultural trends allows them to circumvent this influence on their lives if they so desire—always by subtle evasion rather than open confrontation.

Neptune Sextile Ascendant Trine Descendant (Ψ ✳ Asc. △ Desc.)

This configuration gives the natives a subtle but charming personality and a magnetic ability to gain the support of others. In highly evolved types, the trait will be manifested as sympathy and spiritual love. However, in some individuals, it may merely mean empathy with others, which involves influencing or being influenced by them. The natives are extremely sensitive to all factors entering into their relationships with partners and with the public. They are, therefore, in a good position to react intelligently in such relationships.

This aspect is a general indicator of clairvoyance or other extrasensory abilities. Sometimes the natives know what another person is going to say before he has had an opportunity to voice his thoughts.

Neptune Sextile Midheaven Trine Nadir (Ψ ✳ M.C. △ Nadir)

This configuration gives the natives a sensitive awareness of hidden factors affecting their careers and ambitions, as well as the ability to intuit the responses of their employers or people in positions of authority.

They can exert leadership and influence policy in such a subtle way as to avoid opposition and lead others into acquiescence.

Their sensitivity in domestic relationships creates harmony in the home and rapport with the family group. Sometimes they live near the ocean or another body of water.

Sextiles of Pluto

Pluto Sextile North Node Trine South Node (♀ ✳ ☊ △ ☋)

This configuration gives the ability to exert a transforming influence on social trends, customs, events, and institutions. There is a penetrating awareness of the motivating forces behind social institutions and cultural attitudes. For someone involved in politics, this is a favorable aspect to have.

The natives know how to manipulate the hopes and fears of their societies. Whether this skill is used selfishly or altruistically depends on the rest of the horoscope.

Pluto Sextile Ascendant Trine Descendant (♀ ✳ Asc. △ Desc.)

This configuration indicates awareness of personal consciousness and a corresponding awareness of the consciousness of others. Thus the natives are able to enter dynamically into meaningful relationships that can markedly affect the larger social milieu.

The natives have good powers of concentration. Combined with other similar configurations in the horoscope, this aspect often indicates spiritual insight or clairvoyance. There is the ability to act decisively, both individually and in cooperation with others.

Pluto Sextile Midheaven Trine Nadir (♀ ✳ M.C. △ Nadir)

This configuration indicates considerable professional skill and ambition. They are always looking for ways to improve their chosen careers. They are able to gain the cooperation and support of people in positions of authority.

They have firm concepts of how to organize their domestic affairs. They wield a harmonious yet transforming influence on the domestic situation, which they are continually trying to improve.

CHAPTER 14

The Squares

Squares of the Sun

Sun Square Moon (☉ □ ☽)

The effects of this adverse aspect are not as specific as those of squares from the Sun to the planets. However, the aspect does create a conflict between the conscious will and the unconscious and inherited habit patterns. Self-expression is hampered by these habits, and the disharmony causes them emotional insecurity.

The family and domestic lives of the natives also tend to block creative self-expression. Their early family conditions can cause difficulty in understanding and getting along with the opposite sex.

Sun Square Mars (☉ □ ♂)

Natives with this aspect tend to be their own worst enemies because of their overly vigorous, impulsive behavior. Obstacles to their self-expression in action generate frustration and anger, which in turn cause them to try to achieve their desires by force. This tendency arouses resentment in others, who consider them brash and egotistical.

Natives who have this aspect must work to control it by thinking before they act and by restraining their anger and aggressiveness while cultivating tact and diplomacy. They must learn that only with patience can they accomplish what they want without contention.

Very often they waste energy in arguing. If the aspect is found in cardinal signs, it is manifested as impulsiveness and sudden temper. In fixed signs, it indicates stubbornness and a tendency to hold grudges.

In common signs, it results in irritability and the frittering away of energy in useless activities.

Sun Square Jupiter (☉ □ ♃)

This square often signifies ill-considered extravagance in self-expression. The natives want to accomplish too much too fast, without sufficient discipline or forethought.

Their self-image can be unrealistic and exaggerated and can therefore frustrate them when they attempt to broaden their self-expression. This often leads in turn to egotism as a defense mechanism. The natives must learn patience by cultivating the Saturnian virtues and establishing a solid basis of experience and self-discipline from which to reach self-actualization. This may take time and effort, but it will yield success in the long run.

This aspect can also indicate a tendency toward extravagance and ostentation in the affairs controlled by the houses and signs which the Sun and Jupiter occupy and rule.

The natives should guard against foolish optimism and ill-considered efforts at self-development. They are likely to be indiscriminately generous but frequently with ulterior motives. Restlessness and the desire for change and travel can be detrimental to them.

Sun Square Saturn (☉ □ ♄)

This square places obstacles in the way of the native's self-expression and often indicates a life of hardship and drudgery. Only if there are many other favorable aspects in the chart, or a good aspect from Jupiter to the Sun, can the effects of this negative configuration be offset.

The obstacles which frequently threaten professional and romantic fulfillment can sometimes be overcome through extremely hard work and severe discipline. Everything is earned the hard way; nothing comes freely. Prolonged and repeated frustrations in self-expression lead to a pessimistic outlook.

Because of the oppressive influence of this aspect, the natives are held in check and forced to learn some very difficult lessons relating to signs and houses which Saturn and the Sun occupy and rule. If they are strong, this aspect builds character; but it can also lead to a sour disposition, expressed in a Spartan outlook. It can also be manifested in rigidity, and the natives may be too traditional in their approach to problems. They must cultivate the virtues of optimism and cheerfulness.

This aspect does not favor the health or well-being of the native's children; usually the eldest suffers in some way. The natives may be subject to fatigue. There may be illness, broken bones, bad teeth, or some other chronic health problem.

Sun Square Uranus (☉ □ ♅)

This square indicates a propensity for erratic behavior, eccentricity, and unwise action. The natives have originality, but often their ideas are impractical, or else they do not possess sufficient perseverance, training, experience, and discipline to carry them out. They tend to work in spurts rather than steadily.

Self-will and an inclination to self-dramatization, combined with a dislike for routine procedure, can sometimes be their undoing. Irrational behavior due to nervous tension at critical times can cause the natives to destroy what has taken them a long time to create. Pride and desire for freedom at all cost may cause them to ignore good advice.

These natives can be leaders of groups and organizations, especially those that espouse human brotherhood. They will have many friendships, but often reserved for people who are willing to be their ardent followers.

They can make vehement enemies when their antagonism is aroused through some real or imagined injustice. These tendencies are not manifested all the time, but unfortunately they often appear at critical junctures in the natives' lives. Thus they impair their chances of reaping the rewards of their efforts.

Sun Square Neptune (☉ □ ♆)

This is the aspect of self-deception par excellence. If the natives are mystically inclined, they often consider themselves the chosen vessels of some Master or Divine Being. This belief is often the result of an unconscious desire for importance.

These persons can be vessels in a pure sense, but only if the rest of the horoscope shows a good mentality, humility, and realistic practicality. A well-developed Mercury and Saturn will do much to offset the negative effects of this square.

Very often peculiar emotional desires and romantic tendencies are indicated, which can range from platonic love to the most morbid and debased physical type of sensuality. Secret love affairs and scandal leave confusion in their wake.

The imagination is often overworked and feeds the natives' desires to the point where they indulge in self-destructive acts. Severe weaknesses in character can then develop, distorting perception of reality. But these difficulties will be manifested only if the rest of the horoscope provides indications of a similar nature.

Usually there is a tendency toward escapism as a means of avoiding individual responsibility and discipline. A well-developed Saturn will offset this.

Utmost caution should be exercised to avoid involvement in cults and occult mystical activities of a spurious sort. The motives and character of people who interact with the native emotionally should be carefully and objectively scrutinized.

Unstable and unwise financial speculation should be avoided, since get-rich-quick schemes will end in disaster.

Sun Square Pluto (☉ □ ♀)

This square produces ambition for power and a tendency for the natives to impose their will on others. They are forceful and domineering, with a desire to make people over. This desire should rather be turned inward. Their might-makes-right attitude can cause resentment and dislike in others. There is a tendency to be overly aggressive with the opposite sex.

The signs and houses involved in the square show in which departments it will operate.

Sun Square Nodes (☉ □ ☊ ☋)

This square causes the natives' attempts at individual expression to be out of phase with the current of larger events in their society. Sometimes they hold back when they should go forward, or vice versa.

Circumstances in their lives and in their society tend to block their self-expression and creative endeavors. They find themselves poorly adjusted in their social and romantic lives.

Sun Square Ascendant and Descendant (☉ □ Asc., Desc.)

This square creates a conflict between the native's individuality and the way he presents himself to the world. It is hard for him to project himself as he actually is. Therefore, his outward image, which represents the "now" consciousness, and the Sun, which represents the potential for self-expression, tend to be at cross-purposes. There is also a conflict between spiritual consciousness and personality expression.

The native is likely to propel himself into action in an inharmonious manner. Since he tries to dominate others and has difficulty making himself understood, he will have trouble relating to the public, a partner, and a spouse. He will have to sacrifice his individuality if he wishes to gain the acceptance of others.

Sun Square Midheaven and Nadir (☉ □ M.C., Nadir)

This square tends to create a conflict between the natives and those in authority—their immediate superiors, employers, the government, or their parents. They are likely to encounter obstacles in realizing their ambitions and to have difficulties where their public reputation is concerned. In some way they must sacrifice their individual self-expression in order to gain professional success and public approval.

In some cases this aspect indicates ambition for power.

The natives can also experience conflict in their family and domestic situation and may feel uncomfortable in their homes. Domestic problems often aggravate career problems and vice versa.

Squares of the Moon

Moon Square Mercury (☽ □ ☿)

This square creates a nervous disposition with a tendency for the unconscious mind to interfere with conscious, reasoning processes. The natives' thinking may be so much tied to the past that it interferes with objectivity and open-mindedness.

There can be preoccupation with trivialities and emotional whims, which stand in the way of more worthwhile mental pursuits. Maudlin sentimentality can interfere with clear-headedness.

Some natives talk incessantly about things of no consequence, dissipating the energy of everyone concerned. They can be taken up with family and domestic affairs to the point of boring others with endless chatter about them. This is especially true of women if the square is found in mutable signs.

The natives can be sympathetic toward their friends and are loyal to those they love, but they have a hard time communicating with the public and can be misrepresented or slandered.

This square can create difficulties in the nervous or digestive system, or the fluids of the body and the nerves that control them.

Moon Square Venus (☽ ☐ ♀)

This square tends to create financial and social problems in the domestic sphere.

The affections are bestowed indiscriminately, leading to problems in love and unhappiness in marriage. The natives are too trusting of spouses or partners and as a result are taken advantage of. Unwise romantic and sexual involvements are characteristic. Sometimes this square causes difficulties or delays in getting married, especially if there are confirming Saturnian indications.

Sentimentality and emotionalism may make the natives vulnerable to manipulation by others. Unhappiness and emotional stress are likely to be connected with early childhood and home life.

The natives are sometimes unlucky or careless with money.

Moon Square Mars (☽ ☐ ♂)

This square indicates an emotionally volatile nature—the natives easily become upset and lose their temper. Their tendency to take things too personally leads to emotional outbursts.

They are sometimes too independent for their own good. They want to make their own way in life and resent interference. They have domestic problems and disagreements with their parents. All this can have an adverse effect on their professional standing, reputation, and ambitions.

Being forceful and aggressive, they often have problems getting along with women. Alcohol is especially dangerous for them, because of their inclination to lose emotional control.

Sometimes this square brings poor health in the form of ulcers or stomach problems. Those who suppress their anger, so that it builds up inside, are particularly vulnerable to emotionally linked physical disorders. This characteristic may not be apparent until major transits or progressions activate the square.

Moon Square Jupiter (☽ □ ♃)

This is an aspect of emotional excess. It particularly represents the overly indulgent mother. There is a tendency to be foolishly generous by befriending people who have a good sob story; often these natives lose money as a result. Generosity is a noble virtue, but it must be tempered with discrimination in order to accomplish good results.

The natives are inclined to be imprudent and extravagant sometimes because they desire an ostentatious home environment. Problems with religion may be due to the natives' disagreement with the beliefs of their parents and family. They may be either agnostics or fanatics. In any event, balance in religious attitudes is lacking. Whatever Jupiter does is done in a big way; therefore, this aspect leads to emotional extremism in some form.

There can be wanderlust and unsteadiness of purpose, and a tendency to eat too much, which often results in excess weight. In extreme cases, excessive fluids in the body create a flabby, unhealthy appearance.

The natives may encounter misfortune of some kind in foreign countries. If the general horoscope lacks strength, there is also a propensity for laziness. If the natives are wealthy, this aspect can lead to idleness and luxury. Sometimes it creates grandiose fantasies.

Moon Square Saturn (☽ □ ♄)

This square generates a condition of melancholia and unhappiness. Unless other factors in the horoscope indicate the contrary, the natives have a bleak view of life and lack emotional vitality. Very often they have a mother complex or some other inhibition stemming from early childhood experiences: they tend to be emotional prisoners of the past. Distressing memories block the possibilities of finding happiness in the present. Others may shun them because of their negative outlook. They are depressing, lackluster, moody. Thus, they tend to isolate themselves, creating a self-perpetuating cycle of misfortune and loneliness.

Because the Moon progresses at approximately the same rate that

Saturn transits, Saturn can remain in square aspect to the Progressed Moon for a long period in the natives' lives, placing a perpetual dark cloud over their heads. Sometimes the disappointments brought by this square generate a sour, austere attitude or lead to a martyr complex.

The natives should force themselves to forget the past and face each new day with faith and optimism. Only in this way can they project a positive self-image which will inspire confidence and friendliness in others.

This square often creates difficulty in dealing with women since the natives, especially the males, find themselves awkward and shy in the presence of the opposite sex. It may lead to a general inferiority complex. The natives are their own worst enemies, lacking confidence in themselves and failing to inspire confidence in others.

Moon Square Uranus (☽ ☐ ♅)

This square produces a strong and ingenious imagination and exceptional talent. However, there is a tendency toward emotional perversity and sudden inexplicable changes in moods. Sometimes the natives become bored and throw over one activity for another that promises more excitement and adventure.

Often there are external misfortunes in their lives—accidents, sudden ill health, involvement in social or natural catastrophes or in an unstable domestic situation. Frequent changes of residence are characteristic; something unusual and disruptive may affect the home life.

Sometimes friends and associates upset the feelings of the natives, or vice versa. They seek that which is unusual and mentally stimulating and as a rule take a fresh view of the world. There is a strong desire to throw over the conditions of the past, thus creating scope and opportunity for emotional excitement.

Moon Square Neptune (☽ ☐ ♆)

This aspect indicates confusion and a tendency to become immersed in fantasies, resulting in the lack of a grip on reality.

Domestic life is likely to be muddled and confused, the home environment disorderly or unclean.

This square frequently indicates emotional indulgence which is manifested in addiction, often to drugs or alcohol.

Persons with this square often express mediumistic and psychic tendencies which can be distorted by low-level astral plane influences. Sometimes the outcome is cultism, delusions of grandeur, and unrealistic ambitions.

If the rest of the horoscope agrees, there can be psychosis or delusional insanity, resulting in complete submersion of the natives' conscious ego in the morass of the unconscious, and consequent institutionalization. Natives should be especially careful of dabbling in spiritualism.

Often the natives inherit wealth and become social parasites, and the result may be virtual disintegration. This square also produces the easygoing types who never seem to run out of people to help them through their difficulties.

Moon Square Pluto (☽ □ ♀)

This square indicates an intensely emotional nature, generating a psychic field which can make others, especially women, uneasy.

There is a desire to forget the past or destroy all ties which have a confining effect.

The natives tend to be abrupt with their families and parents and to brook no interference from them. Attempts by families to cast them in a mold of their own choosing generates resentment.

This configuration can give clairvoyant abilities which sometimes lead to disdain or distaste for material things. The natives often are annoyed by trivialities and petty details and want to be concerned only with things that are important or unique in some way. Very often they are impatient when things move too slowly to suit them.

There is a tendency to force actions and relationships with others. Many people with this square will seek to bring drastic changes in their lives or to resort to drastic solutions to emotional problems.

Moon Square North and South Nodes (☽ □ ☊ ☋)

This square tends to make the natives emotionally out of harmony with the trends of their society. Very often the flow of events creates petty problems and sometimes domestic problems.

There is difficulty in gaining social recognition or fulfilling ambitions if women play a part in this. The natives are likely to incur their disfavor or dislike in some way.

Moon Square Ascendant and Descendant (☽ □ Asc., Desc.)

This square generates emotional difficulties with self-expression and the projection of energy into action. It also generates problems with relationships, including partnership and marriage.

Sometimes the unconscious habit patterns of the natives block their ability to act decisively, and they create annoyances which get in the way of partners or others close to them.

The way to overcome this aspect is for the natives to be scrupulously aware of habit patterns, body movement, and personal mannerisms.

Moon Square Midheaven and Nadir (☽ □ M.C., Nadir)

The natives are likely to have emotional problems with parents and family. Sometimes their domestic problems will cause difficulties in their careers and jeopardize their public reputations. Sometimes they will be emotionally dissatisfied with their homes and professional responsibilities.

Their emotional habit patterns will probably annoy their employers, parents, and family. Since the Moon deals largely with the unconscious mind, they may have difficulty in understanding this aspect of themselves.

Squares of Mercury

Mercury Square Mars (☿ □ ♂)

This square produces an active, energetic mind, with tendencies to become overheated, irritable, argumentative, and partisan in view. Very often communications received by the natives make them angry, causing them to react with harsh words.

This aspect indicates a lack of tact and is unfavorable for public relations. The natives are likely to jump to conclusions before giving careful consideration to all the facts and viewpoints. Their reasoning may be one-sided because of interference from the emotions. Thus they fail to gain a balanced understanding of factors on which to base correct decisions. They are fond of debates and arguments.

To overcome the negative effects of this aspect, the natives should strive for more patience, deliberately exercise diplomacy, and learn to be good listeners in order to find insight into other people's points of view. They should bear in mind that their judgment is not infallible: Even if their reasoning is correct, they may not know all the facts.

Sometimes they are not able to express their ideas in a pleasing manner. There is a general need for mental detachment and less ego-involvement.

At times this aspect can endanger health, causing nervous disorders (especially headaches) and breakdowns. This result is due to Mercury's relationship with the nervous system and house of health, and Mars's relationship to the First House, which rules the brain.

Mercury Square Jupiter (☿ □ ♃)

This square is detrimental because the natives' abundant ideas are too grandiose for realization. Unless Saturn is strong, ideas are not worked out in enough practical detail to be useful. Nor, as a rule, are the natives well organized, and they often lack balance and realism.

They are usually in too much of a hurry, wanting to achieve great things, and they promise more than they can deliver. Mentally, they tend to attempt things beyond their capacities.

Persons with this square can be unrealistically optimistic. "Fools rush in where angels fear to tread." Often the mind and the feelings are at cross-purposes over philosophic and religious matters.

The natives are generous and well intentioned, but they may lack common sense and proportion in their thinking. They can be indiscreet, divulging confidential information at the wrong time or to the wrong people. They should be very careful in signing bonds or contracts for others, since they are easy prey to sales talk from people who may not be reliable.

Sometimes their mental endeavors are of an esoteric, scholarly sort, and they abandon the ordinary affairs of life to pursue them.

In many cases there is a tendency toward excessive talking and bombast designed to impress others. Unwarranted egotism and mental pride are characteristic.

Mercury Square Saturn (☿ □ ♄)

This square indicates a tendency to excessive worry. Sometimes the natives are mentally inhibited, or too tied to traditional ways of thinking.

There may be a lack of imagination, or concern over unimportant details. Ironically, when these natives do have ideas of their own, they have difficulty in gaining recognition and acceptance of them because of opposition from the established way of thinking.

Their education is likely to be rigidly disciplined, forcing them to conform to conventional thought. Their creative mental faculties may therefore be dulled.

Often, narrow-mindedness, strict observance of law and order at all costs, and unnecessarily rigid adherence to discipline characterize people with this square. Fearing change, older natives wish to uphold the established order in the face of evolutionary change. They are also inclined toward anxiety based on anticipation of danger or failure. They are prone to jealousy.

Their outlook on life tends to be pessimistic. If the natives occupy positions of authority, there will be instances in which they belittle the ideas of others.

In some cases, scheming and deliberate dishonesty are probable, if the rest of the chart agrees. The natives are likely to get into trouble through written communications and contracts.

Mercury Square Uranus (☿ ☐ ♅)

This square indicates an active, original mind but a nervous disposition with eccentric and often impractical ideas. Mentally, the natives are "way out," and likely to jump to conclusions. They have harebrained ideas which are not based on sufficient knowledge or practical experience to be of use.

The natives can be mentally perverse and will not accept advice from anyone. An individual may change his mind twice in a day, but no one will change it for him. He makes snap judgments, or seeks unusual and exciting ideas as ends in themselves, without regard to their truth or practicality.

There is a tendency to alienate others through tactless remarks, foolishly opinionated views, and intellectual conceit. Sometimes these persons think they are geniuses, when in reality this is far from the truth. If the rest of the map bears it out, there may be exceptional insight, but it is not likely to be wisely used unless the natives learn to overcome their obstinacy and egotism.

Mercury Square Neptune (☿ □ ♆)

This square is likely to cause absentmindedness, woolgathering, and mental disorganization concerning details. It can also indicate unintentional unreliability.

Sometimes the unconscious mind plays tricks on the conscious mind, so that when the conscious mind is preoccupied, the unconscious mind tends to cause the natives to make errors or forget things. This is generally the result of repressed emotions.

There may be an interest in the occult and mystical. If the rest of the horoscope bears it out, there can even be talent in these areas.

At times the natives have difficulty when it comes to matters of secrecy. Not that they disclose confidential information deliberately; it just seems to happen.

They can have trouble communicating with others, because they are too subjective or their ideas are too abstract or mystical for most people to understand. Nevertheless, this aspect can give insight into the actions and motives of others through the natives' ability to perceive rationally the unconscious levels of the mind. Neptune gives the insight and Mercury gives some degree of understanding. Whether these attributes are used in a cunning and underhanded way or constructively depends on the remainder of the horoscope.

Sometimes these persons are mental escapists, although the Saturnian nature of the square can give a feeling of realism if the natives desire it.

Mercury Square Pluto (☿ □ ♀)

This square can give keen mental penetration into the realities of any given situation. The natives do not mince words; they are harsh in speech and thought. (This tendency is more deliberate or calculated in them than in those with Mercury square Mars.) They will "tell it like it is," regardless of how others react to them. For this reason they must often remain silent to avoid creating controversy.

These people tend to secrecy, keeping their own counsel until they are ready to make their moves. Sometimes they are suspicious of others or they plot and use cunning where straightforwardness would be more appropriate. There can also be a desire to shape the ideas of others, generally to conform to the natives' own points of view.

A characteristically strong willpower may be misapplied or used for disruptive purposes. In this case it is extremely destructive because it is such a subtle power, insidious and far-reaching in its consequences.

Mercury Square North and South Nodes (☿ □ ☊ ☋)

This square creates a situation in which the prevailing attitudes of the society conflict with the natives' mental expression and communication. They cannot project their ideas as they would like and therefore tend to be misunderstood.

Often they meet with social disapproval because they speak out at the wrong time or place. They may be in disagreement with surrounding social patterns.

Mercury Square Ascendant and Descendant (☿ □ Asc., Desc.)

This square causes difficulties in self-expression and communication with partners and the public. The natives project their thoughts, whether by speech or writing, in an awkward manner which leads others to misunderstand or disagree with them. This can cause difficulties in marriage, in partnerships, and in communicating with the outside world.

Mercury Square Midheaven and Nadir (☿ □ M.C., Nadir)

This square puts obstacles in the way of communication with the family, parents, landlord, and employer. It is especially difficult in professional matters, since good communication on the job is essential to success in any profession. The effect is stronger if the profession involves mental work or writing.

Squares of Venus

Venus Square Mars (♀ □ ♂)

This square causes emotional problems, especially in romance and relationships with the opposite sex. Sometimes there is a tendency to use members of the opposite sex or to be used by them for purely sexual gratification.

The natives may lack good taste or refinement in their social conduct. Their desires are very strong and unless other factors indicate the contrary, there is need for control. Unbridled passion can cause them great harm.

Men with this aspect are likely to offend women because of their coarse manners. Women with this aspect often exasperate men with their emotional temperaments.

When Mars predominates, there may be a lot of horseplay. But when Venus predominates, the natives are very sensitive and their feelings are easily hurt at rough or coarse behavior.

Though the natives may be emotionally sensitive, they are not necessarily careful about the sensitivity of others. Relationships with the family are not close, harmonious, or satisfying.

Venus Square Jupiter (♀ □ ♃)

Natives with this square tend toward self-indulgence, idle luxury, laziness, and meaningless social niceties. The latter are often used as a camouflage for bad feelings which the natives do not want to admit or openly express—emotional hypocrisy is one of the prime dangers of this aspect.

This aspect will generally produce overindulgence in the affairs ruled by the signs and houses that these two planets occupy and rule. Sometimes the natives lose financially or through marriage and partnerships as a result of legal difficulties or secret involvement.

Women with this aspect may be conceited about their beauty or social status, and they will seek the center of the stage. If combined with other malefic influences, the aspect can cause debauchery and rebellion against moral and religious values. Since the natives are likely to take too much for granted, there can also be waste and lack of appreciation of the true value of things.

Venus Square Saturn (♀ □ ♄)

This square confers a melancholy disposition. The emotions are often blocked, producing shyness in some and a stiff formality in others. The natives may have misfortunes that shut them off from affection or cause disappointment and unfulfilled romance. This circumstance can make them antisocial in disposition, alienating them even further from the affection of others. So a vicious cycle is put in motion.

Sometimes the natives are calculating in gaining wealth, power, or prestige. Or, if they have wealth or influence, they may use it to attract a younger mate. Or younger people may become involved with older people for the sake of the wealth and social position they may thus acquire. The result is often unhappiness or lack of real affection.

As artists, the natives will have certain technical skills but will lack originality unless other factors in the horoscope supply it.

Occasionally this aspect causes extreme material hardship. Happiness may be blocked by excessive responsibilities. Parents may be a burden or exert an emotional oppression. Meanness and jealousy are possible if other factors in the horoscope agree.

It is difficult to achieve peace and happiness with this aspect: Either the circumstances of life are exceptionally harsh, or the natives are oversensitive to ordinary misfortunes.

Venus Square Uranus (♀ □ ♅)

This square generally brings about sudden but brief attractions in the natives' lives. Infatuations which begin under this aspect will be exciting while they last. Since the emotions are likely to be unstable and subject to swift reverses, the natives can be in love today and indifferent tomorrow.

This fickleness is almost certainly present if the square is found in mutable signs. If it is in fixed signs, there is an emotional rigidity which refuses to listen to reason and chooses emotional gratification at all cost. If in cardinal signs, the aspect causes the natives to be socially hyperactive, so that they have difficulty in gaining stability or discovering their real feelings in romantic relationships.

Sometimes love and friendship are confused. The natives want to be friendly with everyone, but they may discover that this is an impossibility, especially when sexual considerations enter the picture. They may be unable to sacrifice some of their personal freedom in order to make a stable marriage relationship. Therefore, this aspect often indicates divorce.

The native's desire for exhilarating, exotic emotional experiences is not always compatible with a practical way of life. Sometimes this square can cause sexual promiscuity or perversion, but only if other factors in the horoscope are confirmatory and if the Fifth House is involved in the pattern. If these natives are not able to find constructive outlets for their desires, nervous disorders may result.

Venus Square Neptune (♀ □ ♄)

This square causes emotional problems connected with the unconscious mind and the imagination. Since emotional and sexual problems may arise out of past experience that lies deep in the unconscious, the aspect can have a karmic connotation.

Escapist tendencies may cause the natives to live in a fantasy world in order to avoid the harsher realities of life. This proclivity may be manifested in alcoholism or drug abuse.

These people are likely to bestow their affections unwisely. There is danger of scandal through dubious relationships and financial involvements. Sex is generally the grounds for attack. Marital happiness can be endangered by a lack of honesty and directness.

Their imaginations can create sexual imagery that inflames the passions. Thus, this aspect can cause emotional complexes of various kinds. Depending on other factors in the horoscope, these tendencies are repressed or are evidenced in overt behavior which is, nevertheless, usually carried on in private.

At times the natives are shy and retiring, but they are inclined to carry on secret romances. In extreme cases there are secret sexual debaucheries. Natives may be homosexuals.

On the positive side, this aspect can give artistic abilities and aesthetic sensitivity. However, unless Saturn is well developed in the horoscope, the natives usually lack the discipline necessary to put these abilities to practical use.

Sometimes the natives are overly sensitive; their feelings are hurt too easily or without real cause. This aspect can also cause laziness and disorderly living habits if other factors in the horoscope do not contradict.

Sometimes the natives are prey to people who play on their sympathies for the sake of getting something out of them. They can be susceptible to dubious get-rich schemes and need to use discrimination in both their financial dealings and their romantic involvements.

In some cases they are too idealistic, seeking relationships that are hardly possible. They should be wary of impractical forms of cultism or strange religious beliefs.

Venus Square Pluto (♀ □ ♀)

This square tends to cause intense emotional and sexual involvements. Sometimes these can have a debasing influence. The natives are subject to being overwhelmed by sexual passions, too strong to be controlled or properly directed. There is often something karmic or fated about the natives' romantic lives.

As is sometimes the case with Venus square Uranus or Neptune, this aspect indicates that social conditions or impersonal cosmic events can interfere with personal happiness and emotional fulfillment. For example, a girl might lose her lover because he is drafted into the army.

Because of the natural opposition between Scorpio and Taurus, this aspect can produce a desire for material wealth. Sex and romance may become tainted with financial considerations, leading in extreme instances to prostitution. Marriage too may be motivated by the desire for financial security rather than by deep, abiding love.

The aspect can give a high degree of artistic inspiration and power of expression, which can provide a means of sublimating some of the emotional forces it generates.

The square may be associated with magic as a means of gaining the favor of the opposite sex, or for influencing the public to gain fame or fortune. It can also indicate secret love affairs.

Venus Square North and South Nodes (♀ □ ☊ ☋)

The emotional qualities of the natives and of their social expressions (these are the persons who flirt in church and giggle at funerals) are not likely to conform to prevailing social mores and attitudes. Marriages and financial dealings especially can meet with social disapproval.

Venus Square Ascendant and Descendant (♀ □ Asc., Desc.)

This square causes emotional difficulties in self-expression and in relating to others. There can be marital problems based on misunderstanding between the natives and their partners. This aspect may make the natives overly sensitive; in the case of males, it can result in a certain effeminacy. Sometimes there is a lack of social grace.

Venus Square Midheaven and Nadir (♀ □ M.C., Nadir)

This square can cause emotional difficulties relating to domestic and professional responsibilities. The natives may regard their job and their home life as mundane and have a certain distaste for both. Career and home responsibilities may hinder the fulfillment of their social, romantic, and aesthetic urges. Emotional misunderstandings with parents are probable.

In some cases the natives lack good taste in decorating the home and office.

Squares of Mars

Mars Square Jupiter (♂ □ ♃)

This can be one of the most destructive aspects because the natives are likely to use collective power and even social sanction for self-aggrandizement and gratification of the passions.

This square is likely to occur in the horoscope of people who glorify war. These natives are also inclined to fight holy crusades to gain social approval of their violent tendencies. Munitions manufacturers may have this aspect in their horoscopes since they seek to gain financially through destruction and violence. Much waste and misuse of resources accompany this aspect, mostly with other people's money.

The natives also are inclined to fanatical religious and social beliefs. At times they get involved in controversial social and political issues.

Extremism and prodigality will affect the signs and houses which Mars and Jupiter rule and occupy, leading to disaster and ruin if the natives are not careful.

There is restlessness and desire for constant activity and stimulation. For this reason the natives find it hard to relax.

These natives are socially outgoing, but not necessarily honorable or reliable in their dealings. There is a strong tendency to hypocrisy: The natives want to whitewash the real motives behind their actions. Sometimes religion is used as a vehicle to further hypocrisy.

Mars Square Saturn (♂ □ ♄)

This square can indicate a harsh and austere disposition. The actions of the natives may be continually frustrated, leading to resentment and negative attitudes.

There can be a sullen anger in the natives' dispositions. Their ambitions are often blocked, and there can be difficulties in relating to others, especially in partnerships and marriage. In some cases, excessive austerity and self-discipline interfere with normal healthy development.

Sometimes the influence of this square is manifested in physical hardship, violence, accidents, and broken bones. There can also be severe restrictions on careers and professions. This aspect is often related to political or military careers.

The actions of the natives are not well regulated or properly directed. Saturn can produce inhibitions of action and does not control or direct, as would be the case with favorable aspects between these two planets. Many natives do not follow through on projects that they have initiated, because they lack a sense of sustained purpose.

Often this aspect produces harsh, dirty, or even dangerous conditions connected with the occupation. Sometimes occupational dangers result in death.

There can be a certain callousness with this aspect. Often the natives are selfish individuals who will not go out of their way to help others unless they gain by it in some way.

Mars Square Uranus (♂ □ ♅)

This square tends to cause recklessness and dangerous sudden action. The natives are too impulsive for their own good. They crave excitement in the areas designated by the houses and signs which Uranus and Mars occupy and rule.

The natives are prone to disagree with their friends and associates. They should be careful with machinery and electrical devices, since there is a definite risk of accidents and even death through these devices. In extreme cases, especially in male horoscopes, thrill-seeking takes the form of reckless driving, hot-rodding, and other dangerous sports or pleasures. Natives with this configuration should be careful of air travel, since this can also be a source of harm.

Sudden temper and impulsiveness are faults to guard against. Willfulness and eccentricity characterize this aspect. There is a need for patience and the willingness to cooperate with others. Often the natives are nervous and excitable. Sometimes, because of the double Scorpio connotation of this aspect, attacks take place, or sudden, violent death.

These natives have a tendency to take risks when unusual experiences and excitement are provided. Their action can be erratic, lacking sustained effort. Their temperaments are generally idealistic. However, they are impatient with the revolutionary desire to overthrow by drastic means the established order of things.

Mars Square Neptune (♂ □ ♆)

This square generates peculiar emotional desires, arising from deep levels of the unconscious. Very often unconscious habit patterns that are not appropriate to the present reality negatively influence the actions of the natives.

This square can have various effects, depending on whether the natives' desires are repressed or expressed. If they are repressed, the square is likely to manifest itself in a form of neurosis, perhaps of a sexual or psychosomatic nature. In extreme cases there may even be hallucinatory phenomena. If the influence of the square is expressed overtly, it may take the form of alcoholism, drug abuse, or sexual excess. In less extreme cases there will be confusion and muddle in the actions of the natives, or a tendency to act with hidden motives. Heavily afflicted horoscopes may even reveal treachery, deceit, and dishonesty.

This aspect, like Venus square Uranus or Neptune, could indicate sexual deviation, but its energy could also be used to advantage in creative art, dancing, drama, music, and other activities that give scope to the imagination.

It gives a tendency to self-deception, since the natives are not always fully aware of their own motivations. (Therefore, it is not surprising that they should cause confusion in their relationships with others.)

The key to overcoming the negative effects of this aspect is to learn to control the imagination, since an uncontrolled imagination often inflames the desires, and the natives find themselves in difficulties.

This aspect is common in the horoscopes of astrologers, for it encourages the expression of the more sublime tendencies of Neptune. The same could be said, no doubt, of the horoscopes of psychologists, since it takes psychic energy to become involved with people's unconscious emotional problems. Proper direction of emotion is very important where this aspect is concerned.

Mars Square Pluto (♂ □ ♀)

This square can be dangerous because of its overly forceful nature. Unless other factors in the horoscope mitigate it, the natives' tendency to use force to gain their ends will override careful planning, diplomacy, and love.

In a good horoscope this square can result in an exalted form of courage, but sometimes the outcome is a do-or-die attitude. The natives should always examine the motivations behind their sacrifices. They may desire to perform some spectacular deed only from egotism. This urge can be carried to unnecessary and foolish extremes.

Natives with afflicted horoscopes can easily lose their tempers and become violent. In very extreme cases, where Mars and Saturn are severely afflicted, the aspect can produce brutality and criminal tendencies. This will not be the case with those who possess only the usual disagreeable tendencies that accompany the aspect (although even they can be overly aggressive in sexual areas).

The willpower of these natives is highly developed, but as a rule it lacks direction. Sometimes a violent death is indicated if the rest of the chart bears it out.

Often the natives are attracted to violent circumstances, such as wars, revolutions, and riots. They can have a dictatorial inclination, stemming from an attitude that "might makes right."

In people with spiritual aspirations, a conflict between the will and the desires is generally indicated. When combined with reason, discipline, and diplomacy, this square can provide the energy for great achievements.

Mars Square North and South Nodes (♂ □ ☊ ☋)

This aspect indicates a condition in which the actions and impulses of the natives are likely to be at odds with current social standards.

These people tend to express their aggressive tendencies at inappropriate times and places. They may appear to have bad luck, because they lack the ability to act in harmony with the events around them. Others then become irritated and the natives themselves frustrated.

Mars Square Ascendant and Descendant (♂ □ Asc., Desc.)

This square indicates that the natives will project themselves aggressively in their personal relations as well as in their dealings with the public. This tendency is usually externalized in the form of marital and partnership problems and in general unpopularity. Sometimes the frustration it causes results in angry scenes and paranoia—the natives feel they must fight to gain their ends.

Heavily afflicted horoscopes may show the natives to be bullies or inclined to gain their ends through aggressiveness.

The negative effects of this aspect can be overcome by cultivating gentleness and diplomacy and by checking impulsiveness.

Mars Square Midheaven and Nadir (♂ □ M.C., Nadir)

This square indicates that the natives may be unable to get along with their parents, family, landlords, immediate superiors, or employers.

Both career and domestic affairs are subject to strife. There is a tendency to transfer to the job the conflicts that result from quarrels at home and vice versa. Thus, problems in the profession or in the home life are likely to aggravate other spheres of activity. The natives must learn to use their heads more and their feelings less.

There is also an inclination to get into trouble with the state and with its legally constituted authorities. Sometimes the natives are unwillingly involved in military affairs; for example, they may be drafted.

Squares of Jupiter

Jupiter Square Saturn (♃ □ ♄)

This square causes difficulties in business and financial affairs. The natives are likely to suffer professionally, through either misfortune or a lack of opportunities.

Their judgments in planning and pursuing long-range goals are likely to be faulty, especially in relation to finances. Sometimes, when Saturn is strong, they lack initiative or the confidence to take advantage of opportunities that do occur. Or they may initiate activities and take on responsibilities without sufficient preparation. In either case, misfortune can follow.

If Jupiter is strong and Saturn is weak, the natives have too little discipline and experience. If Saturn is strong and Jupiter weak, they will work patiently and hard but lack the inspiration and confidence to exact cooperation from others.

Usually their timing is bad; they are not in the right place at the right time. Also, they are unable to present their cases convincingly.

They must learn the value of pursuing long-term goals steadily yet with flexibility. They must avoid the pitfalls of being overly ambitious on the one hand and reluctant to take on responsibility on the other.

They often fill minor governmental and business administration positions.

Too often they are slaves to dull routine, appearing to others like stick-in-the-muds. Their own feelings that life is drab lead to melancholia and depressions.

Sometimes they are oppressed by professional, family, or other problems which limit their freedom to act and expand. There are likely to be difficulties concerning religion: They may be too orthodox, too conservative, too materialistic, or too agnostic for their own best interests. In any case, they are rigid in their philosophical, educational, and religious values.

Jupiter Square Uranus (♃ □ ♅)

This square has impulsive excess as its primary fault. Natives are impractical and idealistic, putting all their energy behind a cause, only to abandon it suddenly. They tend to go overboard and embark on all sorts of ill-defined, grandiose schemes.

This aspect does not favor speculation, because some unforeseen turn of events is likely to nullify the expense and effort. Many people have lost fortunes under its influence.

Natives may indulge in eccentric religious beliefs and practices, and in dangerous forms of cultism. This is an aspect of many so-called mystics, masters, and gurus, who claim to be saving humanity while they are merely feeding off their disciples. Bohemian types who wander the country and the world are also likely to have this configuration.

Friends of the natives cannot be counted upon to deliver what they promise and are often misleading. The natives are usually guilty of the same faults.

A tendency to restlessness will be manifested in an urge for travel and adventure.

Jupiter Square Neptune (♃ □ ♆)

This aspect strongly suggests emotional excesses and impractical, flowery, undisciplined religious idealism. Natives will build castles in the air while the important affairs of their lives are in shambles.

They crave exotic experiences, such as can be had by traveling to far-away places or by involvement in mystical cults. With the wanderlust this aspect produces, they are not likely to remain in the place of their birth but will do a great deal of seemingly aimless wandering, either physically or mentally.

They are usually kind and sympathetic but lack discrimination in the bestowal of their kindness. Often they are merely maudlin, with little inclination to exert themselves enough to be really helpful.

They promise more than they can deliver. In extreme cases, they are downright dishonest. Some are smooth talkers who present a glowing picture of projects which have little substance. Generally lacking is the discipline and natural ability to support these projects.

Unless other factors in the horoscope indicate otherwise, there will probably be laziness and self-indulgence. If the native has money, this aspect can lead to a life of idleness and nonfulfillment.

Overindulgence in eating is characteristic, and a tendency to be overweight or to carry excess fluid in the tissues makes the natives feel and look heavy.

Jupiter Square Pluto (♃ □ ♇)

This square inclines the natives to dogmatism in religion and philosophy, combined with a rebellion against their contemporary forms. They would like to remake institutions or reform ideas in the realm of religion and education.

They tend to be a law unto themselves unless there is good reason for conforming to social norms. Since social niceties mean little, they will not engage in them unless there are definite pressures for doing so.

There can be a certain mental pride and willfulness. Whether or not the natives are justified in their attitudes, this proclivity does not make for popularity.

The desire to accomplish something big and important can obstruct the way to happiness.

Jupiter Square North and South Nodes (♃ □ ☊ ☋)

This square produces a situation in which the natives' religious, educational, and social attitudes are not in harmony with the trends and policies of the culture in which they find themselves. They are likely to have difficulty adjusting to social institutions.

Jupiter Square Ascendant and Descendant (♃ □ Asc., Desc.)

This square hinders the natives' social lives by imparting an awkwardness to their manner of expressing themselves and of relating to others. They are likely to be regarded as grandiose, bombastic, pompous, or "holier than thou."

They try to do too much at once, so that they are either overworked or involved in situations in which their endeavors cannot be brought to fruition. In other words, they spread themselves too thinly.

Jupiter Square Midheaven and Nadir (♃ □ M.C., Nadir)

This square tends to give the natives grandiose ideas of their possible careers and ostentation in the domestic sphere.

They are likely to spend more on the home than they can afford and to have greater ambitions than their abilities can fulfill. There is a need for more humility, practicality, and common sense.

The aspect could also indicate a large family that places a burden on the native.

Squares of Saturn

Saturn Square Uranus (♄ □ ♅)

This square creates a conflict between the natives' conservative and radical tendencies. Much depends on whether Saturn or Uranus is dominant.

If Saturn is stronger, the natives will seek to preserve the status quo by opposing innovations and progressive trends in all social and political matters. If Uranus is stronger, they will revolt against the established order of things. However, in either case they are inflexible.

If they oppose change, whatever they depend upon for security is likely to be suddenly swept away. If they favor drastic innovations, their lack of experience and insufficient attention to practical considerations will probably cause them to fail.

This square produces dictatorial tendencies. Natives who claim to champion progress and freedom may be very oppressive toward those who disagree with them.

They are prone to inconsistency and to contradicting their philosophies by their actions. Egotism and hypocrisy can be prominent, and eccentric forms of obstinacy will make them unpopular and a nuisance to others. They will therefore have few friends.

They are liable to reversals in their careers, which can result in downfall and disgrace. Accidents and sudden misfortune may occur. Their temperaments can be disagreeable at times. In general, they lack common sense and adaptability.

Saturn Square Neptune (♄ □ ♆)

This square has a morbid connotation and is likely to give rise to fears, anxieties, neuroses, and phobias that stem from the unconscious. If the rest of the map indicates it, there is danger of confinement or institutionalization because of mental illness.

The natives can become prey to negative psychic influences and should, therefore, be careful of all astral psychic practices, such as séances or experimentation with psychedelic drugs. Psychic possession is also a danger.

In most cases this aspect will be manifested as some fear of inadequacy or as an inferiority complex. The natives may feel confused about careers and general practical responsibilities. Sometimes they desire to escape responsibility. Although they are likely to work hard, they can lack efficiency. In some cases they are cunning and use devious methods to achieve their ambitions. Or they attract secret enemies and become involved in scandal and intrigue. Their friends can be unresponsive or unsympathetic, or vice versa.

The natives' religious beliefs may be peculiar—dogmatic, rigid, or oppressive in some way. Very often they have martyr complexes and seek sympathy through suffering. Since this stance is usually unappealing, others will shun them and they will feel even more lonely and self-pitying. This vicious circle can ultimately lead to severe neuroses and even psychoses.

Saturn Square Pluto (♄ □ ♀)

Persons with this square often feel that they have the weight of the world on their shoulders. Constantly changing impersonal social conditions are likely to impose disappointments and heavy responsibilities on them. Something somber and mysterious blocks their progress in the affairs represented by the signs and houses which Saturn and Pluto occupy and rule.

There is a danger of plot and intrigue, with the natives either victims or innovators. In extreme cases they can become victims or practitioners of the deliberately selfish use of occult powers.

Natives may resort to extreme measures to attain their professional ambitions. Their personal destiny is strongly tied in with mass karma.

Occasionally someone associated with the native will take on the role of dictator or, conversely, the native may be dictatorial. The natives often have a desire to control and remake the lives of others, and their ambition for power may be extreme.

Saturn Square North and South Nodes (♄ □ ☊ ☋)

This square indicates a thwarting of the natives' ambition and progress by prevailing social forces. Their fearfulness and conservatism may prevent their being in the right place at the right time to take advantage of opportunities which the society affords them. They may be isolated by society or become recluses.

Saturn Square Ascendant and Descendant (♄ □ Asc., Desc.)

This square indicates a condition in which the natives' ability to relate to others with warmth and friendliness is blocked. They can have sour dispositions and, if so, are likely to be cut off from social intercourse. Often people find them cold and unresponsive; they will probably have few close friends. They are likely as well to have difficulties in marriage or in finding suitable marriage partners.

Saturn Square Midheaven and Nadir (♄ □ M.C., Nadir)

This square presents obstacles to the natives' professional success, domestic happiness and general well-being.

Often they find themselves with heavy responsibilities that interfere with personal happiness in their home lives (especially marriages) and professions and limit their self-expression. Sometimes these responsibilities are imposed by their parents, who are likely to be oppressive. Their own families may be a burden, requiring them to work extremely hard at their professions. Employers and landlords may be unreasonable and demanding.

Squares of Uranus

Uranus Square Neptune (♅ □ ♆)

This square is indicative of a generation (those born in the 1950s) whose karma it is to live in a time of exceptional social turmoil.

The natives are prone to emotional and psychic confusion. However, these effects will not be pronounced in the average individual unless Uranus or Neptune is in an angular house or heavily aspected by squares and oppositions from other planets.

The degree to which the above is true and which houses are involved in the square will indicate to what extent and in what manner individuals are affected by the turmoil. Also to be considered are the affairs ruled by houses and signs in which Uranus and Neptune are found and the houses they rule. These will be subject to peculiar, sudden, elusive, and upsetting conditions.

The natives can be somewhat high-strung, willful, and nervous. They are inclined to have set ideas and opinions.

Involvement in seceret societies and intrigues is possible. There can be high idealism, but of a confused and sometimes impractical kind. This feature again depends on the rest of the map. Mediumistic and occult matters can be a source of trouble: The natives must cope with discordant and inharmonious conditions on these levels.

Uranus Square Pluto (♅ □ ♇)

This square is indicative of a generation (those born in the early 1930s) who live in times of drastic upheaval. Very often their lives are disrupted and dislocated by wars, revolutions, economic collapse, and even natural catastrophes.

The extent to which this square will affect individuals depends on the positions of Uranus and Pluto and whether they are found in angular houses or form major aspects to the angles and to other planets. Willfulness, eccentricity, radical political views, and revolutionary tendencies characterize the natives who are strongly influenced by this square.

The square is also an aspect of mass involvements and indicates the manner in which the mass destiny affects the individual. This outcome is dependent upon the planets that aspect Uranus and Pluto and the sign and houses they occupy and rule.

The natives have a strong tendency to reform the established order. Their motives and ideals are usually worthy. However, the fact that they must cope with momentous social problems from birth makes them feel that they do not know what it is to be young and carefree. Natives with this square, even when born into affluence, never feel secure.

These people have serious lessons to learn regarding the sexual function. The aspect coincides with a period in history in which there is much sexual abuse.

Uranus Square North and South Nodes (♅ □ ☊ ☋)

This square indicates a situation in which the natives' desire for freedom and their nonconformist tendencies conflict with social standards.

They are likely to run roughshod over the mores of their culture and will incur the disapproval of the more traditional elements of society. Hence they are prone to misfortune.

Uranus Square Ascendant and Descendant (♅ □ Asc., Desc.)

This square indicates a situation in which nonconformist tendencies create irregularities and spasmodic disruptions in the natives' normal flow of self-expression and social behavior.

The natives are prone to divorce: They do not wish to make the sacrifice of personal freedom necessary to make a marriage work.

Their eccentric behavior is also likely to stand in the way of harmonious relationships with their partners or with the public.

Uranus Square Midheaven and Nadir (♅ □ M.C., Nadir)

This square indicates the natives' lack of ability to conform to professional or domestic routines. There is rebellion against authority—whether parents, an immediate superior, employers, or the government. The natives change jobs and residences frequently, and not always for sound or valid reasons.

There is also impatience with family responsibilities and sometimes a tendency to use the home as a camping ground for the eccentric friends. The typical hippie pad is characteristic of this aspect.

Squares of Neptune

Neptune Square Pluto (♆ □ ♇)

This square denotes a generation that lives in a period of social turmoil and subtle disintegration of the social structure. The individual orientation of a horoscope will indicate how this mass destiny affects the individual. (No one now living has this aspect in his horoscope.)

The natives can be participants in or victims of corrupt social and political institutions. In most cases this aspect will be responded to unconsciously and automatically.

It indicates a need for the spiritual regeneration of religious and cultural thought and of the institutions to which the native belongs.

Neptune Square North and South Nodes (♆ □ ☊ ☋)

This square indicates a situation in which the mystical tendencies of the natives conflict with the more prosaic, down-to-earth customs and social institutions of their culture.

Society is likely to regard them as impractical dreamers or even as subversive influences who undermine traditional religious and social concepts. They are likely to feel alone in a crowd and misunderstood by their peers. Sometimes their preoccupation with visionary pursuits keeps them out of touch with the flow of events around them, so that they react ineptly and confusedly.

Neptune Square Ascendant and Descendant (Ψ □ Asc., Desc.)

This square indicates a situation in which the natives are confused and overly subjective in their self-expression and social relationships. Sometimes they are referred to as "out of it," so to speak; they prefer their own dreamworlds.

This square can also make the natives unreliable and deceptive when it comes to marriage or partnerships. Conversely, they too can be deceived.

Neptune Square Midheaven and Nadir (Ψ □ M.C., Nadir)

This square, unless contradicted by other influences in the chart, indicates unreliability in professional obligations and confusion in domestic affairs. The home will be messy and disorganized, and sometimes the scene of alcohol or drug use.

There can be deception and irresponsibility on the job, in the form of laziness, inefficiency, or both. In rare cases, the natives are deliberately dishonest or deceptive.

This square can also manifest itself in escape from domestic and professional duties through daydreaming.

Squares of Pluto

Pluto Square North and South Nodes (♀ □ ☊ ☋)

This square indicates a tendency to want to reform social and cultural philosophies and institutions. Thus, the natives will be at odds with the established order and will incur its disfavor. Depending on other factors in the horoscope, this can either be mild disapproval or a matter of life and death, in which the natives are regarded as dangerous revolutionaries by their society.

Pluto Square Ascendant and Descendant (♀ □ Asc., Desc.)

This square indicates a tendency to be aggressive in personal behavior and antisocial in marriage relationships, partnerships, and dealings with the public.

It is a divorce-prone aspect and can lead to lawsuits of various kinds.

The natives want to remake others, when it is themselves they should be changing. Such domineering naturally causes resentment and leads to inharmonious relationships and battles of the wills. The natives are also subject to attempts at domination by others of similar character. "Diamond cuts diamond," as the saying goes.

Pluto Square Midheaven and Nadir (♀ □ M.C., Nadir)

This square indicates a situation in which the desire to transform existing conditions can cause conflict with employers, immediate superiors, parents and families, constituted government authority, or landlords.

When the natives are at odds with their employers it is probably because they feel they know a better way of doing the job or because they want more power in the decision-making process. When their revolutionary tendencies are directed against the government and social institutions, they can incur official disfavor.

If they are in positions of domestic or professional authority, they may display autocratic or dictatorial traits, which will usually cause disharmony.

CHAPTER 15

The Trines

Trines of the Sun

Sun Trine Moon (☉ △ ☽)

This trine indicates a harmonious interaction between the conscious expression of the natives' will and power potential and their automatic emotional responses, hereditary influences, and habit tendencies. Strong physical vitality is usually associated with this aspect, and it indicates good health, stamina, and recuperative powers.

There is a fine balance between the masculine and feminine, or yang and yin, facets of the natives' nature. Because of the inner harmony promoted by the trine, the natives are usually attractive to the opposite sex. They are able to function well in their social relationships, other factors being equal. This aspect promotes self-confidence and optimism.

The natives tend to get on well with their families and parents, unless there are serious afflictions to the Sun, Moon, Fourth House, Tenth House, and their rulers to complicate these relationships. They are fond of children and are able to work well with them.

Sun Trine Mars (☉ △ ♂)

This trine gives courage, willpower, leadership ability, and decisiveness. It is especially favorable for men, because it strengthens the traditionally masculine attributes of ambition and self-confidence.

Often considerable physical strength and endurance accompany this aspect. The natives can function at high energy levels for prolonged periods of time and are often fond of sports or other physical activities. However, even with the trine aspect, they may be competitive and more interested in their own pursuits than those of others.

There is a strong sense of honor and integrity. Since nothing is too much trouble for these natives, they enjoy the challenge of a hard task. Their practical experience and their habits of constructive use of energy often provide them with insight into how to perform difficult tasks.

Whatever theoretical understanding the natives have they can put to practical use.

This aspect has a strong fire-sign connotation because of the Sun's rulership in Leo and exaltation in Aries, the Mars rulership of Aries, and the combined Leo-Sagittarius nature of the aspect itself. Mars's position as the right-hand man of the Sun means that the power potential of the Sun flows into creative, inspirational action; therefore, the natives are enthusiastic in a constructive way.

Sun Trine Jupiter (☉ △ ♃)

Since the Sun rules Leo and is exalted in Aries, this trine has many of the same ardent fire-sign qualities as the Sun trine Mars. Jupiter rules Sagittarius, thus bringing the trine a combined Leo-Sagittarius connotation.

The Ninth House and the Fifth House are equally emphasized here. The enthusiastic, optimistic, outgoing quality of this trine, therefore, is directed into religious, philosophic, legal, social, and community affairs rather than into the personal physical action of Mars trine the Sun. The natives are positive and altruistic in their attitudes and consequently gain the confidence and cooperation of others. This attribute leads in turn to good fortune and success.

They are always protected by spiritual forces where their basic happiness and safety are concerned, so they are never completely down and out. They are generous in helping their fellow man.

This aspect confers honesty, and the individuals base their actions on an ethical and religious standard of conduct. They have insight into the future and a degree of farsightedness bordering on prophecy. In some cases they withdraw from worldly affairs in order to pursue a contemplative life with books and favorite friends.

Sun Trine Saturn (☉ △ ♄)

This trine indicates an honest, practical, circumspect, and conservative disposition. The natives do not waste energy or resources; everything is geared toward a useful and practical objective.

Good organizational ability and powers of concentration go hand in hand with this aspect. The natives exercise a high degree of discipline and generally fulfill their ambitions through hard work.

They are never caught short in difficult times because their practical desire for security makes them save for that "rainy day." They are very patient, do not take chances, and therefore live to a ripe old age.

Sun Trine Uranus (☉ △ ♅)

This trine gives personal magnetism, spiritual insight, leadership ability, and creativity. There is the ability to tap the Universal Mind to some extent. Flashes of intuition and genius occur when the trine is set off by transits or progressions. The natives' minds are inclined toward scientific and occult studies. Good astrologers often have this aspect.

The natives have strong wills and are willing to experiment in new realms of experience: They may spearhead reform and champion new ideas and inventions. They tend to be humanitarian and to have a sense of universal human brotherhood which comes from their perception of the underlying spiritual oneness of all life.

Sun Trine Neptune (☉ △ ♆)

This trine, like the Sun trine Uranus, gives intuitive ability. However, this intuition is emotional in nature and often expressed in empathy, whereas that of Uranus is more mental and impersonal.

Intuitive ability often finds expression in art, music, religion, mysticism, and the spiritual guidance of others. The natives possess a quality of universal love which can transcend the personal, sexual, and physical outlets for this emotion. In its highest form it can spiritually uplift and physically heal those who come in contact with the natives.

Unless there are sufficient practical qualities of Saturn and Mercury, the natives may be only visionary dreamers. However, this aspect does have its practical side and can give insight into business and stock market investments. There is also an ability to flow with the subtle currents of life, so that the natives have an instinct for being in the right place at the right time, saying the right thing to the right person.

Sun Trine Pluto (☉ △ ♀)

This trine gives the natives highly evolved powers of concentration and will. There is an ability to regenerate, upgrade, and transform all aspects of life. They can be inspired leaders if the rest of the horoscope indicates advanced spiritual evolution. They have an insight into situations that lets them know just when or where to act with the most efficient use of energy and resources.

Often there is an interest in meditation, yoga, or other systems of spiritual self-development. Clairvoyance and intuitive abilities are frequently present. The natives have almost supernatural energy; they are fiery and creative in their self-expression.

Sun Trine North Node Sextile South Node (☉ △ ☊ ✳ ☋)

This configuration gives the natives ability to exercise their wills and express themselves in harmony with prevailing social attitudes and institutions. This assures a creative, harmonious outcome of effort applied to any given situation.

There is considerable leadership ability, usually indicating public favor and popularity—the configuration favors politicians and those in public life.

Sun Trine Ascendant Sextile Descendant (☉ △ Asc. ✳ Desc.)

This configuration gives vitality, self-confidence, and a positive, optimistic disposition. The natives have willpower and abundant energy. Their magnanimous dispositions usually win the cooperation of others.

This is also a favorable aspect for marriage and for all partnership arrangements, because the power of the Sun harmonizes the natives' relationships.

Sun Trine Midheaven Sextile Nadir (☉ △ M.C. ✳ Nadir)

This configuration gives leadership ability and increases the natives' chances of gaining prominence in their careers. It is favorable for politics and public life and for relationships with people in positions of authority.

Professional success makes possible an expanded scope in the domestic sphere, providing the basis for a happy family life.

Trines of the Moon

Moon Trine Mercury (☽ △ ☿)

This trine indicates a good memory and a good working cooperation between the conscious and unconscious mind. There is constructive thinking concerning personal and domestic affairs, especially in matters of health and diet.

The keynote of this aspect is common sense, and the natives are able to reason accurately and communicate sensibly about the ordinary affairs of life. Often they have keen business ability, especially with regard to food or products for the home.

They are generally fluent in speech and expression, good conversationalists, and fortunate in businesses that are carried on by mail, phone, or other communications media.

Moon Trine Venus (☽ △ ♀)

This trine indicates a harmonious, pleasant disposition. It is especially favorable for women since it enhances the traditional feminine virtues, such as beauty and gentleness of emotional expression and affection. There is a great deal of sympathy and empathy for others. The natives' presence has a soothing effect.

The natives generally possess some artistic ability or at least manifest good taste in cooking, home decorating, and personal appearance. If combined with favorable Neptune aspects, this trine can indicate exceptional musical or artistic talent.

The aspect favors singers, actors, and performers, for Venus rules Taurus, where the Moon is exalted. The voice influenced by this trine has a pleasing, melodious quality.

Moon Trine Mars (☽ △ ♂)

The natives tend to be active emotionally and to have an abundance of psychic energy. They are enterprising in business and in building up the home and domestic life.

There is a great deal of strong feeling, but it is controlled and constructively used. The natives will fight for what is right. They also possess the ability to back their imaginations with will and action. Their robust health and energy lead to an intensity of experience which in turn improves their imaginative faculties.

Moon Trine Jupiter (☽ △ ♃)

This trine inclines the natives toward altruism and religious devotion. There is generally great generosity of spirit and a kind disposition—they will help others whenever possible. Their imaginations are expansive.

Natives are devoted to home, parents, and family, with a desire to maintain domestic peace and happiness. This attribute is due to the Moon's rulership of Cancer, where Jupiter is exalted.

The aspect favors wealth, either through inheritance or through the natives' own business ability.

Moon Trine Saturn (☽ △ ♄)

The natives are cautious and conservative. They are honest and possess a great deal of common sense. They have organizational ability and can endure hardship when necessary in order to achieve long-range goals. They can be shrewd and have business acumen.

By itself this aspect does not make the natives originators of ideas. However, they can build on the foundations of already established or inherited businesses or institutions. This is a favorable aspect for dealing with mining or real estate or matters concerned with the land itself.

At times a Spartan, austere, self-disciplined attitude accompanies this aspect, and the natives then have little concern for the usual physical comforts of life.

Personal dignity and a sense of responsibility in carrying out obligations are characteristic.

Moon Trine Uranus (☽ △ ♅)

This aspect gives an original, spontaneous imagination and business ability where new or inventive enterprises are involved. The personality has a sparkling effervescence that intrigues others. Natives are full of energy and determination.

The home, parents, and domestic situation will be rather unusual. The natives are seekers of unusual experiences; they do not like a conventional existence.

Psychic abilities are often present, accompanied by an interest in astrology or other occult sciences.

Moon Trine Neptune (☽ △ ♆)

Strong mediumistic and psychic proclivities characterize this aspect. Depending on the rest of the horoscope, the natives can have prophetic or intuitive insights into people and future conditions.

There is interest in psychology, psychic phenomena, and related subjects. Hypersensitivity to environmental factors can also be connected with this trine.

The natives possess keen imaginations, which if linked to Venus can produce exceptional artistic talent. In some cases, they are mere dreamers unless other factors, such as Saturn, Mars, or Mercury, well placed or aspected in the horoscope, add a practical side.

Moon Trine Pluto (☽ △ ♀)

This aspect gives emotional intensity, along with the capacity for emotional regeneration of the self and of the environment.

The feelings are under the control of the will and can be expressed with tremendous power. The natives possess great courage and determination to overcome obstacles to material and spiritual success.

Often they have intuitive insight into the underlying causes of objective phenomena. They utilize their wills and imaginations to bring thought into objective, practical manifestation, since they know instinctively that thoughts are things and are powerful when energized by the will.

Moon Trine North Node Sextile South Node (☽ △ ☊ ✳ ☋)

This configuration indicates a harmonious blending of the natives' own emotions and instinctive reactions with the prevailing social trends and attitudes.

The natives instinctively know how to navigate the currents of changing popular beliefs to their own advantage.

Moon Trine Ascendant Sextile Descendant (☽ △ Asc. ✳ Desc.)

This configuration indicates constructive expression of the emotions. Also, the natives are sensitive to this dual expression in others.

They have active imaginations and can function harmoniously in domestic and social situations, including the domestic aspects of marriage.

Moon Trine Midheaven Sextile Nadir (☽ △ M.C. ✳ Nadir)

This configuration favors professional success through the ability to deal with the public and to adapt to the emotional reactions of people in positions of authority, as well as with all who affect the natives' careers.

The security engendered by this aspect creates the opportunity of establishing a secure, harmonious domestic situation. This is further facilitated through emotional sensitivity toward the home and family members.

Trines of Mercury

Mercury Trine Mars (☿ △ ♂)

This trine gives an abundance of mental energy. Since their mental concentration has endurance and depth, individuals with this aspect are capable of serious study and much learning. However, the degree to which they apply themselves will depend upon the natives' ability to control restlessness. Good aspects from Saturn or the outer planets help to give the necessary steadiness of concentration.

While this aspect alone would not make for a scholarly theoretician or pure scientist, it is extremely favorable to the practical application of scientific knowledge, like that encountered in trades dealing with machinery. Often there is an interest in mechanical things and engineering in general. This practical mental capacity is derived from the ambition and competitive drive of Mars.

The natives' ability to be dramatic and forceful in speech and communication makes them well suited for work as reporters or commentators. The aspect is of great help to writers of mystery novels. (This aid comes from the Scorpio side of Mars.)

Because they seek to mold public opinion, these natives often enter politics, the military, law, or any profession which will provide them the possibility of exerting mental authority and leadership.

There is an almost immediate response to all mental stimuli. Mercury's exaltation in Aquarius adds to the Martian zeal a broad understanding, or universal overview, which expands the sympathies and makes the natives more idealistic in promoting what they consider good causes.

Mercury Trine Jupiter (☿ △ ♃)

This trine is particularly favorable for people engaged in higher education—either students or teachers. (Mercury rules the practical reasoning mind, Jupiter is ruler of the mental house of higher education, and the trine itself has a Ninth and Fifth House connotation.) It also favors publishers, foreign correspondents, and writers, especially those who deal with religious and philosophic subjects and with matters pertaining to the Ninth, Third, and Sixth houses.

The mind is broad, tolerant, and quick to comprehend; the natives communicate with ease and confidence. Since they can project their ideas and gain acceptance of them, the trine is good for speechmaking. Politicians and people in public life are favored.

This aspect implies honesty and integrity since it is the natural tendency of the natives to consider the moral and ethical consequences of their thoughts and actions. Consequently, this is also a good aspect for those engaged in the legal profession.

The natives are generally fond of travel. Even if they do not travel physically, their minds are busy with foreign countries and the world at large.

Generous toward their friends, they enjoy entertaining them in their homes. The home is also a place of scholarly endeavor. The natives generally have large personal libraries. They will work hard to have homes conducive to social harmony and intellectual pursuits.

In addition, they exemplify the principle of the power of positive thinking, and their mental optimism helps them achieve success. However, in some cases this position inclines them toward a contemplative life, to the extent that they are not interested in worldly success. (This attitude would be indicated also by other factors in the horoscope.)

Mercury Trine Saturn (☿ △ ♄)

This trine gives mental organization. It especially favors mathematicians and scientists or others who must do exact, systematic mental work in which there is little or no tolerance for error. It confers dexterity with the hands and will often be found in the charts of craftsmen who do precision work. Because of the ability it gives to deal with organizational responsibilities, this is a good aspect too for managerial work or political planning.

The natives make fine students because of their patience and capacity for hard work. While this aspect by itself does not give originality of thought, it does aid in its practical use and expression.

This is also a favorable aspect for writers and teachers, giving a much more practical outlook and more ability to pay attention to details than does Mercury trine Jupiter. Good memory is characteristic of this trine.

The structure-building aspect of the mind in general is improved. Persons with this aspect usually view life seriously and tend to be disciplinarians. Their moral character and self-control are excellent, provided the rest of the horoscope has no strong indications to the contrary.

These natives are loyal friends, but not inclined to flattery. Any compliment from them is well earned.

Mercury Trine Uranus (☿ △ ♅)

This trine confers a special mental ability that is linked to the intuitive faculties. The natives generally have a humanitarian outlook because of the double Aquarian connotation—Uranus's rulership of Aquarius and exaltation of Mercury in Aquarius.

Natives are well suited for investigation and research into new areas of thought. They have a natural understanding of subtle energy forces and are usually attracted to scientific or occult areas of study. They have intuitive flashes whenever their conscious minds become attuned to the Universal Mind, as is their natural tendency.

They may well have genius in some special area but be indifferent to things which do not interest them.

This is an excellent aspect for those in the field of astrology because it confers scientific understanding of occult principles.

The natives are not bound by tradition; they arrive at their own conclusions independent of popularly held views. For this reason they are far ahead of the times in their comprehension of life. They express their thoughts originally and dramatically and often have excellent memories; this aspect favors public speakers.

Also favored are those who work in the field of electronics and electronic artificial intelligence, especially computers. They often possess a specialized skill which is important to their careers.

Mercury Trine Neptune (☿ △ ♆)

This trine indicates an intuitive mind with the capacity to read the thoughts of others. It also confers prophetic ability if other factors in the chart sustain it.

Natives possess highly developed visualization which lets them see mentally any object or process in complete detail, as though they were actually looking at it. Since Neptune rules the picture-making faculties, the psychic premonitions which accompany visions are characterized by this aspect. However, the intelligent nature of Mercury makes the natives generally able to understand these premonitions better than can natives with other Neptune aspects.

This trine, especially if it is combined with Venus, can give artistic and musical ability, especially in the area of composition. The natives write good fiction because of their vivid imaginations and can be skilled in photography and cinematography. They can also become good poets and writers on mystical subjects.

The aspect confers extremely delicate and acute senses, so that the natives avoid harsh conditions.

The natives achieve success through subtly infiltrating the minds of others, rather than openly declaring their attempts to win them over. Therefore, if the rest of the horoscope is favorable, this aspect can be found among successful financial, political, and military strategists. These natives can also be masters at manipulating the public mind from an unconscious level by the subtle use of mass media.

Mercury Trine Pluto (☿ △ ♀)

This trine indicates the kind of mind that is capable of understanding reality in terms of the interplay of energy—that is, understanding the causes of outer manifestations (the ability needed by an atomic physicist to understand atomic structures). Deep involvement in such areas will occur in only a few cases, since many other factors must bear it out. Often this influence is too subtle for the average natives to understand or use to its fullest potential. In ordinary humanity the aspect would merely indicate an ability to get at the root of things.

There is an interest in scientific or occult fields, and this aspect is often found in the horoscope of the physicist, especially if he deals with nuclear energy. However, in such an instance, Saturn and Uranus would need to enter into the configuration along with an appropriate house and sign position.

These people have good powers of concentration and can use their willpower intelligently. They can thus improve their mental abilities, as well as their minds and manner of communication. The aspect favors writers, researchers, and investigators. There can be a special concern with reading or writing mystery and detective stories.

Mercury Trine North Node Sextile South Node (☿ △ ☊ ✳ ☋)

This configuration gives skill in understanding prevailing social attitudes, trends, and institutions. Consequently, the natives communicate with the public to their advantage. It favors those who work in the mass media—promoters and others who must gain public acceptance for their ideas. Politicians, who deal with media to reach the public, are especially favored, as are sociologists.

Mercury Trine Ascendant Sextile Descendant (☿ △ Asc. ✳ Desc.)

This configuration confers keen mental and sensory perception, coupled with a quick, intelligent mind. The natives can express themselves fluently and are easily able to convince others of the worth of their ideas. In this way they gain cooperation to implement their conceptions. Because of their skill in presenting ideas, they make good public relations representatives and diplomats.

There is good mental interchange in marriage and other partnerships and rapport with fellow beings. The high degree of intelligence conferred by this aspect makes the natives good scholars or researchers, especially if Mercury is well aspected from other directions.

Mercury Trine Midheaven Sextile Nadir (☿ △ M.C. ✳ Nadir)

This configuration indicates an unusually close connection between intelligence and professional ambition. It gives the ability to write on subject matter that pertains to the native's profession, and enables him to communicate well with those in authority.

The home is likely to be a place of intellectual endeavor and probably contains a sizable library. The natives want to share their intellectual and educational interests with their families as well as using them in their professional work. The configuration promotes harmony, through good communication, between the domestic and professional spheres of life. At times, relatives play a helpful part in both professional and domestic affairs.

Trines of Venus

Venus Trine Mars (♀ △ ♂)

This trine is emotionally energizing and artistically inclined. The natives are fun-loving and, unless there are factors in the horoscope to indicate otherwise, usually have sex appeal. They know how to appeal to others emotionally and are at ease in their relationships with the opposite sex.

Since Mars is the natural ruler of the First House and Venus is the ruler of the Seventh House, this trine has a Fifth House connotation which promotes happiness in romance and marriage.

The sensitivity of Venus is energized by Mars, giving Venus a more dynamic expression, while Mars is rendered more refined and less destructive. The natives, then, express themselves dynamically and have a natural ability to please.

There is usually creative talent in music, art, and drama and the energy and willpower to give that talent concrete expression.

Venus Trine Jupiter (♀ △ ♃)

This trine indicates a happy, optimistic, sociable disposition. It favors success in music and the arts. The natives are often interested in religious art, or use art to convey philosophic and religious ideas.

There is harmony in marital and domestic affairs. These people are often successful in businesses relating to art, culinary delights, and furnishings and decorations for the home.

This aspect is conducive to teaching or publishing in the artistic field, because of the Ninth House, Jupiter connotation and the Ninth House trine connotation. There can also be interest in hospitals and similar institutions because of the exaltation of Venus in Pisces, where Jupiter co-rules.

The voice has a pleasing, soothing quality. If the Moon is involved in this trine, the native has the potential to be an excellent singer.

The major virtue of the aspect is the ability to spread joy to others. The natives have a great deal of sympathy for the unfortunate. They are especially refined and possess the social graces; consequently, they are much sought after.

In an otherwise weak horoscope, this particular combination of benefic influences can lead to indolence, especially if the native possesses wealth that he did not earn by his own efforts. In an afflicted horoscope, indicating that a person has many crosses to bear, a trine of Venus and Jupiter can be a saving grace, giving a sense of joy in living despite the hardships. Since this trine of itself is not a dynamic aspect, whether its full creative potential is realized will depend upon the rest of the horoscope.

Venus Trine Saturn (♀ △ ♄)

This trine indicates a sense of order, balance, and proportion in art and music. It is frequently found in the horoscopes of artists; it gives an excellent sense of rhythm and structural relationship in time and space. The aspect is also favorable for architects, designers, mathematicians, and people who work with structures that must be both functional and aesthetic.

The natives possess business acumen, stemming from Saturn's rulership of Capricorn and Venus's rulership of Taurus. These signs are also in trine relationship.

Saturn co-rules Aquarius, and Venus rules Libra, where Saturn is exalted. These relationships indicate that while the natives have a strong practical sense, they also have the air-sign intellectuality and the Libra sense of justice and fair play.

Venus's exaltation in Pisces, combined with Aquarius and Capricorn influences and the Libra concern for the other fellow, signifies that the natives have a real and practical understanding of the needs of those less fortunate than themselves. Also implied is an eagerness to help others in such a way that they will eventually be able to help themselves.

These people are loyal friends. They also make good marriage partners, because Saturn gives durability to their relationships. In many ways this is an excellent contact, because the beauty and harmony of Venus are preserved and stabilized by the influence of Saturn.

Even with the trine relationship, the natives can be overly serious and reserved. Superficially, this trait might be mistaken for coldness and unresponsiveness. These natives, however, have a way of growing on people as the relationship goes on.

Venus Trine Uranus (♀ △ ♅)

This trine indicates an effervescent, fun-loving nature that is full of surprises and tends to see the bright side of life. It gives a spontaneous quality which is especially favorable for the performing arts. The natives frequently have exciting romances and marriages, unusual friends, and much popularity. There can also be sudden good fortune in financial matters.

In any artistic endeavor, these people will have a distinctive style; their endeavors are often associated with electronic media, such as radio, television, recording.

The good fortune brought by this aspect is usually the result of the joyous outlook on life which attracts people of importance and money: The natives radiate the happiness which others seek.

They generally possess a lot of sex appeal and have no difficulty attracting romance.

In a horoscope that indicates tendencies toward deep spirituality, this trine can be of assistance. However, by itself, it does not necessarily signify a profound person.

Venus Trine Neptune (♀ △ ♆)

This trine evidences a highly romantic nature. It bestows talent and sometimes genius in music, art, and poetry. However, the natives are not inclined toward practical affairs, unless other factors in the horoscope so indicate.

They are likely to have unusual romances and to meet lovers under unusual circumstances, which appear in some way to be preordained and are often accompanied by premonitions.

People with this aspect are kind and sympathetic toward those in need. However, the way they go about giving help may be impractical.

The trine has a double Pisces connotation which conveys all the mystical beauty of this sign. These people have a certain mystique, along with deep emotional understanding. Highly developed people are often able to exert a healing power by their soothing presence.

The trine can indicate extreme aesthetic, emotional, and even spiritual refinement.

Venus Trine Pluto (♀ △ ♀)

This trine shows an intense emotional nature which is capable of the highest form of love. In its loftiest aspect, it indicates spiritual regeneration through love. There is often something predestined about the natives' love lives and marriages. Love at first sight is not uncommon. Because the emotions have great power behind them, the natives' close relationships will be of a significant character.

They are definitely romantic, but in a powerful, positive way which has more direction than Venus-Neptune, and more constancy than Venus-Uranus. Even in a trine aspect, these two planets indicate a strong sex drive. In the case of the trine, it finds constructive expression. Penetrating understanding of the reality and power of love can have a transforming effect on others, as well as on the natives themselves. Often they or their marriage partners are changed for the better through the relationship.

Venus Trine North Node Sextile South Node (♀ △ ☊ ✳ ☋)

This configuration indicates much refinement of the social graces. The natives' actions in all social situations coincide with the appropriate line of conduct. Thus their popularity is enhanced, but unless other factors in the horoscope give evidence of a deeper sense of values, their concern for the sensibility of others may be superficial.

Venus Trine Ascendant Sextile Descendant (♀ △ Asc. ✳ Desc.)

This configuration bestows graceful, harmonious personal expression and appearance. It is especially favorable for women, since it enhances their beauty and charm. The pleasing quality and gentleness of the native's manner and his awareness of others bring him popularity, romance, a favorable marriage, and the willing cooperation of others. These persons attract happiness because they take the happiness of others into consideration.

The configuration gives some musical and artistic ability or at least appreciation of the arts.

Venus Trine Midheaven Sextile Nadir (♀ △ M.C. ✳ Nadir)

This configuration indicates continuation of the natives' careers and ambitions through the use of beauty, charm, and the social graces, which win the favor of people in important places. The harmony in their homes creates a favorable social atmosphere for furthering professional ambitions.

Performing artists with this aspect will achieve some recognition.

Trines of Mars

Mars Trine Jupiter (♂ △ ♃)

This trine shows an ability to act with energy and enthusiasm. The philosophic and humanitarian impulses of the natives, as represented by Jupiter, find outlet in constructive action, as indicated by Mars. The natives take practical action to help those less fortunate than themselves, instead of merely feeling sorry for them.

These people put their religion into practice. The double-fire quality of the trine gives them ardent enthusiasm. Mars rules Aries, and Jupiter rules Sagittarius, and the trine aspect itself has a Sagittarian Ninth House connotation. The natives therefore gain understanding and wisdom through positive action. This will affect the affairs ruled by the signs and houses in which Mars and Jupiter are found and the affairs of the houses which they rule.

This trine indicates good karma, attained through previous expenditures of energy designed to help humanity at large. The Twelfth and Eighth House connotation of this aspect also evidences the capacity to regenerate negative conditions stemming from the past into positive actions.

Mars, exalted in Capricorn, and Jupiter, exalted in Cancer, work together to expand the ambitions and also provide the basis for an active, constructive home life.

Also indicated is a liking for sports, adventure, and travel. There is an interest in evangelical or religious work. The aspect favors working with young people through psychology, social work, or religious endeavors.

Mars Trine Saturn (♂ △ ♄)

This aspect combines all the favorable qualities of Capricorn (Saturn rules Capricorn, and Mars is exalted there). It indicates an ability for hard work and serious, purposeful action. Energy is seldom wasted but is applied to produce a maximum of useful results. A tremendous willpower applied with systematic patience characterizes this trine.

Since Saturn lends mathematical precision to the combination, the natives often possess engineering skills, especially where precision optical and mechanical devices are required. They are highly ambitious and will work hard to attain positions of authority and managerial command. Often they are shrewd in politics, whether governmental or corporate. Men who seek military careers are likely to have this aspect.

The trine confers patience combined with skill and daring in action. It favors those who must shoulder serious responsibilities, and gives the natives the ability to endure hardships and face, when necessary, dangerous situations. Under stress there is a high measure of stamina and strength.

Mars Trine Uranus (♂ △ ♅)

This trine gives originality and resourcefulness in action. The natives possess willpower and a capacity to act decisively. They are able to reject old conditions and concepts in order to bring about new ones. This regeneration process comes from the double Scorpio influence. Mars rules Scorpio, and Scorpio is the exaltation sign of Uranus. The natives are direct and outspoken and have a superabundance of energy. They are able to use original methods in achieving professional ambitions, and they aspire to leadership in organizations and groups.

They are skillful in the practical application of occult laws. Considerable inventive and engineering ability goes with this aspect. It especially favors those who work with electromechanical devices.

Independence and a demand for personal freedom at all costs are characteristic of these natives. They are adventurous and will go out of their way to seek unusual experiences.

The high pitch of nervous energy the natives are constantly subject to can be difficult to deal with, even though it derives from a trine. They need to cultivate poise and self-control.

Mars Trine Neptune (♂ △ ♆)

This trine indicates an energized psychic nature, which can be used in healing or in occult work. The natives have a special aptitude for sensing danger and making adjustments to offset it. Their keen sensitivity permits them to detect insincerity in others.

The ability to act decisively in a secretive manner also accompanies the trine. This enables the natives to outmaneuver their opponents and achieve their goals without interference from others.

The aspect combines stamina with acute perception. There is an interest in occult forms of physical culture such as hatha-yoga. Skill in the arts, especially those involving the physical body, such as the dance, is characteristic. Natives are likely to have good habits in diet and personal hygiene. They are extremely sensitive to the emotional coloring of their surroundings and thus have an advantage in knowing how and when to act.

This aspect favors chemists, particularly those who work with liquids and organic chemistry.

Mars Trine Pluto (♂ △ ♀)

This trine indicates a well-developed willpower and the ability to regenerate the personal life and all that it touches through decisive, constructive action. Penetrating insight and realism are combined with the will and the power to act.

In some cases there is an interest in advanced forms of science, such as the use of atomic energy. When the natives are highly developed, they can wield occult forces for the benefit of humanity.

Should a situation require, these natives will fight ruthlessly and give no quarter in defending what they consider right. They know no fear and cannot be intimidated by threats or danger.

Some natives have a dynamic attitude toward life. They are more than normally aware of life as a flux of energy rather than as a set of static conditions.

Often there is a strong constitution with an outstanding degree of stamina. They have the ability to recharge their strength by drawing energies from higher spiritual sources.

Mars Trine North Node Sextile South Node (♂ △ ☊ ⚹ ☋)

This configuration gives the ability to act and to time actions so that they are in harmony with socially accepted modes of behavior. Thus the natives gain popularity as social leaders. The configuration favors politicians and others who lead public lives. The energy needed to deal with social trends and institutions is available.

Mars Trine Ascendant Sextile Descendant (♂ △ Asc. ⚹ Desc.)

This configuration gives a strong physical constitution combined with willpower and decisiveness. The natives' strength and directness inspire confidence in others and gain their cooperation. They lead active lives, are quick in their responses, and accomplish much.

Men are especially favored, since the aspect strengthens the traditional masculine virtues of physical power and ambition.

Mars Trine Midheaven Sextile Nadir (♂ △ M.C. ⚹ Nadir)

This configuration strengthens the natives' ambitions and determination to rise to prominence in their careers. They are energetic and hardworking in their chosen fields. Thus by gaining the confidence of those in authority they win the means to provide a good domestic environment for themselves and their families.

Trines of Jupiter

Jupiter Trine Saturn (♃ △ ♄)

This trine is an excellent indication of a generally responsible person with common sense, honesty, and integrity. It confers business, financial, and managerial abilities.

The natives are provident, farsighted, and capable of coordinating large-scale tasks that carry with them heavy obligations. The trine favors a career in politics or public life. These natives make excellent executives and government officials. They have a good public reputation.

This is also a fine aspect for lawyers and judges. Saturn is exalted in Libra, a sign dealing with justice and law, and is ruler of Capricorn, a sign dealing with government. Jupiter rules Sagittarius and the Ninth House, which rules the law as codified cultural thought. This aspect has a Ninth and Fifth House connotation.

The natives are generally serious-minded, dignified, even-tempered. They have a religious outlook on life, which is likely to be along orthodox lines unless the three outer planets are strong. The trine adds much stability to their lives. They are charitable, but discriminating as to how and to whom charity is given.

Jupiter Trine Uranus (♃ △ ♅)

This trine bestows creative ability and inspiration. The natives will be interested in religion, but along progressive, occult, or metaphysical lines. They are often fortunate on account of past karma, which manifests itself in unexpected ways—they may inherit money or find themselves in highly favorable situations.

The optimism, intuition, and flashes of spiritual inspiration characteristic of these natives make it possible for them to take advantage of opportunities which other people would not notice.

They dislike restraint, for personal freedom is important to them. Often they seek excitement, depending on the rest of the horoscope. They will travel frequently and suddenly, usually by air or water. They will have unusual adventures in foreign lands.

These natives may be active leaders in lodges, clubs, or social and religious groups, especially those of an occult nature. They are often involved in such fraternities as the Masons or Rosicrucians. In politics they are likely to be liberal and proponents of reform. Being good leaders, they acquire renown and popularity through the causes with which they choose to identify.

If other planets reinforce Jupiter and Uranus with good aspects, real genius can be in evidence.

Jupiter Trine Neptune (♃ △ ♆)

This is primarily an aspect for mysticism. The natives are receptive to spiritual influences. However, unless Mercury, Saturn, or Uranus is strong, their intuitive tendencies will be more along the path of love and emotion, rather than mental discrimination and insight.

The natives are fond of grand ceremony, drama, mystery, and religious music. They like to be overwhelmed by a feeling of awe and to lose themselves in the sea of religious ecstasy. However, even with the trine aspect between these planets, they can lack the necessary discrimination that a truly spiritual life demands. Unless other factors in the horoscope confer wisdom, they can be deceived.

These natives are generous and hospitable to all who come into their homes. They want to mother those who will subscribe to their pet beliefs or way of life. These people will receive help from others, even if they do not seem to merit it.

They are inclined to live a monastic life or to live in the country near water.

Often they contribute to mental institutions, hospitals, religious societies, and institutions of higher learning. However, natives with this aspect are just as likely to wander around and follow a rather bohemian life.

Of all the aspects, this is probably the most expansive; it confers a boundless imagination which is more suitable for religion, music, art, poetry, and drama than for more mundane endeavors. There is a tendency for this aspect to be too much of a good thing, since Jupiter and Neptune are both expansive, and rule and are exalted in the same signs, and since the trine aspect also has a Jupiterian, Sagittarian, Ninth House connotation.

In a weak horoscope this aspect can indicate a parasitical nature, inclined to laziness and self-indulgence. But in the case of highly developed people it can give real spiritual inspiration, compassion, and generosity which can border on saintliness.

Jupiter Trine Pluto (♃ △ ♀)

In its highest expression, this trine indicates a faith that can move mountains. Vast powers of spiritual regeneration, both psychological and physical, go with this aspect. The spiritual life of the natives is strengthened by willpower directed constructively.

The natives possess the ability to meditate and to focus their concentration in such a manner as to bring their spiritual inspirations into concrete manifestation. Because Jupiter is ruler of Sagittarius, a fire sign, and Pluto co-rules Aries and is exalted in the fire sign Leo, the natives have tremendous creative power, enabling them to transform both their lives and their surroundings for the good of all. They have deep insight, knowing instinctively what is wrong with any situation, and what must be done to make it right.

Jupiter Trine North Node Sextile South Node (♃ △ ☊ ✶ ☋)

This configuration indicates that the natives' moral and religious values are compatible with those of the society in which they live. For this reason, they are likely to gain prominence in the religious and social institutions of their culture. Their instinctive ability to flow with prevailing trends brings popularity and financial gain.

Jupiter Trine Ascendant Sextile Descendant (♃ △ Asc. ✶ Desc.)

This configuration denotes a constructive, optimistic outlook on life. The natives project self-confidence, enthusiasm, and goodwill, inspiring confidence and cooperation in others. The configuration favors happiness in marriage and harmony in partnerships and in relations with the public.

Jupiter Trine Midheaven Sextile Nadir (♃ △ M.C. ✶ Nadir)

This configuration indicates a constructive attitude toward work which facilitates a rise to prominence in the native's chosen profession. His honesty and sincerity will gain the goodwill of people in positions of power, who in turn will help him further his ambitions. This aspect is especially favorable for a career in law or in the ministry.

Professional success ensures the wherewithal for a happy, secure domestic life. The natives love their families and have a positive attitude toward family members.

Trines of Saturn

Saturn Trine Uranus (♄ △ ♅)

This trine gives intuitive insight into the workings of the laws of the universe. The natives understand the meaning of karma and are, therefore, in a position to structure their lives with this in mind.

Strong willpower is combined with the ability to make practical use of creative inspiration. This aspect is excellent for mathematicians, scientists, astrologers, yogis, and occultists in general. The natives can control subtle energies in an exact, systematic, and scientific way.

They have a genius for organization, which, along with their clear vision and insight, makes them excellent statesmen or heads of state, as well as good executives and coordinators of large projects. There is also skill in public relations, with an understanding of human motivation. The natives often work through groups, organizations, and lodges, especially those dealing with religion or the occult.

Saturn's rulership of Capricorn, combined with Uranus's rulership of Aquarius, gives the ability to work in groups, while Uranus's exaltation in Scorpio imparts the ability to manage collective resources and power. Saturn's exaltation in Libra gives skill and diplomacy.

Saturn Trine Neptune (♄ △ ♆)

This aspect gives the ability to carry on organizational plans and professional activities behind the scenes. For this reason it favors investigators and workers on secret projects, especially government projects. Military strategists, generals, and occult investigators are also favored. The natives are skillful at ferreting out secrets and solving mysteries. Few clues, no matter how subtle, will escape their notice.

There can be involvement with secret societies of a mystical, occult, or religious nature. This trine makes for practical creative expression of clairvoyance and insight. The picture-making apparatus of the mind (ruled by Neptune) has precision and form which can contribute to this prophetic insight. The trine favors those who work in the movie industry since Neptune rules photography, the Fifth House nature of the trine rules entertainment, and Saturn rules the managerial organizing ability.

Because of their steadiness of concentration, these natives are good at meditation and at using their intuition. They are also skillful in analyzing the subtle factors involved in investments and the stock market. In this respect they possess a sixth sense, especially if the Fifth or Sixth House is involved in the aspect.

As is the case with Saturn trine Uranus, there is understanding of the law of cause and effect as it bears on the karmic circumstances of the natives and those with whom they must deal.

The influence of this trine will be strengthened if faster-moving planets in the horoscope make favorable aspects to Saturn or to Neptune. Otherwise, the trine may not be strikingly apparent in an ordinary individual.

Saturn Trine Pluto (♄ △ ♀)

This trine gives the natives the ability to understand the laws by which subtle forces are organized, enabling them to use these laws consciously or unconsciously. It favors those who work in such fields as physics, the occult, magic, astrology, or systems of meditation. If other aspects to Saturn and Pluto are also favorable and if the chart as a whole indicates occult leanings, the natives can have a vast comprehension of the nature of life and of the universe.

The natives have tremendous willpower and are relentless in working toward a goal. Because they combine this trait with organizing ability, they have an aptitude for leadership and managerial responsibilities. They are able to work slowly and make fundamental and irrevocable changes in their own and others' lives. Often there is a sense of destiny or a peculiar karmic mission which they must fulfill. This is one of the most profound of aspects.

In the chart of an average person this aspect will not be strongly marked unless Saturn or Pluto is angular and unless other planets tie into the configuration in a significant way.

Saturn Trine North Node Sextile South Node (♄ △ ☊ ⚹ ☋)

This configuration indicates that the natives are careful and conservative, hewing strictly to the codes of social, moral, and business behavior of the culture with which they must deal. They are, therefore, considered somewhat old-fashioned. However, they achieve success by gaining the cooperation of social institutions and the older, more traditional members of society who respect their conservatism. They tend to ensconce themselves in secure positions in established institutions. This aspect especially favors those politicians or others in public life who represent the more conservative elements of society.

Saturn Trine Ascendant Sextile Descendant (♄ △ Asc. ⚹ Desc.)

This configuration gives the natives a dignified and somewhat cautious and conservative manner and does not permit them to act rashly. Both practical and honest, they gain the respect and admiration of others, though they may be considered rather cold. However, they are able to enter into meaningful partnerships and carry out plans in cooperation with others.

These natives can be trusted to fulfill their obligations to others unless contrary factors in the horoscope are present.

This configuration gives stability in marriage but does not in itself indicate opportunities for marriage.

Saturn Trine Midheaven Sextile Nadir (♄ △ M.C. ✳ Nadir)

This configuration indicates considerable professional ambition. The natives will work steadily and hard to achieve their chosen career goals. They are reliable in their jobs and possess organizational and managerial abilities. Thus, they gain the confidence of people in positions of authority and are promoted. This configuration favors a slow, steady climb to the top. It especially favors those in politics and indicates honesty in public office, providing other factors in the horoscope are confirmatory.

The professional success gained through hard work contributes to a secure and well-ordered domestic life.

Trines of Uranus

Uranus Trine Neptune (♅ △ ♆)

This trine indicates highly developed spiritual faculties. Since it is of long duration, it affects a whole generation (roughly, those born between 1939 and 1945) and is not especially significant in an individual horoscope (unless Uranus or Neptune is angular or heavily aspected by other planets, in which case real genius is indicated). It gives the natives a decided leaning toward the mystical and occult.

This generation will be inclined toward clairvoyance and the development of intuition. Therefore, astrology, yoga, magic, the occult, extrasensory perception, etc., will be in vogue. There will be a tendency to join organizations designed to teach and promulgate these subjects. This generation harbors utopian ideals. Its destiny is to raise the overall level of civilization's spiritual realization to a higher plane.

Uranus Trine Pluto (♅ △ ♀)

This trine indicates a generation of people who have a dynamic will to transform civilization and bring about reform. There are strong scientific and occult leanings among them.

They instigate much dynamic progress and sudden change, a large part of which is brought about through science and the occult. They will brook no opposition and tolerate nothing that obstructs progress. New beginnings in civilization are made through these group efforts. There is an awareness of higher forms of energy and a general unfolding of the intuitive faculties. However, the effects of this trine will not be noticeable in the individual, unless Uranus or Pluto is angular and strong aspects are made to one or both of these planets.

There is an interest in death and life after death, and an understanding of spiritual rebirth and regeneration. This trine has a double Scorpio significance because Pluto rules Scorpio and Uranus is exalted in that sign. Therefore, all of the spiritual and occult qualities of Scorpio find their highest expression in this trine.

Uranus Trine North Node Sextile South Node (♅ △ ☊ ✳ ☋)

This configuration indicates an ability to take advantage of changes in prevailing social attitudes and institutions. The natives may even be leaders of social reform. In politics they are likely to be liberal.

Often there is talent for capitalizing on sudden changes in the social structure because of the natives' ability to adapt quickly to new conditions and to seize new opportunities.

Uranus Trine Ascendant Sextile Descendant (♅ △ Asc. ✳ Desc.)

This configuration gives an original, bright, distinctive, intuitive mode of personal expression, combined with willpower. The natives are often tall, and striking in some way.

Often there is some degree of clairvoyance or intuitive insight.

The natives are natural leaders because of their ability to spark enthusiasm in others and gain their support and cooperation.

There is a tendency to enter into relationships through unusual circumstances.

Uranus Trine Midheaven Sextile Nadir (♅ △ M.C. ✳ Nadir)

This configuration indicates professional success and even fame through unique contributions to the natives' professions, which are in unusual fields. Renown may come suddenly.

The configuration favors scientists, occultists, astrologers, and particularly those in electronics.

The home life and family conditions are likely to have an original flair. There can be unusual gadgetry or architecture for the home itself.

Trines of Neptune

Neptune Trine Pluto (♆ △ ♇)

This is a highly occult aspect and one of long duration. Because it affects an entire generation, it will be manifested in the average individual as a set of attitudes and values characteristic of his generation as a whole. Marked results will be noticeable in an individual only if Neptune or Pluto is strongly aspected with the angles, or is placed in one of the angular houses, or if Neptune and Pluto have strong aspects to other planets.

This trine gives a general tendency toward mysticism and clairvoyant and intuitive faculties. There will be interest in the theoretical aspects of science, as well as in various fields of occult endeavor, especially in reincarnation and survival after death.

Neptune Trine North Node Sextile South Node (♆ △ ☊ ✳ ☋)

This configuration indicates an intuitive ability to fathom the trends of prevailing social attitudes and modes of conduct. The natives thus instinctively know how to benefit from the social forces around them. They are in tune with the times and gain success and popularity through this rapport.

Neptune Trine Ascendant Sextile Descendant ($\Psi \triangle$ Asc. $\ast$ Desc.)

This configuration gives the natives a subtle sensitivity to life which sometimes includes clairvoyant ability, or at least a well-developed intuition. The natives are likely to be somewhat intriguing or mysterious in their personal appearance and mannerisms. Their eyes seem to have a magnetic quality.

Their great empathy with their surroundings extends to human relationships. This intuitive ability to sense the moods of others gives them an advantage in winning confidence, popularity, and cooperation. The aspect favors close rapport with the marriage partner.

Neptune Trine Midheaven Sextile Nadir ($\Psi \triangle$ M.C. $\ast$ Nadir)

This configuration indicates that the natives' intuition can be used constructively in their professions, helping them find solutions to problems and giving them the ability to sense the mood of superiors or others in positions of authority.

The configuration especially favors artists, musicians, and actors because it helps them to gain public recognition. It also favors close intuitive domestic relationships and rapport with the parents. The natives' homes are likely to be unusual or artistic in some way, and they may live near a body of water.

Trines of Pluto

Pluto Trine North Node Sextile South Node ($♇ \triangle \Omega \ast ℧$)

This configuration gives the natives the ability to be leaders in transforming social and political institutions and in helping them attain a higher level of expression. The natives know how to influence mass thought. The configuration favors people in public life, politicians, and social reformers.

Pluto Trine Ascendant Sextile Descendant ($♇ \triangle$ Asc. $\ast$ Desc.)

This configuration gives the natives excellent powers of concentration, a keen awareness, which sometimes includes clairvoyance and a highly developed willpower. The natives have the ability to raise their level of expression by altering their mode of personal interaction with others. This will have the additional effect of raising the level of awareness in others. The strength and self-confidence of these natives inspires confidence and cooperation, and for this reason they make good leaders and organizers. They make new discoveries, initiate new projects, and are constantly finding ways to improve any project or process. Thus they have a transforming effect on their environment and relationships.

Pluto Trine Midheaven Sextile Nadir (♀ △ M.C. ✳ Nadir)

This configuration indicates driving ambition toward professional success and leadership status. The natives keep improving their work techniques. They understand power and know how to deal with people in positions of power. To executives, this configuration gives strength, farsightedness, initiative. There is, in short, the will to succeed.

The professional success gained makes possible a regeneration of domestic conditions.

The home and profession may be a base for occult or scientific endeavor. The configuration favors those who work in science, politics, and metaphysics.

Trines of the Nodes

North Node Trine Ascendant Sextile Descendant (☊ △ Asc. ✳ Desc.)
South Node Sextile Ascendant Trine Descendant (☋ ✳ Asc. △ Desc.)

This configuration indicates a strong awareness of prevailing social trends and institutions. The natives know how to express themselves and act effectively in relation to these, thus gaining social support and approval for themselves and their partners. They carry out their endeavors with a minimum of friction and opposition, unless there are other factors in the horoscope which indicate the contrary.

North Node Trine Midheaven Sextile Nadir (☊ △ M.C. ✳ Nadir)
South Node Sextile Midheaven Trine Nadir (☋ ✳ M.C. △ Nadir)

This configuration gives the natives an awareness of social trends, customs, and institutions in relation to their professions, public reputations, and domestic lives. They are thus able to advance themselves in all professional and domestic dealings which require harmony with the prevailing cultural attitudes.

The configuration favors politicians and others who must depend on good public relations and social approval for success.

North Node Trine Descendant Sextile Ascendant (☊ △ Desc. ✳ Asc.)
South Node Trine Ascendant Sextile Descendant (☋ △ Asc. ✳ Desc.)

This configuration indicates a special ability to make use of current social trends and opinions. Such ability is utilized in public relations, partnerships, salesmanship, and legal matters. The natives are, as the saying goes, "hip," or tuned in to what is going on at the present and what will meet with popular approval.

North Node Trine Nadir Sextile Midheaven (☊ △ Nadir ✳ M.C.)
South Node Trine Midheaven Sextile Nadir (☋ △ M.C. ✳ Nadir)

This configuration indicates special capacity for utilizing social trends in the domestic and professional sphere. The talent for making domestic and career matters mutually supportive is characteristic.

There can also be business ability in using popular trends to make money that is then used to support or improve the domestic environment.

CHAPTER **16**

The Oppositions

Oppositions of the Sun

Sun Opposition Moon (☉ ☍ ☽)

This opposition generally indicates a conflict between the conscious will and the unconscious mind and feelings. Stress is often seen in relationships with the opposite sex, though relationship problems are also generally manifested in domestic, romantic, financial, and marital affairs.

Often the conflict will affect the natives' health, since both the lights strongly influence the vitality principle. There may be a tendency toward restlessness, nervousness, or psychosomatic ailments. In any event, the vital forces are not harmoniously regulated, so that the natives' energy fluctuates erratically.

The natives may also have difficulty in the role of parents, often because of bad experiences in their early childhoods. They should learn to let go of the past, since it blocks their present growth and expression.

This aspect is of a general character rather than a specific influence. It deals more with the overall psychological characteristics than with particular abilities and problems. Its influence in the horoscope will be through the affairs governed by the signs and houses which the Sun and Moon occupy and rule.

A trine aspect made by a planet to the Sun or Moon and sextiling the other light will greatly mitigate the tension of this opposition by creating an area of constructive expression for the energy of the opposition.

If this opposition is part of a square configuration, the planet which squares the Sun and Moon will act as the point of focus and particularize the tension through which the natives' problems are manifested, and through which they must be resolved.

The natives should not endeavor to accomplish great things without duly considering the detail and hard work necessary.

Sun Opposition Mars (☉ ☍ ♂)

This aspect is prone to contention and disagreement, in some cases leading to physical combat. The natives are aggressive and are likely to attract others who are also aggressive. Their desire for power brings them in contact with those similarly inclined. The result is a battle of the wills.

Their tendency to resort to coercion, instead of reason and diplomacy, will naturally create unpleasant situations and arouse a good deal of animosity.

The affairs of life which this opposition affects will depend upon the signs and houses in which Mars and the Sun are found, and the houses which they rule.

These persons often adopt partisan causes, they assess others only in black-and-white terms. They are too impulsive in their relationships and lack the ability to make subtle distinctions in dealing with people.

Sometimes they are too aggressive in sex, or get into quarrels that involve the jealousy of a rival.

Often they overwork their hearts because of continual overexertion.

Sun Opposition Jupiter (☉ ☍ ♃)

This opposition indicates a situation in which the natives are much too optimistic and overexpansive in relating to other people.

They promise more than they can deliver, thus damaging their reputations. Sometimes they annoy others by trying to proselytize their religious and philosophic doctrines. Arrogance or pomposity may be exhibited. Often they make impractical or unrealistic demands on others.

They should cultivate a practical, down-to-earth, impersonal attitude, especially when dealing with others. Impulses toward grandiose schemes and ostentatious manners should be curbed.

Sun Opposition Saturn (☉ ☍ ♄)

This opposition tends to block the self-expression of the natives and to make them somewhat cold when they try to reach out to others. Their reserve and formality can cause difficulties in friendship and romance.

Sometimes the natives have to shoulder heavy responsibilities, which may be imposed by friends, partners, or spouses. Sometimes their self-expression is hampered by lack of self-confidence, lack of cooperation, and negative attitudes on the part of other people. They must work arduously, overcoming many obstacles, in order to fulfill their ambitions.

People with this aspect may be denied children, or there may be an unfortunate condition in connection with them. Marriage comes late in life or does not occur at all. Often the parents of the natives are overly strict or may be a burden to them.

This aspect brings low vitality and difficulties with the teeth.

These natives need to cultivate a sense of humor and a happier outlook on life.

Sun Opposition Uranus (☉ ☍ ♅)

This opposition indicates a situation in which self-will, hypersensitivity, and independence make it difficult for the natives to get along with friends and partners. Their insistence that everything be done their way incurs the disfavor of others. If they change their attitudes, they do so unexpectedly and not always for sound reasons.

They are likely to be nervous and high-strung, tense and irritable; thus others are uneasy in their presence.

At times they deliberately flaunt convention merely for the sake of causing excitement and controversy. They are difficult to deal with because of their sudden changes in behavior, eccentric notions, and ego-identification with their current points of view. They often consider themselves mentally exceptional; but while they may have unusual talents, they do not necessarily use them wisely, nor are they as talented as they would like to think.

Their erratic behavior and impatience stand in the way of sustained effort, so that they cannot acquire the education and experience they need to make practical use of their ideas.

Sun Opposition Neptune (☉ ☍ ♆)

This opposition confuses the natives in their romantic, religious, and private relationships. Very often there is distortion in their understanding of others because their perceptions tend to be colored by biases arising from limited and perhaps one-sided emotional experiences in the past.

Therefore, they should strive for objectivity in their contacts with others.

Emotionalism is likely to induce fantasies and wishful thinking in their relationships, and hence they are often deceived by others. Also, they may be almost unconsciously deceitful because of their own unreliability. They are especially prey to illusion where love and romance are concerned.

These natives may regard themselves as inspired from "on high," whereas in reality they are victims of their own desire for importance. At times they are in danger of influence by astral entities and deceptive psychic forces. They should avoid séances and involvement in astral phenomena. They should be absolutely open and aboveboard in all their relationships.

Sun Opposition Pluto (☉ ☍ ♀)

This opposition indicates dangers from the overbearing nature of the natives' will. There may be a tendency to force circumstances, or to dictate to other people. The natives are usually impulsive in exerting their influence, especially in attempting to transform the world according to their conception of its needs. Conflict may arise when others do not agree with them. This aspect indicates a need for self-regeneration as a means of establishing more successful and harmonious relationships.

The direct, forceful quality of the natives' self-expression will either intimidate or annoy other people, so that the natives cannot gain their support or cooperation.

They are likely to be overly aggressive in matters of sex and romance.

They should avoid getting involved in wars and political and social revolutions, since these will be a source of danger to them.

Oppositions of the Moon

Moon Opposition Mercury (☽ ☍ ☿)

This opposition indicates confusion and irritation in social relationships, resulting from the natives' incessant talking about trivial matters. Women especially are likely to become so boring that their friends will try to avoid them.

Unconscious emotional patterns can distort the natives' ability to think and to communicate clearly and objectively. They take criticism too personally.

They are also prone to nervousness and emotional excitability. Their health can suffer from improper diet and personal hygiene, or they may be fanatics about personal and domestic cleanliness. In either case, there can be a lack of balance.

The natives may waste money on unimportant things, usually household items or clothing, or these matters can be out of balance.

There may be confusion in communication involving family and neighborhood affairs. The natives' excessive worry about their families is a source of annoyance for both family and friends.

Moon Opposition Venus (☽ ☍ ♀)

This opposition indicates an inclination to be emotionally oversensitive and to feel unloved. Domestic and material problems may result.

Sometimes there are self-indulgent tendencies and too great a concern for material comforts and luxuries. This aspect has a negative, double Taurus emphasis. There can be sexual excess as well as unhealthy eating habits—usually overindulgence in sweets and carbohydrates.

Sometimes the natives' families will cause problems by interfering in marital affairs, perhaps in the form of the proverbial mother-in-law conflict.

If the natives concentrate on universal aspirations, they may ignore the material comforts of domestic life.

Moon Opposition Mars (☽ ☍ ♂)

This opposition indicates a volatile and emotional nature. The natives often lose their tempers over petty annoyances, especially domestic ones, and consequently damage social and domestic relationships. Men with this aspect are likely to be too brusque with women; women sometimes lack the gentle feminine qualities.

Alcoholism is also a danger. There is a tendency to be very argumentative under the influence of drink.

The natives need to develop serenity and self-control. Their impulsiveness may make them act irrationally. Their tendency to spend too much money can lead to financial depletion and debt. Carelessness with other people's money and property will cause resentment and even conflict.

There are often clashes with parents, especially the mother, which later carry over into the native's own home life.

Impatient with routine, these natives have difficulty in carrying out long-range responsibilities. Their desire for excitement can lead to undesirable associations, dissipation, and sometimes violence or other serious troubles.

They may lose members of their families because of war or violence. It is well for them to take precautions to protect their homes against fire. In heavily afflicted horoscopes, there may be dishonesty and criminal tendencies.

Moon Opposition Jupiter (☽ ☍ ♃)

This opposition indicates a tendency to get carried away by benevolent impulses. The natives lack wisdom and discrimination in bestowing kindness. Problems in their relationships are likely to arise because they are duped by others or they promise more than they can deliver. This aspect can also indicate laziness and self-indulgence. Overeating may cause bodily distress or too much weight. Extravagance, waste, and disorder are some of the vices to which the natives are prone.

Sometimes there is maudlin sentimentality, very often connected with religion.

Often extravagance causes relationship problems with parents or family members, perhaps as the result of religious controversies. There may be difficulties over private family affairs which the natives do not want to face objectively.

The natives often block their own progress because of an emotional attachment to attitudes and habit patterns of the past, which represent security to them.

Moon Opposition Saturn (☽ ☍ ♄)

This opposition indicates a tendency toward emotional depression and stagnation because of a clinging to unfruitful relationships and family ties. Often the parents are responsible for instilling rigid attitudes during the natives' early childhood.

These people lack emotional flexibility and optimism in their relationships with others. Sometimes their stiff, formal manner makes others bored or ill at ease.

There is also an inclination to judge relationships, and to respond to them on the basis of past experiences and disappointments. This blocks the ability to respond to other people in an appropriate and natural manner.

Sometimes the natives' lives and free expression are thwarted by parental and domestic responsibilities, either real or imagined. Financial problems may cramp their style. Either they have difficulty making friends or their families disapprove of their friends.

Their imagination is likely to be limited or blocked by this opposition. Since their emotional nature can be cold and unresponsive, it is hard for other people to respond to them.

There is the strong possibility of conflict between domestic and professional obligations. Employers or superiors can unconsciously remind the natives of their parents, causing difficulty in getting along with those in authority.

Moon Opposition Uranus (☽ ☍ ♅)

This opposition can indicate emotional perverseness and instability. There are frequent, unexpected changes in mood and attitude, which are confusing to others. Undependability and unpredictability may so exasperate family and friends that they will separate from the natives or avoid them as much as possible. There can also be nervous tension which sometimes is manifested as irritability.

Often the natives make many new and sudden acquaintances, but as a rule these will not endure long.

There can be instability in the family life, as well as frequent changes in residence. The tendency to seek unusual experiences can drain too much time and energy from important responsibilities of life and lead to the breaking of domestic ties in order to pursue adventure. At times mothers neglect their maternal duties out of boredom with child-raising routines. Men are often irresponsible toward sweethearts, wives, and families. Women are likely to exasperate men with their erratic emotions.

These natives should be careful with psychic involvements which do not serve a useful purpose in their spiritual unfolding.

Moon Opposition Neptune (☽ ☍ ♆)

This opposition indicates a tendency to project internal emotional confusion onto other people and the world at large. Often there is such a subtle interplay of unconscious telepathic forces in the natives' relationships that they are uncertain as to whether their problems originate in themselves or in their associates.

Extreme impressionability characterizes this aspect because the natives soak up the emotional coloring of their environment. Therefore, they must learn discrimination in choosing their associates.

In this era there is considerable danger that these natives will become implicated in drug abuse because of bad associations. Alcohol is also a danger. They should be careful of dubious moneymaking schemes and financial ventures.

Involvement in the astral plane or psychic phenomena can be risky.

Domestic affairs are likely to be confused and disorderly, either because of laziness and irresponsibility or because of psychological problems originating in the past. Other people will take advantage of the natives by playing on their feelings. Psychosomatic ailments and emotional tension are often in evidence. In weak individuals this aspect can give a parasitical inclination.

Moon Opposition Pluto (☽ ☍ ♀)

This opposition indicates a tendency to control and remake family and friends. The natives display an emotional vehemence in their relationships that makes it difficult for others to respond to them in a relaxed way.

Disputes over money and the use of joint resources often take the form of family quarrels over inheritance. Other altercations with the family can arise from the natives' unwillingness to be dictated to by them.

This opposition can also signify aggressiveness or austerity in love and romance.

Oppositions of Mercury

Mercury Opposition Mars (☿ ☍ ♂)

This opposition indicates an argumentative disposition causing verbal conflict with others when the natives feel abused. At times they will take a contrary point of view for the sake of argument. This trait does not help their popularity.

These people are critical, fault-finding, sticklers for accuracy in thought and word. Nevertheless, their impulsiveness often makes them overlook pertinent details, or they totally fail to see the other person's point of view.

There is a tendency to take ideas too personally or to become ego-identified with them. The natives are therefore often unable to see things from a multifaceted point of view. An attack on their thoughts is taken as a personal affront. The desires and the emotions can often interfere with their reason.

These natives are prone to have nervous, hypersensitive dispositions, and less cultured individuals may use profane language. Generally the tongue is sharp. Naturally, such attributes, which interfere with harmony and communication, do not make for friendly relationships and can affect friends, brothers, sisters, partners, or co-workers.

There can be disputes over the use of joint resources.

Mercury Opposition Jupiter (☿ ☍ ♃)

This opposition can get the natives in trouble because they are inclined to promise more than they can deliver; there will be a lot of talk and insufficient follow-up action. Woolgathering and daydreaming are the other negative attributes of the opposition.

These natives need to acquire thoroughness and attention to detail in their thinking, planning, and communicating to achieve results and to gain the confidence and respect of others. They are likely to have difficulties with religion, because they either are agnostic or hold illogical beliefs. They should not sign bonds or securities for others since they are likely to be unreliable.

In higher education the natives may pursue esoteric, literary, scholarly, or philosophic studies, which lack practical value for earning a living. At times the natives can neglect worldly responsibilities for such pursuits.

Intellectual conceit may go with this aspect. However, the natives are easily flustered and unable to defend themselves under cross-examination because their memories fail them under stress. They are not good at keeping secrets and are likely to divulge confidential information at the most inopportune time.

Mercury Opposition Saturn (☿ ☍ ♄)

The effect of this opposition makes the natives somewhat defensive and suspicious. In highly afflicted horoscopes, it can even lead to scheming and underhandedness.

The natives are prone to depression and anxiety. This tendency to look on the dark side of things can prevent them from recognizing opportunities around them.

Sometimes they are nagging and critical; they therefore have few friends.

They are ambitious for intellectual recognition but encounter many obstacles in achieving it. Their intellectual jealousy arouses antagonism in their colleagues. Communication problems, overly conservative thinking, or rigid attitudes often hamper their careers and public standing. Attacks on their reputations are also possible with this aspect.

In heavily afflicted charts, extreme narrow-mindedness and opinionated attitudes can be in evidence.

These natives are subject to nervous and respiratory disorders. Smoking is particularly harmful to them.

Mercury Opposition Uranus (☿ ☍ ♅)

This opposition indicates eccentric opinions. The natives are inconsistent in thought and stubborn in adhering to their ideas. No one can change their minds for them, although they may do so themselves twice in one day.

Their speech is usually blunt and tactless, unless other aspects indicate the contrary. They are arrogant and conceited. They may consider themselves geniuses or, at worst, extremely gifted mentally, while others often regard them as impractical and strange. These tendencies can annoy others to the point where the natives have difficulty in forming lasting friendships.

They have trouble with group endeavors. Often they think that their ideas should be adopted or else they are unwilling to conform to the ideas of others.

They jump to conclusions or make snap judgments. They generally have considerable nervous tension, unless Saturn is well aspected. Concentrating on one mental task for a sustained period of time is hard for them, and unless they have constant stimulation they are bored.

The natives are likely to start too many projects at once, and except in the presence of a strong Saturn, none is followed through. For this reason, they can gain reputations for unreliability.

Mercury Opposition Neptune (☿ ☍ ♆)

This opposition gives rise to a high degree of sensitivity to other people's thoughts and motivations. An unconscious telepathy often leads to deceitful practices that may or may not be malicious. It is as though the natives were trying to outmaneuver their opponents in a subtle telepathic chess game.

These natives could be more successful by being straightforward; at times they defeat their own purposes by their scheming, which makes other people mistrust them.

If other factors in the horoscope indicate that the natives are naïve or lack astuteness, this aspect is likely to cause false illusions about others. The resultant confusion in relationships makes them prey to deception through the written and spoken word.

They must be careful not to divulge secret information.

Their sensitivity makes it hard for them to shut off environmental influences, so that they may be distracted from important responsibilities. They usually find it difficult to control their imaginations, especially regarding other people.

Mercury Opposition Pluto (☿ ☌ ♀)

This opposition can cause great mental tension because the natives find themselves in situations in which they must deal with secret and potentially dangerous information. Researchers on secret projects often have this aspect.

Often these people are the repository of confidential information. In extreme cases, the natives may actually be involved in spying or detective work and get themselves into difficulties doing it. In extreme cases, it can result in death.

Sometimes these natives are abrupt and harsh in speech, or else others are abrupt and harsh toward them.

They may be engaged in scientific investigations. They also have a tendency to interrogate others or to be curious regarding them. The result is often resentment and bad personal relationships.

Oppositions of Venus

Venus Opposition Mars (♀ ☌ ♂)

This opposition generates relationship problems of an emotional nature, often involving sex. Natives are extremely sensitive and easily hurt by other people's unkindness.

This aspect can work two ways, depending on which planet is stronger. If Venus is stronger, the natives, especially if female, may be the victims of abusive treatment. If Mars is stronger, the natives are likely to use the opposite sex for sexual gratification, without consideration for their feelings and needs.

The aspect is not favorable for happiness in marriage because of its tendency to cause emotional and sexual incompatibility. Often the natives have nothing in common with their spouses except sexual attraction, because Mars is the natural First House ruler and Venus is the natural Seventh House ruler; thus the principles of desire and attraction are involved.

There can also be disagreements over joint finances, money shared with a spouse or business partner.

Sometimes this aspect causes separation in marriage when, for various reasons, one partner is away from home a great deal of the time, causing unhappiness and discontent.

Venus Opposition Jupiter (♀ ☍ ♃)

This opposition is characteristic of the person who is sickeningly sweet, boring others.

Natives with this opposition, especially if they are well-to-do, can be spoiled and overly involved in meaningless social activity. Laziness, self-indulgence, and love of luxury may be in evidence. Females are likely to be conceited, thinking themselves more desirable than they are. Sometimes they have the attitude that everything should be done for them, particularly if they are born into affluence.

The natives can be too maudlin and given to flowery religious sentiments. Often hypocrisy shows itself when something practical has to be done to help those in need.

The natives may take too much for granted concerning others, mostly in regard to things that are done for them. Marital problems may center around matters of religion.

These natives like to be the center of attraction and are far from reticent. Somehow they gain the attention they want.

There can be overindulgence in eating, especially of sweets. Money can be spent wastefully on luxuries.

Venus Opposition Saturn (♀ ☍ ♄)

This opposition is often the cause of emotional frustrations and financial hardships. The natives experience disappointments in love and have few pleasures in life. Often they are depressed, because Saturn frustrates the natural tendencies of Venus toward joy, beauty, and happiness. Their natures may be made cold because of continual deprivations and heavy responsibilities.

This opposition often indicates an unhappy marriage in which the spouse is unresponsive, unfortunate and poor, harsh and dictatorial, much older than the native—the marriage may be based on financial considerations only with a lack of any love.

This aspect can also indicate financial difficulties with regard to employment, since the natives are likely to have jobs they do not enjoy or which do not pay well. Their employers may be miserly and selfish.

Often the natives are misunderstood by their friends, or else their friends are a great deal older than they are.

This opposition can also make it difficult to relate to the public at large and does not favor popularity because the natives always appear to be so reserved.

Marriage may be delayed or prevented altogether. The parents can have an unfortunate effect on the natives by being poor, too strict, cold, or oppressive. Or they may force the natives to assume heavy responsibilities prematurely.

Venus Opposition Uranus (♀ ☍ ♅)

This opposition indicates an unstable emotional nature. It tends to stimulate the desire for all types of exotic experiences, without consideration for the consequences.

Very often there are several marriages ending in divorce. The natives are periodically enthralled in new infatuations and while they last the natives will do anything for their sake. However, these romances break up as suddenly as they start, leaving chaos in their wake. The effect is as though the natives were subjected to an emotional force beyond their control or understanding.

These natives are foolish in their use of money, spending it impulsively in casual friendships or useless pleasures.

Often there is a great deal of emotional willfulness. The natives will not follow the dictates of their own consciences, let alone good advice from others. Powerful desires drive them toward an erratic and sometimes disastrous course of life, especially where relationships are concerned.

Their demand for personal freedom at any cost often makes it impossible for them to adjust to the mutual responsibilities which marriage, partnerships, and friendships require. Other people are likely to give up on them for this reason, making loneliness and estrangement their fate.

There can be unfortunate friendships and associations, based on mere gratification of desire for pleasure, which lead the natives astray.

Venus Opposition Neptune (♀ ☍ ♆)

This opposition indicates that emotions and affections are strongly influenced by unconscious forces.

In matters of money, marriage, social life, and artistic creativity the natives are sometimes their own worst enemies. Their unconscious desires generate wishful thinking and distorted perceptions of reality.

Sometimes laziness and self-indulgence cause them to go astray, partaking in unhealthy and exotic pleasures such as alcohol and drugs. This catering to the senses can deplete their financial resources, placing them in an inferior position or limiting their expression.

This aspect may cause scandals as a result of secret love affairs or alliances, for the tendency of Neptune is to camouflage the private affairs of the natives until the matter is forced into the open.

There is danger of practicing or being the victim of subtle sexual seduction. This can in some cases manifest itself in homosexual tendencies.

If marriage is involved, the aspect can cause divorce. It will do so by gradually undermining a marriage, instead of openly breaking it off, as would be the case with Venus opposing Uranus.

Venus Opposition Pluto (♀ ☍ ♀)

This opposition confers a predisposition for getting involved in intense emotional and sexual relationships which can be demoralizing. The natives are likely to have romantic and sexual problems of some sort, usually because of their uncontrollable passions.

The emotions can distort the will and regenerative power. The natives often attract associations of an undesirable kind. In extreme cases, there are underworld involvements with sex, such as prostitution, or the use of sex in making money some other way.

This opposition can indicate problems in marriage because of the natives' dictatorial attitudes toward the marriage partner or vice versa. They may try to remake those they love rather than reforming themselves.

There will probably be problems with taxes, insurance, joint finances, or inheritances.

Karmic factors can affect the natives' lives, often through so-called sex magic or possession by an outside entity. There is a possibility of suicide attempts due to disappointment in love.

Oppositions of Mars

Mars Opposition Jupiter (♂ ☍ ♃)

This opposition produces extravagant tendencies, especially with other people's money.

Often the natives appear to be outgoing and friendly, but as a rule this attitude only serves their own interest—often their holy crusades are designed to promote their own material well-being, their sense of importance, or both.

They are opinionated and aggressive in promoting their religious and philosophic viewpoints, which trait often antagonizes others. At times this zeal serves to provide a socially acceptable outlet for their self-assertiveness, which often inclines them to attempt great things without the necessary resources to succeed.

This is one aspect of the soldier of fortune. Restlessness and desire for travel and adventure are characteristic. In extreme cases avarice and dishonesty occur.

The aspect does not favor speculation, and partners or business associates should be chosen for dependability. The natives are prone to boast and exaggerate their own importance. They often acquire reputations for wastefulness and unreliability.

In general, there is a lack of steady, sustained, well-regulated effort.

Mars Opposition Saturn (♂ ☍ ♄)

This opposition can produce a resentful and oppressive nature. There is often frustration and a need to demonstrate personal prowess or superiority through some kind of violent, aggressive action as a cover-up for the fear of personal inadequacies in relating to others. The natives' attempts to take action, as indicated by Mars's rulership of the First House, are thwarted by others, as represented by Saturn's exaltation in Libra, the Seventh House sign.

The natives' professional ambitions are stifled by misfortune or by those in authority. Their relationships with parents, especially their fathers, are not likely to be good because the fathers will be oppressive toward them.

Since Mars is exalted in Capricorn, where Saturn rules, the natives may seek status in undesirable or destructive ways, encountering obstacles and opposition in the process. Or they may become victims of this type of behavior in others.

There can be problems with joint finances and corporate resources, which result in strained relationships. Often the natives have unfriendly attitudes and refuse to go out of their way to help others. By the same token, others will not help them.

In extreme cases, cruelty or criminal tendencies manifest themselves. Military involvements are also possible.

Mars Opposition Uranus (♂ ☍ ♅)

The natives with this opposition are inclined to explosive outbursts of energy which can be manifested in quarrels. Ill temper and irritability are common. These people are averse to any kind of routine and discipline. Their efforts are spasmodic; however, when they do work they can over-exert themselves. Lack of moderation is the main vice of this opposition.

There is also danger of violent death because of the double Scorpio connotation, which stems from the rulership of Mars and the exaltation of Uranus in Scorpio. In war situations this aspect, when activated by transits of progressions, can indicate violence from others or from the natives to others.

Stubbornness and the desire for personal freedom at all cost make these natives hard to deal with. They cannot be instructed or led against their will. Lessons have to be learned through hard experience. Youths with this aspect may be reckless and engage in revolutionary activities, especially when other factors in the horoscope confirm it.

The natives' aspirations lead them into dangerous and unstable situations. They can make enemies out of friends through ill-considered actions. They are difficult to get along with because they want their own way under all circumstances.

There can be sudden, drastic changes in their lives. Their desire is to sweep away the status quo, without adequate planning for where to go or what to do next. This unpredictable conduct exasperates those who must contend with it.

The natives tend to confuse their desires with their will.

There is danger through electricity and machinery with this aspect.

Mars Opposition Neptune (♂ ♍ ♆)

This opposition is indicative of a subtle and hard-to-control desire nature. The Mars tendency of aggressiveness and violence functions through the unconscious in such a manner that the natives are not always aware of the motivations behind their actions.

The danger of this opposition is its emotional character. Unless planets of a more mental nature such as Mercury, Uranus, or Saturn aspect either Mars or Neptune favorably in some way, the natives' unconscious desires and actions stemming from them are not checked by conscious reasoning. Distorted conditions in the natives' lives are the result.

At times the natives act secretively. In extreme cases they are deceitful or underhanded. This conduct may not be deliberate but rather an automatic reaction, since Neptune rules the unconscious and the Twelfth House of self-undoing.

Sometimes abnormal or unhealthy sexual desires and alliances affect the natives' home and professional reputation. Often these natives seek unusual emotional gratification, which interferes with the practical necessities of life. They should stay away from drugs and alcohol, which can lead to entanglement in the lower astral realms.

In the horoscopes of respectable or so-called nice people, this opposition can cause various forms of neurosis, resulting from repressed desires.

There may be psychosomatic ailments or other mysterious, hard-to-diagnose mental and physical ailments. If other factors confirm it, this opposition, because of its Eighth, Fourth, and Twelfth House connotation, can bring about a peculiar and mysterious death.

Religious or spiritually inclined natives will experience unrealistic visionary and religious emotionalism. Often this fervor has an unconscious motivation in the desire to be special in some way.

There is danger from associations with dishonest people, and with people who take advantage of the natives' sympathy.

Neptune is the Achilles' heel of the Zodiac. In this configuration, as with other Neptune afflictions, the natives are as a rule perfectly rational except in the areas affected by the sign and house positions, the rulerships of Neptune, and the planets which are afflicting it, in this case Mars. The reason is that the department afflicted by Neptune is subject to the influence of the unconscious mind, over which the natives have no control. In the Mars-Neptune afflictions, this is particularly dangerous because the tendency of Mars is to action without rational thought.

Mars Opposition Pluto (♂ ☍ ♀)

The effect of this opposition is generally to create a conflict between the natives' personal desires and actions, as represented by Mars, and their spiritual will, as represented by Pluto.

Mars, Uranus, and Pluto are the planets that have the most to do with action and fundamental change. Actions stemming from Mars are usually based on personal desire, whereas actions based on Uranus and Pluto are the result of universal forces, evolutionary trends, and the natives' higher consciousness and spiritual will.

In highly developed individuals this opposition can indicate a test on the natives' evolutionary path, which will determine whether the personal desire or the spiritual will is the stronger factor, based on considerations of the universal welfare.

The temptation of this aspect is to use collective power, represented by Pluto, for personal, selfish aggrandizement, represented by Mars. In extreme cases, this can result in the demoniac, the individual of extreme violence. The natives must learn how to use power correctly because their actions will have far-reaching consequences for themselves as well as for others.

In wartime the native is likely to be involved in direct physical combat with consequent danger of violence and death; however, violence or death may come through other facets of war, or through revolution, crime, or natural catastrophe.

The natives with this opposition can be perpetrators of or victims of violence. There is also the tendency to want to rule and remake others. This naturally causes resentment and conflict. In extreme cases there can be thievery and violence.

Oppositions of Jupiter

Jupiter Opposition Saturn (♃ ☍ ♄)

This opposition often creates problems in relationships affecting profession, marriage, domestic affairs, friendships, religion, and group associations. As a rule, the natives must shoulder weighty responsibilities, and their standing in the community will depend on how effectively they deal with them.

Sometimes they are under pressure to perform tasks for which they do not have sufficient time, training, or resources. Financial and professional problems may result from poor planning and bad timing on their part.

Lacking imagination, unless other factors in the horoscope confer it, they are too rigid and conservative and may lead a humdrum life of stagnation. Their ambitions are hard to attain, because of inability, misfortune, or absence of opportunity.

They are seldom happy in their work and perform it out of necessity or a sense of duty. Sometimes they must rigidly conform to the routine practices of a large organization in which they hold minor posts. In order to succeed in such an operation, they must sacrifice their individual ideals to its impersonal requirements. Otherwise, they have to go it alone and are forced to compete with organizations that have more money and influence than they have. Thus, the established structure of society imposes conformity or hardship on the natives.

Sometimes the natives internalize the established social standards and become narrow-minded representatives of them. They are likely to be rigid, traditional, and at times hypocritical in their religious philosophy.

They may encounter obstacles in obtaining a higher education, or they may find themselves in disagreement with the educational institutions they attend. In many cases they must endure a life of privation and struggle in order to achieve even moderate goals. They can lack optimism and become easily depressed. The parents may be intolerant and oppressive toward them.

Legal difficulties and involvements in lawsuits are probable with this opposition. There can also be difficulties in foreign countries and on long-distance journeys.

Jupiter Opposition Uranus (♃ ☍ ♅)

This opposition signifies restlessness and unwise attempts at financial, religious, and social expansion. Often that expansion involves large outlays of money and resources belonging to the natives and their friends. Such projects can run into unforeseen difficulties, leading to financial ruin for the natives and for those who invest in their enterprises. For this to be a serious threat, other factors in the horoscope must confirm it.

For example, if Jupiter in opposition to Uranus is also square Mars, the effect could be disastrous. The natives could be overoptimistic, or overconfident, becoming easy prey to those who approach them with grandiose, get-rich-quick schemes.

This opposition, though highly idealistic and well-meaning, can be one of the most dangerous of all the aspects. It denotes unbridled flights of imagination which have no basis in reality.

It also invites involvement in unconventional religious cults and practices. Proselytizing on behalf of such beliefs and organizations can give the natives reputations for eccentricity and cause problems with their friends and in their social relationships.

Often the natives are in conflict with traditional religious, educational, philosophic, and legal views, holding obstinately to their own opinions, contrary to their common sense.

This aspect is likely to produce wanderlust. The natives may suddenly take off on journeys of adventure, which can bring disaster and financial loss in their wake.

They can be blunt and often abandon diplomacy in dealing with friends and group associates, thereby causing disharmony and inviting personal unpopularity.

Characterizing this aspect is the image of the soap bubble that bursts with the slightest pinprick. The natives generally promise far more than they can produce. They can also be taken in by the unrealistic or dishonest schemes of others.

Jupiter Opposition Neptune (♃ ☍ ♆)

The natives are not deliberately dishonest, but they are absentminded and make promises they are unable to fulfill. In short, they are unreliable and impractical, unless other factors in the horoscope indicate otherwise.

Even then, there is likely to be an unrealistic blind spot somewhere in their character which relates to the signs and houses occupied and ruled by Jupiter and Neptune. In extreme cases, there are delusions of grandeur with religious overtones.

How this opposition is handled will depend on the strength of Mercury and Saturn in the horoscope. Often the natives are inclined to religious mysticism, but their beliefs are likely to be distorted. Their spiritual idealism seldom benefits humanity in any practical way. They can be generous and kindhearted but usually lack discrimination in this regard.

Sometimes the aspect produces maudlin sentimentality and gushy emotions which are an annoyance and embarrassment to others.

The religious inclinations tend to cultism, and worship of supposed masters, or some idealized personality. This is probably an ego mechanism for vicariously bestowing spiritual importance and distinction on the natives, who may imagine themselves as special messengers from on high.

There are often exotic dreams of travel to faraway places, which is the aspect of religious pilgrimages.

There is danger from gases, fumes, drugs, and alcohol.

The lack of practicality is not always favorable for business or financial involvements.

Jupiter Opposition Pluto (♃ ☍ ♀)

Natives with this opposition often try to indoctrinate others in their religious and philosophic views. They feel it is their responsibility to reform others spiritually. Since other people may not agree with their dogma, conflict is likely.

In some cases the desire for great wealth or power tempts the natives to use dishonorable means to attain their ends. Ambition will be manifested in either a material or a spiritual way, so that the desire for importance stands in the way of harmonious relationships with others.

Autocratic attitudes and lack of humility can cause unpopularity. If carried too far, they will result in the natives' ultimate downfall.

Oppositions of Saturn

Saturn Opposition Uranus (♄ ☍ ♅)

This opposition inclines the natives toward inconsistent and dictatorial attitudes. They will rarely practice what they preach. Their philosophy is idealistic, but their actions are oppressive. Desiring freedom for themselves, they are usually unwilling to grant it to others. Naturally their friends will be few. (This opposition appears in the horoscope of the Soviet Union.)

If the natives hold positions of authority, their subordinates will resent them and rebel. Should the natives be in inferior positions, they will be prey to the whims of their superiors.

The natives have little stability or security in their lives, because circumstances over which they have no control may unexpectedly deprive them of whatever they depend upon for this.

They lack humility, being unwilling to admit to the unreasonableness and inconsistency of their attitudes and actions. Despite an ability to work hard, common sense and good planning are often absent, as are patience and the capacity for disciplined, sustained effort. Irritable moods mark their temperaments.

Saturn Opposition Neptune (♄ ⚍ ♆)

This opposition can make the natives mistrustful of others, morbid, and morose. They are subject to irrational fears, stemming from their unconscious minds and past memories, which color their attitudes toward others. Their anxiety and reserve also make other people suspicious.

The virtues of frank and aboveboard dealings should be cultivated, since a conflict which is openly discussed can often be worked out. In extreme cases the natives are cunning and deceitful, or are victimized by others who are.

Sometimes they use underhanded means to achieve worldly ambitions, or they may be victims of the plots of others, which can affect their reputations. Public scandals may even result from these conditions.

There can be a persecution or martyr complex with this aspect. Sometimes the native has to be institutionalized. Psychological problems tend to be deep-rooted and hard to diagnose and cure.

Saturn Opposition Pluto (♄ ⚍ ♀)

This opposition indicates serious karmic problems. The natives can be the perpetrators or victims of oppression, cruelty, and harsh treatment, usually because of their personal connection with adverse conditions of mass destiny which thwart their ambitions and endanger their safety.

Saturn, as the grim reaper, will bring misfortune into their lives. Individuals who are raised in slums, severely underprivileged, cruelly treated, or caught in wars, or who are unjustly imprisoned, are likely to have this opposition. However, its effects will not be strongly noticeable unless the opposition spans angular houses and Saturn and Pluto are afflicted by other planets.

Sometimes the deaths of the natives are fated in some peculiar way. The natives are thwarted in self-expression and creative self-development. This opposition requires regeneration through hard work and discipline.

Oppositions of Uranus

Uranus Opposition Neptune (♅ ☍ ♆)

This opposition, which is of long duration, is indicative of a generation of people who live in a time of social unrest. Destiny forces them to choose sides in large religious, social, and political controversies, and in partisan causes.

The average person will respond to the opposition in automatic ways, often according to the prevailing social trends and the standards of their peers.

If the opposition is angular and heavily aspected by other planets, particular conscious, intuitive sensitivity will be evident.

These natives must be careful how they use their psychic abilities, especially if there are other afflictions to Neptune or Pluto in the horoscope. Destructive astral-plane experiences can have harmful results.

In afflicted horoscopes, this opposition can contribute to neurotic tendencies, escapism through alcohol, or sexual involvements. There may be extremism, rigid, unreasonable attitudes, and in some cases fanaticism.

The emotions can be at variance with the will and the intuitive mind. Psychic problems are sure to be manifested in this opposition.

Uranus Opposition Pluto (♅ ☍ ♀)

This opposition is indicative of a generation of people who must live in times of social and political upheaval. The mass destiny of these natives is beset with drastic changes—war, revolution, and violence.

Fanaticism is likely to be manifested in many ways, often taking the form of extreme political and social doctrines. The natives lean toward occult interests, which can be dangerous unless properly directed. In those who are strongly affected by the opposition extremist tendencies, explosive temper, and radical action should be avoided, lest they bring violence and danger.

Sometimes the lives of the natives are disrupted by economic collapse, war, revolution, industrial revolution, and temporary dislocation of work brought about by these changes.

The effect of this opposition will not be obvious unless Uranus and Pluto are angular and heavily aspected. The average individual will respond to it in an automatic, unconscious way according to the destiny of the times. That destiny will affect the natives through the signs and houses which Uranus and Pluto occupy and rule.

Oppositions of Neptune

Neptune Opposition Pluto (♆ ☍ ♇)

This opposition, which occurs in the maps of a whole generation of people, is noticeable in its effect on individuals only if it is angular and heavily aspected, in which case they will be markedly different from their peers.

This aspect often indicates psychic or occult proclivities which can result in subtle emotional and mental stress.

Conflict between the emotions and the will may cause tension between the unconscious desires and an urge for power. The way this stress is externalized depends on the signs and houses which Neptune and Pluto occupy and rule.

This opposition is likely to cause involvement in racial, religious, and social problems, and in conflicts of various kinds.

Glossary

Ascendant The point at which the eastern horizon intersects the ecliptic. The First House or rising sign.

Aspect The angle formed between two imaginary lines connecting two celestial bodies or points with the Earth.

Conjunction The occurrence of a direct or nearly direct line-up of two planets as seen from the Earth.

Cusp The line of division between two houses. The cusps are normally named for the line between a house and the house below it. Thus, the Seventh House cusp is the line between the Seventh and Sixth houses.

Descendant The point at which the western horizon intersects the ecliptic. It is also the cusp between the Sixth and Seventh houses.

Ecliptic The plane of the Earth's orbit around the Sun extended into space to meet the celestial sphere. From the Earth, the ecliptic appears to be the path the Sun follows around the Earth in a year's time.

Horoscope A map or chart of the position of the planets in the heavens at the exact time and place of one's birth. The map covers the entire sky, a full circle of 360°. Also called a *natal chart* or *map*.

House One of twelve divisions made in the cycle of the Earth's daily rotation. Each house represents an approximate two-hour period during which one-twelfth of the Zodiac appears to pass over the horizon. The houses are named in order, beginning with the First House and continuing through to the Twelfth House. Each house presides over a different department of practical affairs and is associated with a specific sign of the Zodiac.

Meridian A great circle on the celestial sphere passing through the north and south points of the horizon and the zenith, which is directly above the observer.

Midheaven (also written *M.C.* from the Latin *medium coeli*) The point at which the meridian intersects the ecliptic.

Nadir The point on the ecliptic directly opposite the Midheaven looking downward from the observer. Also called the Fourth House cusp.

Node Each of the two points at which a planet's orbit intersects the ecliptic: once when the planet moves north across the ecliptic, and once again when it moves south. In astrology, the Nodes of the moon are especially significant.

Opposition An aspect representing an angular relationship of 180° between two planets. Planets in opposition generally occupy approximately the same number of degrees in two signs directly across the Zodiac from each other.

Quadruplicity One of three fixed groups of signs, each containing four signs. The three quadruplicities relate to three characteristics—cardinal, fixed, and mutable—and are concerned with basic modes of activities.

Sextile That aspect representing an angular relationship of 60°, or one-sixth of a circle. Planets in sextile aspect are placed two signs apart and occupy approximately the same number of degrees in these signs, plus or minus 6°.

Square That aspect representing an angular relationship of 90°. Planets in square aspect generally occupy the same number of degrees in signs which are three signs apart.

Sun signs The twelve traditional signs of the Zodiac. They are Aries (the Ram), Taurus (the Bull), Gemini (the Twins), Cancer (the Crab), Leo (the Lion), Virgo (the Virgin), Libra (the Scales), Scorpio (the Scorpion), Sagittarius (the Archer), Capricorn (the Goat), Aquarius (the Water-bearer), and Pisces (the Fishes).

Trine That aspect representing an angular relationship of 120° or one-third of a circle between two planets. Planets in trine aspect generally occupy the same number of degrees in signs four signs apart.

Triplicity One of four fixed groups of signs, each containing three planets. The four triplicities relate to the four elements earth, air, fire, and water. They are concerned with tendencies of the temperament.

Vernal equinox The intersection of the plane of the ecliptic with the celestial equator. This intersection occurs once a year, at the moment the Sun crosses the celestial equator moving from south to north.

Zenith That point in the celestial sphere directly above the observer.

Zodiac The band of sky 18° wide having the ecliptic as its central line. It consists of twelve parts, each 30° wide, which represent the twelve signs of the Zodiac.

General Index

Cross Index of Aspects

Sextiles

Squares

Trines

Neptune trine Moon (*see* Moon trine Neptune)

Neptune trine Mercury (*see* Mercury trine Neptune)

Neptune trine Venus (*see* Venus trine Neptune)

Neptune trine Mars (*see* Mars trine Neptune)

Neptune trine Jupiter (*see* Jupiter trine Neptune)

Neptune trine Saturn (*see* Saturn trine Neptune)

Neptune trine Uranus (*see* Uranus trine Neptune)

Neptune trine Pluto, 412

Neptune trine North Node sextile South Node, 412

Neptune trine Ascendant sextile Descendant, 413

Neptune trine Midheaven sextile Nadir, 413

Neptune trine Descendant sextile Ascendant (*see* Neptune sextile Ascendant trine Descendant)

Neptune trine Nadir sextile Midheaven (*see* Neptune sextile Midheaven trine Nadir)

Pluto trine Sun (*see* Sun trine Pluto)

Pluto trine Moon (*see* Moon trine Pluto)

Pluto trine Mercury (*see* Mercury trine Pluto)

Pluto trine Venus (*see* Venus trine Pluto)

Pluto trine Mars (*see* Mars trine Pluto)

Pluto trine Jupiter (*see* Jupiter trine Pluto)

Pluto trine Saturn (*see* Saturn trine Pluto)

Pluto trine Uranus (*see* Uranus trine Pluto)

Pluto trine Neptune (*see* Neptune trine Pluto)

Pluto trine North Node sextile South Node, 413

Pluto trine Ascendant sextile Descendant, 413–14

Pluto trine Midheaven sextile Nadir, 414

Pluto trine Descendant sextile Ascendant (*see* Pluto sextile Ascendant trine Descendant)

Pluto trine Nadir sextile Midheaven (*see* Pluto sextile Midheaven trine Nadir)

North Node trine Ascendant sextile Descendant, South Node sextile Ascendant trine Descendant, 414

North Node trine Midheaven sextile Nadir, South Node sextile Midheaven trine Nadir, 414–15

North Node trine Descendant sextile Ascendant, South Node trine Ascendant sextile Descendant, 415

North Node trine Nadir sextile Midheaven, South Node trine Midheaven sextile Nadir, 415

Oppositions

Sun opposition Moon, 416–17

Sun opposition Mercury (astronomically impossible)

Sun opposition Venus (astronomically impossible)

Sun opposition Mars, 417

Sun opposition Jupiter, 417

Sun opposition Saturn, 417–18

Sun opposition Uranus, 418

Sun opposition Neptune, 418–19

Sun opposition Pluto 419

Sun opposition North Node (*see* Sun conjunct South Node)

Sun opposition South Node (*see* Sun conjunct North Node)

Sun opposition Ascendant (*see* Sun conjunct Descendant)

Sun opposition Midheaven (*see* Sun conjunct Nadir)

Sun opposition Descendant (*see* Sun conjunct Ascendant)

Sun opposition Nadir (*see* Sun conjunct Midheaven)

Moon opposition Sun (*see* Sun opposition Moon)

Moon opposition Mercury, 419–20

Moon opposition Venus, 420

Moon opposition Mars, 420–21

Moon opposition Jupiter, 421

Moon opposition Saturn, 421–22

Moon opposition Uranus, 422

Moon opposition Neptune, 422–23

Moon opposition Pluto, 423

Moon opposition North Node (*see* Moon conjunct South Node)

Moon opposition South Node (*see* Moon conjunct North Node)

Moon opposition Ascendant (*see* Moon conjunct Descendant)

Moon opposition Midheaven (*see* Moon conjunct Nadir)

Moon opposition Descendant (*see* Moon conjunct Ascendant)